B

MW01119569

Corporate Governance Around the World

The last Asian financial crisis, coupled with the western series of corporate scandals, has caused investors and citizens to doubt managers' abilities to guarantee credible financial information about organizations. Consequently, legislators all over the world have come to realize the necessity of legislating in the area of corporate governance.

This book explores several national corporate governance reform experiences from around the world (including Canada, China, the United States, and the European Union) and offers an explanatory theory with regard to national systems of corporate governance. It also underlines corporate governance as a management tool and principle. The author argues that each country should be encouraged to build its own system of corporate governance which should be harmonized with its history, culture and the level of its economic development.

Corporate Governance Around the World will be useful reading for advanced students of International Business and Corporate Governance and will also appeal to a professional audience.

A. Naciri is currently Professor of Finance and Accounting at UQAM School of Business and Chairman of the Montreal International Center for Governance. He is internationally recognized for his work on corporate governance, quality of financial information and financial disclosure. His research papers are published in many first class international journals, like the *Journal of Futures Market*, the *Advances in International Accounting* and the *International Journal of Accounting*. He is prize-recipient of the Administrative Sciences Association of Canada.

Routledge studies in corporate governance

Corporate Governance
Around the World

Edited by A. Naciri

Routledge
Taylor & Francis Group

LONDON AND NEW YORK

First published 2008
by Routledge
2 Park Square, Milton Park, Abingdon, Oxon OX14 4RN

Simultaneously published in the USA and Canada
by Routledge
270 Madison Ave, New York, NY 10016

Routledge is an imprint of the Taylor & Francis Group, an informa business

Transferred to Digital Printing 2009

© 2008 Selection and editorial matter, A. Naciri; individual chapters, the
contributors

Typeset in Times by Wearset Ltd, Boldon, Tyne and Wear

British Library Cataloguing in Publication Data
A catalogue record for this book is available from the British Library

Library of Congress Cataloging in Publication Data
Corporate governance around the world / edited by A. Naciri.
p. cm.
Includes bibliographical references and index.
1. Corporate governance—Case studies. 2. Corporate governance—
Government policy—Case studies. I. Naciri, A.
HD2741.C77496 2008
338.6—dc22   2007034961

ISBN10: 0-415-42874-2 (hbk)
ISBN10: 0-203-93067-3 (ebk)

ISBN13: 978-0-415-42874-3 (hbk)
ISBN13: 978-0-203-93067-0 (ebk)

To Sissi, Kiki, Yaya, and Ani

Contents

Figures

Tables

Contributors

Melsa Ararat is Director of the Corporate Governance Forum of Turkey and Professor of Management, Sabanci University, Turkey.

Fabrice Bien is Professor of Law, ESC Clermont Ferrand, France.

David A.H. Brown is Executive Director, Conference Board, Canada.

Jacques Délga is an Attorney and Professorof Law, ESSEC-Paris, France.

Gérard Charreaux is Professor of Management, Université de Bourgogne, France.

Alain Ged is Dean and Professor of Accounting, IAE Université d'Aix-Marseille, France.

Simon S.M. Ho is Dean and Professor of Accounting, School of Business, Hong Kong Baptist University, Hong Kong.

Raymon Leban is Dean and Professor of Management, The International Institute of Management, Paris, France.

Ahmed Naciri is currently Professor of Finance and Accounting at UQAM School of Business and Chairman of the Montreal International Center for Governance.

Brian L. Nelson is an Attorney and Professor of Law, Kogod School of Business, American University, United States.

Tetyana Pasechnyk is Professor of Management, Odessa State Economics University, Ukraine.

Mehmet Ugur is Jean Monnet Reader in Political Economy, University of Greenwich, England.

Masaru Yoshimori is Professor of Management, School of Business, Yokohama National University, Japan.

Foreword

Some terms speak for themselves; they deliver their entire secret only after having acquired the time sanction. The term "corporate governance" (CG) is one of these. Thus, despite the tremendous interest surrounding the issue of CG, acquired at the expense of unprecedented financial scandals, there always remains a quasi general mixed feeling with regard to its exact extent and an international divergence as for the solution to be opposed to the serious problems its absence always generates.

As usual hesitant people always resist change, and CG which was facing first hours rejection, has gradually gained a much broader frame of influence, mainly under the daily facts of life. CG is currently covering all the dimensions of corporate management. Less than a decade ago, indeed, the majority of corporations would consider CG in terms of standards respect but only in their form.

We should recognize that the situation has drastically changed and that, more and more attention is devoted to good conduct in CG. As ever before, managers are required the improvement of their management practices emphasizing business ethic and the respect of the laws. Actually organizations are realizing that the success of their business goes hand in hand with their willingness and ability to gain the respect and the confidence of their shareholders, their employees, their communities, and their market. Indeed, an effective CG system is essential to organization survival. Besides its benefits at the micro level, CG presents advantages at the macro level. Globalization effects of both product and financial markets are causing countries with different legal CG frameworks to compete for international capital and investment and countries with weaker CG systems are served last. National governments and international organizations are therefore striving toward doting countries with appropriate CG frameworks in order to maintain investors' confidence in the capital market and to reinforce world peace.

At the corporate level, transparency and management rigor are becoming two basic organizational values. It is becoming obvious that each organization and all its partners have real interest in having in place, policies, procedures, and equitable and transparent practices of CG. As representative of shareholders, the Board, assisted by its different committees, has the responsibility of overseeing the respect CG, to which everyone in the organization must adhere with honesty and conviction.

The book admirably describes the dynamic of CG in motion, sparing almost no country and no region of the planet. Each country, however, should be harnessed to build its own CG system that can be harmonized with its history, culture, and the level of its economic development. All national systems of CG must, however, respect the same fundamental principles of ethics, justice, and honesty.

This book is a fundamental contribution to the better understanding of the CG phenomenon. It widens our horizon with regards to the development of national CG systems all over the word. The understanding of other systems may help us to better understand our own. While the book leads us to conclude that as regards to CG, there is not a better system, it all depends on the condition of the country, it also informs us, that in the field there is no worse system than a "no system."

Robert J. Giroux

Acknowledgments

This book is the result of a team effort, involving scholars across America, Asia, Europe, Middle East, and North Africa. We would like to express our gratitude to all contributors whose determination and commitment have made possible the production of this book, by alphabetical order: Mrs Melsa Ararat (Sarbanci d'Istanbul of Istanbul), Dr Fabrice Bien (ESC de Clermont Ferrand), Mr David Brown director (Conference Board), Dr Jacques Délga (ESSEC, Paris), Dr Alain Ged (Institut d'Administration des Entreprises, Aix-en-Provence), Dr Gérard Charreaux (Université de Bourgogne), Dr Simon S.M. Ho (Baptist University of Hong-Kong), Dr Raymond Leban (CNAM, Paris), Brian Nelson (American University), Dr Tetyana Pasechyk (University of Ukraine), Dr Mehmed Ugur (Greenwich University), and Dr Masaru Yoshimori (Open University of Japan).

My deepest thanks go to my wife and my three children for their patience, continuous encouragement, and support.

Abbreviations

ACCA   Association of Chartered Certified Accountants
ADACTE   Eurotunnel Shareholder Defense Association
ADAM   Association de Défense des Actionnaires Minoritaires – Minority Shareholder Defense Association
AFEP   Association Française des Entreprises Privées – French Association of Private Businesses
AICPA   American Institute of Chartered Public Accountants
AMF   Autorité des Marchés Financiers – Financial Markets Authority
ANSA   Association Nationale des Sociétés par Actions
ASBJ   Accounting Standards Board of Japan
ASE   Amman Stock Exchange
BAC   Business Accounting Council
BCCI   Bank of Credit and Commerce International
BIS   Bank for International Settlements
BSE   Bahrain Stock Exchange
CA   Chartered Accountant
CAAP   Comptables Agréés et Auditeur Public
CalPERS   California Public Employees' Retirement System
CASC   China Accounting Standards Committee
CASE   Cairo and Alexandria Stock Exchange
CBCA   Canada Business Corporations Act
CCCE   Canadian Council of Chief Executives
CCGG   Canadian Coalition for Good Governance
CDIC   Canadian Deposit Insurance Corporation
CDP   La Caisse de Dépots et Placements
CDVM   Commission des Valeurs Mobilières (Security Exchange Commission)
CEE   Central and East European
CEEC   Central and Eastern European Countries
CEM   Control Enhancing Mechanism
CEO   Chief Executive Officer
CFO   Chief Financial Officer
CG   Corporate Governance
CGWG   Corporate Governance Working Group

CICA	Canadian Institute of Chartered Accountants
CICPA	Chinese Institute of Certified Public Accountants
CIDA	Canadian International Development Agency
CIEB	Chartered Public Accountant Investigation Examination Board
CIS	Commonwealth of Independent States
CIT	Commonwealth of Independent Countries
CLO	Chief Legal Officer
CMA	Certified Management Accountants
CMB	Capital Markets Board
CML	Capital Markets Law
CNAO	China National Audit Office
CNCC	Compagnie Nationale des Commissaires aux Comptes
COB	Commission des Opérations de Bourse – French Securities and Exchange Commission
CPA	Chartered Public Accountant
CPAAOB	Chartered Public Accountants and Auditing Oversight Board
CPAB	Canadian Public Accountability Board
CSA	Canadian Securities Administrators
CSE	Casablanca Stock Exchange
CSR	Corporate Social Responsibility
CSRC	Chinese Security Regulatory Commission
DFM	Dubai Financial Market
DIFC	Dubai International Financial Center
DIFX	Dubai International Financial Exchange
DSE	Damasacus Stock Exchange
DSM	Doha Securities Market
EBITDA	Earnings Before Interest, Taxes, Depreciation, and Amortization
EC	European Community
ED	Executive Director
EEA	European Economic Area
EiT	Economies in Transition
EU	European Union
FASB	Financial Accounting Standards Board
FASF	Financial Accounting Standards Foundation
FIG	Financial-Industrial Groups
FSA	Financial Services Agency
GAAP	General Accounting Agreed on Principle
GCC	Gulf Cooperation Council
GDP	Gross Domestic Product
GEM	Growth Enterprise Market
GITIC	Guangtong International Trust and Investment Corporation
GNP	Gross National Product
HAMS	Hong Kong Association of Minority Shareholders
HKEx	Hong Kong Exchange
HKEx	Hong Kong Exchanges and Clearing

HKLA	Hong Kong Listing Authority
HKMA	Hong Kong Monetary Authority
HKSA	Hong Kong Society of Accountants
HKSCC	Hong Kong Securities Clearing Company Ltd
HR	Human Research
IAS	International Accounting Standards
IASB	International Accounting Standards Board
ICAEW	Institute of Chartered Accountants in England and Wales
ICD	Institute of Corporate Directors
ICGN	International Corporate Governance Network
ICT	Information and Communication Technologies
IDA	Investment Dealers Association
IDT	Insider Dealing Tribunal
IFAC	International Federation of Accountants.
IFC	International Finance Corporation
IFRS	International Financial Reporting Standard
IIA	Institute of Internal Auditors
IIB	Independent Investigation Board
IMF	International Monetary Fund
INED	Independent Non-Executive Director
IOSCO	International Organization of Security Commissions
IPO	Initial Public Offering
ISE	Istanbul Stock Exchange
ISX	Iraq Stock Exchange
JICPA	Japanese Institute of Certified Public Accountants
JSLC	Joint-Stock Limited Company
KBV	Knowledge-Based View
KSE	Kuwait Stock Exchange
KhSE	Khartoum Stock Exchange
LLP	Limited Liability Partnership
M&A	Mergers and Acquisitions
MD&A	Management Discussion and Analysis
MEDEF	Mouvement des Entreprises de France – Movement of French Businesses
MENA	Middle East and North Africa
MI	Multilateral Instrument
MMT	Market Misconduct Tribunal
MOF	Ministry of Finance
MSM	Muscat Securities Market
NASDAK	National Association of Securities Dealers Automated Quotations
NCCP	New Code of Civil Procedure
NED	Non-Executive Director
NI	National Instrument
NPC	National People's Congress
NRE	New Economic Regulations

NSCG	National System of Corporate Governance
NYSE	New York Stock Exchange
OECD	Organization of Economic Cooperation and Development
OMERS	Ontario Municipal Employees Retirement
OSC	Ontario Security Commission
OSFI	Office of the Superintendent of Financial Institutions
OSOV	One Share–One Vote
OTPP	Ontario Teachers Pension Plan
PACOB	Public Accounting Oversight Board
PCCW	Pacific Century Cyberworks
PEEC	Pacific Economic Cooperation Council
PLC	Public Listed Company
PRC	People's Republic of China
PSE	Palestine Securities Exchange
QFII	Qualified Foreign Institutional Investor
RBV	Resource-Based View
ROB	Report on Business
ROSC	Reports on the Observance of Standards and Codes
SAS	Statements of Audit Standards
SCAP	Supreme Commander for the Allied Powers
SCCLR	Standing Committee on Company Law Reform
SCMP	South China Morning Post
SDIO	Securities (Disclosure of Interests) Ordinance
SEC	Security Exchange Commission
SEHK	Stock Exchange of Hong Kong Ltd
SESC	Securities and Exchange Surveillance Commission
SETC	State Economic and Trade Committee
SFC	Securities and Futures Commission
SFO	Securities and Futures Ordinance
SGM	Shareholders' General Meetings
SHSE	Shanghai Stock Exchange
SIDO	Securities (Insider Dealing) Ordinance
SME	Small- and Medium-sized Enterprises
SOE	State-Owned Enterprises
SOX	Sarbanes/Oxley Act
SPE	Special Purpose Entities
SRO	Self-Regulatory Organizations.
SSAP	Statements of Standard Accounting Practice
SSIP	Social Systems of Innovation and Production
SZSE	Shenzhen Stock Exchange
TSX	Toronto Stock Exchange
UAE	United Arab Emirates
VOC	Varieties of Capitalism
WB	World Bank
WSE	Warsaw Stock Exchange

1 Introduction

A. Naciri

Truth exists, only a lie has to be invented[1]

Despite the increased interest in corporate governance (CG), gained recently at the high price of corporate scandals, there is always some confusion, characterizing its general understanding and it is not surprising to see the extreme hesitation expressed by governments, all over the world, regarding the appropriate solution to face CG challenges. For some people, this is actually the result of the relative novelty of the concept, inevitably expected to be characterized by some lack of deep understanding. For others, it is mainly the confusion of the concept of governance with the concept of control, which creates the problem. They are alarmed to see CG often reduced to a simple question of separating control from ownership, within the organization – a simple technical problem of supervision – some would argue. Progressively, however, and under the pressure of daily life, we were forced to concede to governance a much larger recognition, a wider extent and a bigger framework (Cornell and Shapiro, 1987; OECD, 1999).[2]

After all, a corporation is no more than a legal construct based on the separation of the legal identity from its owners and as a legal entity the corporation benefits from specific legal rights and has, of course legal duties. Several fundamental rights were indeed conceded, from the beginning, to corporations.

Two rights, namely the limited liability and the perpetuity, have unsuspected financial consequences: the rational of the limited liability right lies in the fact that it allows anonymous trading in the shares of the corporation by virtue of eliminating the corporation's creditors as stakeholders. Limited liability further allows corporations to raise tremendously more funds for enterprises by combining funds from shareholders. Limited liability also reduces the amount that an investor can lose by investing in a company. This in turn greatly reduces potential investors risk and increases both the amount they are likely to invest and their number, thus adding liquidity and volume to the stock markets. With regard to the perpetuity principle, the fact that corporate assets exist beyond the lifetime of any one of its stakeholders or agents, this allows for stability and capital accumulation which thus becomes available for investment in larger size projects and over longer terms.

At the end, when we think of it, the corporate model proves to be one of the most ingenious human organizational creations and corporations are today shaping every facet of our lives and in a non measurable way. They are deciding the way we live, the way we die, and soon, the way we may be born. On the other hand, recent history indicates that private organizations are also invading political grounds and is directly impacting politics' orientation and development and implementation (Monks and Minow, 1996), and it is only a matter of fairness, to require some minimum level of good governance from them, as it is also a matter of economic growth, democracy and social justice. In his seminal "Wealth of Nations" book, Adam Smith criticized the corporate form of business because of the separation of ownership and management it implies:

> The directors of such [joint-stock] companies, however, being the managers rather of other people's money than of their own, it cannot well be expected, that they should watch over it with the same anxious vigilance with which the partners in a private copartnery frequently watch over their own .... Negligence and profusion, therefore, must always prevail, more or less, in the management of the affairs of such a company.
>
> (Adam Smith, 1776)

Adam Smith also defined the foundation of governance in business, by indicating that:

> Property rights continue to have a rightful moral legitimacy when used to secure the right of each individual as a stakeholder in the assets on which they depend to produce a reasonable living for themselves and their families. They lack moral legitimacy, however, when used by those who have more than they need to exclude others from access to a basic means of living or to absolve themselves of responsibility for equitably sharing and stewarding the resources that are the common heritage of all who were born to life on this planet.
>
> (Smith, 1817)

The governance term "significance" may change by changes in context. In an organizational perspective, the governance system is represented by the legal framework, the ruling institutions, along with the disclosure requirements which impacts the way organizations are managed, not forgetting the financial market, dictating the behavior of organizations. Any corporation is finally no more than a set of agreed conventions, regulating monetary and physical flows it generates. In such context, governance would come down to a relation of power between governing bodies and those who are governed by them. Those governing bodies are hired to set up economic programs and policies, entitled to foster economic development and growth. Up to now, governance remains a broad concept, referring to both internal and external mechanisms to organization, and linked to a precise objective.

One objective of governance emphasizes organization's ownership and the way corporate decisions affect the wealth of stakeholders. More and more often it goes even beyond that limit, by taking into account wealth creation via the maximization of economic efficiency of the organization and ensuring that such wealth is fairly allocated among corporate stakeholders. On the field, like in the case of Microsoft, CG is supposed to serve several purposes:[3]

i   establishing and preserving management accountability to owners by appropriately distributing rights and responsibilities among Board members, managers, and shareholders;
ii providing a structure through which management and the Board set and attain objectives and monitor performance;
iii strengthening and safeguarding our culture of business integrity and responsible business practices; and
iv Encouraging the efficient use of resources, and requiring accountability for our stewardship of those resources.

As far as this book is concerned, governance is defined as the set of organizational and institutional mechanisms that define the powers and influence the managers' decisions, i.e. that "govern" their conduct and define their discretionary space.[4]

CG internal mechanisms

As representative of the shareholders, the Board of Directors is the CG guarantor. Shareholders elect the Board of Directors to oversee management and to assure that stakeholders' long-term interests are served. Through oversight, review, and counsel, the Board of Directors establishes and promotes business and organizational objectives. The Board oversees the company's business affairs and integrity, works with management to determine the company's mission and long-term strategy, performs the annual Chief Executive Officer (CEO) evaluation, oversees CEO succession planning, establishes internal controls over financial reporting, and assesses company risks and strategies for risk mitigation. The Board relies on several committees to fulfill its duties and each committee is led by, and is composed solely of independent directors:

i   Audit Committee;
ii Compensation Committee;
iii Nominating Committee; and
iv Finance Committee.

The Board of Directors develops CG policies and practices to help it fulfill its responsibilities. These policies are usually memorialized in the Corporate Governance Guidelines or Code, to assure that the Board has the necessary authority and practices in place to review and evaluate the company's business operations and to make decisions that are independent of the company's management. The Board routinely reviews evolving practices to determine those that will best serve stakeholders' interests. Special emphasis is placed on the decisive role of the Board of Directors, with regard to CG. Such a role is, of course, delegated to him by the shareholders.

As mentioned before, it is also interesting to represent the organization as a knot of both implicit and explicit contracts, all of them aiming at harmonizing the relations existing between various interest groups (Alchian and Woodward, 1988; Fama and Jensen, 1983a). Such harmonization of interests appears more and more as the effectiveness determinant of the organization and in final analysis as ultimate indicator of its survival (Williamson, 1999). Contractual organization has, however, shown its own limits – contract agreements inevitably incomplete, and not always taking into account temporal changes – have proven to be sensitive to environmental changes and they finally end up losing most of their effectiveness. For this reason early concern was raised with regard to their failure (Berle and Means, 1932).

Theoretically, Board members are supposed to make sure that contractual agreements terms are respected and to run the organization, in shareholders' interest (Shleifer and Vishny, 1997). It should be noted, however, that when an individual is sole owner of its company, the potential of conflict of interest is quasi nil, whereas each time an organization is directed by non owners, the conflict of interest is latent (Cyert and March, 1963; Machlup, 1967; Jensen and Meckling, 1976). Consequently, one of the main responsibilities of the Board of Directors is to make sure that managers act responsibly and effectively, in the exercise of their function. Any responsible Board would, in fact, put all its efforts toward the minimization of conflicts of interest.[5] In order to be able to do so, however, Board members need to be carefully selected and suitably nominated (Bhagat and Black, 1998). This is unfortunately far from being the case, even in most developed countries. The *Chicago Tribune* of November 20, 2003, reported, for instance, that the Security Exchange Commission (SEC) of the United States was inquiring into the Board of the Press giant Hollinger, and has discovered that two of the members of the Board are none other than Henry Kissinger and Richard Perle (former advisor to the Pentagon). This inquiry has also shown several illicit transactions and payments, particularly to the Chairman of Hollinger and Member of the House of Lords, England, Conrad Black.

The most worrying task of the Board, is, undoubtedly, the determination of management remuneration and compensation plans, often indexed to some quantitative data (Rappaport, 1986), rather than to some real organizational performance (Jensen and Murphy, 1990). It is believed that it would be possible to minimize conflicts significantly within the organizations, by simply aligning remuneration plans with real organizational performance (Hausbrich and April, 1994; Core *et al.*, 1999). Some people are also convinced that the supervision capacity of the Board can be tremendously improved by a simple inclusion of independent members (Sarbanes/Oxley, 2003; Fama, 1980; Weisbach, 1988; Brokhovich *et al.*, 1996).

However, Board members are far from being immune to market pressure, constantly inviting them to increase organizations profitability and decrease their variability (Healy, 1985; DeAngelo, 1988; Dye 1988; McNichols and Wilson, 1988; Jones, 1991; Naciri, 2000). Some managers have quickly understood that those unrealistic requirements could only be reached by manipulating the numbers. Consequently, the understanding market structure and mechanisms must also be a priority for the Board. These so-called "corporate governance external mechanisms," enables the Board to fill effectively its role of stewardship. Despite the paramount role in the survival of the organization, the Board role is still neglected or not taken seriously. Four of five CEOs, for instance, still believe that their organization poorly prepare their Board meetings, and 88 percent of them estimate that Board members always fail to allocate the necessary energy and time to their tasks (Laurendeau Labrecque/Ray and Berndtson, 2003).[6]

Shareholders accuse no better a picture, they also seem, not to take seriously, their role, especially when it comes to the choice of Board members. Saucier's report (Chartered Accountants of Canada and Toronto Stock Exchange (TSX), 2001) indicates that an engaged Board of Directors, interdependent and effective adds value to the organization, initially and above all, by the choice of the right CEO. Generally the Board can add value in various ways, but particularly by:

i   approving and evaluating the strategic orientation of the company;
ii making sure that the company has suitable processes for the appreciation and the risk management like for internal control;
iii ensuring the performance monitoring, with regard to some agreed bench marks; and
iv Ensuring the integrity of information on financial performance.

In order to effectively fulfill its governance role, the Board must rely on a formal three dimensional process:

i   strategy dimension;
ii structural dimension; and
iii design dimension.

On the purely strategic dimensional process, development and growth orientation of the organization must be revised in order to include CG considerations. CG must, in fact, transcend all corporate strategic decisions. The Board must support a strategic process, favoring strategic orientation discussions, and Board members must be aware of strategic plans prepared by managers. The Board can adopt various measures to reduce managers' enormous informational advantage, by concentrating on key performance indicators. The Board should also make sure it receives, from independent sources, reliable and specific information on such indicators. Finally, we never emphasize enough the crucial effect of an effective remuneration and compensation model, inciting managers to value creation. It is necessary for the Board to know how to deal with the whole spectrum of stakeholders, seeking good balance of rewards between the short-term and long-term output, the desired amount of total remuneration compared to relevant markets, the protection measures against the handling of measurements and indicators of output, and the required share of internal measurements compared to external measurements of output.

On the structure level, organizational structures must be reorganized to allow the development of CG within the organization. Indeed, certain organizational structures can be more favorable to governance than others.

On the level of organizational design, the one favorable to governance must be privileged and in order to be able to achieve CG goals, the Board must, especially, avoid falling under management control. An efficient system must provide employees with clear indications on how various governance initiatives of the organization are integrated. The Board needs to receive information, usually, not only necessary for traditional control and monitoring, but also strategic information which is particularly relevant to the type of company concerned. It thus, will be able to have access to independent and regular evaluations of the competitive position of the company and of the degree satisfaction of its customers, employees, and personnel retention. The Board should be able to resort, for these purposes, to the services of an effective audit committee. An audit committee would, however, prove to be more effective in protecting CG within the organization, when it is offered capacities and the necessary resources. It must also be insured independence from management.

Previous discussion indicates that major problems of CG; reside within the incapacity of the Boards of Directors to fairly represent shareholders and other stakeholders interests. Any governance reform must address such dimensions.

CG counts

Data from the Worldwide Governance Indicators, for the year 2005, shows that democratic accountability and clean government go hand in hand. Countries that are vibrant democracies show very little corruption, while countries with voice and accountability challenges tend to have much more corruption. It is astounding, however, to learn that it is only recently, following corporate crisis with their unprecedented moral violence, that Boards of Directors have woken up to their basic and long-time neglected corporate responsibility. Governance has, in fact, proven to be crucial, and not only to the organization, but also for the whole of society. Even though, the currently agreed on objective of firm – the so called "shareholders' wealth maximization" – is continuously debated. In fact, it is becoming progressively obvious, that if there is to be a shareholders' wealth maximization, there should also be a protection of other stakeholders' interests.

Sound CG practices are supposed to attract investment, mainly because of the improved management of firms and the resulting reduction of its risk. At the global level, national institutions, regulations, laws, and practices based on international norms and standards would enable countries, especially developing countries, to modernize their corporate sector, allowing them to attract technology and foreign investment and becoming internationally competitive. Furthermore, political and sovereign risks would be reduced and economic performance and outcome would be de-linked from political regimes and dependence from specific resources (Saidi, 2004).

CG as a managerial principle

Once CG was assessed, the question which comes to mind is how to integrate it as a fundamental organization management principle? Experiences of successful organizations, having created value through good governance, may prove to be helpful in shaping a behavior model of good governance. We name such models as "Value creation by corporate governance" (ΔVCG). Let us assume that all the organization stakeholders would find it beneficial when their organization was creating value, and when its managers and employees had the necessary skill, energy, and willingness to accomplish such objectives. The real challenge for the Board of Directors is to create, to the benefit of all, such appropriate climate, motivating all concerned parties. When this happens all the corporate stakeholders will be satisfied, shareholders, customers, suppliers, and society, as a whole. No organization can, in fact, hope to be prosperous in the long run, if its managers are still not remunerated adequately, if its employees rights are constantly defied, or if immoral practices characterize its relations with its customers and suppliers. Management ethic-based practices are likely to allow the organization to grow and expand harmoniously. Figure 1.1 suggests a road map to achieving such objectives.

By moving from left to right, in Figure 1.1, and departing from the Board (step 1), we can see that, as shareholders' representatives and management supervisors, Board members play a key role in the management of the

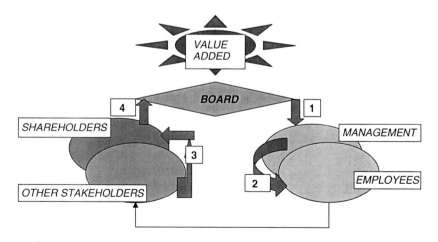

Figure 1.1 The ΔVGG model.

organization and in the consolidation of its ethic. For the Board to be able to fulfill such a strategic role, its credibility, legitimacy, and competency should suffer no exception. Directors' legitimacy in the eyes of shareholders, managers, employers, and other interested parties is reflexive of the criteria used in the selection of Board members. In other words, the way Board members are nominated, and their level of implication in the organization, is tributary of the significance of their shareholding, or dependent of their social commitment (in the case of a non-profit organizations). Unfortunately, we can only take note that processes of Board selection were gradually transformed into futile rituals wholly controlled by managements.

Times have obviously changed; institutional investors are now commonly detaining, in some environments, more than 50 percent of all corporate outstanding shares. They do not hesitate, anymore, in expressing their views with regard to corporate challenges. As a matter of fact, they are even becoming, more and more proactive in this regard. Efficiency along with credibility, are sine qua non conditions to CG. In fact, the credibility of the Board, in the management eyes, has a decisive value. Given that the Board must prove its ability to discuss strategic challenges, to control and supervise the profitability of the corporation, and to conceive fair and motivating compensation plans. Such tasks show a high intensity and quality when they are carried out by a legitimate Boards of Directors, offering better possibilities of wealth creation for stakeholders. As underlined before, the Board needs, however, for this purpose, to get access to applicable valid and precise information. A credible and effective Board takes the necessary action to ensure that the separation of management and ownership, carrying usually destroying germ of conflicts, will not lead to a certain negligence of shareholders' interests and other stakeholders' rights, and finally diminishing employee spirit and leading to customers' and suppliers' skepticism.

Harmonious relation between the Board and management (step 2), is determining the success of CG. Each party in the organization must learn how to respect the other, within the framework of self responsibility and within collaborative climate. Any Board of Directors unable to force the confidence and trust of its managers will experiment difficulties to fulfill its role effectively. However, a management team which understands the role of the Board can only encourage it to fully fill it. In the same way, managers who can do their work in all honesty, force the respect of to their employees and foster their faithfulness to the cause of their organization. For this reason the Board and management can collaborate effectively and intentionally, particularly in areas as:

i   clear identification of links they are operating and specifying why,
ii   hiring appropriate individuals, in terms of personal worth and abilities,
iii lining up their own interests with shareholders interests,
iv   setting up organization objectives, policies, and performance standards,
v   evaluating realization plans for such objectives, along with achievement results, and
vi reacting to results, having in mind management responsibility.

Employees, who are actually convinced about the integrity of their management and its respect for them, will prove to be much more dedicated, motivated, and inclined to make the organization reach its objective of prosperity and growth. All it takes is to show employees the appropriate itinerary to follow, particularly by setting well-structured action plans and by insuring them with the necessary competencies, mainly by putting in place appropriate training programs.

Continuing (step 3), satisfied and professionally qualified employees, can only make customers more happy and loyal to the organization, and so suppliers, creditors, and other external relations. They are all now in relation with a well-recognized organization, for its seriousness and professionalism. In such cases, only increase in value will occur and should be beneficial to everybody, within and outside the organization.

In this regard, the rather disgusting behavior of some corporate managers, interested mainly by their own benefits, rather than by value creation for stakeholders, has proven to be extremely damaging for all, and sometimes decisive for some organizations. Certain managers, blinded by their own interests, learned how to bargain corporate objectives for their own benefit. They, for instance, learn how to buy employees' peace, by granting them generous and non-affordable collective agreements. They also learned how to juggle with numbers to maximize their own option plans, etc. In such cases sub optimality in decision making has become the rule and thousands of billions of dollars were lost, solely in 2000, in this way. The extent of such losses is a real threat to the whole financial system, and has endangered the economic and social accomplished progress.

In step 4, the model indicates that customers, suppliers, and other external parties, once convinced of the seriousness of the organization, are ready to concede their trust and they can even become concerned by its future and to some extent, they become a source value creation.

Operationally speaking, CG is composed of activities of various kinds, strategic, supervision, auditing, control, and evaluation. Given the extent of the Board role in CG, it becomes crucial for shareholders to be assured of the efficiency and credibility of the Board (step 5). We should, however, deplore absence of concern, at this level, especially with regard to the availability of transparent and formal procedures of nominating Board members. Some easy measures can, in fact, improve the situation significantly, and will be discussed. The ΔVCG model shows how important CG is for organizations and for this reason it should be under shareholders' responsibility, via their elected Board of Directors. Such conclusion is shared by Byrne (1996a); Millstein and MacAvoy (1998); and Steward and Walsh (1996). The Board of Directors however, should not only be held responsible for the increase of the organization value, but it should also be held responsible for how such increase is actually achieved. In other words, it must be ensured that the way followed, for this purpose, goes through ethics and respect of others.

In the final analysis, an organization will create more wealth, for itself and for society as a whole, by ethic strategies and good governance, which will bring a reputation of integrity. This is a no surprise conclusion, since good governance aims to increase solidity, viability, and competitiveness of the corporations. Moreover, in an increasingly globalized economy, competition is intense and good governance can make a difference, by influencing the way in which national companies are perceived by the foreign investors.

The same objective and multiple national systems of CG

International competition for capital is becoming a kind of CG competition and even International Financing Agencies are requiring some CG provisions appliance. Two schools of thought currently dominate the governance thinking and dispute its universality. The first school, of Anglo-Saxon origin, places priority on the property right – shareholder supremacy.[7] Consequently, the objective of the organization and the finality of its governance resides, above all, in the maximization of shareholders' wealth. Such orientation is traditionally founded on the argument that other stakeholders, within the organization, ultimately have their own mechanisms of protection. The long-term creditors, for instance, can protect themselves, using specific contractual provisions. Employees can also adhere to trade unions, dedicated exclusively to the defense of their rights, etc. From this point of view, the shareholders are then the only ones to find themselves without specific protection. They have to provide capital under relatively vague conditions, and support the major share of the risk incurred by the organization. They are placed in a position where they can be abused by managers. Anglo-Saxon approach, especially the American approach, also advocates a second argument for shareholding orientation, referring to the difficult task of simultaneously responding to divergent objectives of diverse organizational stakeholders. Professor Yoshimori (chapter 7) suggests yet another explanation. According to him,

> the primacy of the shareholder on the others having rights in the Anglo-Saxon school, dates back to the nineteenth century, when contractors were also the principal shareholders of their companies and were often committed themselves in the management of their own businesses. Since they had the major part, supported the majority of risk and that their wealth was closely related to that of their companies, it was completely normal and right to be considered the primary interested party.
>
> (Professor Yoshimori, Chapter 7)

But is this always the case today?

The second school of thought follows diametrically an opposite direction, it perceives in governance the capacity of the organization to fulfill its social role in all fairness and transparency and thus consider accountability as a social obligation. In some European countries, for example, this vision of the organization and of its governance is very widespread and considers that the organization was to combine several competing interests, including shareholders' interests.

The so-called "homogeneity" among Anglo-Saxon models, according to David Brown (Chapter 5), could be just, yet another judgmental error. He believes that a third governance approach is, indeed, emerging, and it is materialized by the current Canadian approach, wrongly classified as 100 percent Anglo-Saxon. The Canadian approach is based on principles, by comparison to the US approach, the rules approach calling for laws and yet more laws.

The Japanese experience, can be joined by the Turkish in order to form yet other alternative systems, oscillating sometimes toward the European model, sometimes toward the Anglo-Saxon model, depending on political and economic pressures. These models do not cease seeking their own way, which, they hope, will be responsive to their respective country's needs. Other countries, although concerned with the phenomenon of CG, did not yet make their choice and continue in considering in governance only what is constraint free, and always refuse to make the necessary efforts to move toward its true improvement.

No matter, however, which approach is adopted and by which country, the determining impact of the recent American Sarbanes/Oxley Act (SOX) cannot be neglected, and it is commonly argued that countries and companies which apply a CG model focusing on the market mechanisms of CG, as the leading mechanism of CG have a clear competitive advantage. CG is, therefore, of increasing importance for investment decisions. The SOX[8] which has led to the most profound reform of US securities markets legislation for the last decade, has set a pace against which most legislations all over the word has found a proper response for promoting their own CG national system. Indeed, the adoption of the SOX has caused a planetary "tsunami" of governance reforms and the spirit of its provisions is evident in all recent initiatives. In one way or another, whether Chinese, Japanese, Russian, French, Mexican, Canadian, European, etc. national CG systems were significantly impacted by the SOX.

SOX has, however, never intended to be international, it was meant to address a specific domestic American problem and it solely concerned large American listed companies. The SOX unexpected influence can be explained by two phenomena, on the one hand, the high international pressure exerted by international agencies (Corporate Governance: Observance of Standards and Codes) on some countries, to improve their CG systems for financing purposes; and on the other hand, most research on governance comes from the United States, necessarily reflecting their own concerns and offering their own solutions.

Besides a common departure, motivation for governance activities generally differs in various existing governance systems. In environments where organizations are, for instance, strongly dependant for their financing, on the financial markets, the emphasis on governance activity, tends to lean toward the shareholder protection and the achievement of his objective of wealth maximization. This is what it is called "market based governance." The US governance system is a market-based governance system. In such a system, it is also claimed that other stakeholder interests, such as employees, customers, suppliers, creditors, and so on, are automatically respected through the objective of maximization of the wealth of the shareholders. Alternatively, in environments where organizations have to resort massively to banks for their financing, ownership is usually concentrated and gives rise to another governance system, known as "banking governance" or system of internal audit. In addition to ownership concentration, organization control is seldom effective and the financial market is not able to play its role of monitoring funds effectively. Note, nevertheless, that even in some banking governance systems, the shareholding can be sometimes enough diffuse, as is the case in Japan and sometimes very concentrated, as is the case in Germany. Finally, some developing environments have features and mechanisms that are specific to them and they are struggling to find out appropriate solution to their specific governance problems and obviously CG models on the table do not fit their needs.

Obviously, CG issues may vary, not only from business to business, but also across countries. For example, in the field of enforcement, it can identify that the level and quality of the judiciary is a fundamental issue. Mass privatization processes have also created, in a number of countries (former Soviet republics, China, etc.), a class of shareholders who are not fully aware of their responsibilities to other shareholders and the company. In order to help countries to build their own CG systems the Organization of Economic Cooperation and Development (OECD) developed its own principles.

The 2004 OECD Corporate Governance Principles, originally endorsed by OECD Ministers in 1999, have since become an international benchmark for policy makers worldwide. These Principles have been advanced in five main areas:

i   Ensuring the Basis for an Effective Corporate Governance Framework;
ii   The Rights of Shareholders and Key Ownership Functions;
iii The Equitable Treatment of Shareholders Disclosure;
iv   Transparency; and
v   The Responsibilities of the Board.

National experiences with regard to CG systems seem to point out to management's Board supervision, within organizations as the fundamental element of all known CG systems today. Such supervision is supposed to be ensured by the Board of Directors, by delegation from shareholders, banks, and other stakeholders. But, since the production of information is a costly process, for anyone who is not part of the organization, an effective supervision activity will only be possible, when a reliable internal information system is in place.

Overview of the book

In Chapters 2 and 3 a synthesis of governance theories is offered by Charreaux (University of Bourgogne), mainly by conducting a survey of existing theories. Micro theories are presented by opposing the disciplinary view to the knowledge-based view and macro theories or national system theories are separated into theories based on appropriation of the organizational rent, and those attributing a dominant role to production. Market oriented governance, in the author's view, is but one model with many limits. He concludes, that in the long term, no current national system of governance seems to distinguish itself at the efficiency ıd usefulness levels.

In Chapter 4, we are introduced to the national CG system of the United States by Nelson (Kogod School of Business). The author believes that while the recent initiatives (SOX and the New York Stock Exchange (NYSE)) are undoubtedly important, their significance can best be understood in the context of the existing frameworks under corporate and securities law. He shows us that the American governance system is actually twofold: on the one hand, the recent NYSE initiatives, are attempting to improve the degree of independence among directors of listed corporations to meet corporate law. On the other hand the SOX, attempts to improve the independence of external auditors and corporate directors to meet the US securities regulations. There are finally provisions intended to enhance the care with which corporate officers prepare required public disclosures.

In Chapter 5, David Brown of the Conference Board of Canada, indicates that away from stereotypes, the Canadian national CG system is far from being a copy of the American system. The Canadian landscape of governance is characterized by the point of view of those, which to an extreme defend vigorously the system of governance containing principles, and those, to the other extreme, suggesting that Canada will be better served by the adopting SOX provisions. The Canadian CG model is interesting in the sense that it embodies a constructive reflective of a contemporary tension between, the Anglo-Saxon traditional model on one side, and the continental Europe model on other side.

We are introduced, in Chapter 6, to the French national CG system by Délga *et al.* (ESSEC-Paris, University of Montpellier and IAE-Aix-en Provence). The authors underline that the Anglo-Saxon model of CG has recently made a spectacular breakthrough in French law. They strongly regret the fact that businesses practices evolution has been made at the expense of a cultural legal heritage disavowing.

The Japanese national CG system is introduced to us in Chapter 7 by Yochimori (National University of Yokohama). The author underlines that although the Japanese CG is converging toward the American model, such convergence is confined to the structure and functions of the Board of Directors, aiming at the improvement of its supervision effectiveness. With regard, however, to corporation concept itself, another component of governance, namely the specific ideology to the country remains the determining factor. The author notes that even highly profitable Japanese companies, leaders of their sector, like Toyota, continue supporting, strongly, the traditional Japanese CG model, centered on the employee.

We are introduced, in Chapter 8, to the Hong Kong CG system by Ho (Baptist University). The author indicates that enhancing of the CG regime is a priority of the Hong Kong government, particularly in terms of protecting minority shareholders' interests. The government and all relevant sectors have attached much importance, and dedicated considerable efforts reforming legislation, rules and guidelines to keep them up to date. Although, Hong Kong is ahead in the region in CG, he cannot rely on stringent legislation and enforcement alone to enhance CG standards. Education and culture change should also be on the menu.

Simon Ho also introduces us to the Chinese national CG system in Chapter 9. The author underscores the fact that both Shareholding Corporation and CG are new concepts in China and "corporatization" or "privatization" of state-owned enterprises (SOE) in China has led to new agency problems generating conflicts of interest among different stakeholder groups. Recently, however, a number of efforts have been undertaken to improve China's business culture in the area of CG. China acted more decisively to improve CG since 1998. The Chinese Security Exchange had issued guidelines on independent directors, established a delisting mechanism for non-quality companies, and promulgated a systematic set of codes of CG for all listed companies, among other initiatives. Learning from the experiences of other countries, the author suggests a number of ways to improve CG standards in China.

The Turkish CG system is revealed to us by Ugur and Ararat (Universities of Greenwich of London and Sarbanes of Istanbul, respectively) in Chapter 10. The authors explore the evolution of the Turkish CG system during the last few decades and show that macroeconomic instability is itself a determining factor of governance quality. They also examine new evidence to ascertain the extent to which the quality of CG standards can be related to the emergence of a rule-based economic policy framework and the subsequent reduction in macroeconomic instability. The analysis suggests that the positive impact of the change in the economic policy framework is still evident, but there is still significant resistance to change in a number of areas of CG in Turkey.

Economies in transition CG is dealt with by Leban and Pasechnyck (CNAM Paris and Odessa Ukraine, respectively) in Chapter 11. We learn that CG in the Commonwealth of Independent States (CIS) cannot be dissociated from the privatization process and it is suffering from all the traditional privatization setbacks. The CIS is composed of Azerbaijan, Armenia, Belarus, Georgia, Kazakhstan, Kyrgyzstan, Moldova, Russia, Tajikistan, Turkmenistan, Uzbekistan, and Ukraine and is faced by unprecedented political, economic, and social change after the break-up of the Union. Challenges included deep economic distortions, major trade disruptions, the absence of market-oriented institution, and CG. Things are slow to change.

CG efforts and advances in the Mediterranean and North African Region (MENA) are assessed by Naciri (Uqam) in Chapter 12. The author remarks that MENA countries have undergone, in the last decade, a number of reforms and restructuring on legislative and infrastructure fronts, especially in the field of CG. The author warns that some CG initiatives in MENA may miss the point. According to him what is mostly needed in MENA are CG systems, guidelines, and rules dealing with non-listed companies and family businesses.

The European Union (EU) CG system is examined by Naciri in Chapter 13. The author indicates that corporate scandals have fuelled the European worries about CG and financial markets were pushing European companies to give priority to governance approach based on shareholder supremacy. In 2003, the EU, therefore, launched an Action Plan, "Modernizing Company Law and Enhancing Corporate Governance in the European Union – A Plan to Move Forward." For the last five years, the EU was working for the development of a strong, reliable European model of CG which should essentially be enshrined in European and national legislation. The EU CG initiative is mainly inspired by the US legislation which sets the scene for the most important national CG systems in the world.

The described governance systems in this book are only but a few benchmarks, in a spectrum with multiple intermediate positions. Certain governance environments, such as the Canadian model can share certain similarities with that of the United States, in terms of organizational structure or dynamics of capital market, but show notable differences in the system of governance adopted. In Canada, however, as in Australia, the shareholding is less diffuse and banks are relatively important and are engaged actively in financing organizations, moreover, a large numbers of organizations are under family control, diverging significantly by family or group.

Currently, CG models seem to evolve to form a much more complex system, one that is much more systemic and disputing the universality of the Anglo-Saxon model (Charreaux, Chapter 3) but the majority of authors recognize the impact of the American governance model and the corporation model which underlines it. Such influence, they think, is, however, confined to the supervision structure. Authors have, in fact, identified that country specific social and historical environment remain the crucial factor.

Conclusion

The last Asian financial crisis, coupled with the black series of modern corporate scandals demonstrates how organizations have let themselves relax from corporate ethic principles and to opt for information manipulations and sometimes for fraud. The curse does not limit itself to advanced economies and all countries of the world seem to have had their own misfortune. Everybody is to blame and we are all paying the price today, as investors and citizens doubt about managers' ability for guaranteeing credible financial information about organizations. Consequently, legislators all over the world have come to the conclusion of the necessity of legislating in the area of CG. Like a newspaper page set on fire in a dry forest, the SOX, had tremendously impacted CG reforms all over the world. In a way the huge progress in governance reforms scored during the last few years can be attributed to the American awareness, initiated by the Enron collapse. Such progress is especially reinforced by the work of people and organizations dedicated to the cause of governance and convinced of the accuracy of its ideals.

This book relates several national CG reform experiences around the world: Canada, China, Economies in Transition, France, Hong Kong, Japan, MENA,

Turkey, the United States, and the EU, and offers an explanatory theory with regard to national system of CG. It also underlines CG as a management tool and principle. The book presents real interest for legislators, Board members, mangers, auditors, lawyers, accountants, and students alike. The book material is original in every way and it contains a mine of new information. It also demonstrates authors' mastering of the subject and high expertise.

The reader with a clear understanding of other national CG systems, will help him better understand his own, we hope.

Notes

1 Georges Braque, in "Le Jour et la Nuit," Gallimard (Free translation). Literal translation.
2 OECD, for example, identifies five fields of the CG, of which, of more importance is responsibilities for the Board of Directors.
3 www.microsoft.com/about/companyinformation/corporategovernance/default.mspx#gov, as visited on July 27, 2007.
4 See Charreaux, Chapter 2.
5 An inefficient manager, even quite disposed, can prove as dangerous as one leading dishonest person.
6 www.rayberndstson.ca, as visited on July 20, 2007.
7 Financial Statement No. 2, Financial Accounting Standards Board (FASB).
8 Adopted in July 2002.

2 Micro theories of corporate governance

G. Charreaux

Introduction

A history of corporate governance (CG) research shows that it has been essentially devoted to Anglo-Saxon large public corporations. Thus, the study of CG systems was conducted within a particular national institutional context of formal rules (in particular, law and legal organization and organization of financial markets) and informal rules (religion, moral and national culture). It, therefore, led to the promotion of mechanisms such as the board of directors, managers' markets and takeovers, disconnected from their national specificities.

The development of research comparing the different national systems revealed that to understand both their diversity and their internal functioning logic, it was necessary to account for the national institutional architectures, for example, the nature of the legal or political systems. In an extension of this evolution, this chapter will be devoted to the theories based on the manager and the firm.[1] Once introduced, it will present approaches comprising the paradigm of governance based on both the efficiency and review of the present attempts to unite them into a synthetic theory of governance. Finally, it will conclude by providing a synoptic presentation of the different views that form the micro approach to governance.

CG in historical perspective

Contrary to what the term "corporate governance," however ambiguous, may mean, sometimes leads us to conclude, the objective of governance theories is not to study how managers govern – that would lead us to confuse the term governance with management – but rather how they are governed. To clarify the meaning we could use the analogy of the role of a child's governess. This role is mainly to supervise children and define the rules of the game and their latitude. Therefore, the governess performs two interconnected functions: a "constraining" disciplinary function and an "enabling" educational function: while the definition of the play area and nature of the games makes supervision easier, it also encourages learning.

According to an early analysis by Berle and Means (1932), performed following the crisis of 1929, the problem of governance of managers arose from the separation of ownership, into a disciplinary function, supported by the incentive and supervision systems – supposed to be performed by the shareholders – and a decision-making function – supposed to be the managers' prerogative – which came about at the beginning of the century during the emergence of the large public corporations with a broad shareholder base, the "managerial" firm, where the managers do not hold a significant share of the capital. This separation would have provoked a decline in the companies' performance and spoliation of shareholders due to the failure of the systems responsible for the discipline of the top managers.

Due to the separation of the functions usually combined under the responsibility of a single entrepreneur, Berle and Means concluded that the maximization of shareholder value should not be retained as the objective of the firm. The shareholders of the large public corporation, having renounced the performance of the "active" aspect of ownership and only performing the "passive" aspect (risk assumption), would lose their legitimacy of being the only residual claimants, in other words, the exclusive right to appropriate the profit, this status should have been held only by actors who perform active entrepreneurial functions. They consequently recommended a stakeholder approach: the large public company having to account for the interests of all the companies' stakeholders. Their theory, however, would be at the origin of a strengthening of stock market regulations in the United States resulting in the creation of the Securities and Exchange Commission, responsible for protecting financial investors. As of the beginning, the question of governance came within the scope of the "regulation" perspective of the manager's behavior, defining the "rules of the game for managers." Expressed as such, this matter was reflected only in the earliest literature dealing with the governance of political leaders.[2] Whether we are concerned with the relationship between government leaders and the people or between managers and shareholders, the problem remains one of governance. In this regard, constitutional lawyers and political scientists have had a longstanding preoccupation with governance and the traditional problem of separation of powers is typically a governance problem. In this last case, however, the rules of the game are not only directed at protecting financial wealth and revenues of constituents but other more fundamental rights as well. More recently, based particularly on the works of Roe (1994), political sciences have taken on greater importance in explaining the emergence of different national systems of corporate governance (which we will refer to as NSCG from now on), as well as legal analysis grids, even certain sociological approaches, with explanatory factors such as culture or religion. Furthermore, through the research regarding compared efficiency and the evolution of the NSCG, a traditional topic has re-emerged; that of comparing economic systems, to the point that certain authors speak freely of "New Comparative Economics" (Djankov et al., 2003a).

These developments and interdisciplinary reconciliations are hardly surprising. The very definition of governance as a system of managerial regulations leads directly to an institutionalist perspective, a natural result in sociology, law and political sciences, and strongly renewed in economics over the past three decades with the emergence of the neo-institutional approach. This perspective, applied to CG, may be considered as a specific case related to North's (1990) approach. The latter (North, 1990, pp. 3–4) defines institutions as "the rules of the game in a society" or more formally, "the humanly devised constraints that shape human interaction." The governance system therefore represents a set of institutional mechanisms – an institutional "matrix" – designating the rules of the game for managers. In this spirit, governance is defined as the set of organizational and institutional mechanisms that define the powers and influence the managers' decisions, in other words, that "govern" their conduct and define their discretionary space.

Micro theories of governance: the governance of the firm and its managers

Most micro theories focus on efficiency, but also on a particular interpretation of economic Darwinism, leading to the creation of a relationship between selection through inter-firm competition and the efficiency of the governance systems. According to the principle of natural selection adapted to the field of governance, only efficient systems that ensure the regulation of firms leading to the creation of sustainable value, survive in the long term. Consequently, the systems observed would be considered efficient. This association between survival and efficiency, contested by certain modern biological works,[3] produces a critique known as "Panglossianism."

In the field of CG, this critique aims for a conclusion, often associated with the functionalist perspective, according to which the governance systems observed would be the most efficient possible. In other words, the efficiency of first-degree would be guaranteed and the systems should systematically and automatically reach optimum performance. There are two approaches of the paradigm of efficiency: (i) the disciplinary approach and (ii) the knowledge-based approach.

The theories of governance relating to the paradigm of efficiency are all based, more or less explicitly, on a particular model of creation and allocation of value, associated with a theory of organization that is based on efficiency. The objective of every organization should be to produce a surplus, through cooperation – the organizational rent – with regard to the resources used; the allocation should be done in such a manner as to guarantee the perenniality of the organization by obtaining assistance from the different stakeholders. The view of governance as a set of rules of the game for managers can be adapted to the model for creation and/or allocation of value retained, which itself is associated to a particular conception of efficiency, and the firm. We will distinguish between the disciplinary approach and the knowledge-based approach.

The first approach is based on the contractual view of the firm, in its standard version founded on disciplinary arguments. The firm is represented as being a "nexus of contracts," in other words, a decision-making center responsible for centralized negotiations and management of all contracts required for its activities.

Due to the asymmetry of information between the economic actors and the conflicts of interests, the spontaneous management of all the contracts by the market – i.e. the only price mechanism – does not create maximum value, in other words, it does not make the best use of the investment opportunities considered as being given. For certain contracts, an authoritarian management run by the orders issued by the hierarchy was revealed to be more efficient.

This argument is at the origin of the "contractual theories" of the firm. However, it reflects a restrictive and negative view of the productive project. The source of efficiency is "disciplinary;" incentives and supervision are necessary to avoid dissipation of the profits resulting from cooperation. The firm exists because it is better able than the market to succeed in reducing loss of efficiency due to conflict of interests between the stakeholders, losses that should be measurable by the first rank Pareto optimum, sometimes referred to as "Nirvana economy" (Demsetz, 1969), which would be introduced if there were no flaws or conflicts of interests in market coordination.

The concept of efficiency that underlies this perspective may be presented as an adaptation of the allocative efficiency criteria of Pareto. According to Milgrom and Roberts (1992), an organization is inefficient if another exists that produces better average results in all possible states of the environment for all the stakeholders involved. The stakeholders should be free to negotiate and to implement and enforce their decisions.

Efficiency, defined as such, depends on the value created but, because of its Paretian origin, it also depends on the allocation of this value, and except for very particular cases – corresponding to Coase's theorem – in which allocation costs are negligible, the creation and allocation are no longer independent and separable. In other words, the method of allocation influences the level of value created. Due to the difficulties in applying this approach, it is often abandoned in favor of productive efficiency only (Rutherford, 1994), evaluated by reporting production in relation to resources consumed.

However, if the concept of information, confounded with that of knowledge, is a central part of contractual theories of the firm and the associated CG theories – the organizational problems originate in the asymmetry of information – the "knowledge-based" theories of the firm distinguish between the concepts of information and knowledge, favoring the latter. If, according to Fransman (1998), information refers to an objective closed set of data – that all individuals can potentially acquire – related to the consequences of possible events, then knowledge, on the contrary, represents an open subjective set resulting from the individuals' interpretation of the information, according to their cognitive models. For Langlois (2001), knowledge is a complex structure, based on experience and consisting of a system of action rules that determine the meaning and the utility of the information.

If, through a contractual perspective, the creation of value results only from the resolution of conflicts of interests based on asymmetry of information, then knowledge-based theories would have other bases linked to knowledge acquisition and innovation: this enables the firm, a well identified entity, to acquire the faculty of learning and to create knowledge. The process of creating value does not always take the disciplinary path, but sometimes a production path based on skills. The Pareto (allocation) efficiency or the simple productive efficiency in the static sense are abandoned in favor of a dynamic or adaptive approach, inspired by Schumpeter, who places great importance on innovation and flexibility and therefore the ability to creating sustainable value.

Let us specify that the two paradigms are separated mainly by an argument deemed crucial to the process of value creation – disciplinary vs knowledge-based – rather than the opposition between the "nexus of contracts" firm and the "productive entity" firm, which is possible to transcend by retaining a constitutionalist view (Vanberg, 1994) of the nexus of contracts. In the latter, the contracts network is interpreted as a constitution defining the common rules that allow the firm to act as an entity.

The disciplinary view of CG

The disciplinary perspective has numerous variants based on the representation of the nexus of contracts and the analysis of the process of value creation. Traditionally, we distinguish the financial or shareholder view as dominating the stakeholder view.

The shareholder model of governance

Resulting from the debate opened by Berle and Means regarding the large public corporation, the financial model of governance is normally associated with the agency theory. Paradoxically – the initial analysis relating to the entrepreneurial firm opening its capital – this model originated in an analysis of Jensen and Meckling (1976) that focused on two main objectives. The first very ambitious objective was to propose a contractual theory of the firm seen as a team of pro-ductive inputs (Alchian and Demsetz, 1972), inspired by the theory of property rights and focusing on the agency relationship concept. The second more limited objective was to illustrate the explanatory power of this theory with regard to the problem of the capital structure of the firm.

If, in the beginning, Jensen and Meckling considered the firm as a nexus of contracts, associating the firm and the entire group of resource contributors (the team of productive inputs), their limited objective of explaining the capital struc-ture led them to construct a more simplified model taking into consideration only two agency relationships. The first linked the manager to the shareholders and the second linked the firm (represented by the managers and shareholders) to the financial creditors.

This initial modeling, that gave priority placement to the analysis of the rela-tionship between the manager-entrepreneur opening his capital and the new shareholders – the shareholders playing the role of "principal" and the manager that of the "agent" – was to lead to the shareholder approach that still dominates normative research and reflections today. Traditionally associated with the legal approach to ownership, presumed[4] to recognize only the shareholders as the owners – or the only "residual"[5] claimants – it attributes the unique role of "securing" the financial investment (Shleifer and Vishny, 1997) to the governance system. According to this disciplinary perspective, the governance mechanisms constitute a means of forcing the managers to "maximize" the shareholder value. This perspective has particularly dominated the studies relating to the board of directors, the annual shareholder's meeting, the remuneration systems for managers, the legal and accounting regulations and takeovers as well.

However, the shareholder model is most often based on the normative branch of the agency theory – referred to as "principal-agent" – claiming through hypothesis, in its dominant model, that the shareholders are the only principals and the managers are the only agents. Moreover, it is possible to justify the shareholder objective in a different manner, to better conform to the positive branch of the agency theory resulting from the analysis of Jensen and Meckling. In accordance with the natural selection principle, we need only maintain (Jensen, 2001) that organizational practices have emerged in endogenous fashion, reinforcing the probability of survival of the firms that adopted them. However, the question is now to justify this argument by attempting to identify the sources of the advantage granted.

A first justification, developed by Williamson (1984, 1985), consists in assuming that if the stakeholders, other than the shareholders, are effectively protected by their contracts, the particular characteristics of the transaction that constitute the contribution of financial capital, render the shareholders particularly exposed to risks of opportunism and they would assume the major part of the residual risk. Consequently, the governance system would be constructed by entrusting the control to the shareholders in order to protect their interests and reduce the costs of this particular transaction. Hansmann (1996) completed this first argument by retaining the manager's control costs. A cost that is too high could do more than compensate for the economy of transaction costs realized by entrusting control only to the shareholders. As such, the shareholder value is also required since the presumed homogeneity of the shareholders interests would lead to a low cost, collective decision. The shareholder objective is therefore based on two hypotheses: (i) the shareholder investment is the least protected against the opportunism of managers; and (ii) there is homogeneity of interests between the different categories of shareholders. The latter hypothesis becomes invalid if conflicts exist between the dominating shareholders, holders of controlling interest and minority stockholders.

In the perspective opened by Jensen and Meckling, completed mainly by the analysis of Fama (1980), devoted to the large public corporation, the system of governance is comprised of "internal" mechanisms, implemented intentionally by the stakeholders or by the legislator, and "external" mechanisms resulting from the spontaneous functioning of the markets. The "internal" mechanisms, such as the voting rights attributed to the shareholders, the board of directors, the remuneration systems, the audits decided by the managers ... or "external" mechanisms, such as the market of managers and takeovers, are all mechanisms that appeared and persisted due to their ability to reduce agency costs resulting from conflicts between managers and shareholders. Other mechanisms such as contractual guarantees, rules of bankruptcy procedure, the financial information market, even an informal mechanism such as reputation, are justified by the resolution of conflicts of interests existing between the firm and the financial creditors.

These different mechanisms do not necessarily have the same significance. A hierarchy exists that varies according to the type of company. As such, according to Fama, for large public corporations, the dominating mechanism is the market of managers – the managers attempt to maximize the shareholder value to improve their reputation and value on the market – that is based on the evaluation of the performance by the financial market. This first mechanism is completed by internal mechanisms such as hierarchy, mutual monitoring between members of the management team and, most of all, the board of directors. The latter has only one disciplinary function, based either on incentive by linking the remuneration of the managers to the shareholder value (bonus, stock-options), sanction through the eviction of the manager or the monitoring performed, for example, by the audit committee. To be efficient, the board must simultaneously include inside directors (members of management) for informational purposes and outside directors whose independence should be guaranteed by the existence of a competitive market of directors. The takeover market, a brutal and costly disciplinary mechanism, intervenes only as a last resort.

The loss of value, depending on the nature of the conflicts (managers/shareholders or shareholders/creditors), has various origins (underinvestment, "private benefits" resulting from the appropriation of part of the organizational rent in the form of perquisites or additional compensation). Certain models (Shleifer and Vishny, 1989) integrate entrenchment strategies implemented by the manager. The latter, to avoid being dismissed – he would therefore avoid the loss of human capital and could continue appropriating rents – may make his replacement more costly for the shareholders by preferring to invest in "idiosyncratic" investment projects or projects with reduced visibility. In the first case, the profitability is dependent on the presence of the manager as leader of the company; his dismissal would result in a loss of part of the organizational rent for the shareholders. In the second case, it would be more difficult for the shareholders to value the opportunity of a replacement and there is less pressure from the managers' market. This process of taking the managers' defensive behavior into account as well as their strategies for seeking rents is not inconsistent with the paradigm of efficiency. Since entrenchment increases agency costs, the governance systems are supposed to adapt in order to reduce a priori the negative effects of this type of strategy.

This first governance approach focuses on financial investors. The creation of shareholder value involves the discipline of the managers. The financial model constitutes the principal foundation for debates regarding the remunerations of managers and directors, the role, the composition (whether outside directors – or not), the form (single or two-tier) of the board of directors, the disciplinary role of takeovers, the measure of performance assured by the financial market, freedom of expression and the protection of small investors. This predominant model, inspired directly by the Anglo-Saxon large public corporation, has, however, greatly evolved, influenced by the concentration of equity capital in the non Anglo-Saxon countries and by the considerable spoliation of small investors by the dominating shareholders, in particular, during privatizations in the former Eastern bloc countries. Originally focused on the manager, the attention was moved to the dominating shareholders who would take advantage of their position to appropriate the major part of the rent. In a sense, the financial model is more concerned, today, with the dominating conflict between shareholders/small investors rather than the conflict between managers/shareholders.[6]

Since the shareholders are the only residual claimants, the efficiency of the different mechanisms is measured only according to shareholder value, which resulted in numerous empirical studies thanks to the availability of financial data banks. These often ambiguous results (Becht *et al.*, 2002), in all probability due to the effects of complementarity and substitution arising between the various mechanisms, conclude that the explanatory ability of the shareholder model is limited. The limitations of this model, in particular, for explaining the structure and functioning of non Anglo-Saxon systems and the small degree of realism in view of the minor role the shareholders play in the financing of companies or the ambiguous relationship connecting the disciplinary systems to shareholder performance, contribute to an extension in order to take other stakeholders into account, such as employees.

The disciplinary stakeholder model

The disciplinary stakeholder model also finds its origin in the representation of the firm as a team of productive inputs of which the synergies are the basis for the organizational rent. Modifications to the model for value creation, as compared to the shareholder model, are related to distribution by calling into question the shareholders' status of exclusive residual claimants. The abandonment of this hypothesis led to a questioning of the sharing of the rent that, due to the fact that the investment/financing are not separable, also has an influence on value creation. The contributors of production factors, other than the shareholders, would be encouraged to contribute to value creation only if they were to receive a share of the rent, therefore attaining status of residual claimant. In other words, as specified by Zingales (1998), governance only has an impact on the creation of the rent through distribution: "the governance system is simply a set of constraints governing the negotiations ex post for the sharing of the rent between the different stakeholders."

This view is a result of the renewal of the analysis of property rights within the incomplete contract theory (Grossman and Hart, 1986; Hart and Moore, 1990).[7] Ownership is defined as much by the residual control rights[8] as by the allocation of residual gains. The ownership status can be extended to all the parties to the nexus of contracts. A salaried employee, who is assigned the power of decision in order to better utilize his knowledge, becomes part owner. He therefore has a greater incentive to contribute more effort when he would collect a share of the organizational rent, in the form of over-remuneration, regardless of its form (monetary or not), in comparison to his reservation salary. This extension of the analysis puts special emphasis on human resources (Blair, 1995, 1999).

The attention given to managers, of great importance with regard to the question of governance, led Castanias and Helfat (1991) to question their role in the production of the organizational rent, that is to say, the importance of the managerial rent due to their specific skills. Even if the model does not provide direct reference to the concept of extended ownership, it supposes that the more rent the managers are able to appropriate the more incentive they will have to produce the rent. Then the problem of sharing the rent with the shareholders arises, which can be explained by the respective contributions of the shareholders and the managers and the shortage of skills offered. If the shareholder function is limited to the contribution of equity capital – "passive" ownership – and the financial market is competitive, shareholders hold less power; consequently, they must be remunerated at their opportunity cost that is presumed to be equal to the market equilibrium rate, to keep them in the nexus of contracts. However, it is best for the managers to share the rent with them in order to avoid dismissal; therefore, their interests converge to a certain extent with those of the shareholders. This situation changes the view of the governance system – the intensity of conflicts considered as being less significant than within the financial model – and results in different interpretations of certain mechanisms.

Thus, contrary to the traditional analysis, the managers' entrenchment strategies do not necessarily lead to a destruction of value (Garvey and Swan, 1994; Charreaux, 1996). Entrenchment, by securing the profitability of the human capital investment specific to the firm, encourages further investments on the part of the manager, which can produce a higher organizational rent. This reasoning can be transposed to the managerial latitude: excessive discipline by reducing latitude can produce a drop in efforts and initiatives of the managers further provoking a drop in efficiency (Burkart *et al.*, 1997).

The issue of the origin of the rent put emphasis on the specific skills of the employees in addition to the managerial capital. As emphasized by Rajan and Zingales (1998a), it plays a determining role, particularly in the New Economy. However, the specificity of human capital, if it is the basis for the rent, renders it vulnerable to attempts at expropriation. The governance system is therefore justified by its ability to protect this capital. The firm becomes a nexus of specific investments: a combination of co-specific assets and persons[9] (Zingales, 1998, 2000; Rajan and Zingales, 1998a, 2000). The organizational rent depends on the process of accumulation of specific assets associated with the critical resources brought by the manager. The sustainability is ensured if the growth of the rent is sufficient to encourage the different stakeholders to develop their specific investments, in particular, the employees to invest in their human capital. Furthermore, as specified by Rajan and Zingales (2000), due to the increasing inalienability of the critical assets, allocation rather than managerial shirking would become the major problem with regard to governance.

Finally, the logical conclusion to the stakeholder approach is its generalization to all the parties to the nexus of contracts, contributing to the formation of an organizational rent. The latter also depends on the particular skills offered, notably in long-term cooperation relationships, by certain suppliers, sub-contractors or customers. Such an approach assumes that the relationships between the firm and the different stakeholders are not reduced to simple market exchanges governed by prices, but are rather frequently co-constructed. As proposed by Charreaux (1995) and Charreaux and Desbrières (1998), this approach studies and evaluates the governance system in accordance with its ability to create stakeholder value[10] – for all stakeholders – by reducing the loss of value due to conflicts relating to the redistribution of the rent among the different stakeholders.

Modeling of the formation of value in the stakeholder model is summarized, essentially, by the resolution of conflicts of interests by influencing distribution, even if certain knowledge-based aspects superficially appear (Charreaux, 2002a). Then, according to Alchian and Demsetz, the manager acquires a particular skill relating to the other production factors and stricto sensu plays a much greater role in management than simply monitoring or "metering." However, the process of value creation itself remains unexplored. Also, Fama and Jensen (1983a, 1983b), Jensen and Meckling (1992) or Jensen (1998) are satisfied with their restricted view that organizational architecture, the forms of ownership and governance systems are organized in such a way as to optimize the use of knowledge, the latter not being truly differentiated from information. The models of Rajan and Zingales (1998a) and Blair and Stout (1999) offer little more. If the first model considers that the organizational rent is due to specific investments made by the different stakeholders and the second model insists on the importance of both vertical and horizontal cooperation to produce this rent, we may not really view this analysis of the process of value creation in terms of comparative advantages linked to production. The theory of the firm of Rajan and Zingales, in particular, remains traditional in its view of value creation and investment. Consistent with the theory of the firm of Hart and Moore (1990) but proposing a more extensive and complete model, its view of governance remains exclusively disciplinary. The objective is to reduce the loss of efficiency resulting from the conflicts associated with the sharing of the rent and, most particularly, those linked to underinvestment resulting from the specificity of assets and the hold-up phenomenon in the tradition of Williamson. This conclusion also applies to the more general analyses (Pagano, 1993; Pagano and Rossi, 2002; Nicita and Pagano, 2002), which emphasize the two types of causality existing between the structure of ownership rights and the development of skills. If, according to Grossman and Hart's theory of property rights, it is the characteristics of the assets, including human assets, which determine the structure of the ownership, the reverse may also be true.

The definitions of stakeholder governance confirm this interpretation. Zingales and Blair[11] mention only the decision and appropriation rights of the rent.

Berglöf and Von Thadden's (1999) definition, considering governance as a set of mechanisms that translates the signals emitted by the goods market and the production factors in the behavior of the firms, is seemingly different, but its justification based on two arguments: (i) the importance of recognizing the existence of categories of actors other than only the financial investors and managers; and (ii) the necessity of considering a larger context involving the competition on the goods market and inter-firm connections, apart from the fact that it is introduced in a purely normative manner, is based only on disciplinary aspects.

However, the role of organizational knowledge appears to be more important in the theory of the specialized firm (Demsetz, 1991), resulting in a transition, maybe even a primary synthesis, of the disciplinary and knowledge-based theories of the firm. The latter is represented as "a bundle of commitments to technology, personnel, and methods, all contained and constrained by an insulating layer of information that is specific to the firm, and this bundle cannot be altered or imitated easily or quickly." While remaining consistent with the contractual perspective, this definition presumes that there are only three conditions under which a nexus of contracts is a firm: (i) specialization: the firm must be a specialized production unit for others; (ii) continuity of association: the nexus of contracts must be durable; and (iii) reliance on direction: the coordination must be governed by corporate management. Demsetz adds that, in addition to market coordination costs and monitoring, the third factor determining the productivity of the firm relates to the acquisition and use of knowledge. Finally, firms are defined as "repositories of specialized knowledge and of the specialized inputs required to put this knowledge to work" (Demsetz, 1991, pp. 171–172), their boundaries determined, in particular, by "the economics of conservation of expenditures on knowledge" (Demsetz, 1991, p. 173).

The knowledge-based approach of governance

The disciplinary view of governance remains captive to the limits of the theories of the firm on which it is founded and either ignores the productive dynamic or offers a restricted view limited to the impact of incentive systems on production choices. If the link between skills and organizational rent is recognized, if the stakeholder value apparently has better explanatory potential than that of shareholder value, the view remains based on static and reactive conceptions of efficiency. The value is maximized at a given moment with the managers presumably aware of all investment opportunities, the choice of investment made according to an analogy of the "menu." The main aspect, in conformance with the disciplinary perspective, remains the organization of rent distribution sufficiently incentive to maximize value. The process of value creation through the emergence of the investment opportunity set, in particular, is still neglected.

To comprehend this process, we must call on the knowledge-based theories of the firm. Contrary to the disciplinary theories that can be interpreted lato sensu as extensions of the neo-classical economic model, these theories break away from this model. They particularly reject the hypothesis of calculative rationality, limited or not, in favor of procedural rationality. Rationality is assessed not according to the consequences of decisions but rather their governing processes. In these theories, value creation depends mainly on the identity and the skills of the firm, viewed as a coherent entity (Teece *et al.*, 1994). Its specificity is linked to its capacity to create knowledge and therefore long-term profitability. A dynamic concept of efficiency is retained.

Much the same as the disciplinary theories, the knowledge-based theories include numerous perspectives that favor knowledge-based arguments. By caricaturing these aspects, due to their frequent imbrications, we can identify three main perspectives:

i   The behavioral perspective introduced by Simon (1947), March and Simon (1958) and Cyert and March (1963): the firm is a political coalition and a cognitive institution that adapts itself through organizational learning.[12]

ii   The neo-Schumpeterian evolutionary economic theory developed mainly by Nelson and Winter (1982), that led to a very important line of research.[13] The firm is defined as an entity coherently uniting activities, a repository of productive knowledge (Eliasson, 1990; Winter, 1991), an interpretive system (Loasby, 2001b), that favors the concept that competition is based on innovation. This theory substitutes, in particular, the representation of investment choices as a pre-existing menu with a conception in which the menu is constructed from knowledge acquired by learning and stored in the organizational routines.

iii   The strategy theories based on resources and capabilities (the Resource-Based View – RBV) that results mainly from the growth theory of the firm proposed by Penrose (1959). The firm appears to be a set of resources and an entity for accumulation of knowledge guided by the vision of the managers and depending on the experience they have acquired. The origin of sustainable growth is found in the ability to learn and in the specificity of the stock of accumulated knowledge. This theory is at the origin of an extensive[14] current of research that considers the knowledge-based theory of the firm stricto sensu (the Knowledge-Based View of the Firm[15] – KBV) as one of its components.

The framework of creation and allocation of value that underlies the knowledge-based theories differs profoundly from the one underlying the contractual-disciplinary theories, in which the productive aspect is either ignored or reduced to the incentive perspective (Langlois and Foss, 1999). It results in an approach that is different from the reasons for the firm's existence that not only distinguish it from the market but also from its competitors, in other words, that defines its identity. For example, according to Foss (1996a), firms exist because they can more efficiently coordinate the process of collective learning. According to Dosi (1990), firms represent a set of core competencies and complementary assets associated with these competencies and the boundaries of the firm must be understood not only in terms of transaction costs but also in terms of learning, path dependence, technological opportunities, selection and complementarity of assets.

The main element is the importance attributed to the productive aspect as much from the viewpoint of innovation as coordination. Therefore, according to Loasby (2001a), the problem of coordination cannot be relevantly expressed by defining the firm as a simple informational system in which coordination is performed only through incentive methods. It must be reformulated in relation to an objective of growth based not on the use of information but on the use of knowledge, which is not only the collection of information but the processing and interpretation as well. This reformulation also implies a more complex conception of the firm seen as an open system and the rejection of the equilibrium concept in favor of the process concept. In a similar perspective, Hodgson (1989) defines production as a social process that involves people with their own personal aspirations and as constraining their interactions. Efficiency depends not only on technology but also on the motivation and abilities of the manpower, organization and managerial supervision, the latter two based on the institutional structures and routines as well as the cultural norms inherited in the past.

The perceptive aspect of the entrepreneurial function linked to the management's ability for imagination, perception and construction of new opportunities (Prahalad, 1994), also plays an important role, more important than the restructuring or reconfiguration of the firm's business portfolio in response to the evolution of the environment. Let us recall that the objective is to ensure sustainable value creation, in particular, through the creation of growth opportunities.

In summary, the firm when viewed as a processor or repository of knowledge is based on the following applications of the knowledge-based argument:[16] (i) orientation of the activity in accordance with the managers' view; (ii) the creation of knowledge as a basis for innovation and all investment opportunities, this knowledge possesses a tacit and social character that makes it difficult to imitate; (iii) protection of the knowledge database; (iv) coordination of the productive activity that involves aspects such as construction, exploitation and transfer of knowledge that go above and beyond the simple transfer of information (Hodgson, 1998);[17] (v) resolution of conflicts, that goes above the conflicts of interests to take on a knowledge-based aspect.

This last point deserves a special comment. A significant difference between the nature of conflicts of interests and cognitive conflicts is determining although it is advantageous to reduce conflicts of interests to a minimum; this objective seems less than optimal for cognitive conflicts. Innovation, even simple adaptation, seems favored by the coexistence of conflicting cognitive frameworks (Foss, 1996b). In other words, the increases in efficiency resulting from the reduction of cognitive conflicts may be more than compensated for by the reduction of the potential for innovation or adaptation. We find here the traditional opposition between "exploitation" and "exploration" (March, 1991) or between "static efficiency" and "dynamic efficiency" (Dosi, 1990).

The knowledge-based approach to the firm leads to a reconsideration of the role of governance. It must support the identification and implementation of profitable investments within a dynamic efficiency perspective. According to Demsetz (1969), to comprehend the influence of the institutional framework – and hence of the governance system – on dynamic efficiency, we

> must strive to balance three objectives: (1) a wide variety of experimentation should be encouraged; (2) investment should be channeled into promising varieties of experimentation and away from unpromising varieties; (3) the new knowledge that is acquired should be employed extensively.
>
> (Demsetz, 1969)

The critique addressed by Prahalad (1994) regarding the financial view of governance supports this approach: this view must be expanded to consider the quality of the relationship between managers and investors and its potential for increasing the efficiency of the firm, to identify and create growth opportunities. In a broader perspective, the knowledge-based approach results in studying governance systems according to their influence on the different cognitive aspects of the value creation process.

The knowledge-based approach also involves a reconsideration of the traditional financial approach to governance, in which the relationship between the firm and the financial investors is limited to the contribution of capital and where the only objective is to secure the financial investment by disciplining the managers as best as possible. Therefore, as suggested by various authors, finance also includes a cognitive aspect. Accordingly, Aoki (2001) believes that, in the governance model associated with venture capital, it is not the ability of the venture capital investor to contribute funds that is the most important factor, but his ability, based on his knowledge and experience, to select the most promising projects and refuse the financing (or refinancing) of the less interesting projects, without delay. Similarly, Charreaux (2002a, 2002b) proposes an interpretation of the financing policy based on cognitive arguments that explicitly involve the contribution of expertise from the shareholders, in particular, industrial shareholders. Such developments plead in favor of a reconstruction of the financial view of governance extended to include cognitive aspects.

Attempting a synthesis

Of course, following the examples of Winter (1991), Foss (1996b) and Foss and Foss (2000), we may wonder if the knowledge-based theories are incompatible with the disciplinary theories.[18] As their analyses show and as the constitutionalist approach to the nexus of contracts suggests, a certain number of intersections are possible. The fundamental considerations of the disciplinary theories, in particular in terms of conflicts of interests, can be useful to better understand the performance of the firm viewed as a collection of competencies. For example, the sharing of common cognitive frameworks can lead to a reduction in conflicts of interest, the concept of specificity can be applied to organizational abilities, the protection of knowledge and the appropriateness of rents can explain corporate acquisition policies. However, the cognitive aspects directly linked to the productive function, possessing a tacit and social character associated with organizational learning, cannot be comprehended through disciplinary arguments only.

The concept of access to a "network of specific investments" introduced by Zingales, which he compares to that of organizational capital, can indeed be directly transposed in terms of access to the knowledge database. However, this analysis, that promotes the disciplinary aspects (of control and incentive), is unable to integrate the cognitive aspect of the creation of organizational capital. In contrast, the works of Lazonick and O'Sullivan (Lazonick, 2000; O'Sullivan, 2000, 2001; Lazonick and O'Sullivan, 1998, 2000) focusing on the governance of innovative firms and the more ambitious works of Aoki may be considered, to a certain extent, as attempts at a study for constructing a theory of corporate governance where disciplinary and cognitive aspects are simultaneously at work.[19]

The presentation of these works would be an occasion to illustrate the structure of the links that exist between the micro and macro levels of governance. This approach does not mean that we begin the second part devoted to the presentation of the theories of the NSCG, but we must correctly show the imbrications of the different levels of analysis – in particular organizational and institutional – in the different theories of corporate governance. If considerations on the macro level are introduced, particularly in the presentation of the Aokian theory, they are only to better understand the architecture of all the governance systems governing the firm and its managers, while the specificities of the different NSCG are not presented.

Lazonick and O'Sullivan: governance of the innovative firm

The works of Lazonik and O'Sullivan resulted in the formulation of a theory of the innovative firm. While based mainly on knowledge-based theories, they represent one of the best illustrations of recent attempts at considering the disciplinary and knowledge-based aspects jointly to model value creation. The concept of innovation retained is very broad; it is not based only on the technological aspect but also includes administrative and marketing aspects.

These works have succeeded in defining synthetic governance, attributing a central position to investment. According to O'Sullivan (2000), "a system of corporate governance shapes who makes the investment decisions in corporations, what types of investments they make, and how returns from investments are distributed." The focus on the innovative firm leads to the proposition of a governance theory centered on organizational control – as opposed to control by the market – to obtain a framework that can analyze the institutional conditions that support the innovation process. To be efficient, this process must comply with three conditions: (i) it must facilitate development: the resources must be committed long term because of the irreversible and uncertain character of the investments that support organizational learning; (ii) it must possess an organizational aspect (organization of work): organizational learning can only be executed through the interactions inside the firm; (iii) it must have a strategic character because it results from decisions that not only depend on the subjective interpretation of the environment but that evolve in accordance with the experience, which determines learning and modifies the very context of the decision. To sum up, the allocation process must be "developmental, organizational and strategic."

The characteristics of the innovation process lead to a complementary conception and analysis of the governance system also based on three conditions:

i   financial commitment to support the development of expertise, but also to obtain sufficient time for the innovation investments to be profitable;
ii organizational integration that offers incentives for the insiders to invest their expertise and efforts in accordance with the objectives of the firm, and;
iii insider control over the allocation of corporate resources and returns, to ensure that those who exercise control have the abilities and incentives to make innovative investments.

This micro analysis leads to a macro analysis of the NSCG based on the concept of a "skill base" (Lazonick and O'Sullivan, 1998), deemed to be a determining factor in understanding the motivations of individuals to commit to a collective and cumulative learning process. The example of the Japanese domination in certain sectors leads to the conclusion that only the "broad and deep" skill bases can procure a sustainable competitive advantage. Inversely, the American situation, characterized by organizational methods that are based on three types of segmentation – hierarchical, functional and strategic – would not be the most conducive to producing efficient organizational learning. It would result in a type of innovation based on "narrow and concentrated" skill bases, unsuitable for sustainable growth.

Based on this view, three categories of conditions resulting in the emergence of the innovative firm were defined: (i) industrial (technological, market and competitive); (ii) organizational (cognitive, behavioral and strategic); and (iii) institutional (financial, employment, regulatory). The analysis otherwise focuses on the dynamic interactions between organizational and institutional conditions emphasizing four main types of institutions: (i) the "executive" institutions in charge of setting out the responsibilities and qualifications of the decision makers with regard to allocation of resources and returns within the companies; (ii) the "supervisory" institutions whose role it is to determine which stakeholders the decision makers will be accountable to; (iii) the "consultative" institutions whose function is to specify the stakeholders to be consulted (unions, shareholders, company groups, etc.) as well as the consultation procedures; and (iv) the "regulatory" institutions that define the laws and rules for company decisions relating to the allocation of resources and returns.

This governance theory, based on the innovation process, recommends methods of redistribution of rents other than those normally retained in shareholder or stakeholder models, for example, favoring entrepreneurs responsible for launching new projects. It also contributes to the analysis of certain mechanisms such as the board of directors, in relation to their ability to encourage organizational learning and to conclude, for example, that this body should include representatives from every entity (organizations of employees, companies, financial institutions, training institutions, public bodies, etc.) in agreement with this objective. Finally, more generally, the State is attributed the important role of structuring the institutions in a manner so as to facilitate the organizational learning process.

This resolutely prescriptive approach is critical with regard to the financial view of governance as well as the stakeholder approach; they are criticized for ignoring the dynamics of innovation. Beyond its normative aspect, it recommends an analysis of governance systems, based on their ability to facilitate innovation.

Aoki and the comparative institutional analysis

Initially, Aoki's research regarded the theory of the "cooperative" firm (Aoki, 1980, 1984) based on the cooperation between shareholders and employees, attributing as much importance to the horizontal and participative dimension of coordination as the vertical dimension, and on the complementarity of mechanisms within the Japanese firm (Aoki, 1988, 1990). More recently, extending his research on the firm, Aoki (2000a, 2000b, 2001) proposed a "comparative institutional analysis" that very likely, at the present time, constitutes the most advanced and ambitious study on governance systems, simultaneously taking into consideration the disciplinary and productive aspects. Although the latter analysis is conducted at the macro level, the central role of the firm in the model justifies that it be included in the first section.

In a framework of analysis based on the subjective evolutionary game theory – in which the different players are supposed to possess individual and incomplete cognitive views of the game – Aoki defines the institutions of governance as self-enforcing mechanisms that govern the strategic interactions between the players.[20] These mechanisms (formal or informal) regulate the choice of actions of the stakeholders (investors, employees and managers) in the organizational field. The analysis of governance systems is consistent with a very general issue that primarily tries to understand the complexity and diversity of the different NSCG from a static perspective as corresponding to the multiple Pareto equilibria solutions for the same game. Second, the objective is to analyze the dynamic mechanism of change within these systems in accordance with the view that institutions are equilibria solutions for an evolutionary game, while taking innovation into consideration.

This analysis strays from the normative analyses of governance, such as those that most often dominate the financial approach or that underlie discussions regarding the governance of the innovative firm. Aoki's objective is to understand the bases of the diversity of governance systems, while admitting that the least efficient systems and mechanisms can be eliminated in the long term due to the competition between firms, in conformance to the natural selection principle.

An economy is a game characterized by a set of domains (the domains of common resources – "commons," trade – economic exchange, organizational, political economy – "polity" and social exchange) connected by a group of institutions that comprise an "overall institutional arrangement," or in other words, a system.

The developments in organizational architecture, based on the theory of the cooperative firm, represent a particularly important aspect of the analysis. This architecture is defined in relation to the division (vertical and horizontal) of the cognitive labor, in other words, information and knowledge processing activities between the different components of the organization. Aoki's objective was to identify the main types of architecture in relation to building blocks based on the different methods of informational connection and to study their ability for adapting to the evolution of the environment as much in the commercial aspect as the technological one.

Based on the distinction between vertical and horizontal relationships as well as the opposition between systematic information and idiosyncratic information (specific to a task), Aoki defines a certain number of organizational types (functional hierarchies, network-integrated functional hierarchies, hierarchical-controlled teams, horizontal hierarchies, participatory hierarchies, suppliers keiretsu, Italian industrial districts, third-party information mediation – Silicon Valley clustering, etc.). He shows that their efficiency depends on the nature of human assets and skills and, more generally, that there must be a concerted evolution – a co-evolution – between organizational structures and the nature of human capital expressed in terms of competence. He also shares certain conclusions with Zingales (2000), but within a larger framework, attributing a central place to the cognitive aspects, particularly to mental models able to interpret the environment. In this analysis, the State is considered a full player with its own objectives but also as a constraint through its interactions with the other players. This integration of public power introduces the political aspect within the governance systems and studies its influence as it interacts with the rest of the system.

This very general framework contributes to the method of analysis of governance that is based on a structure that involves three types of players: the financial investors, the employees – the investors in human capital – and the managers who decide on the use of the resources and assume a central role. In order to discuss the self-enforcing character of governance mechanisms, Aoki puts a special emphasis on the institutionalized links that exist between the organizational domain – in relation to the different types of organizational structure – and the domains of financial transactions, work relations and polity, in particular evaluating their interactions.

This analysis identified numerous models of institutional arrangements, classified into three groups. The first group includes two referential and theoretical models: the Walrasian model and the model of the firm associated with the theory of Grossman, Hart and Moore. The second unites different national models based on stylized observations of the main developed countries such as the United States, Germany and Japan, before the transformations resulting from new information technology. Aoki specifies that other models representing, for example, France, Italy or the Scandinavian countries may have been added, but an analysis remains to be performed. Finally, the third group is comprised of two emerging models, the globalization model and that of venture capital associated with the Silicon Valley. The analysis continues with an examination of outcome of national models in comparison to the emerging models. Will the latter dominate them or replace them altogether? Or will the national models evolve in order to efficiently meet the challenges set out by these new models?

The work of Aoki seems to best express the micro and macro aspects of governance, even if it is debatable in many regards. Among other things, we may regret that the framework of the game theory as well as the way of considering information/knowledge prompts a sometime superficial integration of the cognitive aspects, in particular the production of knowledge through organizational learning. We can also regret the often arbitrary character of the typologies used and contest them by re-examining the critique expressed by Coriat and Weinstein (1995) addressing the Aokian theory of the firm, the advanced causality model, based on the generic modes of information connectedness, that may seem inadequately adapted for taking organizational innovations into account. The magnitude of the reflection undertaken concerning the links between the types of organizational architecture and the institutional systems, as well as the effects of complementarity between the different types of institutions, resulted however, in all probability, in the most elaborate governance theory as of yet. Table 2.A1 provides a summary of the principal characteristics of the different micro theories of CG of the firm.

Conclusion

Most micro theories of governance come under the perspective of efficiency, but also on a particular interpretation of economic Darwinism, leading to the creation of a relationship between selection through inter-firm competition and the efficiency of the governance systems. The function of a governance mechanism or, more generally, a governance system, is to contribute to the efficiency of the firm. Thus, mechanisms such as the board of directors or hostile takeover bids would, by ensuring a better discipline of the managers, contribute to the increase of efficiency of the firm that creates more value. However, if most of the theories retain this criterion, they attribute it differing contents. In the disciplinary perspectives of governance the existing governance systems are, however, not presumed efficient in the absolute, but only in a relative and precarious manner – particularly because of institutional and organizational innovations – and after taking the costs of adaptation into account, according to the principle of remediability.[21] In particular, this principle is not opposed to path dependence and therefore, the contingent nature of efficiency according to the historical development of the institutional framework.

Other theories belonging to economics or more often to sociology or strategic management, propose an explanation other than efficiency in the sense that the reasons put forth are connected, for example, to research and appropriation of rents produced by firms by coercion, creation of dependency or influence. Mechanisms, such as the board of directors, the directors' network or the hostile takeover bids, are therefore viewed as means of acquiring power in order to collect wealth and not as a disciplinary lever to achieve greater efficiency. These theories are sometimes based on an integrative logic in which the managers or the firm are supposed to obey a collective rationality greater than themselves, for example, of a social class or a network. In other cases, particularly in connection with the New Institutional Sociology approach, they provide justification of an inter-organizational nature for certain governance mechanisms. For example, the board of directors and directors' network would serve only to fulfill a function of social legitimization, ensuring the distribution of cognitive or normative models between organizations – for example, shareholder value – without this function necessarily having an effect on the efficiency of the organizations. The latter theories, however, rarely focusing on the firm, do not strictly speaking; constitute micro theories of governance systems, as do the theories of efficiency.

Notes

1 The next chapter will present the different macro theories, the objective of which is to identify and explain the main configurations of the NSCG.
2 This anteriority of the political analysis of governance is particularly evoked by Becht *et al.* (2002) who show that the political model was explicit at the time of the creation of the American Corporate Law.
3 According to these works, the concepts of selection and adaptation are not necessarily connected, since selection does not depend only on adaptation but also on the ability of the species to procreate.
4 This interpretation of the legal view is contested, including in the United States. See, in particular, Blair and Stout (1999).
5 The "residual," similar to profit, is what remains after remuneration of the various production factors. The resource contributors, other than the shareholders, should be remunerated at their opportunity cost corresponding to a price fixed on the presumed competitive markets. The shareholders are the only stakeholders that have the status of residual creditor and who are attributed a rent. Their interests therefore converge with those of all the other parties to the nexus of contracts. This hypothesis assumes that the remunerations paid to stakeholders other than the shareholders, take into account all the consequences of the decisions made by the firm, therefore, no externality exists.
6 This evolution led La Porta *et al.* (2000a, p. 4) to define "corporate governance is, to a large extent, a set of mechanisms through which outside investors protect themselves against expropriation by the insiders."
7 For Grossman and Hart (1986, p. 692) the firm is defined in terms of ownership of assets and the authority associated with holding residual control rights resulting in an ex post allocation of a substantial share of the rent. It will consequently influence ex ante investment decisions. Hart and Moore (1990, p. 1121) specify that the only right held by an asset owner is his ability to prevent others from using it. This authority, over the use of physical assets, results in retaining that of the employees.

8 That is to say the decision rights that are not explicitly provided for by the contracts or the law.

9 Co-specificity signifies that profitability depends on the cooperation of the combination of different factors. There is a reciprocal dependence.

10 The stakeholder value is defined by the organizational rent generated, which is equal to the difference between the sum of the revenues evaluated at opportunity price and the total of the opportunity costs.

11 Zingales (1998), in a spirit similar to that of Williamson, defines the corporate governance system as being "the complex set of constraints that shape the ex-post bargaining over the quasi-rents generated by a firm." For Blair (1995), "Governance systems, broadly defined, set the ground rules that determine who has what control rights under what circumstances, who receives what shares of the wealth created, and who bears what associated risks."

12 Organizational learning presumes there is interdependence between the individuals to build knowledge within the firm. This knowledge is of a collective nature and learning is an institutionalized social process of interpretation, trials, feedback and evaluation. This is a process of formulation and resolution of problems rather than acquisition and accumulation of information (Hodgson, 1998).

13 For a recent synthesis of the evolutionary approach to economics, see Nelson and Winter (2002).

14 Foss (1997) constitutes an excellent introductory book on this current of research.

15 For a critical synthesis of the KBV, see Kaplan *et al.* (2001).

16 In Kaplan *et al.* (2001), we find a more developed analysis of the courses through which knowledge can influence value creation.

17 This cognitive aspect concerns intra-firm and inter-firm transactions, which presumes that the latter cannot be reduced to simple exchanges governed by prices but also involve relational modes of governance. The argument according to which cognitive expansion (of rationality) allowed by the firms renders contracts less incomplete and brings greater flexibility can be included in this aspect.

18 We also find numerous developments regarding this confrontation in Foss and Mahnke (2000), see, in particular, Dosi and Marengo (2000).

19 Analyses, such as those of Grandori (2001) may also contribute to the construction of a theory of the firm that can act as a basis to the development of a synthetic governance theory.

20 This definition, contrary to that of North, presumes that organizations are a sub-group of institutions.

21 According to the principle, an existing situation is considered efficient unless an achievable alternative for producing a net profit (after deduction of implementation costs) can be described and implemented

Table 2.A1 Micro theories of CG

Governance theories	Disciplinary		Knowledge-based	Synthetic
	Shareholder	Stakeholder		
Theories of the support firm	Mainly Agency theory (normative and positive)	Mainly Agency theory (normative and positive) extended to numerous stakeholders	Behavioral theory Evolutionary theory Resources and competence theory	Attempts for a synthesis between disciplinary and knowledge-based theories
Aspects favored in the creation of value	Discipline and distribution Reduce the loss of efficiency connected to the conflicts of interests between managers and financial investors. Only the shareholders are residual claimants	Discipline and distribution Reduce the loss of efficiency connected to the conflicts of interests between stakeholders (employees, in particular) Numerous categories of residual claimants	Productive-cognitive aspects Create and seize new opportunities	Disciplinary and cognitive aspects
Type of efficiency	Constrained static efficiency Shareholder view of efficiency and ownership	Constrained static efficiency Stakeholder view of efficiency and ownership	Constrained dynamic efficiency Cognitive aspects of production	Constrained dynamic efficiency Cognitive and disciplinary aspects of production
Efficiency criteria	Shareholder value	Stakeholder value	Ability to create a sustainable organizational rent through innovation in particular	Ability to create a sustainable organizational rent through innovation and resolution of conflicts
Definition of corporate governance systems	All mechanisms that secure financial investments	All mechanisms that maintain the nexus of contracts and optimize the managerial latitude	All mechanisms possessing the best potential for value creation through learning and innovation	All mechanisms that have a simultaneous effect on the disciplinary and cognitive aspects of the value creation/distribution process

3 Macro theories of corporate governance

G. Charreaux

Introduction

The opposition between the disciplinary and cognitive functions of governance that support the presentation of the different micro theories, could also, in the continuum, identify the analyses of national systems of corporate governance, (NSCG). This dichotomy would result, first, in the presentation of disciplinary analyses of the NSCG that presume that the essential influencing factor of efficiency – often measured according to the productive perspective by the growth of the national economy – is based on the protection of the interest of the different contributors of production factors, with precedence given, under the influence of the shareholder view, to financial investors. Second, this presentation would be followed by the analyses attributing primacy to the cognitive aspect. Like the firms, the nations are supposed to have comparative advantages (Porter, 1990) resulting from their abilities and justifying an international specialization, reinforced by globalization. To present a clearer and more balanced presentation of the different theories of the NSCG, this logic will, however, not be followed. Instead of making the distinction between the disciplinary theories and knowledge-based theories, we prefer to use the one, although quite similar, that opposes the theories that overlook the productive aspect of value creation and those that support it. The productive aspect would therefore be considered globally; whether it is based on disciplinary or cognitive aspects.

The literature assembled comes from relatively separate fields. In the first approach, we find mainly law and finance literature, neoclassical economics and political theories based on rent-seeking. In the second approach, researches come under a larger perspective of the NSCG than the one effectively illustrated in the comparative institutional analysis of Aoki. They regard, in particular, the national systems of innovation and production, and more generally, the explanation of the different forms of capitalism and their evolution.

The disciplinary theories of the NSCG based on rent appropriation

The analyses supporting the disciplinary perspective based on the appropriation of organizational rents and the protection of the financial investor's rights are of financial origin. They begin with the hypothesis that the financial system plays a central role in explaining economic growth and prosperity. Levine (1997) presents literature that explains and tests the role of this system in relation to information and transaction costs. Its influence is exercised through five functions:

i   risk management: the facilitation of the trading, hedging, diversification, and pooling of risk;
ii   allocation of resources;
iii   the monitoring of managers and control of corporations;
iv   the mobilization of savings; and
v   the facilitation of the exchange of goods and services.

The financial system would then promote accumulation of capital and innovation (Beck *et al.*, 2000).

This positive effect appears to be confirmed by numerous empirical studies (Levine, 1997). Different indicators representing the liquidity of the financial system, the role of the central bank in relation to the commercial banks, and the importance of credit attributed to companies are positively correlated to growth and productivity.[1] The initial level of financial development is also a good predictor of future growth, once the effects linked to income, education, political stability, and the monetary, trade, and fiscal policies have been considered.

However, the question of the respective significance of different influencing factors for growth remains open. (Barro and August (1996) underline the fact that growth is maximized when the following variables are improved: level of education, life expectancy, law quality, inflation control and exchanges' efficiency and inversely when birth rate and taxation are out of control.) A high performance financial system, whether it is the reason for growth or accompanies it, is supposed to play a significant role. And then it is a matter of knowing which institutional factors support the development of such a system through a corporate governance (CG) perspective.

The dominant explanation belongs to La Porta *et al.* (1998), which is based on the corporate legal institutions, which certain authors (Roe, 2003) call "the quality of corporate law argument." Since this approach is of great significance, it will be presented first. Then we will continue by presenting the critiques that were addressed to the approach before examining the explanatory theories – political, endowment-based, and socio-cultural – that are either competitors or provide completion.

The law and finance view of the NSCG: the quality of corporate law argument

Within a financial perspective, efficiency depends on the protection of the financial investor's rights against attempts at expropriation by the managers or dominating shareholders. La Porta *et al.* (1998) concluded that the capacity of the law to ensure this protection – the quality of law – constitutes an influential explanatory factor of the financial policy and the ownership structure of firms. The different NSCG must therefore be analyzed according to the protective ability that appears to fundamentally depend on the origin of the legal tradition seen through the opposition between the Anglo-Saxon Common law tradition and that of Civil law,[2] inspired from Roman law and including many branches (French, German, and Scandinavian). To summarize, the two legal systems function according to different principles. The civil systems are based on professional judges, legal codes, and written procedures; inversely, in the Common law system, jurors are not professionals, the laws are not codified, and the procedures are oral (Glaeser and Shleifer, 2002).

According to the dominant interpretation (La Porta *et al.*, 1997b, 1998, 1999a, 1999b, 2000a), these differences between legal traditions have a political origin based on the power relationship between the monarchy and the landlords. Hence, British Common law appeared and evolved so as to ensure the protection of the owner's interests against the monarchy. This protection especially ensures the confidentiality of the transactions, therefore, facilitating financial development. Inversely, the creation of the French and German civil codes in the nineteenth century, by reinforcing the domination of the State over the courts, led the governmental power to prevail over individuals' rights and to a greater regulation of the economic activity. These different legal traditions were subsequently circulated through conquests, colonization, or simply imitation. Civil law would therefore be associated to a greater governmental intervention, a weaker protection of private interests, corrupt, and less efficient governments, even less political freedom (La Porta *et al.*, 1999b; Djankov *et al.*, 2003a).

Another explanation, also of political nature, given by Glaeser and Shleifer (2003) contrarily puts emphasis on the protective role of the State. In order to avoid that the local judges be totally beholding to feudal lords, it was necessary in France, where their powers were particularly strong, to appoint judges who would answer to the central authority. According to this logic – that follows the path of efficiency – regulation leads to obtaining a superior level of development – it is the countries that originally had the least efficient system of protection of rights that opted for the civil system. We remark that this second argument supporting the State does not necessarily oppose the preceding claim: protection ensured by the State can be considered as compensation for its own power of predation.

We may also go above the political explanation – either Civil law is imposed because it facilitates governmental intervention or the Civil law structure itself requires governmental intervention (Glaeser and Shleifer, 2002) – by claiming that Common law acquires its superiority from its inherent advantages.[3] Therefore, for Beck *et al.* (2002), the most important element is the adaptability conferred by Common law, which provides for a better adaptation to the needs of economic development. From an evolutionary perspective, the non-adapted, inefficient laws would be eliminated. Beck *et al.* (2001a) therefore contrast a "dynamic" law and finance view to the political perspective supported by La Porta *et al.* (2000a). Evidently, however, the two paths – political and adaptability – of influence of law regarding finance are not independent of each other: jurisprudence has as much of a chance of developing as the legal system is independent of the State (Glaeser and Shleifer, 2002).

LLSV[4] analyze the systems of protection of financial investor's rights (shareholders and financial creditors) based on legal traditions. They conclude that, independently of the level of national prosperity, the systems based on Civil law – most particularly those of the French branch – offer less protection than those based on Common law. This conclusion should, however, be weighted in accordance with its ability to execute legal decisions. Hierarchy is modified on these criteria: the German and Scandinavian countries with a Civil law tradition appear to be the top performers, followed by the countries of Common law and finally, the countries that follow French law. Of the two criteria considered – quality of the protection and ability to execute the law – the French tradition appears to be the less protective. However, the authors often differentiate between the countries where legal tradition originated and those where it has been transplanted (Djankov *et al.*, 2003b). If, in the first case, the hypothesis that the Civil law tradition constitutes an efficient solution (in particular to guarantee the independence and impartiality of the legal procedure) is sometimes accepted, this hypothesis is rejected in the case of transplantation. In this second scenario, the legal regime appears exogenously, either because it has been imposed or because it has been adopted for linguistic reasons, or a reason of political philosophy (La Porta *et al.*, 1998). Consequently, it does not necessarily ensure efficient protection of investors. According to the argument for "transplantation" (Berkowitz *et al.*, 1999), countries that were able to adapt the law to their local conditions or that had a population already accustomed to the law, had more of a chance of building efficient legal institutions.

La Porta *et al.* (1998) conclude from the imperfection of the Civil law systems that governance mechanisms must appear to remedy the insufficiencies. They justify, in this manner, the persistence of concentrated ownership and the predominance of dominating shareholders in countries of Civil law. Their theory, according to which the legal tradition is the main explanatory factor for the ownership structure, appears to be confirmed due to the negative correlation existing between the concentration of ownership and the protection of investors. The same argument also explains the development of financial markets. The capital markets appear less developed in countries of Civil law tradition, in France, in particular, since they are less protective of investors.

The law and finance theory led to an abundance of research attempting to confirm the relevance of the distinction between Common law and Civil law. The research led in three directions. The first direction consists of studying, precisely, the functioning and the cost of legal mechanisms in the different systems. Hence, Djankov *et al.* (2003b), based on indicators measuring the formalism of contentious procedures, show that the latter is systematically higher in countries of Civil law tradition. The procedures are longer, less coherent, less honest, less fair, and more subject to corruption. They conclude that ownership rights are much less protected in these countries.

The second direction, and the main one, concerns the impact of legal institutions on finance. Various studies, apart from exceptions, which confirm the relevance of the legal variable, addressed the issues of corporate valuation (La Porta *et al.*, 2002), the maturity structure of debt, access to external financing or growth (Demirgüç-Kunt and Maksimovic, 1998, 1999, 2002), the dividend policy (La Porta *et al.*, 2000b), the allocation of capital between firms or industries (Wurgler, 2000; Beck and Levine, 2002; Claessens and Laeven, 2003), the informational efficiency of stock prices (Morck *et al.*, 2000), financial fragility (Johnson *et al.*, 2000a), possession of excessive liquid assets (Dittmar *et al.*, 2003), the operating and bankruptcy risks of companies (Claessens *et al.*, 2000), the effects of diversification on value (Fauver *et al.*, 2003), the legal procedures that an entrepreneur needs to carry out to begin operating a firm (Djankov *et al.*, 2002), the value of voting rights and private benefit associated with control (Nenova, 2003), or, finally, the State's share of bank capital (La Porta *et al.*, 2000c).

The third direction evaluates the influence of the legal tradition on non financial aspects of governance, for example, employment and social security legislation. Hence, Botero *et al.* (2003) stress that the most prosperous countries, while ensuring better social protection, display less interventionism. If socialist countries or French Civil law countries of legal tradition are greater interventionists than those of Common law, the influencing factor seems to be the legal tradition and not the political factor evaluated using the ideology of the government party.

The law and finance view has evident normative implications. This view considers the market-oriented governance systems, based on Common law and a limited intervention of the State, to be more efficient. The causality model resulting in efficiency and measured by growth is very simple, maybe even over-simplified. By ensuring effective protection of financial investors and limiting the role of the State, the Anglo-Saxon NSCG should achieve a better performance. An intervention from the State is justified only when the level of conflict – linked to the risk of spoliation of private interests through other private interests – is too great to be resolved by private means or by the courts (Djankov *et al.*, 2003a). This concept is based on numerous empirical studies that, apart from exceptions, seem to confirm the relevance of the legal factor, if not to explain the superior performance of Anglo-Saxon NSCG – a certain number of studies show, that in the long term, this result is not a foregone conclusion (Boyer, 2001; De Jong, 1997; Hall and Soskice, 2001) – at least with regard to the protection of financial investors and the financial policies followed.

Critiques of the law and finance theory

The law and finance theory is based on a simple argument. The Common law systems, recognized as being more flexible, would ensure a better protection of financial investors, in particular minority shareholders, and would result in a better development of the financial market. This argument was subject to numerous critiques contesting, in particular: (i) the presumed advantages of Common law and the interest in the distinction between legal categories regarding the importance of governmental regulations; (ii) the presumed connection with the development of financial markets; (iii) the homogeneity and the relevance of the legal categories.

Is the common law system superior to the civil law system?

The first critique is regarding the presumed superiority of Common law: the Anglo-Saxon law would lead to a better adaptation to the variations of the economic environment. Lamoreaux and Rosenthal (2000) studied the possible choices of legal forms available to companies in the nineteenth century in France and the United States and arrived at a different conclusion. First, the French commercial code offers more flexibility. Second, this flexibility was used effectively by French entrepreneurs while their American counterparts were only able to imperfectly recreate it by contractual methods due to the difficulty of executing the contracts. Third, with regard to the rights of creditors as much as those of minority shareholders, the two systems ensured similar protection with the French form seemingly presenting a slight advantage. Globally, it seems that the rigidity of the French form had been over-evaluated and was inferior to that of the American form.

Furthermore, the evolution of the legal framework since the nineteenth century seems to show that it is the American corporate law that took the example of French law rather than the opposite. The present lag of France, regarding the protection of minorities, would be due to the fact that, contrary to the United States, the management of retirement benefits does not go through the financial market. Such protection is therefore not as important in the United States where it only appeared later due to the scandals that arose in the 1929 crisis. Unable to explain the superiority of the Anglo-Saxon system in view of the characteristics of the French legal framework, the authors put forth the hypothesis that the latter, more complex, could only be applied effectively if the higher legal skills required were present in sufficient quantity. The French form, despite its higher quality, is less efficient in developing countries due to the shortage of competent legal officers.

To a certain extent, this conclusion resembles that of Beck et al. (2001a), who consider that in the French case, there was a deviation from the spirit of the Civil law tradition. If the original objective of codification performed under Napoleon I was to expel the jurisprudence, the necessity of adapting the law to economic requirements and the prior legal tradition would have required the preservation of the important role of jurisprudence leading to the adaptation of the system. However, this relaxation resulting from the jurisprudence in France would not have come about in countries that adopted the French legal framework.[5]

The eventual superiority of Common law constitutes an acceptable argument only if the traditional legal systems play a decisive role. But, according to Pistor and Xu (2003), during the last century, as regulatory intervention greatly developed, they would play only a secondary role. The rapid socio-cultural and technological evolutions would increase the incomplete character of the laws. The inability of the legal framework to adapt quick enough would motivate a growing regulatory intervention by public authorities, regardless of the country's legal tradition. This more flexible intervention was less subjected to the procedural constraints resulting in a better adaptation but at the cost of aggravating the problem of control by the regulator. The main question would no longer be the origin of the legal tradition but that of the structure of State governance.

Is the nature of the legal system a primary factor in the development of financial markets?

If we admit to the superiority of the Common law system, then must we establish that it is at the origin of the superior development of the financial markets? This link is strongly contested by Franks *et al.* (2003) in the British case where the concern for the protection of minorities appeared only recently. According to the law and finance theory, a concentrated ownership structure should have resulted. However, since British legislation has evolved over the twentieth century, from an almost total absence of protection to a very strong protection, a parallel increase in the dispersion of ownership should have resulted. On the contrary, the study of the structures of ownership of English corporations assessed in 1900 and in 1960, shows that ownership was not concentrated in the beginning of the twentieth century and there was little difference in the rates of dispersion between these two dates, invalidating the law and finance theory. The authors assume that in the absence of legal protection, the security of the investors is ensured through implicit contracts based on informal trust relationships facilitated by the geographic location of the investors, often in proximity to the companies in question. The external growth by means of takeovers would have resulted in the severance of these trust relationships and the implementation of substitute mechanisms ensuring a formal legal protection.[6]

However, if the rates of dispersion are similar in 1900 and 1960, the structures of ownership appear more unstable during the second half of the century. The strengthening of the formal protection of investors seems to be a factor for the growth of market liquidity and the rotation of investors. Finally, the dispersion of ownership in Great Britain did not result in the separation of ownership and control as noted in the United States. The boards of directors remained firmly controlled by the founding families even if they no longer held a substantial share of the capital. Coffee (2000, 2001a) achieved a similar analysis for the United States. For the greater part of the nineteenth century, the interests of the minorities were not well protected; the situation was comparable to the recent one in the Eastern Bloc countries. Also, for the financing of infrastructures by foreign investors, two protection mechanisms appeared, first, investment bankers were given a seat on the board of directors and second, regulation mechanisms were implemented with regard to the stock market. The American and English experiences led Coffee to reject the law and finance theory: the law is not a preliminary condition to the development of financial markets. Causality would be the opposite. In the beginning, these markets could develop based on the substitute mechanisms applied, of private origin, but in the end the legislator had to intervene upon the request of investors, to reinforce their protection.[7]

The study of Rajan and Zingales (2003), regarding the development of financial markets throughout the twentieth century, also invalidated the law and finance theory. This study predicted that either financial development would be guaranteed indefinitely or it would be perpetually blocked or restrained if the protection of financial investors was insufficient. On the contrary, on the basis of the usual financial indicators, most of the nations appeared more developed in 1913 than in 1980, the level of 1913 was surpassed only recently. Also, in total contradiction to the predictions of the theory, in 1913, the French financial market presented a market capitalization/GNP ratio almost equal to twice that of the United States, while the French legal system, presumably hostile towards investors, should have produced opposite results. More generally, at the beginning of the century, the Common law countries were not as developed on the financial plan as those of Civil law tradition.

Are the legal categories homogenous and relevant?

The validity of the law and finance theory is also dependent on the homogeneity of the legal categories that is strongly contested. Coffee (1999a) is not convinced that the American and English systems can be put in the same category. The quality of the protection of investors seems to him to depend mainly on the ability to apply the law; he shows that the minorities are much less protected in Great Britain than in the United States and that this difference is in all probability of the same nature as that existing between the United States and France. In addition, the role of judges is quite different. Hence, if American judges seem very active in the creation of new legal regulations in the absence of a specific law, their British colleagues seem contrarily passive. Then what is the difference with countries of Civil law tradition? What seems to matter most to Coffee, is not so much the quite contestable proximity between the American and the British corporate laws but rather the real proximity between the financial market regulations, which would explain the similarities in the development of the financial markets.

Coffee (2001a), starting with the analysis of the development of German, English, American, and French financial markets, also proposes an interpretation of the role played by the State, as opposed to that of LLSV, according to whom the financial markets cannot develop in the absence of a legal system to protect financial investors. The English and American experiences support an opposite model: substitute mechanisms of private nature appeared to offer this protection. The legal system is important not to offer a technique for the protection of investors' rights but as a framework supporting the decentralized development of methods for private regulation and facilitating the development of financial markets. This conclusion is backed up, a contrario, by the French case. The governmental control over the stock market, ensuring a monopoly status, was an incentive for the latter to not engage in innovations. Due to the governmental regulation, private initiatives that ensured protection of the investors in Anglo-Saxon countries were discouraged.

To a certain extent, this theory is similar to the very radical critique of the law and finance theory expressed by Pistor *et al.* (2003a). The indicators used by LLSV to evaluate the protection of minority shareholders is often associated with the legal practices that, in Common law countries, have either been abandoned early on or they have only been recently adopted for reasons of European harmonization. The argument according to which these practices would proceed from more favorable attitude with regard to the protection of ownership rights therefore does not seem well founded. Consequently, the presumed link between legal traditions and the development of financial markets must be found in aspects other than those covered by these practices. For Pistor *et al.*, the most important element is the ability of the legal system to adapt to the requirements of economic, political, and social situations. The essential criteria would not be the protection of minorities but rather the flexibility of the legal framework.

The political view

The numerous flaws in the law and finance theory make us turn to the earlier political theory of the NSCG. The first version was proposed by Roe[8] (1990, 1994, 1997) to explain the configuration of the American financial system. It is sometimes called the politics and finance view (Beck *et al.*, 2001a) due to the role attributed to politics in the construction of financial institutions. While the theory of LLSV dominates the law and finance perspective, that of Roe occupies an equal position within the political perspective. For this reason, it will be presented first.

The political theory of Roe

Roe's analysis is centered on the organization of the American financial system, in particular on the emergence of large public corporations and the dispersion of stock ownership. The configuration of this system cannot be explained exclusively by the search for efficiency (ability to realize economies of scale resulting from the possibility of financing large entities; superior portfolio diversification linked to the better liquidity and the greater size of financial markets; greater competence of professional managers, etc.) but also and maybe more so by the political constraints that were exercised in the past and have influenced its path of development.[9] In support of this theory, Roe devotes himself to a historical analysis of the American system explaining its inability to finance the expansion of the economy because of insufficient concentration. This would be mainly due to political factors with either an ideological foundation – the American populism would have prevented the creation of organizations sufficiently powerful to jeopardize the interest of the citizens – or interest-based, certain interest groups profiting from the fragmentation of the financial system. These obstacles to the emergence of a banking power, will have also affected other forms of financial power such as insurance companies and to a lesser extent, investment funds. The argument is therefore based on the excessive regulations, the political constraints rendering a NSCG a priori less than optimal (Coffee, 1999b).

The absence of powerful financial organizations would have had significant consequences on the discipline exercised by the investors over the managers. In accordance with agency theory, the fragmentation of ownership results in an increase in agency costs that could lead to higher capital costs, even if the concentrated ownership retains its own costs. The American system, however, endured, since it was able to invent substitute disciplinary mechanisms to control the managers (competitive markets for goods and services, an active takeover market, incentive remuneration systems, etc.), and take advantage of dispersed ownership that facilitated financing and the creation of managerial capital (and a managers' market). The recent evolution toward institutional ownership of capital (via investment funds) and a more active and direct control of managers may, however, be interpreted as a recognition of advantages associated with concentrated control. In the end, Roe concluded that neither of the two main systems – dispersed ownership against concentrated ownership – seem to be systematically superior and we must make space for competition between the systems.

In his initial studies, Roe gave precedence to the analysis of the American system, but then he tried to understand why the dispersion of ownership did not occur in non Anglo-Saxon nations, therefore, preventing the emergence of large public corporations. The explanation is also political (Roe, 2000). In social democracies that support the interest of employees, the managers have less incentive to perform their managerial duties in the best interest of the shareholders; the political constraint opposes an alignment of interests between shareholders and managers and reduction in agency costs. Codetermination, which results in a highly rigid labor market, is one of the main obstacles for this reduction. The dominating forms of ownership in social democracies would consequently be family-owned firms or concentrated-ownership firms. A contrario, the emergence of the large public corporation in the United States appeared only because of the absence of a dominant social democracy. Roe finds corroboration for his theory in the significant statistical correlation that exists as much between the dispersion of ownership and the political positioning of nations as between the importance of the financial market and income inequality.

The latter argument completes those expressed previously, supporting the fact that political factors were obstacles in the emergence of a strong financial power. Regarding efficiency, the arguments are however different, since the existence of a financial power was supposed to reduce agency costs between shareholders and managers while the presence of a social democracy ideology caused an adverse effect. Roe decided to abstain from evaluating the combined effects of financial power and social democracy, therefore, the result remains undetermined.

Roe (2001) extends his theory by considering the competitive character of markets that is supposed to determine the level of appropriable rents. Therefore, social democracy would be more frequent in smaller nations with lower competitive character. This weakness would result in the existence of higher rents that, on the one hand, would procure greater latitude for managers, and on the other hand, would become a stake for different interest groups. In both cases, there would be an increase in agency costs, managers would be less constrained and employees would have a higher incentive to seek rents. Due to the electoral importance of employees as compared to the shareholders, this situation would most often result, on the national level, in a domination of the social democratic parties. In this scenario, the protection of the shareholders interests that is not ensured through the political or legislative paths would be carried out privately by the concentration of ownership. This causality model differs from the previous one, since it uses the industrial structure to determine political positioning and corporate governance systems. The strong correlation that exists in developed nations, between the protection of workers and the concentration of ownership on the one hand and the market power on the other hand, supports this model.

Roe's theory, affirming the primacy of political factors over the influential legal factors, also contributes to the criticism of the law and finance theory. To justify this primacy, Roe (2002, 2003) shows that the explanatory power of the law can only be limited. To do so, he decomposes the managerial agency costs into two categories: (i) the first is associated with "private benefits" that the managers try to appropriate in accordance with their opportunism; and (ii) the second is linked to managerial errors, based on the ability of the managers to exploit investment opportunities in the best interests of the shareholders, these "errors," of course, could be considered as relevant decisions from the managers or employees point of view. If the law is able to efficiently reduce the first category of costs, then it is revealed as incapable of eliminating the other costs. This duality would explain that the concentration of ownership is maintained in most European nations while the legal protection of the financial investors is of comparable quality to what it is in the United States. This concentration would, therefore, not be because of insufficient legal protection but rather the necessity for reducing the costs related to managerial errors.

Another limit of the law and finance theory is therefore emphasized. If the concentration of ownership endures in a nation, we do not know whether it is because of insufficient protection of financial investors against appropriation maneuvers from managers (or dominant shareholders), or of managerial errors presumed to be more frequent in the absence of dominant shareholders. The results of a test confirm the superior explanatory power of the political theory in developed countries. Roe does not conclude however that the law and finance theory should be totally discarded: the argument of legal protection remains relevant, in particular, in developing nations or nations in transition, but it is far from being exclusive or even an influencing factor in developed nations. Let us also recall that in the law and finance theory, the role of politics is not denied but is limited to explaining the emergence of the legal tradition.

As shown by Gourevitch (2003), the political view of Roe contains in fact three critiques of the law and finance theory. The first one relates to the importance of the legal protection of financial investors: effective protection does not suffice to guarantee diffuse ownership because other reasons exist for the existence of control blocks. The second presumes that it is not the law that determines the request for legal protection, but rather the competitive character of the markets. If the markets function well, the rents are limited and the conflicts between the stakeholders hoping to appropriate the rents are minor. Finally, if competition determines CG, it is in itself caused by political factors that are therefore the main explanatory variable.

Other political models and the critique of the political view

Roe's political theory was also subject to many critiques, propositions for development or expansion. As specified by Gourevitch (2003), since Roe opened the door for political interpretations of governance, other models may be equally proposed. In particular, Roe's analysis, based on the ideological opposition between right and left and the conflict between employees and financial investors, seems incomplete. Other scenarios, based on different relationships between the three main interest groups – the financial investors, managers and employees – may be designed.

The models proposed by Rajan and Zingales (2003) and by Pagano and Volpin (2001a, 2001b) illustrate some of these scenarios. According to Rajan and Zingales, the main explanatory factor of financial development resides in the relative power of the beneficial political forces. Their scenario reveals that this development constitutes a threat for the dominating interest groups whether they are industrial or financial. The established (and mature) industrial interests are presumed not to be beneficial for the following reasons: (i) since their opportunities for growth are limited, there are few advantages; (ii) they can easily be financed, either by a bank – for they can use the collateral from existing projects and their prior reputation to borrow, or on a financial market that is modestly developed with limited transparency – because of their past history and position; (iii) their relative strength efficiently protects their investments. Regarding the financial interests, development compromises their comparative advantage, based on the relational aspect of financing. Financial development, therefore, threatens the interests in place by increasing competition and by obstructing the progression of existing relationships. The vigor of the opposition depends on their respective powers and the profitability of this strategy.

In the past, how have dominating interest groups been able to slow financial development in order to protect their rents? The main explanatory factor of development seems to have been the international openness of the economy through its influence on the competitive character of markets. The political analysis is therefore expressed in terms of opposition to this openness. In a crisis situation popular pressure is exercised requiring reinforced protection from the State. The barriers that result do not only reduce international competition but also national competition and supports maintaining the rents appropriated by the dominating interests. In contrast to the analysis of Roe, which places workers and financial investors in opposition – the cause of higher agency costs in social democracies and the preservation of the concentration of capital – that of Rajan and Zingales, which attempts to explain the re-concentration of capital in European nations, is more balanced and dynamic. The result depends on the alliances between the interest groups. On occasion, it is possible for workers to make a pact with the industrial and financial interests so as to oblige the government to slow down the international extension.

Pagano and Volpin (2001a) propose another model. If politics play an influential role in the construction of the legal framework in response to the request of various interest groups, the structure of political institutions also intervenes by influencing the possible alliances. Since the entrepreneurs/managers are presumed to have little influence, the political debate mainly opposes the financial investors and workers. In order for the entrepreneurs to appropriate private benefits at the expense of the financial investors, they can conclude an agreement with the workers guaranteeing them better protection where their job is concerned. The possibility of such an agreement depends on the structure of the political institutions. The "consensus" systems, based on coalitions, are in opposition to the "majoritarian" systems. In the first systems, Pagano and Volpin obtain a solution characterized by a poor protection of financial investors and a strong protection of workers. In majoritarian systems, the solution is reversed. The results of the model are sensitive to the diffusion of ownership: the greater the diffusion, the higher the chance that protection of the capital will be essential. The "corporatist" nations offer greater protection for workers and a poorer protection for financial investors, and most often have a "consensual" political system favoring coalitions, as confirmed by the results of a test.

Gourevitch (2003) tries to generalize the political theory with its previous models constituting special cases. First, his theory is based on a representation of political preferences and interest groups, different from the traditional right/left or capital/labor opposition, hardly relevant when accounting for different types of conflicts. As revealed by Rajan and Zingales, in certain circumstances, industry-based logics may prevail over the capital/labor opposition; alliances may be formed between workers, shareholders, and managers in order to protect the specific industry-based investments against the effects of globalization. Gourevitch and Shinn (2004) conducted a systematic study of coalitions that can be formed between these three groups.

Second, according to Pagano and Volpin, an important role is attributed to political institutions for the aggregation of preferences, such as electoral laws, the degree of federalism and the relationships between the legislative, executive, and party systems. A fundamental opposition is also present between the majoritarian and the consensus systems. It does not reflect the right–left distinction, a left wing regime may result as much from a majoritarian logic as a consensual one. If majoritarian systems are conflicting and facilitate sudden modifications and extreme solutions, it is entirely different for the consensus systems based on negotiation and compromise. A system of corporate governance beneficial for shareholders (or, inversely, only for the workers) is only possible in a political majoritarian context. The credibility of long-term commitments that influence specific investments, in particular those made by workers is only as strong as the system is consensual.

Such an analysis is, therefore, based more on the protection of specific investments made by the different stakeholders than the reduction of opportunism with regard to financial investors only. This analysis resembles that of Blair and Zingales, in that it focuses on the protection of specific investments made by workers; arguments of cognitive nature are not present.

The political theories were also criticized. Roe's theory, regarding the political origin of the dispersion of ownership in the United States, is particularly contested by Coffee (2001a). If this theory is valid, how can we explain that in Great Britain, in a political context that is much less constrained, the financial investors are organized in similar fashion? Coffee is not convinced by the political explanation for the concentration of ownership – and lack of transparency – in Europe, for which the function would be to offer protection to the private investors against attempts at expropriation from the social-democratic States. He finds this explanation to be fallacious, because it implies that these States would have a special interest in favoring transparency to increase the dispersion of ownership and weaken the financial investors in order to obtain better control over the private sector. On the contrary, in the past, these States were rather opposed to the development of these financial markets. He finds the theory of Rajan and Zingales to be more plausible: the poor development of the financial markets could be explained by the comparative advantage of banks to constitute a lever of governmental interventionism. Once the banks had established their power, it was in their best interest to oppose the emergence of markets.

Coffee, however, does not deny the importance of politics (Gourevitch, 2003) that intervene on two different levels in the alternative theory, based on the institutional investors' demand for liquidity, that he proposes (Coffee, 1999b): (i) once the diffusion of ownership is accomplished, the shareholders put pressure on political leaders in order to obtain a legal regulation to protect their interests – the law can be adapted but is not foregoing; (ii) politics plays a central role in relation to the key variable of the theory, in other words, the intervention of the State in economic life that influences the emergence of private mechanisms of governance.

The decisive influence of politics on the constitution of NSCG however appears difficult to deny but it does not take only one direction. Coffee's critique presumes that, for Roe, only the causality model underlying the American system would lead to the dispersion of ownership. As such, this type of interpretation is based on naïve determinism, foreign to Roe's approach (Roe, 1996; Bebchuk and Roe, 1999), which does not exclude the fact that other earlier paths may have resulted in the same effects (the equifinality principle).[10] Gourevitch (2003) and

Gourevitch and Shinn (2004) have emphasized the complex character of the paths which have led politics to influence the forms of ownership.

Of course, the State is an essential link for political analysis. For Beck *et al.* (2001a), the political view leads to the conclusion that a centralized, strong government is not compatible with financial development due to the threat of governmental predation and the risks of interventionism that could hinder the proper functioning of the financial markets. Similarly, the existence of powerful interest groups or majoritarian electoral systems would constitute as much of a threat for the development of financial markets. Such a conclusion is far from being totally accepted. Furthermore, Rajan and Zingales show that certain configurations of a balance between the interest groups can be beneficial to the development of financial markets. There are early examples of how a centralized State can try to develop the financial markets, such as the case in France under the socialist government two decades ago or even earlier under the French Second Empire.[11]

The endowment theory and the socio-cultural theory

Two other theories propose different or complementary explanations of the legal-financial and political theories. The first, the "endowment" view or theory (Beck *et al.*, 2001a, 2003b), is a study of the emergence of financial institutions in ancient colonized countries, in connection with their endowments in natural resources and their health status. This theory helps us to better understand the failure or success of transplanted institutions and to qualify the law and finance theory that presumes structural inferiority of the countries that adopted the French law without considering the context. The second theory comprises all the works that retain socio-cultural variables (religion, trust, norms in general, etc.) as explanatory factors for the risks incurred by financial investors and for the level of agency costs.

The endowment theory

An important line of research (see, for example, Sachs, 2001), claims that the geographic differences (climate, endowments in natural resources, etc.) and health-related differences (in particular, mortality factors) have played an influential role in development. The countries that are not well endowed should have experienced more difficulty in creating efficient institutions, particularly financial. Acemoglu *et al.* (2001) put particular emphasis on the health situation that was present during colonization.

The argument underlying this theory is as follows (Beck *et al.*, 2001a, 2001b). First, according to historians, the types of institutions created depend on the policies for colonization. Implantation strategies, contrary to the resource extraction strategies, led to the creation of institutions to protect ownership rights and facilitate development. Second, if the health status is unfavorable, the extraction strategies had a greater chance of being established. Third, the initial state of the institutions has been extended until today. Therefore, institutions that turned to extraction of resources, generally centralized and authoritative, were upheld by the subsequent governments inasmuch as they were beneficial.

Acemoglu *et al.* (2001) reveal that the level of development depends greatly on the institutional variable that represents protection against expropriation, itself depending on the mortality of the colonists. The presumed superiority (La Porta *et al.*, 1999b) of the British legal tradition would in fact be due to a lower mortality in British colonies. However, the French legal origin remains associated with the institutional framework that is least performing, even after controlling for the mortality rates. In addition, the religious, climatic, ethno-linguistic, endowment and natural resource variables have little effect on the results.

The institutional theory proposed by Acemoglu *et al.* supports the role of institutions in development and is opposed, at least in part, to the "geographic" determinism theory. In support of their theory, Acemoglu *et al.* (2002) show that, among the countries colonized by the European powers, there has been a regression: the richest countries of the beginning of the sixteenth century have become the poorest ones today. The Europeans would have created institutions beneficial to investment – protecting private interests – in the regions historically less developed where implantation was easier. In the nineteenth century, the nations using the institutional framework would have better success at industrialization. Such a scenario does not exclude the influence of the geographic factor, but this influence was accomplished through institutions.

The institutional theory is also reinforced by Easterly and Levine (2003). They compare, among other things, the "geographic" and "institutional" theories with the "policy view" theory, which implicitly inspire the actions taken by multilateral development institutions. In the latter, the historical heritage plays only a minor role; to guarantee the extension of international trade and the freedom of capital flows. The results reveal that the endowments have a significant influence on the level of development, with mortality explaining more than half of the variance. The influence of endowments, however, passes through the institutional path. Mortality and geographical latitude explain almost half of the institutional variation, with control variables – legal, ethno-linguistic, and religious – that are often significant.[12]

Of course, it is important to know whether endowments explain development beyond their influence on institutions. A procedure of simultaneous equations shows that this is not the case; it is the institutional framework that is the decisive factor. The development policies theory is also rejected, which would imply that a political action that is not accompanied by an institutional reform is not very efficient. The variables associated with the legal origin lose all their significance which also invalidates the law and finance theory. The same is true for the variables that represent the ethno-linguistic diversity but not the religious variables.

The imbrication of the different variables obviously impedes a clear perception of the causality relationships. Endowments, however, seem to play a key role only through an institutional framework, therefore confirming the institutional theory.

The socio-cultural theory

Tests of the endowments theory often reveal a significant effect of the religious and ethno-linguistic variables. For example, Beck *et al.* (2003b) find that the ethno-linguistic dispersion is negatively correlated to the degree of financial intermediation, or that the financial development of ancient colonies depends on religious practices: it seems weaker in populations that are mostly Catholic or Muslim. In certain studies, the inclusion of these variables renders the legal-financial and political variables insignificant. These results are hardly surprising. The disciplinary theories attribute a central role to opportunism; we intuitively expect that these variables, associated with religion, trust, and civil and social capital play an important role.

La Porta *et al.* (1997a) study the role of trust and social capital consistent with the works of Coleman (1990), Putnam (1993), and Fukuyama (1995) who consider that these variables represent the propensity of individuals to cooperate socially in order to increase productive efficiency. Trust seems greatly and positively correlated to the efficiency of the legal system, the absence of corruption, the quality of the bureaucracy, the acceptance of taxes and civil participation. The hypothesis according to which the highly hierarchical religious organizations (Catholic, Orthodox, and Muslim religions), supporting vertical links of authority, would have impeded the construction of trust, is also tested. The hierarchical character appears to have a strong negative correlation with trust and seems to have a detrimental influence on the quality of institutions and the level of development.

Stulz and Williamson (2003) also try to evaluate the influence of religion on financial development, by distinguishing between the rights of the shareholders and those of the creditors. It is only religion that has a decisive influence on the rights of creditors; its explanatory power appears superior to that of language, openness of international trade, individual income level and the legal origin. Countries that are predominantly Catholic offer less protection of creditor's rights and turn less often to financing through medium- or long-term debts. The openness of international trade reduces the influence of religion. In turn, with regard to the shareholder's rights, religion loses its explanatory power if the legal origin is taken into account. Globally, the study confirms the role of religion and language.

Beyond the financial development, Barro and McCleary (2003) attempted to better define the influence of religion on economic growth by separating church attendance and beliefs (hell, paradise, etc.). Economic growth seems to be positively correlated to the importance of beliefs, but negatively to attendance. Since beliefs reinforce morals they reduce opportunism, they constitute the output of religious systems. Most particularly, it would seem that the fear of hell has a greater effect on growth than the perspective of paradise. As for attendance, it would represent the resources consumed in the religious activity. At a given level of belief, greater attendance would result in less productive efficiency. The authors also study the influencing factors of religiosity through an analysis of the supply and demand of religion. Religiosity is positively correlated to the presence of State religion and negatively to the intervention of the State in the appointment of religious leaders. These results open the door to reintroduce the political analysis with regard to religious values. Finally, the religious diversity has a positive influence on church attendance and beliefs.

In these different studies, the legal and religious variables are supposed to be independent. Certain results, however, lead us to presume that they interact. In particular, the hypothesis according to which a greater level of morality substitutes for strict legal control seems plausible. The complementary hypothesis is, however, also valid: greater moral standards facilitate the application of the law. In this perspective, Coffee (2001b) questions the interaction between moral norms and legal systems. His approach is based on an apparent anomaly: private benefits acquired by control, traditionally used to evaluate the quality of legal protection, are the lowest in the Scandinavian nations of Civil law tradition while this result should have been obtained in countries of Common law. According to Coffee, this anomaly originated in the social norms that were substituted for law to ensure efficient discipline in the Scandinavian countries. This hypothesis, if it seems to be corroborated by Russia, Mexico, and Brazil, is less valid in numerous Common law countries, such as the United States.

Licht (2001), considering that the national culture is the principal determinant of efficiency, proposes the use of concepts and methods of intercultural psychology in order to evaluate the cultural differences between nations and their effects on the NSCG. To characterize the national cultures, he uses the works of Hofstede (1980, 1991) and Schwartz (1999) as a basis. The explanatory power of national cultural profiles relating to the protection of minority shareholders and creditors is tested by Licht et al. (2002), based on national scores established from three aspects identified by Schwartz (the opposition of embedness (of the individual) in a group/autonomy; hierarchy/egalitarianism; master (control of the natural and social environment)/harmony, and four aspects from Hofstede (uncertainty avoidance; individualism/collectivism; power distance (attitude toward power and inequality); masculinity/femininity). The protection of shareholders is negatively correlated to the values of harmony and avoidance of uncertainty that would lead financial investors to avoid confrontations and hence renounce the respect of their rights. Similar results relating to harmony are obtained for the protection of creditors. The inclusion of a legal-financial variable shows that the cultural factor prevails over the law. Finally, the cultural classification of the nations does not reflect the legal typology of La Porta et al. (1998, 2000a). The countries that offer better protection to shareholders and creditors simultaneously are the Common law countries in the Far East. The Anglo-Saxon countries ensure excellent protection of shareholders but a poor protection of creditors.

The disciplinary perspective, dominated by the law and finance theory, views the main source of prosperity in the financial development supported by the protection of the investors. The law and finance theory, which leads to opposing the NSCG based on legal origin, is strongly contested because it attributes a decisive role to legal variables only. Other studies show that the political and social variables as well as those representing endowments have an explanatory power preceding or exceeding that of legal variables. These studies, however, do not question the disciplinary origin of performance; they only contest the hierarchy of influential factors and the links to causality. To go beyond, we must account for the productive aspect of value creation.

Productive analyses of NSCG

Productive analyses simultaneously involve incentive (protection of human and financial capital) and cognitive aspects. This leads us to consider, like Hodgson (1988, 1989, 1993), Nelson (2002), or Nelson and Sampat (2001), that institutions display not only an incentive matrix but also a cognitive one that plays a central role in the construction and transmission of knowledge through the learning process. Charreaux (2002a, 2002b) even presumes that the financial aspects are not exclusively incentive but also cognitive.

If the role of institutions simultaneously takes an incentive and cognitive path, then theoretical reflection therefore takes a systemic form going much beyond the legal-financial aspects, eventually completed by the politico-cultural aspects, to integrate educational, technical and work relationship aspects into the social systems of production (Streeck, 1992; Hollingsworth and Boyer, 1997), the varieties of capitalism theory (Hall and Soskice, 2001, 2002), the comparative institutional analysis (Aoki, 2001), or finally, social systems of innovation and production (Amable *et al.*, 1997), within which the interdependencies play a central role. The field of CG theories is then included in literature regarding the economic systems using a much larger framework than that considered by Djankov *et al.* (2002). Let us specify that the productive analyses of NSCG are not confounded with the technological theory – in its neoclassical or evolutionary form (Nelson, 1998) – that retains technology as the main influencing factor for growth.[13]

A presentation based on the incentive/cognitive distinction is hardly relevant due to the imbrications of the incentive and cognitive aspects. Another distinction enables a classification of productive analyses into two categories: (i) one originates with an analysis of NSCG supported by a micro analysis of corporate governance based on the firm; and (ii) the other originates in direct position with the macro level.

These different analyses identify numerous types of NSCG that, apart from exceptions, do not reflect the opposition based on legal categories as emphasized by the law and finance theory. If, on occasion, the theories that attribute a dominant role to the productive aspects, distinctly oppose two types of systems, most often, they result in more complex typologies.

Productive analyses of the NSCG connected to the micro theory of governance

The main studies that integrate the productive aspect and are based on the firm may be grouped into the "Varieties of Capitalism" (VOC) theory. The theories of Aoki and Lazonick and O'Sullivan presented[14] in the first section, developed on a macro level, can be considered as particular cases. However, the presentation will be centered on the VOC version deemed to be dominant[15] by Hall and Soskice (2001, 2002), which opposes two leading types of economies and NSCG inside capitalism: "liberal market" economies and "coordinated market" economies.

The dominant vision of the VOC: the opposition between liberal market economies and coordinated economies

An objective of the dominant VOC view, consistent with the continuing research realized regarding the different forms of capitalism (Hall, 1999; Hall and Soskice, 2001, 2002; Boyer, 2002), is to explain the coexistence of the different economic systems based on the strategic behavior of economic actors, particularly firms. According to Hall and Soskice, the VOC reflects a "relational" perspective of the firm that integrates the contractual and cognitive conceptions of the firm and attributes an important place to the productive aspect. However, despite firms being viewed at first as actors attempting to build and then exploit competencies within the Resourced-Based View (RBV) perspective, Hall and Soskice refer mainly to the contractual perspective.

Coordination is broadly considered with regard to the development of competencies and involves both disciplinary and cognitive aspects. Five institutional domains have been recognized as significant: (i) industrial relations institutions (remuneration, working conditions, etc.); (ii) education and training systems; (iii) "CG" interpreted restrictively such as the financial system; (iv) inter-firm relationships that include exchange and joint-venture cooperative relationships; and (v) internal firm relationships with employees in order to pursue the objectives assigned to them.

Hall and Soskice (2001, 2002) oppose two main types of NSCG based on dominant coordination systems: "liberal" and "coordinated" market economies. Since this vocabulary is ambiguous, we will therefore describe these two types of economies as "arm's length" and "relational." In the first type, coordination is based mainly on market mechanisms. It is an "impersonal" spontaneous coordination, based on prices and attributing a central role to formal contracts. In the second type, coordination exists mainly through non-market relationships, strategic interactions of the actors as described by game theory. These relationships particularly involve reputation and information exchange mechanisms within the networks. As specified by Hall and Gingerich (2001), the choice between the two methods of coordination depends on the institutional framework. If markets are deemed imperfect and there is strong institutional support allowing the creation of credible commitments, the relational method will dominate. Contrarily, market coordination would be favored.

Taking professional training and education as well as inter-firm cooperation relationships into consideration implies the integration of the cognitive component of value creation but, for Hall and Soskice, the role of institutions, however, passes mainly through the disciplinary channel. The primary factors are the ability of institutions to facilitate the exchange of information, the surveillance and the sanctioning of non-cooperative behavior, the objective being to guarantee the enforcement of the commitments by reducing uncertainty.

Hall and Soskice put a particular emphasis on the role of deliberation institutions that provide for the exchange of information regarding the interests and beliefs of the actors in order to increase trust. The function of expanding the cognitive abilities, which would translate into an increase in the actor's ability for strategic action when faced with new situations, appears secondary with regard to the fight against opportunism. This cognitive aspect is attributed more to the informal institutions such as cultural. The informal rules, the shared mental models, are supposed to facilitate coordination by guiding it toward certain equilibria focal points. This aspect also appears in inter-firm relationships that distribute technology or in common technological standards established by industrial associations. In both cases, the objective is to create a common base of skills to facilitate coordination.

This institutional framework within which companies evolve is, at least in part, presumed to be exogenous and to play a dual "enabling" and "constraining" role. In particular, one of the fundamental hypotheses is that the specificities of each NSCG lead to systematic differences in strategies between companies. However, this influence does not reflect total determinism; the national framework only sets the space within which managers have great latitude while their actions and skills are viewed as central variables.

If arm's length economies have institutions encouraging flexibility and redeployment of resources, inversely, relational economies constitute a framework suitable for strategic interactions and (co)specific investments (industry-specific professional training; collaboration in relation to research and development), by better protecting this type of investment against risks of opportunism.

The opposition between the two types of economies, based on the dominant type of coordination, does not exclude the existence of hybrids. However, and this is the main thesis of the dominating version of the VOC, only the "coherent" systems in terms of institutional complementarities, favoring either mechanisms for market coordination or inversely, non-market mechanisms, could dominate due to a greater productive efficiency. For example, significant development of the financial markets would be accompanied by a poor protection of employees, fluid and slightly regulated job markets, training systems based on general skills and impersonal inter-firm relationships based on formal contracts.

Certain complementarities are deemed central (Hall and Gingerich, 2001). The first connects work relationships and financial governance. The financial systems that do not forbid cross-shareholdings by facilitating the concentration of power into the hands of the managers would limit hostile takeovers and would support financing granted on reputation rather than financial results. These systems would increase the efficiency of institutions that govern work relationships, by offering a better guarantee of employment security and to encourage long-term contracts as well as the negotiation processes between labor unions and employers unions. The second complementarity associates the systems of labor relationships and training. In market coordination systems, characterized by a substantial mobility of manpower and salary negotiations decentralized at the level of the firm, the training systems oriented toward general skills would be more efficient than those based on industry-specific human capital that requires training supported by close collaboration with the companies. Finally, the third complementarity is between financial governance and inter-firm relationships. If the pressure exercised by financial markets over managers, to ensure they pursue an objective of maximization of shareholder value, is not as great, it would be easier for them to establish credible commitments for inter-firm cooperation with regard to research, development of products or transfer of technology.

These three forms of complementarity are far from being the only ones. Accordingly, Estevez *et al.* (2001) emphasize a complementarity between social policies beneficial to employees and production strategies based on (co)specific assets. As for Casper (2001) and Teubner (2001), they illustrate how the legal systems are connected with the forms of inter-firm cooperation. Finally, according to Hall and Soskice (2001), by limiting the intensity of inter-firm competition, the regulation of the goods market may be complementary to the relational-based financial disciplinary systems (banks as opposed to financial markets), to the wage systems based on negotiation and to the systems of inter-firm relationships that are aimed at developing cooperation with regard to research and development.

This analysis of institutional complementarities resembles the view of Aoki to which authors make frequent reference. However, Hall and Soskice seem to stray from this view when they conclude that hybrid NSCG are less performing because they are less coherent in terms of coordination. If we limit ourselves to the two main types of NSCG – the most coherent – and their traditionally associated nations, neither of these two systems dominate the other over an extended period (from 1960 to 1998), regarding criteria for the growth rate of the GDP, the GDP per head and the rate of unemployment.

The VOC analysis emphasizes the concept of institutional comparative advantage: the institutional structure of a NSCG provides the companies of this system a competitive advantage in certain types of activities. Opposing radical innovation, characterized by important changes, with incremental innovation, Hall and Soskice show that arm's length economies favor the first type of innovation, which would attribute them an advantage in the industries of rapid technological evolution. Inversely, in the more traditional industries where quality is the main competitive dimension, the systems favoring incremental innovation would, on the contrary, be more performing. This analysis is similar in certain respects to the studies of Lazonick and O'Sullivan. It differs, however, in that the cognitive aspects of the innovation process appear secondary in comparison to the disciplinary aspects, the function of protection of (co)specific assets are deemed dominant.

The political aspect of the VOC

The VOC view attributes great importance to the political aspect. As political action must be defined so as to encourage cooperation, the political organization must be compatible with the dominant coordination method, either impersonal or relational. Consequently, Hall and Soskice emphasize the complementarities between the political and the other institutions, which ensure the coherence in the two main types of NSCG. The relational economies should be based on a political system within which the employer and union organizations are sufficiently strong in order for the State to respect the commitments made by these organizations. A strong executive power, based on a majoritarian political system, even possibly a threat to these commitments, would oppose an efficient relational coordination. Inversely, the consensual regimes, since they are more stable and avoid sudden political reorientations, would make such coordination easier. An effective protection with regard to risks created by the interventionism of the State would encourage the investment in (co)specific assets. In relational economics, the social policies are more beneficial for employees, not only for electoral competition or ideological reasons, but because they ensure a better protection of (co)specific investments.

Gourevitch and Hawes (2002) consider, however, that such an analysis is incomplete and sometimes confuses the different levels of politics. Political influence is supposed to be exercised mainly by the institutions seen only from a formal angle (existence of governmental coalitions or parties able to enforce the respect of the interests of the groups representing the productive forces; multiple possibilities of veto). Then, if the complementarity between the majoritarian systems and arm's length economies and between the consensual systems and relational economies, appears strongly corroborated, then certain formal variables retained, such as the number of "veto points" and the regime (presidential/parliamentary), have a slight correlation to the type of NSCG.

Furthermore, Hall and Soskice bring up another aspect beyond the opposition between majoritarian and consensual systems, by introducing a variable associated with the political representation of the interest groups, which raises the question of taking "corporatism" into account to model political institutions. Iversen and Soskice (2001), therefore, propose a theory predicting that nations where employees have a human capital that is highly specific should be dominated by parties or governments that would protect this capital through social measures, so as to attract the votes of employees. Gourevitch and Hawes criticize this causality model that, by making corporatism one of the determinants of the political system, while it is more of a product of this system, results in confusion between the independent variable and the dependent variable in the test of the relationship between the type of NSCG and the nature of the political system.

Moreover, according to Gourevitch and Hawes, such an analysis presumes that the preferences of the actors are identical regardless of the NSCG. However, the preferences and interests seem to differ between types of economies, due to the protection objective of (co)specific investments. In a relational economy, interdependence between the actor's investments influence the composition of the alliances; for example, the financial investors may have common interests with the employees, which can encourage the two groups to join in the search for a protectionist policy. Inversely, in an impersonal economy, the traditional opposition of capital/labor would appear.

Finally, Gourevitch and Hawes also specify the importance of social networks in understanding the differences that exist between the NSCG. These networks determine the options with regard to political action. Although the German State can rely on a condensed network to apply certain policies (training of employees, normalization, price, and production control), the French State does not have equivalent structures available. On the whole, the influence of politics on the NSCG would depend on the imbrications between the different factors presented: the form of institutions, preferences of interest groups, and the structure and importance of the social networks.

Empirical tests of the VOC

Based on a synthetic indicator, taking into consideration the type of coordination present in the financial sectors, remunerations, and work relationships, Hall and Gingerich (2001) reveal that the results obtained by the main developed nations confirm the relevance of typology opposing arm's length and relational economies. As such, the different types of complementarity presented appear to be confirmed within the two types of economies. At least, the hypothesis according to which greater systemic coherence results in a better economic performance is also corroborated.

The complementarity between this typology and the political characteristics is tested by Gourevitch and Hawes (2002). Significantly positive correlations exist between the type of system and the political variables representing the electoral system (majority/proportional representation), political cohesion (between the government parties) and the number of "effective" political parties that would have a chance of coming to power (bipartism/other systems).

However, a certain number of tests provide results that contradict the theory of Hall and Soskice by invalidating some of their key hypotheses regarding the two viewpoints. First, the mobility of the production factors presumed to be less prominent in relational economies and second, the presumed inferior performance of hybrid economies.

Hiscox and Rickard (2002) contest the least mobility hypothesis because of the imperfect character of the measurements of specificity of labor normally retained (costs of dismissal and the importance of professional training). Considering it more relevant to study the mobility of employees using inter-sectoral mobility rates, they illustrate that, for the countries of the OECD over the period 1970–1992, the labor mobility rates are higher within relational economies. In addition, the intra-type variance of these rates appears as high as between the different types of NSCG. Certain results however conform to the predictions of the VOC. Therefore, the differences between nations with regard to social protection are positively related to the specificity of human capital. But other factors such as programs for retraining and reconversion of employees, as well as the nature of the technology also intervene, contributing to distend the presumed link between the specificity of human capital and the nature of the economy.

Kenworthy (2002) doubts the empirical results obtained by Hall and Gingerich, concerning the association between institutional coherence and economic performance: (i) only three of the five institutional domains proposed by Hall and Soskice are considered in the tests; (ii) nearly half of the indicators retained are based on the financial governance domain only; (iii) the results from certain nations appear barely plausible. The results obtained through a different measurement of coherence invalidate the hypothesis: performance is equivalent for the three groups constituted according to the degree of coherency and the intra-group variance appears quite superior to the inter-group variance. Kenworthy, however, does not reject the theory according to which institutions through their effects on cooperation (Hicks and Kenworthy, 1998) influence performance. He only doubts the ability of the statistical studies to take into consideration the presumed effects of causality, due mainly to the imperfect character of the measurement of the variables. The theory, opposing two types of coordination, appears to him to be over exaggerated also, due to the recent American developments that seem to have resulted, at least in part, from the relational mechanisms borrowed from the Japanese model. Such an example raises the question of relevance of the link between systemic coherence and performance and, more generally, of the evolution by hybridization of the corporate governance systems.

Productive analyses of NSCG not connected to the micro theories of CG

The approach of Hall and Soskice originates from a particular conception of the firm to define the NSCG. It attempts to explain the coexistence of numerous NSCG according to their ability to realize equal performance in conformance to the principle of equifinality. The two polar forms, the most coherent, would result in equivalent performances. In turn, the less performing hybrid forms would eventually be condemned for lack of evolution. This approach, however, is only one particular form of the VOC, based on the two modes of coordination retained. As shown by Boyer (2002), it is possible to define other modes of coordination that results in a typology opposing, not two, but four types of systems, also considered as coherent. As well, Aoki proposes a more complex typology. The position of Hall and Soskice is sometimes ambiguous regarding the relative efficiency of hybrid forms. The characteristic aspect of the VOC is, therefore, not connected to the opposition between arm's length and relational economies; rather it is more a matter of importance attributed to the complementarity between the different institutional domains. It explains the coexistence of numerous national systems, simultaneously accounting for the cognitive and disciplinary aspects, the latter occupying a more important place.

Another viewpoint, the regulation theory – "la théorie de la regulation" – also gives a central role to the complementarity between institutions and hence, institutional coherence. This theory shares a certain number of common elements with the VOC (Boyer, 2002), in particular the refusal to consider that a unique optimal institutional architecture exists, but it diverges on numerous other points.

Initially, the objective of the regulation theory, which emerged in the middle of the 1970s, was not to explain the variety of capitalisms but rather to study the viability of the capitalist accumulation process focusing on crises. The holist and macroeconomic analyses emphasized the concept of the "regulation mode" that represents

> all the procedures and individual and collective behaviors that reproduce the fundamental social relationships, guide the accumulation regime in force and ensure the compatibility of a myriad of decentralized decisions, without the actors necessarily being aware of the adjustment principles of the entire system.
>
> (Boyer and Saillard, 2002; our translation)

The regulation mode is supposed to depend on five fundamental institutional forms: the wage labor nexus; forms of competition; the monetary regime; the place and role of the State; and the relationship with the international economy.

This theory however led to an interest in the diversity of capitalisms because of two phenomena: (i) different modes of regulation can be a basis for the same type of growth regime; and (ii) the different regimes can be supported by different institutional architectures. To explain this diversity and distinguish it from the technological theories, the regulation theory puts emphasis on the political institutional factor that relays the social conflicts and determines the legal framework.

This causality model results a priori in as many forms of capitalism and NSCG as States and political configurations, due to the national specificity of governmental interventions and institutional compromises. However, the regulation theory identifies a lower number of configurations – most often four – based on a dominant mode of regulation. The first, the market-based system, associated with market regulation within a legal framework guaranteeing the enforcement of commitments, can be compared to arm's length economies or to the Common law system of the law and finance theory. The second, described as "social democratic," retains the tripartite negotiation between management, unions and the State as a foundation for the institutional forms. It corresponds to the relational economy model for which the Scandinavian countries constitute an archetype. In the third configuration, called "meso-corporatist," the adjustments are performed mainly at the intermediary, or "meso-economic," level of the large conglomerate companies considered less sensitive to fluctuations in the overall economic situation. The Japanese and Korean economies illustrate this form. Finally, the fourth configuration – the "public" system – attributes a central role to intervention by the State and involves the continental European countries active in European integration. Contrary to the interpretation provided by the VOC viewpoint, the two latter configurations do not constitute hybrids presumed to be less performing, between arm's length and relational economies, but rather fully performing types because of the originality of the mechanisms used to overcome crises.

There are three reasons that justify this reduced number of configurations (Boyer, 2001, 2002). First, if institutions are presumed to have a political origin, their viability depends on their ability to survive in a context of economic competition. Second, the existence of an isomorphism between institutional and organizational forms would reduce the number of possible configurations in accordance with the different regulation modes. Finally, for each important phase of capitalism, the existence of either a hierarchy or a specific complementarity between the different institutions would contribute to explaining this reduction.

If, within the VOC view, the NSCG theory is constructed by changing from a micro to a macro dimension, inversely, in the regulation theory, the micro aspects were originally ignored. Various attempts have however been made to base the regulation theory on a theory of the "regulationist" firm (Coriat and Weinstein, 1995; Boyer, 2002), with causality based more on a macro aspect than micro. Despite these attempts, the view remains fundamentally macro.

Finally, in accordance with its initial objective of explanation of the crises, the regulation theory considers time in a different manner. While the VOC supports a static analysis of complementarity and retains an exogenous explanation of crises, due to important shocks linked, for example, to globalization, inversely, the regulation theory proposes an explanation of endogenous nature.

Although the regulation theory stresses the political factor, it does not ignore the role of innovation, which seems to be influenced by the dominant mode of regulation. The theory of social systems of innovation and production (SSIP), which can be considered as being derived from the regulation theory, assigns it more importance. With the presence of six institutional sub-systems (science, technology, industry, labor markets, education and training, and finance), it focuses on the interactions in terms of hierarchy and complementarity in order to evaluate coherence and the viability of the system over the long term, the objective being in particular to understand the phenomenon of endogenous growth. The SSIP retains the same typology of the NSCG as the regulation theory with each of the four major configurations characterized in accordance to the six sub-systems. It leads to certain predictions regarding innovation, industrial specialization and evolution (Amable, 2000; Amable and Petit, 1999) that are particularly important when studying the question of convergence of the different NSCG.

The main contribution of the regulation theory relates, first of all, to the extension of the analysis of institutional architectures using the concepts of "institutional hierarchy" and "institutional complementarity" and second, to the dynamic study of the systems, for example, the crises provoked by financial globalization. Compared to the VOC, it also puts greater emphasis on production and innovation through the cognitive aspects while the VOC favor the disciplinary considerations for the protection of (co)specific assets.

The macro analyses of the NSCG that integrate the productive aspect place the greatest importance on the interactions between the different institutional domains; this importance is confirmed by different empirical studies. Hence, Nicoletti *et al.* (2000, 2001), using the nations of the OECD, outline the interactions between the policies for the regulation of the goods and services markets, the level of wages and employment, job protection, the degree of innovation, the distribution of the size of the firms, and the degree of specialization of the different nations. The VOC and the regulation view both consider that there is a link between coherence and the performance of the systems even if the form of this link varies according to the complementarities considered or the number of typical forms retained.

The regulation theory deals particularly with the dynamic coherence of institutional architectures and the origin of the crises that are presumed endogenous. It is therefore consistent with the traditional debates on the possible conflict between static efficiency and dynamic efficiency, between static institutional coherence, a source of stability that could result in "ossification" (Olson, 1982; Hodgson, 1989), and the ability of the NSCG to adapt. If Olson focuses on the ossification factors associated with the appropriation of rents – that correspond to the disciplinary aspects of governance – Hodgson, on the contrary, stresses the ability of the different architectures to facilitate the creation and transmission of knowledge. Inspired mainly by Polanyi and Schumpeter, he proposes (Hodgson, 2001) an analysis of the adaptation abilities of the different systems in relation to the "impurity principle" according to which an economic system must contain at least one "foreign" structural element in order to adapt. If the static coherence, connected to high institutional homogeneity, is too great it would impede the possibility of a proper adaptation. In this perspective, the hybrid systems would appear, not as systems hampered by a lesser degree of coherence but, rather, as offering a superior ability for adaptation.

The VOC and the regulatory perspective both attribute an important place to the productive/cognitive aspects while emphasizing the possibility of interactions with the legal and financial domains. They also extend, on a macro level, the synthetic attempts at studies that exist with regard to micro theories. This integration results in an analysis of the national structures of ownership as an alternative to the law and finance explanations of LLSV and the political explanations of Roe. As such, Charreaux (2002b) proposes a model involving cognitive aspects, in addition to the disciplinary variables, which explain the ownership structures, not only in terms of concentration of ownership, but also in accordance with the nature of the shareholders and the skills they contribute.[16]

The complexity of the institutional interactions raises a question regarding the possibility of understanding the impact of institutional structure on the performance of NSCG working only on the macro level. Aguilera and Jackson (2003) therefore propose a model for NSCG, based on the actors and involving the three traditional categories of stakeholders, which particularly shows how institutions influence their conflicts and their strategic behavior. This influence is also considered by Thomas and Waring (1999) to explain the investment policies related to NSCG and also by Kogut *et al.* (2002), for the diversification strategies. Table 3.A1 provides a summary of the principal characteristics of the different theories of the NSCG.

Conclusion

From the financial model based on the protection of shareholder's interests, the CG theories have evolved toward more complex models involving all stakeholders and attributing greater importance to the productive/cognitive aspects of value creation. This evolution, influenced by that of the theories of the firm, leads to considering human capital as being more and more significant since the formation of the competitive advantage seems to be based mostly on skills. The recent developments result in a better understanding of the functioning and the evolution of the corporate governance systems, in particular outside the Anglo-Saxon world. The theoretical critiques and the results of empirical and historical studies that reveal a significant influence of political and cultural factors seriously question the dominant law and finance view. This crisis of the paradigm of financial governance, which is but an expression of the more general financial paradigm crisis (Zingales, 2000; Charreaux, 2002a), does not lead to a theoretical impasse. On the contrary, alternative theories are numerous and open up new horizons. Perspectives have not been addressed and deserve an extended examination.

Analysis, taking the political aspect into account, shows in all probability that the different NSCG offer advantages and disadvantages simultaneously, more or less sensitive according to the economic situations and the nature of the activities, which would explain the coexistence of systems producing equivalent performances (Charreaux, 1997; Gourevitch and Hawes, 2002). The validity of the presumed link between the development of the New Economy and the Anglo-Saxon CG system can be questionned. It would appear that this system, under traditional representation, is neither a necessary condition, nor a sufficient one. According to Aoki (2000a, 2001) and Rajan and Zingales (1998b), the emergence of new forms of firms and the model for the development of the New Economy are based on a configuration that is very different from the model associated with financial governance.

On a predictive level, theories result in variable responses to the question of convergence of the NSCG. For Aoki (1995), in view of the effects of globalization, four scenarios are possible: (i) the convergence by reciprocal imitation;

(ii) the destabilization of a system due to the integration of elements harmful to coherence and resulting in a protectionist attitude; (iii) the disappearance of dominated systems; (iv) the emergence of a hybrid system with its own institutional architecture, of which the European integration is an incomplete example. The supporters of the law and finance theory most often predict a type 3 scenario; the arm's length Anglo-Saxon system would ultimately prevail due to its greater efficiency while the other theoretical perspectives are far from sharing this conclusion. The regulation theory, for example, claims that the arm's length system may dominate, not because of its greater efficiency but rather its destabilizing effect provoked by the integration of certain of its elements into other NSCG. Most analyses, however, consider the hypothesis of evolution toward a single form – either by progressive convergence or by the disappearance of dominated forms – as hardly plausible, as much due to the cultural and political rigidities as the contingent character of the efficiency of the systems according to the stage of economic development. The complete hybridization hypothesis also seems barely probable as proven by the difficulty of implementation in the European Union (EU). Also, certain recent unfortunate transplantation examples, in particular, in the former Eastern Bloc countries.

Notes

1 These results are confirmed and extended, in particular, by the studies of Rajan and Zingales (1998b), Demirguç-Kunt and Maksimovic (1998), Levine (1999), Levine and Zervos (1998), Beck and Levine (2004), and Carlin and Mayer (2003).
2 For a brief history of the different traditions, in addition to La Porta *et al.* (1998), see also Beck *et al.* (2001a, 2003b).
3 For an analysis of the supposed benefits alleged to Common law, see Coffee (1999b).
4 We will use the initials LLSV, in accordance with tradition, to designate the generic position of La Porta, Lopez-de-Silanes, Shleifer and Vishny.
5 According to Pistor *et al.* (2003a, 2003b), legal systems have a greater ability for adaptation and innovation in their countries of origin.
6 Cheffins (2001) also notes that minorities receive limited protection in Great Britain and this situation has barely evolved in the second half of the twentieth century. The evolution of ownership structures toward more large public firms is based on a certain number of substitute mechanisms, such as the concern for the reputation of finance professionals and the regulatory role played by the London Stock Exchange.
7 Similarly, according to Roe (2003), in the United States, Common law was completed by the creation of the Security Exchange Commission (SEC) that led many authors to believe that the SEC was the first mechanism for the protection of minorities and that the main function of Common law was not that of ensuring this protection.
8 We may also mention Pound (1993) as one of the founders of this approach.
9 Path dependence in the CG systems is analyzed in depth by Roe (1996) and Bebchuk and Roe (1999). For Williamson (1984), in accordance with the criterion of remediability, efficiency must be evaluated relatively and taking into consideration the costs for exiting the path, in other words the adaptation costs for the system.
10 The principle of equifinality states that there are a number of different paths to any given outcome.
11 As specified by Roe (2003, p. 69, note 19), Coffee's explanation based on the role of the State is contradicted by two factual elements. Financial markets were developed in France and Germany under the two conservative governmental regimes, the French

Second Empire and the Imperial Regime of Bismarck. Furthermore, the United States (through the SEC budget) spent much more – after controlling for the effects of size – to regulate their financial market than the European nations and therefore based on this point, governmental intervention in the United States appeared more intense.

12 These results are similar to those of Beck *et al.* (2003a), whose study based on the influencing factors for development of financial institutions confirms the role of endowments and the legal systems, with endowments offering the better explanatory power. The French legal origin looses its significance when the religious variable is introduced. The political variables would only have a secondary role.

13 According to Nelson (2002), institutions influence the creation of technology and its adoption as illustrated in literature regarding the "national innovation systems" (Lundvall, 1992; Nelson, 1993; Mowery and Nelson, 1999) and its extensions that, in certain regards, can be considered as being based on the innovative firm theories.

14 We could also include the analyses of the complementarities inside the different systems of capitalism, proposed by Pagano (2002) and Nicita and Pagano (2002), in a perspective based on the protection of assets.

15 This reference to Hall and Soskice may be criticized since it is far from representing all the VOC literature. For a synthetic presentation of the main studies in this objective see Boyer (2002).

16 The importance of the nature of the shareholders is confirmed by Pedersen and Thomsen (2003).

Table 3.A1 Macro theories of the NSCG

	Type of efficiency	Underlying micro theory	Typology of national systems	Institutional interactions	Uniqueness of the optimal system or equifinality
The disciplinary theories of the NSCG based on appropriation of rents (excludes the productive aspect)					
Law and finance theory (LLSV)	Productive efficiency (growth rate of GNP or GNP by head) Disciplinary argument: quality of the law to protect the interests of financial investors	Shareholder theory	Civil law systems (French system) against Common law systems (Anglo-Saxon system) Possible nuances between Civil law traditions	Politics are at the of the legal framework system but once established it is the only one that determines the financial development	Superiority of the origin Anglo-Saxon offering more flexibility and better adaptability
Evolutionary law and finance theory (Beck *et al.*, 2001b; Coffee, 2001a; Pistor *et al.*, 2003a)	Productive efficiency Disciplinary argument (with evolutionary aspects) Flexibility and adaptation to economic and social conditions Trade-off between agency costs and flexibility	Mainly shareholder theory	Transplantation theory Opposition between the countries of origin and countries of transplantation	The law adapts in interaction with the other economic and social aspects (endogeneity) Usually preceded by politics	The Civil law system is more rigid but the equifinality is not excluded, the main influencing factor is the origin Maladjustment would result from transplantation
Politico-financial theory (Roe, 2003)	Productive efficiency Disciplinary argument	Mainly shareholder	Opposition (1) of social democracy to	Politics influences the law and is the decisive	Possibility of equifinality

	with numerous aspects (opportunism, management errors) Protection of shareholders interests Law allows for the reduction of costs of opportunism but not those of management errors		liberal countries (2): (1) weak protection of investors + strong protection of employees + weak competitive character of the markets (2) strong protection of investors + weak protection of employees + strong competitive character of the markets	factor in the separation of ownership/decision Coherence between protection of investors, protection of employees and competitive character of the goods and services markets	Trade-off between monitoring costs linked to dispersion and waste linked to the importance of rents due to the weak competitive character Globalization threatens the coherence of the social-democratic system
Extension and generalization of the political theory (Roe, 2000; Pagano and Volpin, 2001a, 2001b; Rajan and Zingales, 2003; Gourevitch, 2003; Gourevitch and Shinn, 2004)	Productive efficiency Disciplinary argument Protection of minorities or protection of specific investments of stakeholders Three categories of stakeholders: managers, investors, and employees.	Shareholder or stakeholder	Majoritarian vs consensus systems: opposition of capital/labor is not the only possible model; other alliances may be established between the employees, investors, and managers aggregation of preferences depends on political institutions (majoritarian systems vs consensus systems)	Politics constructs the law according to the interests represented within the coalitions	Possible equifinality; multiple equilibria within the games

continued

Table 3.A1 continued

	Type of efficiency	Underlying micro theory	Typology of national systems	Institutional interactions	Uniqueness of the optimal system or equifinality
Endowment theory (Beck et al., 2001a; Acemoglu et al., 2001)	Productive efficiency and disciplinary argument The initial endowments (natural and human resources) influenced the creation of institutions by determining the type of colonization (extraction or implantation). The main variable is institutional	Mainly shareholder	Applies to colonized countries Opposition between countries of implantation and those of extraction No overlapping with the opposition between the Civil law and Common law framework	The endowments have an influence on institutional development The role of institutions has priority over the only geographic determinism The legal and religious factors also seem to intervene as explanatory factors of development	Possible equifinality
Socio-cultural theories (La Porta et al., 1997b; Coffee, 2001a; Licht, 2001; Stulz and Williamson, 2003)	Productive efficiency and disciplinary argument Socio-cultural values, in particular religious, have an influence on agency costs, mainly by reducing opportunism	Shareholder	Countries with strong social cohesion vs countries with weak social cohesion	Imbrications of socio-cultural values and legal aspects Effects of substitution or complementarity with regard to legal-financial variables Predominance of the cultural variable	Possibility of equifinality because of the imbrications of variables

The disciplinary theories of the NSCG based on production (disciplinary and cognitive aspects)

	Type of efficiency	Underlying micro theory	Typology of national systems	Institutional interactions	Uniqueness of the optimal system or equifinality
Varieties of capitalism theory	Productive efficiency with distribution aspects	Stakeholder and (in an	Opposition between "arm's length" (market)	Complementarity between five domains:	Equifinality of the two main forms

(Hall and Soskice, 2001, 2002)	(unemployment and inequality) Productive efficiency with disciplinary predominance but with cognitive aspects Efficiency depends mainly on the protection of (co)specific investments Two regulation modes: arm's length (market) vs relational	accessory way) cognitive	and "relational" economies The less coherent hybrids are less efficient	industrial relationships; training and education; financial governance; inter-firm relationships; and internal firm relationships Complementarity and coherence are central concepts	The most coherent forms dominate
Regulation theory and the SSIP theory (Amable et al., 1997; Boyer, 2002; Boyer and Saillard, 2002)	Productive efficiency (static and dynamic) with considerations of inequality Productive with disciplinary and cognitive considerations Politics determines the emergence of forms, but the viable systematic configurations in terms of static coherence and dynamic ability are selected by the competition The SSIP emphasizes the innovation and production systems	A priori, no underlying micro theory Try to propose a theory of the "regulationnist" firm and to link macro to micro theories	Four viable types: market; social-democratic; meso-corporatist; and public	Regulation theory: complementarity between five institutional forms: wage-labor nexus; forms of competition; monetary regime; place and role of the State; and relationship with the international economy SSIP theory: six sub-systems: science, technology, industry, labor markets; education; and finance	Possible equifinality of viable forms Questioning of the endogenous emergence of crises Conflict between static institutional coherence and ability for adaptation

4 The American national system of corporate governance

B. L. Nelson

Introduction

Corporate governance (CG) has recently been extensively discussed, intensely debated and variously defined in the United States. For the purposes of this chapter, CG shall mean the internal arrangements within a corporation intended to provide reasonable assurances that corporate directors and officers make and implement decisions in accordance with their duties of care and loyalty to their corporations. CG in the United States is often associated with the recent initiatives taken in the wake of corporate scandals such as Enron and MCI. While the recent initiatives are undoubtedly important, their significance can best be understood in the context of the existing frameworks under corporate and securities law.

The current initiatives in the United States (i.e. the recently adopted CG provisions in the listing requirements for the New York Stock Exchange (NYSE) – and the provisions of the Sarbanes–Oxley Act of 2002 – often called "Sarbanes–Oxley") in important ways simply add to the governance measures already in place pursuant to corporate law and securities regulation in the United States. Only after understanding foundations in corporate law and securities regulation in the United States is it possible to understand the significance, and the limitations, of the recently adopted NYSE listing requirements and of Sarbanes–Oxley.

In general, the recent NYSE initiatives attempt to improve the degree of independence among directors of corporations listed there so that they are better able – and more likely – to meet the performance standards currently applicable to directors under corporate law (i.e. duties of care and loyalty), but the NYSE does not change those standards. Unfortunately, the NYSE listing requirements do not have the force of law.

Sarbanes–Oxley, on the other hand, in general, attempts to improve the independence of external auditors and corporate directors so that they are better able – and more likely – to prepare public disclosures in form and substance required by US securities regulations. There are also provisions intended to enhance the care with which corporate officers prepare required public disclosures. Unfortunately, Sarbanes–Oxley applies only to disclosure requirements under US securities regulations. With limited exceptions, Sarbanes–Oxley is not specifically intended to apply to directors' or officers' broader obligations to their corporations or the standards applicable to their performance of those obligations.

Corporate law in the United States

Corporate law – at least in the United States – is often discussed but rarely understood, in part because corporate law is not federal law and in part because there is no government agency actively enforcing it. Securities law is better understood, in part because it is a federal law actively enforced by a government agency. The provisions of corporate law can be divided into three large topics: corporate formation, corporate constitutions and the potential personal liability of corporate directors and officers.

First, corporate law in the United States contains provisions concerning the formation of corporations. In general, corporations are formed when one or more investors transfer assets into a separate account (i.e. the corporation) and, in exchange the investors are granted a divisible common interest (i.e. shares) in that account. The result of these two, simultaneous operations is the separation of share ownership from both corporate ownership of those assets and from corporate control of those assets.

Second, corporate law contains provisions concerning corporate constitutions. Such provisions deal with each corporation's arrangements for the exercise of control over the corporation's accounts, i.e. arrangements for proposing, making and implementing decisions concerning the disposition of corporate assets. Within the scope of these provisions, corporate law is similar to the constitutional provisions of national governments and so can be referred to as corporate law's "constitutional provisions." Generally, corporate directors (the shareholders' elected representatives) delegate authority to corporate officers the obligation to manage corporate affairs in the ordinary course of business. Accordingly, corporate constitutional arrangements also include the obligation of corporate officers to report to corporate directors on the discharge of their management obligations.

Third, corporate law contains provisions concerning directors' and officers' personal liability for actions taken in their corporation's name and for its account. These provisions of corporate law are taken largely from rules of agency law. Generally, corporate directors and officers can be personally liable for failing to act with due care and loyalty on the corporation's behalf.

Corporate formation

In order to form a corporation in the United States, investors are required to contribute some form of capital – i.e. money or assets – to the corporation, a fictitious person with the legal right to own and dispose of assets.

Corporations, in turn, own all of the assets contributed by the investors. As a condition to each shareholder's contribution, the corporation agrees to use the contributed assets in the conduct of a legal business (or a more precisely specified business). In addition, the corporation – not its shareholders – owe all of the liabilities incurred in the corporation's conduct of the business.

The investors' ownership in their corporations is usually divided into "shares," which are often, but not always, evidenced by share certificates. In the absence of classes of shares (i.e. shares with preferential rights), each share constitutes an equal undivided right to participate in distributions made by the corporation to its shareholders, either in the form of (a) dividends in the normal course of business, or (b) distributions in partial or total liquidation of the corporation.

In the absence of classes of shares (i.e. shares with preferential rights), each share also has an equal vote in all decisions made by the shareholders in respect of the corporation. Finally, in the absence of an agreement between or among shareholders, shares are freely transferable and the corporation survives the transfer of shares, whether the transfer is by sale, testament or the laws of intestacy.

Corporate constitutions: separating share ownership and corporate ownership

As explained above, there is a clear separation of shareholders' ownership of shares and the corporation's ownership of assets. Shareholders can directly exercise their ownership rights in shares, either personally or by delegation to others, but shareholders cannot personally exercise private property rights in corporate assets. Instead, corporations alone own the assets transferred to them by their shareholders and exercise private property rights in those transferred assets in the same manner and to the same extent as individuals, i.e. natural persons.

Corporate constitutions: separating share ownership and corporate control

In general, in partnerships in the United States, each partner can act in the partnership's name and, therefore, for the account of all other partners in disposing of partnership assets. Unlike partnerships, corporations in the United States can exercise their private property rights only by delegation to one or more individuals.

In other words, unlike partners, shareholders in corporations cannot act in the name and for the account of their corporations. Instead, all of the authority to act in the corporation's name and on its behalf is delegated to a single individual. This person is designated the "president" by corporate laws in the United States but is also, typically, given the title of "Chief Executive Officer" (CEO).

The CEO typically delegates some of his or her power – in a manner allowed or required by the corporation's constitutional documents – to one or more subordinate individuals, all of whom are then authorized to act in the corporation's name within the scope of that delegation. The person or persons entrusted with the power to exercise the private property rights in corporate assets are called "corporate officers."

CEOs have the authority and, in exchange for their compensation, the obligation to make and implement decisions in the ordinary course of business concerning the disposition of corporate assets. Corporate officers also have the obligation, pursuant to corporate law, to report on the results of operations to their corporations' directors, the shareholders' representatives. This reporting obligation under corporate law arises from the separation of corporate ownership and corporate control, as described above.

Corporate constitutions: shareholders' and directors' control

Shareholders' control of corporations under corporate law is limited to the election of directors and auditors – often nominated by CEOs. Relying on the following provision of corporate law, directors, in turn, typically limit their role to selecting CEOs (and, sometimes, other corporate officers) and to supervising their performance: "The business and affairs of every corporation ... shall be managed by or under the direction of a board of directors" (Delaware General Corporation Law, § 141 (a)). The only additional element of shareholders' and directors' control under corporate law is making decisions on matters outside the corporation's ordinary course of business, e.g. the payment of dividends, changes in the corporation's business, mergers, acquisitions, divestments and the liquidation or partial liquidation of the corporation. On such matters, shareholders and directors typically make decisions on the basis of proposals initiated by their corporation's CEO.

In any event, shareholders and directors in the United States never have authority to take action in the corporation's dealings with third parties. All such corporate action – both in the ordinary course of business and extraordinary matters – are implemented by the CEO and other officers. Only the CEO and other corporate officers can sign documents and otherwise act in the corporation's name and for its account, i.e. only they can act as a corporation's "legal representative" (as such a term is understood in many civil law jurisdictions).

Corporate constitutions: CEOs' and other officers' control

With the limited exceptions described above, in most US corporations all corporate decisions are made and implemented solely and exclusively by corporate officers. In fact, in the first instance, only one corporate officer, i.e. the corporation's CEO, is authorized to propose, make and implement all corporate decisions in the ordinary course of business.

However, CEOs can delegate – and often are required by their corporations' charters to delegate – to other corporate officers the authority to make and implement certain decisions. In those instances where CEOs are required to delegate authority to certain officers (e.g. the chief financial officer (CFO), or the chief legal officer (CLO)), the CEOs tend to have the sole authority to appoint the individuals who fill those offices.

Even in those instances where directors or shareholders make the final decisions, only officers often have the ability to make the initial proposals and to organize the decision-making process. For example, even though shareholders typically elect directors and external auditors, CEOs alone usually have the ability to select the sole nominee for directors and external auditors. In addition, presidents or CEOs organize and administer the election process.

Finally, as previously noted, officers have the duty to report to their corporations' directors, the shareholders' representatives. This reporting obligation under corporate law arises from the separation of corporate ownership and corporate control. In other words, the officers' reporting requirements arise from the fact that they act in a corporation's name and for its account – not in their own name or for their own account.

Officers' personal liability to their corporations

As evidenced by the foregoing discussion, some corporate law in the United States is dedicated to issues surrounding procedures for proposing, making, implementing and reporting on corporate decisions. Directors' and officers' personal liability to their corporations is another important topic under corporate law. The discussion in this section will focus on the potential personal liability of corporate officers. The potential personal liability of corporate directors will be discussed below under the heading of "special topics under corporate law."

Within the scope of their authority, CEOs and other corporate officers have no liability to third parties, i.e. persons other than the corporations they serve. While corporations might incur liability to individuals and other corporations under the law of general obligation or contract law for their CEOs to act in their corporations' names and for their accounts, CEOs generally do not incur any liability to other individuals or corporations on the basis of those acts. Such is the risk for individuals and corporations in doing business with a corporation's CEO.

On the other hand, CEOs and other corporate officers can be liable to their corporations under corporate law for their actions on behalf of their corporations. As regards possible personal liability to their corporations, corporate officers are similar to bailees, such as warehousemen and common carriers. Like bailees, managers take possession of corporate assets – not title to them – and only as a necessary incident to performing their personal services. Just as bailees, warehousemen or common carriers can be liable to the individuals who entrust assets to them if they fail to discharge their obligations, so corporate officers can be liable to their corporations for their failures in proposing, making, implementing and reporting on corporate decisions. Neither the recent NYSE listing requirements nor Sarbanes–Oxley increase CEOs' or other corporate officers' potential personal liability under corporate law.

Finally, CEOs and other corporate officers can be held legally responsible by the United States government, and even subject to criminal sanctions, if the CEOs and other corporate officers violate a government regulation in the performance of their duties on behalf of their corporations. While the NYSE listing requirements have no effect on potential criminal sanctions, Sarbanes–Oxley increases the sanctions potentially applicable to CEOs and other corporate officers for violations of US securities regulations.

Officers' personal liability to their corporations: "fiduciary duties" are performance standards

Corporate officers are required under corporate law to report to directors on the results of operations, but they are not required to inform or consult with directors or shareholders before making and implementing decisions in the ordinary course of business. In the absence of prior guidance from directors and shareholders, officers cannot be held accountable for failing to honor specific wishes of directors and officers.

Corporate officers can, however, be held accountable for failing to meet the standards which all corporations can reasonably expect from their officers in making, implementing and reporting on corporate decisions. More precisely, corporate officers are subject to two specific performance standards, traditionally called "fiduciary duties." The two duties are the "duty of loyalty" and the "duty of care."

Officers' personal liability to their corporations: duty of loyalty

By accepting appointment, all corporate officers are bound by corporate law to the "duty of loyalty" in all obligations they undertake on behalf of their corporations: i.e. the officers will avoid conflicts-of-interest between their corporations' interests and their own interests. There are three elements to corporate officers' duty of loyalty.

First, corporate officers agree to make decisions in their corporation's best interest – without regard to their own best interests.

Second, corporate officers agree not to acquire interests in conflict with their corporation's best interests. This element of the duty of loyalty prohibits corporate officers from maintaining or entering into competitive undertakings and from appropriating corporate opportunities for themselves.

Third, in the event that officers' interests inevitably conflict with the best interests of their corporations, officers agree to disclose the conflict of interest to disinterested directors and to defer to them in making corporate decisions.

Officers' personal liability to their corporations: duty of care

By accepting appointment, all corporate officers are bound by corporate law to the "duty of care," in respect of all acts they undertake on behalf of their corporations: i.e. the officers will pursue their corporations' goals as prudently as if they owned the corporations. The officers' duty of care has three elements.

First, the officers must be acting "within the scope of their authority." This element of the duty of care relates to the corporation's by-laws, corporate resolutions and specific authorizations. If officers are not acting within the scope of these charter documents and authorizations, then the officers have breached their duty of care.

Second, the officers must not be acting "negligently." This element of the duty of care relates to the diligence exercised by officers in collecting facts relevant to their decisions. In collecting facts, corporate officers breach their duty of care if they do not use the diligence of an ordinarily prudent corporate officer in similar circumstances. This element of the duty of care focuses on the facts available and known to officers at the time they make their decisions.

Third, the officers must be acting "in good faith." This element of the duty of care relates to the diligence exercised by officers in reaching conclusions based on the facts known to them at the time they make their decisions. In reaching conclusions, corporate officers breach their duty of care if they do not exercise the judgment of an ordinarily prudent businessperson in similar circumstances. This element of the duty of care focuses upon the manner in which officers decisions are made.

The application of the duty of care to officers' decisions is subject to the "business judgment rule." Pursuant to this rule, courts apply the duty of care on the basis of the facts reasonably available to corporate officers at the time that they are making and implementing their decisions – not on the basis of facts which the officers could not have known, even if they had been diligent. Moreover, pursuant to the "business judgment rule," courts apply the duty of care on the basis of results corporate officers can reasonably expect to achieve, not on the basis of results actually obtained. The business judgment rule does not apply to the duty of loyalty or compliance with government regulations, such as securities regulations.

Special issues under corporate law in the United States

In addition to the foregoing general observations on corporate law in the United States, it is important to understand some special issues raised by the NYSE listing requirements, Sarbanes–Oxley and CG initiatives in general.

Special issues under corporate law in the United States: there is no national corporate law

The most important special issue about corporate law in the United States is that there is no federal corporate law in the United States. Under the US constitution, the power to enact corporate laws is a power reserved for many states in the United States. The most important corporate law in the United States is in the law of the State of Delaware. Delaware first adopted its current corporate law in the early 1900s. Since that early date, Delaware has been by far the most popular state for corporate incorporations. (Corporations with operations any where in the United States are generally free to locate their legal domicile in any state in the United States. For example, a corporation with all or most of its operations in New York State is free to incorporate in Delaware.)

Special issues under corporate law in the United States: obligations of trust

To the extent that corporate officers can make and implement decisions without first consulting with directors or shareholders, their relationship to their corporations is based on trust. Since corporate officers make and implement practically all decisions in the ordinary course of a corporation's business without consulting or even informing shareholders or directors beforehand, the trust placed in corporate officers is considerable.

In fact, shareholders typically do not learn about their officers' individual decisions even after those decisions are made and implemented. On the contrary, shareholders typically know neither the individual decisions made by their corporations' officers, nor the results obtained from those individual decisions.

This situation is not changed by officers' requirement to report to corporate directors under corporate law. Unless the directors impose an obligation on the CEO to inform or consult with them before making and implementing a decision, CEOs have no legal obligation under corporate law to report to directors on decisions they make and implement in the ordinary course of business.

Similarly, this situation is not changed by US securities regulations. Pursuant to US securities regulations (as discussed below), shareholders know only the aggregate results of all decisions made by their corporations' officers – and shareholders know those results (not the individual decisions made) only after the decisions are implemented. Pursuant to US securities regulations, shareholders know those aggregate results only on a periodic basis – typically once each three-month, six-month or one-year period.

Special issues under corporate law in the United States: directors' personal liability to their corporations

The same performance standards applicable to officers, as outlined above, also apply to directors. In other words, in performing their obligations, directors are subject to the duty of loyalty and the duty of care, just as officers are subject to those duties.

There is, however, an important difference. The standards applied to corporate officers are "professional" standards while the standards applicable to directors are lower, "unprofessional" standards. In other words, corporate officers are expected to demonstrate the care and loyalty of corporate officers. Corporate directors, on the contrary, are only expected to demonstrate the care and loyalty of a reasonable person.

There are even cases which suggest that the performance standards for corporate directors are subjective, "personal" standards. In other words, each corporate director is expected to demonstrate the care and loyalty which can be reasonably expected of him or her – having due regard for all relevant facts and circumstances, including his or her background, his or her previous tenure with the corporation and the amount of time he or she dedicates to the corporation.

With one exception, neither the NYSE nor Sarbanes–Oxley sought to impose a professional standard on directors' performance as a part of their CG initiatives. The only exception is the requirement under Sarbanes–Oxley that one member of a corporation's audit committee should be a "financial expert."

Special issues under corporate law in the United States: delegations of authority

Delegations of authority are fundamental to the creation of corporate organizations. The shareholders' delegation of all corporate management to directors is the initial delegation necessary for corporate formation. The next delegation of authority is the directors' delegation to the CEO of all corporate management in the ordinary course of business. Subsequent delegations are made by the CEO to other corporate officers, all in the manner previously described.

Delegating directors and officers can be personally liable for acts and omissions of officers, employees or agents to whom they have delegated authority if the delegating directors or officers have not complied with their duties of care and loyalty in making and implementing the delegations. Most importantly, delegating directors and officers can be personally liable if they violate their duty of care in failing to supervise the subordinate individuals to whom they have delegated corporate authority.

Director supervision of the CEO and other corporate officers is an important issue addressed by both the NYSE and the Security Exchange Commission (SEC) through their CG initiatives. Without changing the performance standards of directors under corporate law, both the NYSE and SEC attempt to rearrange corporate constitutions so that directors will in fact exercise more supervision of senior officers. They attempt to do so by requiring an increase in the independence of directors who serve on boards and important board committees, i.e. audit, compensation and nomination committees.

Special issues under corporate law in the United States: shareholder derivative actions

Generally, there are no government agencies in the United States to enforce officers' personal liability to their corporations. Instead, in the United States the enforcement of such personal liability depends on legal action by corporations against their officers. Needless to say, such action presents significant difficulties.

First, corporations take such legal action, if at all, only after corporate officers' positions are terminated. At the same time, corporate officers typically negotiate waivers from further personal liability in the context of their termination agreements.

Second, in the first instance such legal action needs to be authorized by the corporation's board of directors. At the same time, boards of directors often hesitate in bringing legal action against corporate officers, in part because of the morale issues such action raises for continuing corporate officers.

Third, in the absence of legal action by boards of directors, shareholders are authorized to bring legal action against corporate officers for their personal liability to their corporations. At the same time, allowing individual or small numbers of shareholders to bring legal action against corporate officers can lead to confusion and wasting corporate assets. Such lawsuits are called "shareholder derivative action."

In response to this third difficulty, shareholders who want to sue their corporate officers must follow procedures established under most corporate laws. Typically, shareholders are not allowed to sue in their own names; they are required to sue in the corporation's name. In addition, shareholders holding a relatively small percentage of outstanding shares are not allowed to sue; their lawsuits are subject to annulment by the corporation's independent directors; and they risk having to pay all expenses if they do not prevail in their claims against the corporate officers.

The difficulties encountered by shareholders in bringing shareholder derivative action undermines the effectiveness of the performance standards (i.e. duty of loyalty and duty of care). In the absence of any government agency action enforcing those performance standards, they remain ineffective in too many cases. The initiatives from the NYSE and Sarbanes–Oxley do not eliminate any of the barriers to shareholder derivative action or create an agency responsible for enforcing corporate law in the United States.

United States securities regulations

Just as it is important to understand corporate law in the United States in order to understand the recent CG initiatives there, so it is important to understand securities regulations in the United States. In fact, securities regulations take on added (arguably disproportionate) significance because (as noted above) there is no federal corporate law in the United States. In this context, "national" regulators necessarily (also sometimes called "federal" regulators in the United States) rely exclusively on securities regulations in order to introduce CG reforms.

Summary of US securities regulations: corporate law and securities regulation are different

Corporate law and securities regulation are usually considered to be closely related and indeed they are related in some ways. Most importantly, both include corporate reporting requirements. At the same time, the public disclosure requirements under securities regulation differ in important ways from the reporting obligations of corporate law.

First, corporate law promotes the legal institution of corporations. Securities regulation promotes securities exchanges, another institution which could not exist without legal support.

Second, corporate law is intended primarily for the benefit of shareholders, i.e. corporate investors for the periods of time that they hold their shares. Securities regulation is intended primarily for the benefit of share traders, i.e. corporate investors at the moment that they sell or buy their shares.

Third, pursuant to corporate law, corporate officers report in privacy to corporate directors (the shareholders' representatives). Pursuant to securities regulations, corporate officers report directly to the entire public as the only feasible means of reporting to all potential share sellers and all potential share buyers.

Fourth, the reporting requirements under corporate law exist separately – and in addition – to the public disclosure requirements under securities regulation. One of the duties for corporate officers of publicly traded companies is to prepare and release public disclosures under securities regulations. Those public disclosures under securities regulations are not a substitute for complying with officers' reporting duties under corporate law. In other words, if directors request information in addition to disclosures required under securities regulations, then the CEO and other corporate officers are required to provide that information pursuant to corporate law.

Fifth, corporate law is based on trust while securities law is based on disclosures. Pursuant to corporate law, directors and officers are not required to disclose any material information to shareholders before the directors or officers make decisions on behalf of their corporations. Instead, shareholders trust their corporations' officers and directors. Share buyers do not trust share sellers in a similar fashion. Instead, pursuant to securities regulation, share sellers are required to disclose all material information before share buyers make their decisions.

In publicly traded corporations, shareholders do not have direct access to the data required to provide the material information share buyers demand. As a result, publicly traded corporations are required under securities regulations to disclose all relevant information publicly, i.e. to all potential share sellers and potential share buyers. Accordingly, the most important element of trust in securities transactions is the trust placed both by potential share sellers (i.e. current shareholders) and by potential share buyers (i.e. the entire public) in the corporate officers who prepare the public disclosures required by securities regulations. Since 1976, breaching this element of trust (more precisely, breaching this "duty of care") has been subject to sanctions enforceable by the SEC under securities regulations since 1976.

Summary of US Securities Regulations: securities regulation is like consumer protection law. In the absence of "consumer protection" statutes, sellers of goods are allowed to keep secrets – even important secrets – about the goods they offer for sale. Similarly, in the absence of securities regulations, sellers of corporate shares are allowed to keep secrets – even important secrets – about their shares and the corporations underlying those shares.

Securities regulation is, in fact, intended as a type of consumer protection for buyers of shares in corporations. This principle is evidenced by the following famous question and answer during the public debates concerning adoption of the US securities regulations in 1933:

US CONGRESSMAN: You think, then, that when a corporation ... offers stock
   to the public ... the public has no right to know what [the corporation's]
   earning power is or [to] subject [the corporation] to any inspections...?
CEO OF AMERICAN SUGAR REFINING COMPANY: Yes, that is my theory. Let
   the buyer beware ... that is the way men are educated and cultivated.

(1933 Congressional Testimony)

Securities regulations give buyers of company shares the "right to know" about their purchases just as consumer protection statutes give buyers of goods and services the right to know about their purchases. If the information supplied by sellers to buyers is complete in all material respects, then the market price for all items (goods, services and shares) is presumed to be fair.

Unlike other forms of consumer protection – which focus exclusively on the buyers' "right to know" – securities regulation is intended to benefit both buyers and sellers of shares in publicly-traded corporations. Because of the separation of ownership and control in publicly-traded corporations, shareholders – i.e. potential share sellers – have no immediate information about corporate affairs. As a result, securities disclosures provide information to share sellers, as well as share buyers, concerning the value of shares purchased and sold on securities exchanges. In other words, disclosures under securities regulations are made on behalf of share sellers but for the benefit of both share sellers and share buyers.

Summary of US securities regulations: required securities disclosures are detailed

As with other consumer protection regulations, securities regulations seek to protect buyers by requiring sellers to give information to buyers. In the case of securities regulation, that information relates to the business of the company whose shares are being issued or traded.

More concretely, public disclosures pursuant to US securities regulation (for our purposes, disclosures concerning shares in the company's equity) can be divided into two general categories: (i) disclosures by corporations and their initial investors concerning securities they are issuing, i.e. selling, securities to the general public – usually called an "initial public offering," and (ii) disclosures by corporations concerning their publicly-traded shares, i.e. shares resold and purchased on public exchanges.

The Securities Act of 1933 (the "1933 Act") generally governs the issuance of securities by corporations, including disclosures issuing corporations are required to make in connection with the shares to be issued. The Securities Exchange Act of 1934 (the "1934 Act") governs the trading of corporate securities on public exchanges, including disclosures issuing corporations are required to make in connection with the already-issued shares available for sale to the public.

Summary of US securities regulations: securities disclosures must be made periodically

The periodic disclosure requirements for companies whose shares are already issued and are being traded, i.e. the rules under the 1934 Act, are more important than the disclosure requirements for companies at the time of the initial public offering, issued by the SEC is the important element of securities regulation, i.e. the rules under the 1934 Act.

The annual and quarterly reports to shareholders (in fact, disclosures to the entire public) are the most important periodic public disclosures required from corporations whose securities are traded on exchanges in the United States. The annual report is intended as a "state-of-the-company" report, providing financial data, results of continuing operations, market segment information, new product plans, subsidiary activities and research and development activities on future programs. The quarterly report provides regular updates of the annual report at three-month intervals. Between annual and quarterly reports, current reports and/or press releases are required whenever there is a material change in a corporation's business.

In addition to the periodic reporting requirements, disclosures for publicly-traded shares include "proxy statements." Proxy materials differ from other public disclosures in that they are intended solely and exclusively for shareholders as opposed to share traders. Proxy statements contain disclosures needed by shareholders in those few instances when shareholder approval is required to take a corporate action. In the normal course of business, the only actions required by shareholders of corporations in the United States are the election of directors and external auditors. Accordingly, most proxy statements focus on providing information reasonably required for shareholders to make informed decisions concerning the election of directors and auditors.

Summary of US securities regulations: misstatements and omissions are not allowed

As described above, the SEC has established an integrated system of public disclosures: (i) beginning with the prospectus, (ii) continuing with the annual, quarterly and current public disclosures, and (iii) including forms and procedures for proxy solicitation materials.

In general, the SEC requires the disclosure of all information it considers reasonably necessary to assure the "full and fair" disclosure of the character of the securities, publicly available for sale in the United States.[1]

At the same time, the specific disclosures mandated by the SEC in each instance are rather detailed. For example, the SEC requires disclosures on over twenty topics in a corporation's annual report to shareholders, including: general development of business, business by segments, financial information about segments and geographic areas, description of property, legal proceedings and changes in accounting methods.

Having established specific disclosures requirements, the SEC mandates that corporations avoid misstatements and omissions in meeting those requirements. More precisely, the SEC requires that corporations avoid all "material" and all "intentional" misstatements and omissions. In other words, misstatements and omissions are acceptable only if they are both immaterial and unintentional.

Special issues under US securities regulations: the SEC has no power to adopt corporate law

In keeping with the arrangements of many other regulatory schemes in the United States and around the world, the statutes governing the issuance and trading of corporate securities in the United States (the 1933 Act and the 1934 Act) are very broad, "To provide full and fair disclosure of the character of the securities sold in interstate commerce and through the mails, and to prevent fraud in the sale thereof" (Preamble to the 1933 Act).

Those powers do not, however, include corporate law. Under the Constitution of the United States, the power to adopt corporate law is reserved for several States of the United States.

As a result, the SEC's recent initiatives have been limited to requirements related to public disclosure requirements for corporation's whose shares are publicly traded in the United States. As a result, the CG reforms initiated by the SEC do not apply to US corporations whose shares are not traded on stock exchanges in the United States, even if those corporations are very large.

In addition, the SEC does not have the power to adopt regulations concerning corporate constitutions or concerning performance standards for corporate directors or officers unless those regulations are reasonably necessary in order to regulate public disclosures. In the absence of such a connection, the SEC must rely on reforms made to the NYSE and other stock exchanges in the United States.

Special issues under US securities regulations: the NYSE is a private association

This chapter contains several references to securities exchanges. Securities exchanges in the United States, including the NYSE, are private associations, not government agencies. Securities exchanges in the United States – as well as other participants in US securities transactions, such as brokers, dealers and mutual funds – are regulated by US securities laws, primarily in the 1934 Act and regulations adopted pursuant to the 1934 Act. In SEC parlance, securities exchanges are called "Self-Regulatory Organizations" (SROs). The various governmental regulations applicable to securities exchanges are not immediately important to corporate executives.

It is important to corporate executives that, in the first instance, securities exchanges regulate themselves. In other words, securities exchanges such as the NYSE adopt their own governing regulations – in much the same way that corporations adopt their own charter documents. In fact, securities exchanges such as the NYSE are required to create rules that "allow for disciplining members for improper conduct and for establishing measures to ensure market integrity and investor protection."

The NYSE and other exchanges are subject to SEC regulation and can include their listing requirements (i.e. their requirements for companies to be listed on the exchanges) requirements which affect corporate constitutions and the performance standards of corporate directors and officers. At the same time, listing requirements adopted by the NYSE and other exchanges do not have the force of law. The only sanctions available to exchanges against those corporations and individuals who violate their listing requirements are delisting of the corporation whose directors and officers violate its rules and the disqualification of such persons from serving in such a capacity in the future.

Special issues under US securities regulations: the SEC does not approve contents of disclosures

All public disclosures made pursuant to the US securities regulation – other than press releases – must first be filed with the SEC as a preliminary or tentative disclosure, but the SEC does not approve any public disclosures. The SEC is given an opportunity to review and comment on the filings but the SEC's failure to make objections or take exceptions with filings does not mean that the SEC approves. In fact, the SEC requires that all prospectuses contain the following disclaimer:

> Neither the Securities and Exchange Commission nor any state securities commission has approved or disapproved of these securities or determined if this prospectus is truthful or complete.
>
> (See e.g. 17 CFR 229.501. Item 501(b) (7))

Rather than having the SEC approve required public disclosures, securities regulations mandate that corporations engage a firm of external public accountants to audit and issue a report on its required periodic public disclosures. If a corporation's external auditors detect a material or intentional misstatement or omission, then they report the misstatement or omission to the corporation. If the misstatement or omission is not corrected in the normal course of the audit, then the external auditors are obligated to call it to senior management's attention (i.e. the CEO or CFO). If senior management does not correct the consequential misstatement or omission, then the auditor is required to call it to the directors' attention (typically through the board's audit committee) and, in addition, within one day, thereafter, to disclose the misstatement or omission to the SEC. The auditor is also required to qualify its audit report concerning any uncorrected misstatement or omission and is authorized to resign as the company's external auditors.

The SEC's reliance on the auditing professional to provide reasonable assurances that public disclosures comply with securities regulations places a great importance on the competence and, of equal importance, the independence of certified public accountants in their discharge of auditing functions for publicly traded corporations.

Recent CG initiatives

The remainder of this chapter focuses on recently adopted CG initiatives in the United States to provide reasonable assurances that boards are loyal and diligent in their supervision of corporate business and affairs. The NYSE, through its listing requirements, and the US Congress, with the adoption of Sarbanes–Oxley, have both recently adopted authoritative measures in respect of supervising a corporation's most senior management.

These two organizations, one a private association and the other a governmental body, have acted in concert but separately, so that the recent initiatives in the United States preserve an important characteristic of the US system for CG: it is not a unified system. Two separate organizations have acted in part because there is no federal corporate law in the United States (only the various laws of the various states, with Delaware remaining the most important); in part because there is no government agency within the United States (not even at state level) actively enforcing corporate law in the United States (not even state corporate law); and in part because there is no corporate law in the United States specifically intended for publicly-traded corporations (not even at the level of the various states).

As you will see, the NYSE has attempted to improve the degree of independence among directors of corporations listed there so that they are better able – and more likely – to meet the performance standards currently applicable to directors under corporate law (i.e. duties of care and loyalty), but the NYSE does not change those standards. More precisely, the NYSE initiatives are intended to improve directors' independence without increasing requirements for directors' competence or diligence. Unfortunately, the NYSE listing requirements do not have the force of law.

In general, with the adoption of Sarbanes–Oxley, the US Congress attempts to improve the independence of external auditors and the diligence of corporate officers and directors so that they are better able – and more likely – to prepare public disclosures with the form and substance required pursuant to securities regulations. With limited exceptions, Sarbanes–Oxley does not augment the substance of the disclosure requirements. Sarbanes–Oxley also does not significantly modify the performance standards applicable to the preparation of those disclosures.

Corporate law gives those with the power to manage a corporation's business (senior corporate officers) wide latitude to make and implement decisions in their corporations' names. The decisions they make and implement are subject to legal challenge by the corporation – usually at a shareholder's initiative – only to the extent that senior corporate officers violate their duty of care and duty of loyalty in making and implementing their decisions.

Senior corporate officers can generally satisfy their "duty of loyalty" with confidence by following the simple procedure in making full disclosure of conflicts-of-interest to independent directors and negotiating directly with them – or their designee. In the absence of violation of law including federal securities regulations, senior corporate officers are rarely found to have breached their "duty of care." Such findings are rare because courts' review of senior officers' decisions is subject to the "business judgment rule," i.e. senior corporate officers' decisions are not reviewed on the basis of facts unavailable to them at the time of the decision or on the basis of the results obtained. Their decisions are reviewed only on the basis of the facts available to them or which, through due diligence, could have been available to them at the time that they made their decisions – and without regard to the results obtained.

Within the context of the broad authority directors delegate to senior corporate officers pursuant to corporate constitutions, typically only three powers are reserved for directors: the power to appoint senior corporate officers, the power to regulate compensation and the power to dismiss them. For practical and sometimes contractual reasons, directors frequently have limited discretion in reducing senior corporate officers' remuneration. Accordingly, once senior corporate officers are appointed, directors' ability to supervise them is effectively limited to the power to dismiss them.

NYSE listing requirements

Recent corporate scandals suggest that directors may have abused their right to regulate compensation and, in appropriate cases, neglected their obligation to dismiss senior corporate officers. Compensation of senior corporate officers at some US corporations – already very high by international standards – has increased geometrically in recent years, even without a corresponding increase in corporate results.

Too frequently, it even appears that directors have not dismissed senior corporate officers even though, on the basis of facts eventually disclosed to the public, at least a few senior corporate officers may well have egregiously breached their duties of care and loyalty over long periods of time. It even appears that, too often, directors have not obtained fair results for their corporations in those instances where senior corporate officers have disclosed conflicts-of-interest and negotiated corporate contracts directly with directors.

In the absence of US corporate law applicable to publicly traded companies, the NYSE has – at the prompting of the US SEC – taken some initiatives in an attempt to correct directors' recent apparent abuses and neglect. More specifically, the new "CG" guidelines require that companies traded on the NYSE have committees of independent directors for the purpose of (i) determining executive compensation, (ii) nominating senior corporate officers and directors and (iii) auditing information provided by senior corporate officers to boards of directors.

By addressing the corporate constitutional issues of (i) who should be corporate directors and (ii) how they should make their decisions, the NYSE is attempting to ensure that directors exercise their rights in respect of senior corporate officers discharge of their supervisory obligations in a manner consistent with their duties of loyalty and care.

NYSE listing requirements: brief background

The NYSE is a private association subject to regulation by the US SEC. The SEC imposes many requirements for corporate securities listed on the NYSE, most of which relate to the size of the issuer and the nature of the securities. Traditionally, the NYSE has deferred to the General Corporation Law of the State of Delaware for determining CG requirements and to the SEC for determining disclosure requirements for companies listed on the NYSE.

On February 13, 2002, the SEC asked the NYSE to review its CG requirements for companies listed on the NYSE. After receiving extensive public comment, on August 16, 2002, the NYSE filed its Corporate Governance Proposals with the SEC. After making the original August 16 filing, the NYSE filed separately with the SEC proposals requiring approval by beneficial shareholders of equity-compensation plans. The NYSE's CG listing requirements are set forth in the new section 303A of the NYSE's "Listed Company Manual." All of them are outlined below. Prior rules are briefly summarized for the purpose of highlighting changes.

Independent directors should supervise senior officers: "independent directors"

As evidenced by the following specific requirements, it is most important for the NYSE listing requirements that directors be independent. For a director to be deemed independent, the board must affirmatively determine that the director has "no material relationship with the listed company." In the past, independence was defined as having no "relationship with the company that may interfere with the exercise of the director's independence from management and the company." It appears that the acceptance of "immaterial" fees from the listed company – in addition to directors' fees – will not jeopardize the "independence" of directors.

Neither former employees of a listed company nor any employees or partners of its independent auditors – including the immediate families of any such employees or partners – may be classified as "independent" directors for a period of five years after the end of their engagement with the listed company. In the past, the applicable period of time, called a "cooling-off" period, was three years.

Independent directors should supervise senior officers: a majority of all directors must be independent

Unless a listed company has a controlling shareholder, corporate boards must have a majority of independent directors. This is a new requirement.

Independent directors should supervise senior officers: compensation and nomination committees: entirely independent.

Listed companies must have compensation and nomination committees and those committees must be composed entirely of independent directors. This is a completely new requirement. In the past, neither separate compensation nor nomination committees were required.

Independent directors should supervise senior officers: audit committee: entirely independent

In the past, listed companies were required to have an audit committee and the audit committee was to be composed of at least three independent directors. Now, audit committees must be composed entirely of independent directors, as defined above. In addition to the rules for "independence" applicable to all directors, audit committee members must limit their compensation from the company to the fees they receive as directors.

Directors should supervise with clear policies and procedures: board committees must have and disclose charters

In the past, there was no obligation for listed companies to have nomination or compensation committees or for audit committees to adopt charters, i.e. rules for procedures and decisions. Now, the boards of listed companies must adopt charters for each of their nomination, compensation and audit committees and the charters must be published.

Directors should supervise with clear policies and procedures: companies must have and disclose codes of conduct

Listed companies must adopt and disclose governance guidelines and codes of business conduct applicable to the senior corporate officers, including the CEO and the CFO. This is an entirely new requirement which follows an identical new requirement from the SEC.

Directors should supervise with clear policies and procedures: non-management directors must regularly hold separate meetings

The independent directors of listed companies, now sometimes called the "executive committee" or "executive session" are required to meet regularly without members of senior management for the purpose of reviewing corporate business and affairs. This is a completely new requirement.

Directors should supervise with clear policies and procedures: shareholders must approve most stock option plans

In the past, shareholder approval was not required for many stock-option plans. Now, shareholder approval is required for all such plans, other than employment-inducement options, option plans acquired through mergers, and tax-qualified plans such as 401(k)s.

Directors should supervise with clear policies and procedures: internal auditors are required

In the past, listed companies were not required to have an internal audit function. In other words, audit committees received all information from senior corporate officers or external auditors. Now, all listed companies must have an internal audit function, available to the audit committee for investigations and other information.

NYSE listing requirements: penalties include reprimand and de-listing

Under the new CG listing requirements, the NYSE is allowed to issue a public-reprimand letter to listed companies who violate requirements and, as in the past, to terminate the listing of violating companies. While self-regulation through the NYSE listing requirements has certain advantages over government regulation, the only sanctions available to the NYSE are, in effect, punishment for corporations and their shareholders – not for corporate directors and officers.

NYSE listing requirements: application to foreign companies

The NYSE has determined that it will not apply any particular CG listing requirement to a foreign company with securities listed on the NYSE (a "foreign issuer") if the foreign issuer provides a written certification from legal counsel in its country of incorporation that the foreign issuer complies with the CG rules (i) of that country, and (ii) of any security exchange in that country on which the issuer's securities are listed.

US securities regulations

Sarbanes–Oxley has received much attention as the most important US CG initiative in the wake of the recent corporate scandals in the US.

As indicated above, the NYSE's CG requirements are probably more comprehensive because they are intended to provide reasonable assurances that directors diligently and loyally supervise their delegations of authority to CEOs and other corporate officers. In contrast, the authority of the SEC – and, therefore, the scope of Sarbanes–Oxley – is limited to adopting measures reasonably necessary for reliable corporate financial reporting and the prevention of fraud in corporate securities trading.

Sarbanes–Oxley addresses three broad issues related to public disclosures pursuant by corporations to securities regulations: (i) the substance of those disclosures, (ii) the independence of auditors of periodic financial reports and (iii) the procedures whereby corporations prepare and present those periodic reports. The Sarbanes–Oxley also imposes (iv) increases in the potential personal criminal penalties for violations of securities regulations by corporate officers.

As with the NYSE listing requirements, each summary summarizes the state of the law prior to adoption of Sarbanes–Oxley. The term "issuers" in the following summary refers to corporations with securities publicly traded on US exchanges.

The substance of securities disclosures: material changes must be disclosed rapidly and clearly

Issuers are required to disclose "on a rapid and current basis … material changes to the financial condition or operation if the issuer, in plain English" (Sarbanes–Oxley, § 409 (a)).

Since 1934, issuers have been obligated to report on Form 8-K and in press releases, the occurrence of any material events or corporate changes of importance to investors. It will not be clear what § 409 adds to previous regulations until the SEC issues regulations pursuant to this new statute.

The substance of securities disclosures: off-balance sheet accounting and contractual obligations

Issuers must explain its off-balance sheet arrangements in a separately captioned subsection of "Management's Discussion and Analysis" (MD&A) in the annual report to shareholders. Issuers must also provide an overview of certain known contractual obligations in a tabular format (Sarbanes–Oxley, § 401 (a) and January 27, 2003 SEC Release, No. 33–8182).

These provisions change the presentation but not the substance of certain financial disclosures. Material off-balance sheet arrangements are already disclosed in footnotes to the financial statements. Material contracts must be described and provided as exhibits.

The substance of securities disclosures: use of non-general accounting agreed on principal (GAAP) financial measures

Issuers that disclose or release non-GAAP financial measures must include, in that disclosure or release, a presentation of the most directly comparable GAAP financial measure and a reconciliation of the disclosed non-GAAP financial measure to the most directly comparable GAAP financial measure. (Sarbanes–Oxley, § 401 (b) and January 22, 2003 SEC Release, No. 33–8177.)

This provision is new. It responds to issuers' recent practice of disclosing pro-forma accounting statements in press releases. Pro-forma financial statements have not been permitted as part of the regular periodic disclosures (quarterly and annual reports to shareholders), except in certain circumstances – such as acquisitions during the accounting period covered by the report – and only as an addition to mandated financial statements prepared and presented in accordance with generally accepted accounting principles (GAAP).

The substance of securities disclosures: companies must disclose codes of ethics

Issuers shall disclose whether it has adopted a code of ethics that applies to the company's principal executive officer and principal financial officer. A company without such a code must disclose this fact and explain why it has not done so. A company also will be required to promptly disclose amendments to, and waivers from, the code of ethics relating to any of those officers. A code of ethics shall require: honest and ethical conduct, reliable financial disclosures and compliance with applicable regulations, including "the ethical handling of actual or apparent conflicts of interests between personal and professional relationships" (Sarbanes–Oxley, § 407 and January 27, 2003 SEC Release, No. 33–8177.)

At least some issuers have had codes of ethics, but the SEC apparently suspects that – either in principle or in practice – too many of such codes have not been applicable to a corporation's most senior officers. The new rules require disclosure of a code of ethics applicable at least in principle to senior officers and, importantly, whether any waivers from the code have been granted for any senior corporate officers.

As previously noted, US securities regulations are concerned exclusively with reliable financial reporting and the prevention of fraud in the sale of securities on US exchanges. At the same time, as evidenced by the SEC's provisions on internal accounting controls (Securities Exchange Act of 1934, § 13 (b-2), the SEC cannot overlook issues of corporate due diligence to the extent that due diligence is required in order for corporations to prepare and present required financial statements and other public disclosures. Similarly, in Sarbanes–Oxley, the SEC has prescribed that publicly traded corporations must adopt and publish a code of ethics specifically applicable to its CEO and CFO.

Auditor independence: create a "public accounting oversight board" (PACOB)

The SEC shall establish an independent board for the purpose of regulating accountants who audit public companies and establishing auditing standards. The board will consist of five members, only two of which shall have been certified public accountants. The board will be funded by companies with securities publicly traded on US exchanges (Sarbanes–Oxley, §§ 101–109).

There already is – and since 1933 – has been an independent board for the purpose of regulating accountants who audit public companies and establish auditing standards. It is the American Institute of Certified Public Accountants (AICPA). In addition, there already is – and since 1933 – an independent board for the purpose of developing generally accepted accounting principles, the Financial Accounting Standards Board (FASB).

Auditor independence: limitation of auditors' non-audit services

Issuers are prohibited from engaging their auditors for non-audit services except with (i) pre-approval from the audit committee, and (ii) public disclosure related to services provided. An accountant would not be "independent" from an audit client if an audit partner received compensation based on selling engagements to that client for services other than audit, review and attest services (Sarbanes–Oxley, § 208 (a) and January 28, 2003 SEC Release, Nos 33–8183, 34–47265).

There has been a wide-reaching SEC rule concerning Auditor Independence. Consistent with existing rules, independence would be impaired if the accountant or any covered person has a direct or material indirect business relationship with the audit client, other than providing professional services since February 5, 2001.

Corporate procedures for periodic disclosures: "internal controls over financial reporting"

In each annual report to shareholders, issuers shall state management's responsibility for establishing and maintaining internal controls over financial reporting, together with an assessment of the effectiveness of those controls. "Internal controls over financial reporting" is defined as a process designed to provide reasonable assurance regarding the reliability of financial reporting and the preparation of financial statements for external purposes in accordance with generally accepted accounting principles (Sarbanes–Oxley, § 404 and Rules 13(a)–15(f).

Since 1976, "issuers" have had the obligation to maintain internal accounting controls, pursuant to § 13 (b) of the 1934 Act. Since 1976, management has voluntarily confirmed its responsibility for internal accounting controls in each annual report to shareholders. This provision is virtually identical to the 1976 requirement and the practices evolving out of the 1976 requirements except that (i) senior management must review internal controls for changes and effectiveness on a quarterly basis and (ii) that senior officers and directors must be involved in design and implementation as follows: the controls must be "designed by, or under the supervision of, the issuer's principal executive and principal financial officers, or persons performing similar functions, and effected by the issuer's board of directors, management and other personnel" (1934 Act, Rules 13(a)–15(f)).

Corporate procedures for periodic disclosures: "disclosure controls and procedures"

Publicly traded corporations must implement controls and other procedures of an issuer that are designed to ensure that information required for public disclosure pursuant to securities regulations is recorded, processed, summarized and reported, within the time periods specified for such disclosures (1934 Act, Rules 13(a)–15(f)).

The difference between "internal controls on financial reporting" and "disclosure controls and procedures" is that regarding disclosure controls and procedures, the public disclosures and related filings with the SEC must be timely. It is clear from the regulations that internal controls on financial reporting are a part of the disclosure controls and procedures. Senior management must review each for changes and effectiveness on a quarterly basis.

Corporate procedures for periodic disclosures: CEO and CFO certification of quarterly and annual reports

CEOs and CFOs of issuers must personally certify their companies' annual and quarterly financial reports, subject to civil and criminal penalties.

Civil and criminal penalties already exist for intentional material misstatements and omissions in financial statements. Since 1976, CEOs and CFOs have voluntarily made statements confirming their responsibility for financial statements and internal controls.

Corporate responsibility for periodic disclosures: audit committee: all independent directors

Issuers must have an audit committee composed entirely of independent directors and disclose the name of at least one financial expert together with whether the expert is independent of management. An issuer that does not have an audit committee financial expert must disclose this fact and explain why it has no such expert (Sarbanes–Oxley, § 406 and January 27, 2003 SEC Release, No. 33–8177).

Under NYSE listing requirements, it is already required for at least three members of the audit committee to be independent. Since January 31, 2000, issuers have had to disclose certain matters concerning their audit committees in the proxy statement incorporated by reference with each annual report to share-holders, including whether the audit committee has: (i) reviewed and discussed the audited financial statements with management and independent auditors; (ii) received from the auditors disclosures regarding their independence; and (iii) based on the review and discussions with management and auditors, recom-mended to the board of directors that the audited financial statements be included in the annual report to shareholders. Issuers have been required to disclose whether their board of directors has adopted a written charter for the audit com-mittee, and if so, include a copy of the charter as an appendix to the company's proxy statements at least once every three years (December 22, 1999 SEC Release, No. 34–42266).

Corporate responsibility for periodic disclosures: no improper influence on auditors

> Issuers' directors and officers shall not "fraudulently influence, coerce, manipulate, or mislead any independent public or certified accountant ... for the purpose of rendering ... financial statements misleading."
> (Sarbanes–Oxley, § 303 (a) and 1934 Act, Rule 13 (b2–2))

Since 1933 and 1934, it has been illegal, subject to potential personal criminal penalties, to engage in fraudulent or manipulative practices in connection with the issuance or trading of corporate securities in the United States. Since 1976, it has been expressly illegal, subject to potential personal criminal penalties, to make, or cause to be made, a materially misleading statement or omission to an accountant in connection with the preparation of public disclosures pursuant to securities regulations.

Corporate responsibility for periodic disclosures: standards of conduct for securities lawyers

An attorney must report evidence of a material violation of securities laws or breach of fiduciary duty or similar violation by the issuer up-the-ladder within the company to the CLO or the CEO. If the CLO and CEO do not respond appropriately to the evidence, requiring the attorney to report the evidence to the audit committee, another committee of independent directors or the full board of directors. The SEC is still considering the "noisy withdrawal" provisions whereby a securities lawyer must "report-out" if the board does not respond appropriately to the evidence (Sarbanes–Oxley, § 307 and January 29, 2003 SEC Release, No. 33–81851).

This provision is substantially identical to the responsibilities and procedures of external auditors in respect of consequential violations of law discovered by them in the course of their audit activities pursuant to securities regulations (1934 Act, § 10A and Rule 10(A-1)). Noisy-withdrawal applies to accountants and involves a notification to the SEC.

*Penalties for corporate officers and directors: increased criminal
penalties for destroying or falsifying audit records*

Officers, directors and employees will be subject to enhanced criminal penalties –
up to 20 years – for destroying audit records or falsifying documents and for
knowing other violations of the securities regulations (Sarbanes–Oxley, § 1102
and the Federal Sentencing Guidelines).

In addition, CEOs and CFOs are required to forfeit bonuses, incentive compensation or gains from the sale of company securities during the 12-month
period after the initial publication of financial statements that have to be rein-
stated as a result of misconduct.

There is already the possibility of criminal penalties for (a) obstruction of
justice and (b) for "knowingly circumvent[ing] or knowingly fail[ing] to implement a system of internal accounting controls or knowingly falsify[ing] any
book, record, or account required [as part of the system of internal accounting
controls]" (1934 Act, § 13(b) 4 & 5).

Acts and omissions constituting violations of securities regulations can, of
course, also be violations of duties of care and loyalty under corporate law. On
the other hand, it is possible to violate securities regulations without having
breached the duties of care and loyalty. It is worth noting that violations of securities regulations, like violations of at least some other laws, are not subject to
the business judgment rule.

Special issues under CG: nominating and electing directors

The focus on the independence of directors, both in the NYSE listing requirements and in Sarbanes–Oxley, is prompted at least in part by the current
arrangement in publicly-traded US corporations, whereby senior corporate officers nominate candidates for their boards of directors. In effect, senior corporate
officers select their own supervisors and, in addition to paying directors fees for
director services, also commonly pay them investment banking and consulting
fees. The selection of directors by senior management, together with the payments to directors from senior management, is widely perceived to compromise
directors as supervisors of senior management.

Corporate law does not dictate that senior corporate officers nominate candidates for their boards of directors. On the contrary, corporate law simply provides the flexibility whereby senior officers can take the initiative in nominating
candidates. Whether candidates are nominated by senior officers, other directors
(e.g. the nominating committee) or by shareholders themselves, corporate law
stipulates that shareholders must elect candidates as directors.

Senior officers are able to nominate practically all candidates for the boards
of directors of publicly traded US corporations largely because senior officers
are responsible for preparing the proxy solicitation materials pursuant to which
directors are elected. At the same time, there is no routine process for solicit-
ing nominations from shareholders. In this context, the candidates nominated

by senior officers are typically the only candidates on the ballot for election as directors.

On July 15, 2003, a SEC report recommended the following actions (i) improved disclosure to shareholders concerning the procedures whereby directors are nominated and (ii) improved shareholder access to the director nomination process. Among other things, the July 15 report recommends that corporations (a) establish and disclose specific procedures by which shareholders can communicate with the directors of the corporations in which they invest, and (b) require that major, long-term shareholders (or groups of long-term shareholders) be provided access to company proxy materials to nominate directors, at least where there are objective criteria that indicate that shareholders may not have had adequate access to an effective proxy process.

Conclusion on CG in the United States

Experience with political organizations indicates that a good method for avoiding abuses of power is their separation and balance. Some elements of recent CG initiatives separate some powers at the level of corporate boards of directors (e.g. creation of separate committees for nominating officers and auditing financial statements) and at the level of corporate officers (e.g. both the CEO and CFO signing certificates concerning the annual report to shareholders). Yet, it seems that little consideration has been given expressly and directly to introducing a "separation and balance of powers" as a fundamental principle for CG.

No modification to securities regulation, for example, can possibly constitute a fundamental "separation and balance of power" within a corporation because the entire financial reporting function (i.e. the object of securities regulation) comes into play only in respect of operations which are complete on, and as of, the date that the financial statements are issued, to the extent that CG has as its goal avoiding the abuse of power by corporate directors and officers (i.e. in the form of either a breach of their duty of care or their duty of loyalty), then a modification in securities regulation can act only to deter such abuses – not to prevent them. Moreover, modifications in securities regulation avoid such abuses only to the extent that public disclosures deter them. In too many cases, it seems that the possibility of disclosure is not an effective deterrent.

In order to avoid abuses of power by corporate directors and officers, it seems better to prevent those abuses than to attempt to deter them through possible disclosure. In order to prevent abuses of corporate power, it seems that separating and balancing those powers is an obvious alternative.

One alternative would be to establish a chief corporate officer for each area of fundamental corporate concern (e.g. operations, legal compliance and financial reporting) with the "constitutional" arrangement that corporations would not make or implement decisions unless all three agreed on that action.[2]

Notes

1 The SEC expressly provides that registrants must provide such other information as is necessary to make the mandated statements "full and fair." The best known formulation of this is Rule 10 (b–5) of the 1934 Act: "It shall be unlawful, in connection with the purchase or sale of any security, for any person, directly or indirectly … to make any untrue statement of a material fact or to omit to state a material fact."

2 The "Internal Control – Integrated Framework" – first released by the Committee of Sponsoring Organizations of the Treadway Commission in September 1992 – suggests that operations, legal compliance and reliable financial reporting are the three fundamental objectives for all corporations. In September 2004, COSO expanded its framework to include strategic considerations, with the specific intention and effect that, according to COSO: in addition to operating concerns, legal compliance and reliable financial reporting should be incorporated into a corporation's strategic direction ("Enterprise Risk Management – Integrated Framework" (September 2004) by the Committee of Sponsoring Organizations of the Treadway Commission, AICPA, Jersey City, New Jersey 07311–3881, USA).

5 The Canadian national system of corporate governance[1]

D. A. H. Brown

Introduction

Canada has been at the forefront of corporate governance (CG) reform through each of its three recent iterations or generations: In 1994, the Dey Report was published by the TSX.[2] Entitled "Where Were the Directors," the report was a landmark document both citing failures in CG in a series of major failures (e.g. Canadian Commercial Bank, Northland Bank, several Trust companies), and introducing 14 guidelines that are regarded as effective standards of CG in Canada and internationally. This "first wave" of CG reform was sparked by watershed reports from the United Kingdom (Cadbury Committee 1992) and the United States (Treadway Commission 1987), but TSX Committee Chair Peter Dey went further than both, introducing guidelines for boards' responsibilities for strategy and risk, independence, evaluation and disclosure. Even today, a benchmarking of the Dey Guidelines to leading practices in the US (2002 Sarbanes–Oxley Act (SOX) and subsequent SEC requirements) and the UK (Combined Code and 2003 Higgs Report) reveals that these are the core capacities that an enterprise's board should concentrate on. In 2001, the Saucier Report was published jointly by the TSX, and the Canadian Institute of Chartered Accountants (CICA), in response to the "second wave" of governance reform punctuated by the Greenbury, Hempel and Turnbull Reports in the UK, and Blue Ribbon panels in the United States culminating in the Blue Ribbon Report on Audit Committees (New York Stock Exchange (NYSE) and National Association of Securities Dealers Automated Quotations system (NASDAK), later incorporated into the SOX). In 2003–05, the Canadian Securities Administrators (CSA) published a series of National Instruments in response to the "third wave" of governance reform characterized by the SOX sparked by a series of major US CG and accounting scandals.

Figure 5.1 shows that Canada's corporations adopted new governance practices in the years immediately following the Dey Report, which raised the bar significantly. As the unprecedented economic boom continued through the late 1990s, most corporations paused in, and some backed away from, adopting new governance practices.

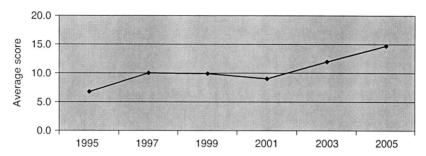

Figure 5.1 The governance index plateaus, then jumps[1] (average score of all corporations that completed surveys in each year).

Note
1 The Conference Board of Canada's Governance Index is calculated based on a suite of leading governance practices reported: maximum score is 20.

There is a second jump in 2003–05, and these trends in particular have been identified as a substantial number of corporations:

i   undertook comprehensive reviews of their CG,
ii   focused on the independence of their board of directors, in particular, the board chair, Audit and Compensation Committee members,
iii reviewed their use of committees, many corporations discontinuing the use of Executive Committees in favor of Governance Committees, and
iv   changed stock option plans for executives and directors, expensing or disclosing these in accounting reports, and limiting or tying benefits to results, ensuring shareholders receive a net benefit (increased share value in exchange for dilution).

Responding to:

i   the public and media attention paid to CG since the massive failures of late 2001 and 2002 (Enron, WorldCom, etc.),
ii   the SOX of July 2002,
iii the slowing of the economic boom, in fact recessionary periods and significant stock market drops in many sectors, and
iv   increased attention to CG in Canada in from the Saucier Joint Committee Report,[3] through the establishment of a public oversight body for the accounting profession, to new TSX listing requirements, CSA releases and more aggressive stances from institutional investors.

Canadian CG, a principle-based governance

Geographically situated next to the US, yet initially populated by founding immigrants from the UK and continental Europe, Canada faces a constant tension among these competing cultures. This is true in every major field, and CG is no exception. The US has adopted a "rules-based" approach to governance, prescribing standards down to small details and enforcing these through a strong adversarial justice system. At the heart of this system is the objective of protecting shareholder value and therefore of ensuring effective capital markets. The UK has adopted a "comply or explain" approach to governance, where practices are voluntary but disclosure is mandatory; however in recent years a large number of rules and regulations have crept into this framework. Continental Europe continues to promote social democracy and co-determination, where CG practices are designed to serve the needs of greater society, communities and stakeholders in general.

Canada has chosen to adopt a principle-based governance framework, where a consensus is reached among diverse players (including regulators, investors, corporations and governments) on the overarching principles[4] that CG aims to achieve, then guidelines[5] are promulgated (by regulators or self-regulating organizations in sectors and industries) to guide corporations, and finally practices[6] are selected by individual corporations based on their own needs, then disclosed publicly to ensure effective capital markets.

The principles used encompass, build on, and go beyond major Canadian and international reports on CG, including the Organization of Economic Cooperation and Development's (OECD) Corporate Governance Task Force and Principles, the United Kingdom's Combined Code and Canada's Toronto Stock Exchange Guidelines. In terms of principle area, Canada's corporations show the greatest strengths in the principle areas of leadership and stewardship, and empowerment and accountability. Boards and executives in Canada typically set the corporation's mission, vision and strategic direction together, explicitly codify a code of conduct and formalize responsibilities and authorities (in terms of reference, job descriptions and delegation of authorities). Since ethical leadership lapses have been at the heart of the most visible failures it is heartening that most of Canada's Chief Executive Officers (CEOs) and boards take this area so seriously.

While some progress has been made, Canada's corporations generally have not yet mastered the principle areas of communication and disclosure, and accomplishment and measurement. In particular, many corporations are still working on developing performance scorecards that are both effective and transparent, and extending these to CEO and board evaluations. Very few corporations conduct individual director evaluations (beyond self-evaluations), and fewer still have embraced ongoing development programs for either their boards or executives. Beyond this, many corporations continue to face challenges in communicating successfully with shareholders and other stakeholders, particularly important in light of recent breakdowns in trust.

Each of these governance dimensions is explored in more depth in the main body of the chapter following.

Canada's CG players

A key advantage to principle-based governance is that it helps organizations address difficult choices posed by competing governance values or viewpoints.

This is especially true in Canada where governance choices are influenced by a diverse group of corporate leaders, or governance "players":

Canada's executives

Central to the Dey Report, and to all subsequent discussions, has been the appropriate balance between the authority of a corporation's board and its executives. While not widely acknowledged, Canada's corporate executives have played a leading role in innovating and championing excellence in governance. Even before the Dey Report they surpassed those of the vast majority of other countries. Canada's CEOs are at the forefront of the CG debate. The Canadian Council of Chief Executives (CCCE) speaks for Canada's CEOs collectively. CCCE's main governance contribution in the post-Enron era was a September 2002 report[7] calling on Canada's CEOs to lead by example in business conduct and ethics, and to demonstrate, in practice, that we do not need onerous new rules like those of SOX.

Balancing the tension between management and boards is a central issue for executives and CCCE. Management theory argues that today's corporations are too complex for real direction and control to be entrusted to volunteer or part-time directors; owners may still "own," but control has been ceded to a professional class of full-time managers who alone understand the firm's complexities and, therefore, effectively must both govern and manage it. Agency theory, on which modern governance reform is based, carves out a clear role for boards of directors as the arbiters between principals (owners/investors) and agents (managers/executives) in corporations. The economic role of boards is to minimize agency costs: any money agents spend in the corporation that does not align with the owners' purpose. Agency theory refutes the claims of management theory: since the CEO is the head of the management team (the agents), it is circular to imagine the CEO can fulfill this arbiter (governance) function as well; accountability becomes circular without a strong independent board.

While today 87 percent of Canada's board chairs do *not* serve as the CEO, 37 percent *are* "related" to the corporation – and 45 percent do not meet today's tougher "independence" standards. The chair/CEO split reflects agency theory; does the lack of independence show that management theory still holds a lot of sway in Canada's boardrooms?

A move toward agency theory is what both Cadbury and Dey espoused by explicitly handing governance (leadership and stewardship) roles to the board, meaning that the CEO cannot oversee and hold himself/herself accountable. The board must be responsible for governance.

Canada's boards of directors

The Institute of Corporate Directors (ICD) represents Canada's board members. The ICD has, in the recent past, partnered with the TSX in reviewing CG practice, with the CICA in discussing Audit Committee effectiveness, and with the

University of Toronto's Rotman School in introducing a national director education program (second to the Directors College in Canada which pioneered director certification in Canada). Just as the CCCE seeks the right balance between management and agency theory, to reflect the views of its CEO members, so the ICD seeks to balance agency theory and stewardship theory in setting its direction.

Stewardship theory argues that directors and executives are all on the same corporate team, responsible for stewarding the corporation and its resources. As a result, the board's primary role is to support and advise management. Agency theory counters that the board's primary role is to direct (lead and steward) and control (monitor and report on) the corporation's management. In putting in place programs for Canada's corporate directors, ICD weighs these competing models of board authority.

Thirty-five percent of Canada's widely-held, publicly-traded corporations conduct no form of individual director performance evaluation (including self) ... less than one in five has a formal ongoing education or development program for directors. Given the drop in terms and tenure, and the rise in responsibilities and compensation, what is holding us back from more robust evaluation and education?[8]

Canada's investors

The first line of defense against CG lapses is market discipline. The Basel II Accord clearly stakes out two concepts that are fundamental and instructive to understanding CG and regulation today. The first is that the best way to determine capital adequacy (and other critical corporate strategies) is through an effective risk management system, led by the corporation's board and executives. This system needs to reflect a much broader range of business risks than traditional functional risks. The Bank for International Settlement's (BIS) second concept is that the best way to ensure that corporations actually follow sound business practices is through market discipline. This means that capital markets will reward sound – and punish unsound – practices by varying the availability and cost of capital. BIS argues this is much more timely and effective than regulators (self-regulatory organizations (SROs) supervisory bodies like the Office of the Superintendent of Financial Institutions (OSFI) and the Canadian Deposit Insurance Corporation (CDIC) and governments) at ensuring and enforcing sound practices.

While these conclusions relate to capital adequacy, both are readily extended to CG: board and executives should take a risk-based approach to governance;[9] and investors in the capital market should exercise discipline as the first line of defense to ensure and enforce sound governance practices.

Institutional investors have long taken the lead in setting, rating and publicizing CG practices in the United States, at least until the massive government intervention of SOX. In Canada, large pension and mutual funds have taken longer to become as active and vocal, despite the fact that they own about 70 percent of Canada's outstanding equities.

US reports indicate that CEOs alone now control approximately 12 percent of outstanding equities, a phenomenal jump from about 2 percent, 15 years ago.[10] SOX deals with the high profile question of stock compensation by requiring Board Compensation Committees to deal with the firm's compensation consultant directly.

The Ontario Teachers Pension Plan (OTPP) has been at the forefront of CG change in Canada, and internationally through the International Corporate Governance Network (ICGN). OTPP has taken public voting positions against management in executive compensation and shareholder voting class resolutions, and typifies the new "active" investor that will not just sell shares if it senses a governance lapse. Instead, it will communicate with management and the board, act to vote its shares and even litigate to further its interests.

The Ontario Municipal Employees Retirement System (OMERS) has pioneered the publication of proxy voting guidelines and how it actually casts its votes. The Canada Pension Plan Investment Board was Canada's first institutional investor to publicly announce it will oppose most executive stock option plans, in February 2003. La Caisse de Dépots et Placements (CDP), Québec's leading institutional investor, has also moved to stake out a position of activist governance leadership, particularly with regard to corporate disclosures and trying to break the vicious cycle of earnings guidance and analyst calls.

Canada's leading institutional investors have banded together to form the Canadian Coalition for Good Governance (CCGG). Determined to concentrate on CG practices that promote long-term shareholder value, CCGG will be publishing governance principles on issues like executive compensation and enforcing them through proxy voting. Behind the scenes, CCGG scored an early success: challenging Canada's large banks on splitting the offices of board chair and CEO (all agreed). This implies that the CCGG embraces agency theory, and it will be interesting to see if its future standards are consistent with empowering the board. As do all investors, institutional investors have limitations as the guardians of "good governance": they are driven by acceptable market returns (versus peers, rather than shareholder value maximization), and are interested in getting real time, accurate (and inexpensive) information from corporations. Market discipline fundamentally requires transparent disclosure; this is the cornerstone of Canada's CG system, where the one "rule" is "thou shalt disclose."

Cadbury pointed out that shareholders have three core rights or duties:

i   to appoint the directors,
ii   to appoint the auditors, and
iii to assure themselves that the corporation has an effective CG system (by diligently reviewing and questioning the directors' and auditors' reports at the annual general meeting and other occasions).[11]

Effective shareholder governance therefore requires shareholders to exercise their franchise diligently, by appointing skilled, experienced, independent-minded directors and auditors.

As they make these critical selections, shareholders need to reflect on the tension between democratic governance theory and agency theory. Democratic theory espouses a "lay" board, where directors are qualified through how well they represent the shareholder. Co-operatives, not-for-profits and even public sector corporations in Canada tend to reflect democratic theory in practice, selecting board members based on the degree to which they represent owner constituencies. Agency theory contends that directors must have considerable functional skills and experience in order to effectively oversee and monitor management (sometimes called a "professional" board).

The 1996 Treasury Board Guidelines strongly endorsed an agency theory role for Crown corporation boards, yet several years later, it was found that the process of selecting those board members did not change, often resulting in gaps in skills to fulfill this role. SOX requires Audit Committee members to be financially literate, another example of the continued swing toward agency theory and moving power to boards.

In widely-held publicly-traded corporations, the top five criteria for selecting directors are character, financial knowledge, skills, industry and business experience; in Crown corporations they are skills, financial knowledge, geographic representation, industry experience and gender representation. Representation criteria reflect democratic theory's influence, skills and experience, agency theory. Since "character" is so difficult to assess, how much of this is really "who knows whom?"

Canada's auditors

Auditors are the third pillar of CG, alongside executives and directors. Canada's auditing firms were the first off the mark to institute governance reforms in the wake of Enron's collapse. In fact, six months before SOX, the leaders of Canada's major accounting firms agreed with regulators that they would take two major steps voluntarily. They would split their consulting and auditing arms into independent firms and set up an independent board to oversee their profession.

Within weeks, firms with names like "Bearing Point" and "Cap Gemini" entered the corporate landscape. The Canadian Public Accountability Board (CPAB) was announced on July 17, 2002 (just as President Bush was putting his weight behind SOX), and Gordon Thiessen was named as its first chair later that year. Before the new fiscal years were out, every major audit partner had met with their clients' Audit Committees and reviewed a course of action to strengthen the Committee and the board's role in audit oversight and internal control. The CICA, the SRO and the national association for Chartered Accountants (CAs, i.e. external auditors) in Canada, have also played a leading role in board governance for many years. It has partnered with the TSX and ICD in undertaking reviews, publishing studies and holding seminars, and has itself published guidance for boards of directors in Canada: the Criteria for Control (COCO) and 20 Questions series. Recently, the CICA has moved the bar on auditor independence, conduct and disclosures.

The Society of Management Accountants of Canada, the SRO and national association for Certified Management Accountants (CMAs) in Canada, also champions strong governance within and beyond its membership.

Internal auditors have played an increasingly visible role in CG, beating out the likes of George Bush for *Time Magazine*'s "Person of the Year" in 2002. The Institute of Internal Auditors (IIA) is active in internal auditor standards and education, including the recently updated and expanded Committee of the Sponsoring Organizations of the Treadway Commission (COSO) standards.

Canada's stock exchanges and SROs

Investors have another set of institutions to defend them beyond auditors: the securities industry and Canada's stock exchanges. Traditionally, stock exchanges have played a major role in setting and ensuring governance practices in English civil law countries (referred to colloquially as the "Anglo-Saxon" governance tradition), including the United Kingdom and Canada.

In September 2002, the TSX benchmarked Canada's governance standards to SOX, outlining areas where the TSX or other bodies ought to be doing more, and staking out the position that further rules would be counterproductive to the Canadian principle-based system. Subsequently, the TSX upgraded listing requirements to require a majority of independent directors on boards and audit committees.

TSX's subsidiary Venture Exchange has published a separate, lower set of governance requirements, opening the door to tiered governance in Canada. The TSX argues this is necessary to encourage a junior capital market in Canada. Of course, stock exchanges like the TSX face internal tensions that must be carefully balanced as well. High governance standards are meant to prevent costly failures (agency theory) and enhance investor confidence. On the other hand, lower standards make capital markets more accessible, especially to small caps, and enhance stock exchange market share and profitability.

Barely 40 percent of Canada's boards receive measures on the perception of their corporation's image or professionalism on a regular basis. If we really do "get what we measure," how are boards ensuring a high level of public trust and investor confidence?

Canada's analysts

The Investment Dealers Association (IDA) is responsible for articulating a policy governing analyst standards. Financial analysts play a pivotal role in obtaining and analyzing information from corporations and guiding investors on their decisions. To the extent this work is timely and robust; it contributes a great deal to the efficiency of capital markets and can be a strong influencer of governance behavior. Analysts and brokers, however, are not immune to challenges. Enron's experience at successfully influencing its own stock's "buy" rating through withholding "sell" business was a jarring lesson in the United States that may not have been learned here. In Canada, the housing of both "buy" and "sell" side brokers within Canada's monolithic financial intermediaries (who are concurrently also large institutional investors) begs questions of independence. Further, the whole system of guidance, consensus calls and compensating analysts and brokerages invites both boards and investors to set realistic expectations of the industry, rather than viewing it through rose-colored glasses.

One gap in the self-regulation of corporate governance in Canada has been enforcement. Despite very public malfeasance and major collapses, stock exchanges have been slow to delist or even punish offenders. Research into SROs in related industries (e.g. law and accounting) demonstrates that it takes both aggressive standards and enforcement to keep public trust in a profession.

Seventy-five percent of listed companies do not have a board approved policy or plan for communicating with/disclosing to shareholders. ... Ninety-five percent of companies only discuss executive compensation in very general terms, without explaining specifically how compensation was determined or how it related to company performance. Why have these practices not been more universally adopted in Canada?[12]

Canada's regulators and governments

As 20–20 hindsight demonstrated with both Enron and WorldCom, the governance team of executives, directors, investors, auditors, stock exchanges and SROs and analysts can completely fail to exercise due diligence, leaving us with the rear guards to defend us: supervisors and regulators. Again, this is a balancing act: the appropriate role of government regulation in governance, balanced with market self-regulation. It is when market discipline and self-regulation prove inadequate, that regulatory bodies must step in to set and enforce basic standards of disclosure and behavior.

The bulk of corporate and securities regulation is the responsibility of the provinces, each of which authors its own Corporations Act and operates its own Securities Commission. The Ontario Security Commission (OSC) is acknowledged as Canada's lead securities regulator, within the national framework of the Canadian Securities Administrators (CSA). Within a few weeks of SOX, the OSC required market participants, including the TSX, to share their responses and actions. The OSC decided to strike a middle course, agreeing with the TSX and CCCE that a "robust, made-in-Canada" solution is appropriate, offering "equivalent but not identical" protection (compared with the United States) that reflects the higher proportion of small cap and controlled corporations trading on Canadian markets.

While the provincial Acts generally do align in important aspects, often the CSA's policies and rulings differ a great deal, reflecting underlying political leanings and partisan objectives. A National Instrument or "NI" on the table below reflects agreement among the provinces, a Multilateral Instrument or "MI" means that at least one province has opted out. Balancing the need for tougher rules with sensitivities to Canada's markets, the CSA has introduced these new regulations or guidelines in key areas of CG, see Table 5.A2.

More than 80 percent of publicly-traded corporations' boards or Audit Committees have already instituted steps to assess and ensure the independence of their external auditor ... less than 60 percent of the directors of publicly-traded corporations currently meet new higher independence standards. Director search firms are used by only a quarter of publicly-traded corporations; at most places, there is a fairly tight circle of people making these critical selections. Why have higher standards of independence won the day in terms of auditors, but not with directors yet?

Beyond the provinces, the federal government does still have at least three major ways to influence CG across the country:

The Canada Business Corporations Act (CBCA), federal legislation (Industry Canada, with input from the Senate's Standing Committee on Banking, Trade and Commerce), sets the standard for corporate law for the provinces. Currently under further review, it speaks to central questions of governance such as the duties and qualifications of directors. One alternative being considered is expanding mandatory standards of corporate responsibility, including a corporation (and its directors) owing a duty to stakeholders beyond the shareholders. This is the fundamental tenet of the final governance theory, stakeholder theory, whose implication is that boards need to reflect the diversity of stakeholder interests. Leading stakeholder and corporate social responsibility practice derives from continental Europe, where boards do include representatives of lenders, employees, unions, small shareholders and other stakeholder groups. A recent poll found that a majority of Canadians would favor "public directors" appointed by the government or some other independent body to represent the public interest inside the boardrooms of Canada's biggest corporations. Incorporating either of these changes in the CBCA would change the face of Canadian CG and is consequently the focus of intense lobbying.

While the purpose of this chapter is not intended to go into detail on Canadian corporate law (and readers are cautioned not to treat this as more than a precis), Table 5.A1 gives an overview of the legal situation as it relates to CG and should be instructive. The financial services industry is federally regulated, through both constitutional and delegated authority. Finance Canada, OSFI and the CDIC are the leading players here. Each has a solid international reputation. OSFI's CG guidelines, which include the use of committees and requirements for disclosure, have influence well beyond Canada's financial community, as do CDIC's sound business practices, which embrace a risk management approach to control.

Under its national interest mandate, Finance Canada searches for ways to harmonize securities regulation across the country, including through its "wise-persons" committee. Two alternatives are possible: a single regulator (federal or trans-provincial) or a "passport" system where issuers could deal with a single regulator. Of course, a third alternative, the status quo, is always feasible. Other recent efforts to reform securities regulation, including the Crawford Report in Ontario, have met with mixed reviews from the provinces. The four leading provinces fiercely defend their claims. As some wry commentators have noted, one way or another, Canada will end up with a national securities commission ... even if it's the SEC!

While 97 percent of Canada's boards take responsibility for their corporation's approach to governance, and 90 percent take responsibility for ensuring a Code of Conduct, only 47 percent take responsibility for ensuring their corporation's approach to corporate social responsibility.

Stakeholder theory has advanced further in Europe than in North America. At a G8 summit, leaders (including Canada and the United States) named corporate social responsibility, transparency and integrity, the foundation for sound macro-economic growth and CG. Table 5.A3 summarizes the key influencers of governance thinking in Canada, their mandates and viewpoints implied from positions taken publicly.

Canada's CG performance

Having painted a landscape of the main players in CG in Canada and their effect on governance practice in recent times, we now move to a more detailed portrait of CG practices and performance in Canada.

Governance practices and trends in Canada are illustrated, and benchmarked where metrics are available, organized by governance principle area alongside each of the 14 TSX guidelines. As mentioned earlier, a key advantage to adopting a principle-based governance system is that it can be applied in practice to organizations regardless of which governance theory they ascribe to, what industry or sector they operate in.

Leadership and stewardship

Leadership[13] and stewardship[14] are the starting points of CG. These include basic steps such as setting the strategic direction, stewarding shareholder and stakeholder resources, overseeing risk and prioritizing objectives, and putting corporate leadership in place. This is the first principle for two main reasons:

i   this is where the board, executive and shareholders (and/or stakeholders) first interact, factoring expectations into plans, deciding what corporation plans to do (with their capital), and selecting the individuals (board and CEO) who will steward the corporation on their behalf; and
ii it is at the heart of both the Cadbury and Dey Reports: Dey's Guideline 1 focuses on leadership and stewardship, and more than half of the TSX Report deals with components of this.

Strategic planning and risk management

Boards of directors work hand-in-hand with management to assume responsibility for setting the strategic direction and adopting a strategic planning process. Ultimately, these leaders must ensure that all of the activities of the corporation are aligned with and work toward the accomplishment of the strategic vision and mission of the corporation.

Even here, at the foundation of CG, there is no consensus on the appropriate delineation of roles between the board and management. Some have argued that only the management team is equipped to draft a corporate mission, vision, objectives and priorities. Others, including Dr Chris Bart who authored 20 Questions Directors Should Ask About Strategy[15] have conducted research showing that corporations whose boards of directors get involved early in setting the mission and direction tend to be more successful.

In this view, setting the strategic direction for the company is the first and best opportunity for directors to exercise their leadership role and authority over the enterprise. Setting goals and objectives that align to the overall mission is critical. Boards must exercise discipline and restraint to ensure they do not stray over the invisible but critical line between board and management responsibilities.

Over 80 percent of Canada's boards are actively involved in the development, as well as the approval, of the corporation's strategic plan, objectives, strategies and tracking systems (see Table 5.1).

Spencer Stuart's research found 86 percent of Canadian boards were involved in strategic planning: 39 percent approved the final strategic plan, 63 percent reviewed the plan, but only 7 percent met with management to develop the plan.[16]

This is an area where Canada's boards of directors became engaged early, in the 1970s and 1980s, even before the broader interest in CG emerged, and clearly this involvement has continued to grow through the 1990s.

Good governance also calls for Canada's boards explicitly to assume responsibility for the stewardship of the corporation. One of the greatest challenges facing boards is to effectively oversee resource application in a manner that remains

Table 5.1 Boards taking responsibility for strategic planning, 1995–2005

Percentages of boards explicitly assuming responsibility to:	1995	1999	2005	Improvements in ten years
Develop corporate strategy with management	67	74	85	+18
Set objectives to measure management performance	68	72	85	+17
Identify criteria to measure strategy	51	56	74	+23
Ensure systems that track the process	54	70	79	+25
Monitor the implementation of the strategy	72	79	92	+20
Assess management in meeting objectives	78	83	92	+14
Ensure an effective succession plan is in place	66	77	87	+21

strategic and does not involve transactional activities rightly belonging to the CEO, staff, internal audit committees or the external auditor.

Stewardship is the thrust of key reports on governance, including the United Kingdom's Turnbull Report that calls for boards to take a risk-based approach to internal control, and the US SOX that focuses on engaging independent directors in oversight and control.

Canada's guidelines, and CG performance, pre-date these reports by several years. As strategic leaders, the board is entrusted with resources, material, environmental, financial and human and should endeavor to safeguard and shepherd those resources with diligence, care and integrity. In general, boards are more effective in oversight than control, which often requires financial skills and access to timely and verified information.

How is this accomplished? As part of its overall stewardship, the board should ensure that the principal risks of the business are identified and that appropriate systems to manage those risks are implemented. Here again, there have been improvements in the board's role in risk management in recent years (see Table 5.2).

Board and CEO selection and succession

Having the right people at the top of a corporation, people with character, skills, competencies, engagement and the right degree of independent-mindedness, is an essential ingredient in both the structural and cultural dimensions of CG. Choosing the best individuals to lead the corporation, its board and CEO, is "where good governance begins."[17] The key objectives of the leadership renewal process are:

i   ensuring effective succession planning and board renewal;
ii   discerning the right mix of desired and needed qualities in leaders;
iii   locating individuals with this mix of experience, skills and personal qualities;
iv   ensuring that the board can function independently of management and individual shareholders; and
v   gaining strength from a diversity of leaders.

The composition of a board is important, since chemistry and character will contribute to unity, perhaps the single most important and elusive component of board effectiveness.[18] A key thrust of the Dey Report in 1994, and indeed

Table 5.2 Boards taking responsibility for risk management, 1995–2005

Percentages of boards explicitly assuming responsibility to:	1995	1999	2005	Improvements in ten years
Identify principal risks	67	79	91	+24
Ensure implementation of systems to manage risks	72	77	91	+19

the SOX, is that a sizeable majority of corporate directors need to be "independent" of management, so that they can exercise due diligence in the best interests of the corporation as an entity, and not its agents or management (see Table 5.3).

While most governance data are not readily comparable from country to country, it is fair to say that these indicators of director independence would put Canada at or near the top of industrialized countries. However, some observers have commented that Canada's small population and concentrated business centers result in a related but different problem: a high number of interlocking directorships, where a small number of people serve on a large number of major corporate boards. The implication is that their independence may be impaired by the effect of their deliberations from one board to another.[19] Interestingly, this allegation was at the root of the 2003 Higgs Report in the United Kingdom, which concluded that, despite public perception, there was no significant interlocking of directorships there.

Core competencies of individuals are key to them being selected for boards. This includes the skills they have acquired and the experience and education they have had that can immediately contribute to the company's and board's effectiveness. Beyond these, the personal character and background of directors are considered critical. Directors must lead the corporation in its ethical practices, so they must have integrity. For teamwork, they require compatibility. Figure 5.2 illustrates who has the main influence in selecting Canada's board members.

In the 1995 baseline year, 55 percent of Canada's business corporations followed a formal process for nominating directors to the board (one of Dey's guidelines). As the chart indicates, over 80 percent of corporations follow such a process in 2003, with input sought broadly from board members, committee(s), shareholders and management.

Another big shift has been the increasing influence of the board in selecting new board members, and the lessening influence of management. A trend that began in the early 1980s, this is reflective of boards taking on responsibility for overseeing and controlling (governing) the corporation rather than management doing this alone – one of the first steps an "independent" board takes is to take responsibility for board and CEO selection. The use of outside search firms is something that is growing, but still barely one in five corporations use these for director search (they are more popular for executive search).

Table 5.3 Independence of board members, 1995–2003

Percentages of board members in Canada who are:	*1995*	*1999*	*2003*
Outside (i.e. not currently management)	78	74	82
Unrelated (as defined by companies)	63	62	64
Fully independent (new higher standards)	n.k.	n.k.	57

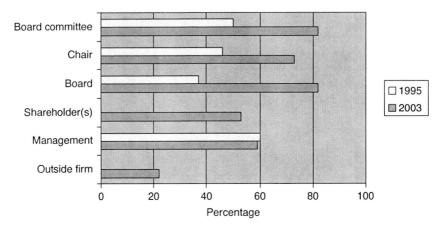

Figure 5.2 Who selects Canada's board members? (Rating of degree of influence in selecting board members of corporations).

The benefit to using outside search firms is that the universe of candidates would be much wider, and boards need to be less reliant on "who knows whom." Figure 5.3 illustrates what main criteria are used in selecting Canada's board members.

While specific business and financial skills have always been of importance in seeking director candidates, these are reinforced in the post-1990's environment of corporate reporting adjustments and drops in public confidence. Board renewal is a continuous process, from identifying needs and profiling skills to recruiting the right candidates, developing and applying their skills and competencies, and evaluating their performance and feeding this information into the succession plan.

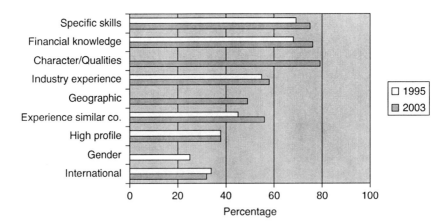

Figure 5.3 How are Canada's board members selected? (Rating of top criteria used in selecting board members of corporations).

Empowerment and accountability

The board delegates authority to management to manage the organization, and ensures further delegation of authority to the lowest levels of the firm compatible with their capabilities (Principle of Empowerment). The board holds the CEO accountable for the organization's success, compatible with delegated authority, and is in turn accountable to the principals (Principle of Accountability). Empowerment and Accountability encompass these CG performance areas:

i articulating right roles and responsibilities
ii the board and executive functioning effectively together ensuring accountability of the board and executive.

Once plans, capital and leaders are in place, the next step for corporations is to articulate "who does what," and to put in place a CG structure that will include basics such as board and CEO work plans: meetings, agendas, committees and accountability mechanisms.

Allocating responsibilities

At the heart of successful governance is the appropriate balancing of roles among the board, management and shareholders. When these roles are out of balance, significant risks are taken which may contribute to or lead to failure of the corporation.

Many boards in Canada are routinely examining and formalizing roles and responsibilities of boards and executives. Better performance and stronger boards are reflective of many corporations that have succeeded in implementing assessment and evaluation systems. Identifying the ongoing specific responsibilities and goals to be assigned to the CEO, chair, board and committees is the crux of this process (see Table 5.4).

Table 5.4 Allocating responsibilities practices, 1995–2005

Percentages of business corporations where:	1995	1999	2005	Improvements in ten years
Board takes explicit approach to governance	67	87	97	+30
CEO has formal written position description	62	67	85	+23
Board as a whole has formal written position description	21	56	69	+48
Individual directors have formal written position description	15	26	43	+28
Committees have formal written position description	n.k.	72	90	

Independence and committees

The concepts of director independence and effective board committees were hallmarks of 2002's SOX in the US, but were by no means new (see Table 5.5).

For example, the key recommendation of the 1992 Cadbury Committee in the UK was to increase the number of independent directors (non-executives) on boards. The formation of audit committees composed entirely of independent directors were central recommendations of both Cadbury and 1987's Treadway (US). The key recommendations of 1994's Canada's Dey Committee are concerned with board independence[20] and the need for boards to explicitly and expressly assume responsibility for the stewardship and governance of the corporation.[21]

Almost 90 percent of Canada's corporations separate the chair and CEO positions, putting Canada well ahead of its major trading partners on this important indicator (see Table 5.6).

This is perhaps the biggest change in governance practice in the past 30 years. When the Conference Board began its board surveys in 1973, the question of CEO and chair separation was not even asked. In 1977, research noted that "vesting CEO and chair role in one person is being questioned," yet the vast majority of companies in Canada continued the practice.

Unlike many governance practices, this one varies by industry and sector. In fact, financial service and high-technology firms often still retain a single CEO/chair, despite widespread calls for these positions to be separated. As shareholder "activism" has increased in Canada, boards of these firms are being challenged at annual meetings. Several banks and high-profile hi-tech companies have named different Chairs and CEOs since 2001. Many corporations with an effective separation of duties at the top, report that their boards function more effectively and assume a larger number of strategic responsibilities than those without a separate chair or lead.

Table 5.5 Independence practices, 1995–2005

Percentages of business corporations where:	1995	1999	2005	Improvements in ten years
Chair is not the current CEO (separate people)	66	71	87	+21
"Lead" director in place	9	21	22	+13
Outside chair or Lead director	75	92	99	+24
Policy is that chair not be a member of management	47	31	61	+14
Periodic sessions at board meetings held without management present (in camera)	21	42	87	+66
System in place to engage outside advisor	29	58	90	+61

Table 5.6 Corporations separating chair and CEO positions (percentages)[1]

Year	Canada	United States
2005	87	30–35
2003	77	25–35
2000	75	25–35
1998	79	20–25
1995	66	19–24
1990	55	10–15
1986	50	10–15
1984	"CEO typically chairs"	(no data)
1977	"Vesting CEO and chair role in one person is being questioned"	(no data)

Note

1 Canadian data: Canadian Directorship Practices, The Conference Board of Canada; US data: Directors' Compensation and Board Practices (The Conference Board Inc. Annual Reports, New York); previous US data: various published surveys: the low end of the range is based on securities disclosures of larger, publicly traded corporations, while the high end of the range is based on broader surveys, including smaller and privately owned firms when available.

In the 1970s, the four most common committees of the board were the Audit, Compensation, Executive and Pension Committees. In the 1980s, Nominating Committees became more widely used, reflecting the increasing formalization and transparency of the process for selecting new candidates for the board. Prior to this, many new directors were essentially chosen by top management. In the 1990s, Compensation Committees were often renamed Human Resources Committees to reflect a broader mandate, and new committees developed to aid the board in specific areas of strategic significance: Environment, Ethics/Conduct Review, Risk and, since the 1994's Dey Report, Governance. Figure 5.4 illustrates the use of board committees across Canada since then.

In 1998 the Governance Committees surpassed Executive Committees. Executive Committees are on the decline largely because of the recognition of director personal liability; hence, the decision not to delegate board authority to a subset of directors when the concomitant responsibility – and liability – cannot be so delegated. Governance Committees received a further boost in 2002 when the US became the first country to mandate their use, in the SOX. Many Canadian corporations are folding their Nominating Committees into these.

Communications and disclosure

The next CG principle involves ensuring an effective flow of information both within the corporation and with its external stakeholders, including the shareholders. The board ensures an effective two-way system of information flow in the organization – gathering credible information from, and directing management. "The board of directors of every corporation should explicitly assume … responsibility for the following matters: (i) a communications policy for the

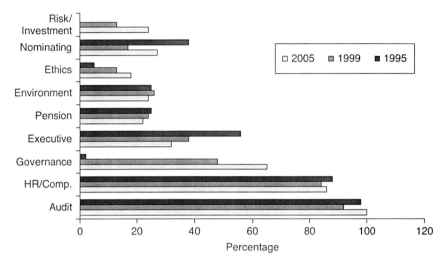

Figure 5.4 What committees do Canada's boards use? (Percentage of corporations reporting each practice).

corporation; and (ii) the integrity of the corporation's internal control and management information system."[22]

Communications and Disclosure encompass these CG performance areas:

i collecting information with integrity,
ii effectively communicating: two-way and proactively,
iii effectively reporting: with transparency, clarity and accountability.

These principles involve structural practices:

i Determining information requirements: the board has to take a lead role in selecting what information it needs, from whom and to what degree. The "agency problem" means that management (agents) always have access to more and better information than boards and principals.

So boards must also decide on:

ii Periodicity: How often does the board need specific information? This is best answered in layers, where core/the most significant risk measures are reported to the board every meeting in a "dashboard" or "scorecard," then periodic reports are reviewed on "drill down" metrics. An example of a dashboard is shown below.
iii Validation: the board needs to decide what checks and verification needs to be conducted to assure itself that management information is accurate and complete. This involves a close relationship with, and understanding of, the

internal audit function and the external auditor in particular, as well as access to outside professional advisors when needed.

As well as cultural practices:

i   Determining degrees of transparency: the board has to weigh the "disclosure dilemma": balancing the competing legitimate interests of stakeholders to access all information in the enterprise, and management to protect competitive, sensitive information.
ii Continuous disclosure: not only reporting on an annual or interim basis, but disclosing material changes (significant events) throughout the year.

Taking responsibility for CG requires timely, accurate and useful information that can be relied on. This is especially important in the area of verifying the integrity of information through internal and external audit processes. For this reason it is essential that corporations, through their boards of directors ensure that an appropriate system exists whereby they receive necessary information (see Table 5.7).

The information needs of the board are another area in which effective relationships among board, management, stakeholders and shareholders are critical. The board should be able to obtain any extra or special information it deems necessary. Conversely, it should be able to communicate extra or special information. Boards should periodically assess the access, quality, integrity and general information needs of the corporation.

Despite fairly strong performance results here, a body of outside research indicates that corporate boards are not as active in information and communication as they should be. A 1999 Ontario Securities Commission Report concluded that 75 percent of listed corporations did not have a board-approved communications or

Table 5.7 Boards taking responsibility for communication and disclosure, 1995–2005

Percentages of boards explicitly assuming responsibility to:	1995	1999	2005	Improvements in ten years
Ensure information flows to the board	75	77	88	+13
Ensure communication with stakeholders	60	71	79	+19
Ensure audit system in place	93	93	95	+2
Verify integrity of audit information	84	83	91	+7
Ensure compliance with accounting principles	90	92	95	+5
Review and approve financial information	94	93	96	+2
Report on internal controls in the annual report	71	75	81	+10

disclosure policy in place. This study led directly to this being a major focus of the Saucier Joint Committee struck by the TSX and CICA in 2000.

Service and fairness

The board is a servant, ensuring fairness in service to all stakeholders – beginning with management and employees, through customers and shareholders, to stakeholders and communities' The board balances the commercial, financial, fiduciary interests of the principals, with the social, environmental, cultural expectations of stakeholders.

Service and Fairness encompass these CG performance areas:

i   dealing fairly with clients, staff and others,
ii   conducting business ethically and professionally with integrity,
iii promoting sustainable development and environmental best practice.

CG is about more than its four core players (shareholders, directors, executives and auditors). For corporations to succeed, they must effectively serve all their legitimate stakeholder groups. Failing to excel in customer service, deal fairly with employees, or sensitively with communities and the environment can threaten the business model and a corporation's financial viability. Ethical lapses can contribute to, or accelerate a business collapse. There are no specific TSX Guidelines related to stakeholder relations. In recent years, the TSX, along with most CG authorities, has endorsed the need for a board-approved code of ethical conduct. However, there is still no consensus among regulators or at the TSX on the appropriate weight to be given to (non-shareholder) stakeholder relations and issues such as social responsibility and sustainable development. One way to look at corporate performance in this area is to separate it into different stakeholder elements.

In the next section, on Accomplishment and measurement, we will examine the use of non-financial performance measures by Canadian corporations, a good indicator of their interest in, and responsiveness to, different stakeholder groups (especially employees and customers).

The subject of corporate conduct and ethical leadership has loomed large in recent years, with a number of major corporate failures (especially in the US). At least partly blamed on ethical lapses at or near the top of a corporation. In 2003, the Conference Board of Canada added these questions to its CDP research (see Table 5.8).

Table 5.8 Boards taking responsibility for ethical and social performance

Percentages of boards explicitly assuming responsibility to:	2005
Ensure code of conduct for the corporation	90
Ensure conflict of interest guidelines	90
Address issues of corporate social responsibility	47

Most boards in Canada do formalize codes of conduct and conflict of interest policies that include policy on the steps to take in a breach of ethical conduct or a conflict of interest, to ensure that high standards of integrity are maintained; far fewer ensure that broader social responsibilities are dealt effectively by the corporation. It is fair to say that social and environmental responsibility has not been universally adopted and can be regarded as an emerging issue in Canada and in the international community in general. Despite major advances in Western Europe in the areas of social responsibility and environmental sustainability, and significant research linking corporate performance to corporate social responsibility (CSR) and stakeholder relations, many corporate leaders have yet to fully embrace leading practices in these areas or to consider them core to good governance.

This is both a philosophical and legal question. What is the right thing to do? What is my legal duty? In Canada, at least, the Business Corporations Acts, courts and regulators have come down clearly in favor of the corporation's interests first; the shareholders' interests second; and other stakeholders' interests considered beyond those. Of course, social and environmental responsibility is not just about costs. Many leading Canadian corporations have undertaken significant initiatives in these areas, partly because they realize that social and environmental stewardship contribute to sustainable shareholder value, customer loyalty and employee satisfaction.

Accomplishment and measurement

The board is ultimately responsible for the organization accomplishing its purpose, to its principals, stakeholders, regulators and beyond, and so must be fully engaged in understanding the industry and business model. The board also "gets what it measures" and "gets what it rewards" – the organization's performance management and incentive system must align with the purpose and direction. Accomplishment and Measurement encompass these corporate governance performance areas:

i   effectively measuring performance: of the corporation, of management and the board
ii achieving financial results and overall success
iii effectively accomplishing strategic objectives and missions.

All the planning, empowering, communicating and serving in the world (the first four principles) are of absolutely no use unless the corporation accomplishes something, unless it generates value and fulfills a purpose. This principle area involves defining what a corporation means by "success," then measuring, monitoring and ensuring this/these. "Every board of directors should implement a process to be carried out by the nominating committee or other appropriate committee, for assessing the effectiveness of the board as a whole, the committees of the board and the contribution of individual directors."[23]

Corporate performance measurement

There is a great deal of truth to the phrase "you get what you measure." Best practice dictates that boards ensure effective mechanisms for measuring growth that align from the corporate mission down through the entire organization. Boards often measure performance in these key areas: Human Resources; Innovation; Service/Product; Financial; Community; Environment. Most corporate boards measure both financial and non-financial performance (see Figurer 5.5).

There has been an across-the-board increase in the use of non-financial performance measures over the years. Employee, customer and social performance indicators are used regularly by most boards of directors, and one can deduce from this that CG systems are evaluating and ensuring stakeholder relations. Increasingly, boards are relying on performance dashboards or scorecards that roll-up corporate performance metrics in key areas (see earlier illustration under Communication and disclosure, Table 5.7).

Performance evaluations

Corporations need to ensure that both the board and executive are accountable, as part of the corporation's overall accountability to its owners and stakeholders. Director accountability, while improving, still has some room to go in Canada (see Figure 5.6). However, our performance is comparable to our major trading partners: Spencer Stuart's research shows that Canadian boards are much more dedicated to formal board and director evaluations than US boards (see Table 5.9).[24]

i   Boards of directors, as the directing mind and legal power of the body corporate, are ultimately responsible and accountable for the

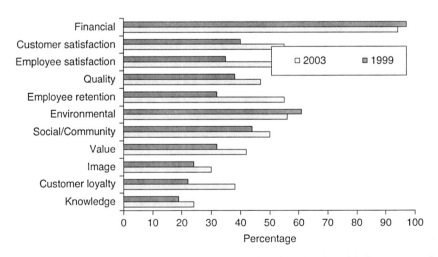

Figure 5.5 What performance measures are reported to Canada's boards? (Percentage of boards regularly receiving measures in each area).

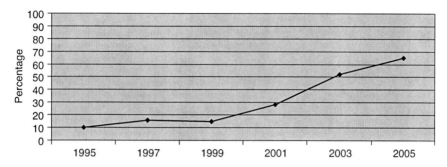

Figure 5.6 Rising accountability for individual directors[1] (percentage of Canadian corporations who perform formal performance).

Note
1 Canadian Directorship Practices, The Conference Board of Canada.

Table 5.9 Performance evaluation practices, 1995–2005

Percentages of business corporations where:	1995	1999	2005	Improvements in ten years
CEO has formal written performance evaluation	64	78	88	+14
Board as a whole has formal written performance evaluation	21	49	75	+54
Individual directors have formal written performance evaluation	10	13	65	+55
Committees have formal written performance evaluation	15	30	70	+55

organization's performance and the accomplishment of its mission,
mandate and goals. As we have seen, most Canadian boards are quite
active in strategic planning, financial monitoring, and even holding the
management accountable for results through formal annual CEO performance evaluations. It is a logical step to argue that board accountability can
only be achieved through a similar form of assessment and evaluation at
the board level, at the top of the organization. Of those corporations that do
undertake individual director evaluations, two-thirds use self-assessments
and only one-third (about 20 percent overall) use peer or outside assessments of performance. Unless corporations really understand why they
should, and are, undertaking an evaluation of the board and its directors,
they risk causing division among participants and inappropriate use of
results. This fear is perhaps the biggest reason that so many directors do
not use peer evaluations despite the fact that most directors (80 percent)
support both.[25] Despite the fears associated with board and director evaluation, which can be mitigated through effective methodology and implementation, there are a number of benefits to be gained. In fact a proper
evaluation promotes positive change and builds a road map to success for

the whole organization ... all governance practices should contribute to the accomplishment of the mission/mandate.

Board evaluation can be a helpful exercise in compliance or a powerful tool to add value to a corporation – there are a number of options in how board evaluations can be conducted, and the right choice will depend on what is being sought as outcomes. As with so many things in life: "the value you will get out of board evaluation is directly correlated to the investment you put into it."

Continuous learning and growth

The board sets a "tone from the top" to encourage and reward a learning organization, capable of innovation and change. The board is never satisfied with the status quo, ensuring a culture of risk management, not risk avoidance, and change management to ensure growth. Continuous Learning and Growth encompass these CG performance areas: (i) changing, improving and learning from the past, (ii) excelling in human resources development and (iii) promoting innovation.

The final governance principle acknowledges that change will always be with us, and the challenge is how we respond to change as a corporation. By embracing change, and fostering a culture of continuous learning and growth, enterprises will not only have more effective governance, but are more likely to sustain success. "Every corporation, as an integral element of the process for appointing new directors, should provide an orientation and education program for new recruits to the board."[26]

Governance guidelines around the world call for orientation, training and development programs to be in place for the board. Leaving a legacy of learning that extends beyond the boardroom will make for lasting accomplishments that boards and directors can be proud of (see Table 5.10).

Table 5.10 Human Research(HR) development practices, 1995–2003

Percentages of business corporations where:	1995	1999	2003	Improvements in eight years
Individual directors have formal orientation program	34	55	63	+29
Committees have formal orientation program	n.k.	26	29	n.a.
CEO has ongoing education program	n.k.	10	13	n.a.
Board as a whole has ongoing education program	n.k.	13	25	n.a.
Individual directors have ongoing education program	n.k.	13	20	n.a.
Committees have ongoing education program	n.k.	9	16	n.a.

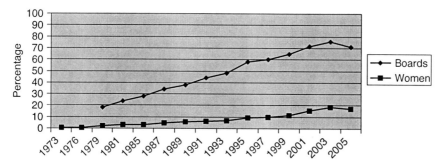

Figure 5.7 Women on Canadian boards (percentage of boards with at least one woman, and women as a percentage of total directors).

Canadian CG studies generally find corporations wanting in all three capabilities here. For example, Patrick O'Callaghan's assessment of Canadian CG highlights the small number of corporations that undertake formal director education, peer assessments and other accountability and learning tools.[27] This is an area that is changing rapidly, however. Anecdotally, both the Directors College (launched by the Conference Board and McMaster University) and the ICD's Governance College have been greeted with strong registrations and participation. Empirically, preliminary data for 2005 indicates that upwards of two-thirds of Canada's corporations have examined and promote ongoing director education for individual board members. Another indicator of corporate culture is the degree to which women are represented in Canada's boardrooms and executive suites (see Figure 5.7).

While most reports suggest that Canadian boards trail US boards in this measure, Spencer Stuart points out that Canadian public boards with revenues above $1 billion have roughly the same gender balance as similar sized US firms.[28] Again, while there has been slow and steady improvement, it is easy to see why many observers are calling for more progress here: the rate of growth is slowing, or even reversing, in terms of broadening diversity in Canada's boardrooms. That is even more compelling when research links between board diversity, leadership style, CG and organizational performance have begun to be made.[29]

What is being strived for in this governance principle is not simply structural enhancements or compliance with standards, but the adoption of a corporate culture that embraces learning, innovation and excellence, including in CG practices.

Canadian CG performance in an international context

The bulk of this chapter explores CG practices and trends in a Canadian context. A key related question is: How does Canada's CG benchmark worldwide? This is almost an impossible question to answer directly, because there is no reliable central source that compares governance activities and results of countries including Canada. Yet there is one useful and instructive proxy. Annually, McKinsey & Co. conducts a comprehensive investor survey that asks "Which premium investors

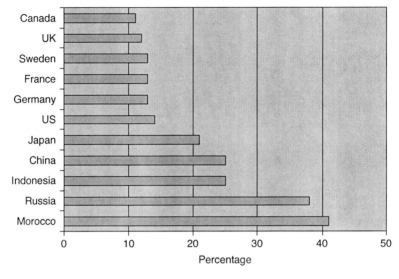

Figure 5.8 Which premium investors would be willing to pay for a well-governed
company?

would be willing to pay for a well-governed company" (Figure 5.8). Canada was
added to this research for the first time in 2002, with the following results.[30]

Of 31 countries in the McKinsey Report, Canada reports the lowest premium
investors would pay for better governed companies. One implication of the
research (and it is an implication not a direct finding) is that governance in
general is more stable and predictable in those countries with lower premiums,
and more volatile and changeable in those countries with higher premiums.
A glance at the list reinforces this anecdotally.

Canadian CG future directions

Reflecting constructive, contemporary tensions between traditional "Anglo-
Saxon" governance and continental European models, and between fiduciary
(shareholder value) and stakeholder perspectives, the future of governance in
Canada is a microcosm and a crucible of the future of governance worldwide.
What direction Canada, or any other country, heads in will depend a great deal
on how they answer the question: "What should we learn from Enron and
SOX?" In turn, how people answer this question depends on how they believe
corporations ought to be governed and where real power should lie: which fundamental CG theory they subscribe to, implicitly or explicitly. Canada's governance guidelines and practices appear to be among the most rigorous and
comprehensive in the world. Canada was among the first major nations to
publish a national code of governance guidelines. This occurred in 1994, barely
two years after the landmark Cadbury Committee report.[31]

There is another, less tangible advantage that Canada has in CG. Traditionally, Canada has used a process of multi-stakeholder consultation and consensus-building in developing its CG guidelines. The 1994 Dey Report followed extensive public consultations; the 2001 Saucier Report went through several iterations in draft before being finalized. Contrast this with the United Kingdom and the United States, two leading nations in CG worldwide: in both nations, a three-way pull is observed among corporations, investors and regulators. Even though many corporate leaders want to embrace best governance practices, they are perceived to be resisting shareholder-driven or government-imposed initiatives.

Canada's CG is "principle-based," as contrasted with the more "rules-based" approach in the United States.[32] Canada's governance landscape can be characterized as having highly committed individuals and institutions in search of the right balance. Those at one extreme vigorously defend Canada's "principle-based" governance system with few changes to the status quo. Those at the other extreme argue that we would be better served by adopting sweeping governance standards ("rules") along the US SOX model. These two concepts, borrowed from the field of accounting practices, essentially mean:

i   "Principles-based": consensus is reached on broad areas of principle, then corporations/practitioners have flexibility to select and apply actual practices within these. Canada has a single fundamental governance "rule": all corporations must disclose their CG practices, though they are free to select practices from a broad range. The Dey Report is the best example of this approach in Canada.

ii "Rules-based": explicit, often complex, prescriptive requirements are promulgated by central authorities. Enforcement is based on corporations implementing practices in keeping with these standards. The SOX, that involves both criminal and civil law, is the best example of this approach in the United States. Leading Canadian corporations have already adopted most of the provisions of SOX, some because they must and others in recognition of the benefits that will accrue to those meeting the highest global standard.

So what? What can or should one do about all this? The outcome of this dialogue will set the stage for Canada and the rest of the world for years to come, affecting international competitiveness and image. In pursuit of the highest global standard, Canada's corporations, investors, regulators and other key players in the CG domain are confronted with a number of different, although frequently interrelated, challenges and opportunities. While Canada's performance generally reflects considerable progress in CG over recent years, it also points to certain challenges and opportunities that could be pursued to achieve further improvements.

In the areas of measurement and communications, while boards receive a great deal of information, generally from management, there is too often a disconnect in really understanding and monitoring the "success" of the corporation. Traditional financial, lagging and quantitative measures of success will continually be updated and enhanced by the development and adoption of innovative, non-financial, leading and qualitative measures of corporate performance.

Perhaps the biggest change in boards will be in their diversity. The whole area of director "recruitment" is undergoing a vitalization of major proportions as companies recognize the competitive advantage that skilled and diverse directors bring: this is increasingly true in an era when companies are differentiated less on product or price than on people and quality.[33]

Further, the types of corporations that implement best governance practices continue to expand, encompassing smaller businesses and those that are more closely held. Canada's public (Crown or state) enterprises, spearheaded by major CG reviews by the federal, Saskatchewan and British Columbia governments, have taken major strides in board functioning, responsibilities and accountability in recent years. Canada's privately held and family businesses can be expected to follow as the link between good governance and strong corporate performance becomes more widely acknowledged.

Conclusion

Canadian CG is now in turning point. Indeed, as both management and boards of Canada's corporations take strides to ensure excellence in CG, the onus will be on shareholders, the third member of the governance team, to embrace improved practices. A chain is only as strong as its weakest link.

Excellence in governance is more about balance as it is about choosing one course over another. Success in CG in Canada's – and the world's – future will undoubtedly involve corporations effectively balancing these critical tensions:

  i Overall, between governance structure and culture, between getting the right practices in place, and practicing governance relationships well.

  ii In responsibilities, between an active and engaged board and committees, and an empowered and strategic management team led by the CEO.

iii In independence, between directors completely independent of the management and corporation and those closer to management and the corporation whose relationships and expertise could benefit the corporation in the long run.

iv Among stakeholders, between large institutional investors and individual members of the community, each of whom have legitimate stakes in CG, though differing power bases.

  v In disclosure, between the expectations of stakeholders for complete transparency, and the legitimate need to protect sensitive and competitive information.

vi In standards, between the voluntary guidelines but mandatory disclosure of "principles" and the mandated standards of "rules."

vii In geography, between seeking a "Canadian way" and making our way in an increasingly convergent global world of business and governance.

As the managers, directors, owners and stakeholders of Canada's corporations work together in raising the corporate governance bar, Canada's access to global markets of capital, labor, resources and customers will be assured and strengthened. The rest of the world is watching – and learning – from Canada's corporate governance journey and success.

Notes

1 The author gratefully acknowledges the major contributions of research and insight to this chapter from Brown Governance Inc., The Conference Board of Canada and Industry Canada.
2 Where the Directors (the "Dey" Report), Toronto Stock Exchange (Toronto 1994) www.tsx.ca.
3 Report of the Joint Committee on Corporate Governance, the "Saucier Committee Report," Toronto Stock Exchange, Canadian Institute of Chartered Accountants and Canadian Venture Exchange (Toronto: November 2001.)
4 Leadership and stewardship, empowerment and accountability, communications and disclosure, service and fairness, accomplishment and fairness and continuous learning and growth.
5 TSX/Dey 14 Guidelines, CSA National Instruments, Sarbanes–Oxley Act, Combined Code (UK), Industry/sectoral guidelines, e.g. OSFI/CDIC for financial sector; CICA for accounting/auditors "Policy" governance.
6 Size and composition of board; frequency and content of board meetings; number and mandate of committees; chair and CEO: combined versus separate; roles, delegation of authority; performance metrics, evaluation and reporting; annual, interim and continuous disclosure.
7 www.ceocouncil.ca.
8 Data came from the Conference Board of Canada's, Canadian Directorship Practices board governance research, based on comprehensive surveys conduct every two years from 1973 through to 2005. Published reports and insight are available at: www.conferenceboard.ca.
9 Required by the London Stock Exchange as a result of adopting the Turnbull Report.
10 Lou Dobbs Tonight, CNN-TV. www.cnn.com.
11 The Cadbury Committee Report, op. cit.
12 Studies published in 2000 by the Ontario Securities Commission (www.osc.gov.on.ca) and in 2002 by the Canadian Securities Administrators (www.csa-acvm.ca).
13 The board has a strong hand in setting with management, and approving, the purpose and long-term direction of the organization, which defines everything else in governance and management, and in selecting corporate leaders of unquestioned character and integrity.
14 The board shepherds resources and capital that belong to others – the principals – so ensures effective systems to control (measure and account for) these. Leadership and stewardship encompass these CG performance areas: (i) establishing a clear sense of purpose, direction, strategy, policy, priorities and criteria, (ii) overseeing management and control of resources and (iii) ensuring the best mix of corporate leaders.

15 One in a series of popular and practical guides published by the Canadian Institute of Chartered Accountants www.cica.ca.
16 Canadian Board Index, Spencer Stuart with the Clarkson Centre for Business Ethics and Board Effectiveness, p. 13.
17 "Where Good Governance Begins" is the title of the Conference Board of Canada's Practical Guide to Selecting and Appointing Directors and the CEO, part of its Practical Guide to Corporate Governance series authored by Debra and David Brown.
18 Jon Grant, former Chair of the Boards of Laurentian Bank and Canada Lands Company.
19 The Globe and Mail's Report on Business was among the first and more vocal to voice this.
20 "Where Were The Directors?," Guidelines 2, 3, 4, 9, 12, 13 and 14: Appendix 5.A2 contains all guidelines.
21 "Where Were The Directors?," Guidelines 1 and 10.
22 TSX Guidelines related to Communications and Disclosure, Guideline 1b.
23 TSX Guidelines related to Accomplishment and Measurement, Guideline 5.
24 Canadian Board Index, Spencer Stuart with the Clarkson Centre for Business Ethics and Board Effectiveness, p. 10.
25 McKinsey & Co. director survey, published in the McKinsey Quarterly. www.mckinsey.com.
26 TSX Guidelines related to continuous learning and growth, guideline 6.
27 Patrick O'Callaghan and Associates publishes an annual review of CG in association with Korn Ferry.
28 Canadian Board Index, Spencer Stuart with the Clarkson Centre for Business Ethics and Board Effectiveness, p. 17.
29 Women on Boards, The Conference Board of Canada examines not only the empirical data here, but the case for using the number of women on boards as a proxy for board culture and CG.
30 McKinsey Global Investor Opinion Survey on Corporate Governance, 2002.
31 Report of the Committee on the Financial Aspects of Corporate Governance (London: December 1992), "The Cadbury Report."
32 The Toronto Stock Exchange and the Canadian Council of Chief Executives have published viewpoints espousing "principles" as opposed to "rules" as the preferred approach to CG in Canada.
33 Where Good Governance Begins: A Practical Guide to Selecting Directors and the CEO (The Conference Board of Canada; Ottawa: 1998).

Table 5.A1 Overview of CG legal framework

Statute Law (Acts of legislatures and regulations):

Corporations Acts	• Corporations are viewed as "persons" under the law – they have the capacity and powers of a natural person • The board of a corporation has all its powers and duties • The board generally delegates management authority but retains supervisory (governance) authority • Board members have a duty of loyalty and a duty of care (fiduciary duties) • The duty of loyalty = to act honestly, in good faith, in the best interests of the corporation (ahead of stakeholders and even shareholders) • The duty of care = to exercise the care, diligence and skill of a reasonably prudent person

Other Statute Law	• Board members can be held responsible and liable for failure of the corporation to meet certain statutory obligations, most commonly:
	
	  • Employment standards, including employee pay, benefits, statutory deductions, health and safety
	  • Environmental standards, including causing damage to the environment, failing to clean up, lending money to a polluter
	
	• Many new Statutes contain a director liability clause

Common Law
(the body of court rulings that set precedents for legal conduct, "case" law)
	• The "Business Judgment Rule": courts will not review board decisions in hindsight as long as the board exercised their duties of loyalty and care
	• Implications of some major recent Canadian court cases:
	
	  • Standard Trustco: the board is responsible for ensuring the accuracy of financial disclosures and regulatory rulings
	  • Repap: the board and its Compensation Committee must exercise diligence and independence in approving CEO pay; it cannot just rely on outside experts
	  • Peoples/Wise: the board is not responsible to protect creditors and other stakeholders' interests, but the corporation and its shareholders
	  • YBM Magnex: the board must disclose significant risks to shareholders, not just proven facts

Table 5.A2 CSA guidelines

CSA instrument	Summary of content

NI 52-108 Auditor Oversight
MI 52-109 Certification of Disclosure (equivalent to SOX section 302)
MI 52-110 Audit Committees
	• Auditors of public companies must be in good standing with the CPAB
	• CEOs and CFOs must certify quarterly that financial disclosures are fair presentations, and that their corporations have effective internal controls
	• Minimum standards of financial literacy and independence are required for Audit Committee members, and expanded duties of the Audit Committee include leading the external auditor relationship
	• Audit Committees are not required to have a financial expert, just to disclose whether they have one
	• Two exclusions have been allowed by the OSC:
	
	  • Controlling corporations may name the same (independent) directors to the Audit Committees of affiliates and subsidiaries as the parent's
	  • Small cap companies are exempt from the independence, financial literacy skills and financial expert disclosure requirements. The first exclusion aligns better with governance principles than the second: it is difficult to justify endorsing unskilled individuals to be responsible for oversight and control, although it is understandable on practical grounds

MI 52-111 Internal Control (equivalent to SOX section 404)	• Corporations must conduct an evaluation of the effectiveness of internal controls over financial reporting and report on material weaknesses • An audit must be conducted of internal control over financial reporting
NI 58-201 Corporate Governance Guidelines (i.e. voluntary not mandatory) (these incorporate the original 14 TSX Dey Guidelines)	• The board should have a majority of independent directors • The chair of the board should be independent; if not, an independent director should be appointed as "lead director" • The independent directors should hold regular meetings without management • The board's written mandate should include ensuring the integrity of the executives, strategic planning, risk management, succession, etc. • Individual directors should have comprehensive orientation and continuing education • The board should adopt a written code of conduct and ethics • The board should use a Nominating Committee and a Compensation Committee, composed entirely of independent directors, following a clear charter and process • The board, committees and individual directors should have regular assessments of their effectiveness

Table 5.A3 Influencers of governance thinking in Canada, their mandates and viewpoints implied from positions taken publicly

The players	Their mandates	Their positions
London Stock Exchange (UK)	Sets and enforces listing requirements for UK, regarded as global benchmark	1992: Cadbury Report set out new standards for active boards and committees, independent directors 1994–99: Hempel and Greenbury Reports add to standards ("Combined Code"); Turnbull Report produces guide for directors to take risk-based approach to internal control
SEC (United States)	Sets and enforces securities requirements for US markets including NYSE and NASDAQ	July 2002: US Congress passes SOX, requiring sweeping changes to CG including independent directors, three core committees with expanded mandates, skills on Audit Committees and CEO/CFO certifications July 2003: SEC's roadmap to implement SOX runs 12 months. Wide-reaching reforms on director elections are promised in July as well
TSX	Sets and enforces listing requirements for Canada's major market	1994: "Where Were the Directors?" Dey Report echoed and built on Cadbury, putting in place 14 guidelines that TSX companies must disclose against. 2000: Saucier Joint Committee Report focuses on building a culture of governance and on the board's role in ensuring disclosure September 2002: TSX expands listing requirements, emphasizing independence of directors; TSX favours principle-based approach, made-in-Canada solution and tiered standards (large caps/small caps)
CSA; Ontario Securities Commission (OSC)	Sets and enforces securities requirements for Canada; OSC for Canada's largest province, regarded as Canadian benchmark	June 2003–January 2005: Adopts some SOX requirements, on CEO/CFO certifications, auditor independence and Audit Committees (52/108, 109 and 110), but gives exemptions to controlled and small cap companies (creating tiered system), and leaves Compensation Committees, Governance Committees, independence requirements and evaluations as guidelines voluntary) April 2005: Draft 52/111 proposes Canadian version of SOX 404 – external audits of internal controls,

continued

Table 5.A3 continued

The players	Their mandates	Their positions
		to be phased in over several years based on market capitalization
Finance Canada	Federal government department responsible for economic issues	March 2003: Appointed "wise persons" committee to suggest changes to current system of securities regulation
Industry Canada and Senate	Legislative branch of federal government	Ongoing: Hearings and studies to revise the Canada Business Corporations Act and other options to set governance standards
CCGG	Nineteen leading institutional investors joining together to set and enforce standards	May 2003: New chair, Michael Wilson and executive director, David Beatty set out CCGG's mandate to promote strong CG, including director independence and skills, stock compensation voting and disclosure
CPAB	New independent body to oversee auditors of public companies, set standards and carry out inspections	November 2002: Chair Gordon Thiessen takes reins in June 2003; OSC and 11 fellow regulators introduce rules to give CPAB clout in effectively licensing auditors
OSFI	Sets and enforces standards for Canada's financial institutions, regarded as benchmark by provinces	January 2003: New CG guidelines for Canada's financial services firms
CICA	Self-regulatory body and association for chartered accountants in Canada	September 2002: Proposed new rules for professional conduct and independence. Also amended accounting standards for stock options. Continues to release 20 Questions series
CCCE	Association of many of Canada's CEOs of leading corporations	September 2002: CCCE publishes CEO commitment to high standards of CG, including codes of conduct; favors principles over rules
The Globe and Mail Report on Business (ROB)	"Canada's national newspaper"	October 2002: ROB publishes five day series on CG, including a controversial new rating system, and extensive interviews and examples. Series repeated annually as "Board Games"
The Conference Board of Canada and McMaster University	Independent research institute and university	March 2003: Announced The Directors College, a joint venture to provide systematic development to new and prospective directors, leading to a comprehensive examination and university accreditation: Chartered Director
ICD	Association of directors from some of Canada's largest corporations	May 2003: ICD launches a second director education program in Canada in conjunction with Rotman School (University of Toronto); expanded in 2004 to Calgary, Montreal, Vancouver

6 The French national system of corporate governance

F. Bien, J. Délga and A. Ged

Introduction

Corporate governance (CG) did not really take off in France until the beginning of the 1990s in reaction to the various financial frauds and the arrival of foreign shareholders in the capital of major listed companies, pension funds and the organization of minority shareholders in defense associations, to such a degree that a certain number of general meetings of listed companies have been quite stormy (Rhodia, Vivendi, etc.). Taken together, these three elements have led legislators, practitioners, academics and politicians to raise questions as to the reiteration of critiques on how listed French companies are operated, both in terms of management and in terms of financial transparency. This chapter is a reflection on the impact of CG on the evolution of French law and practices.

Historical context

The understanding of the evolution of the French CG system requires a reminder of the context of the notion and its concrete textual translations into French law. Although the context in which CG appeared in French law was first of all international before being a domestic French issue, a distinction can definitely be made between before the mid-1990s and after the mid-1990s in terms of legal analysis, whether in the acceleration of the legal and regulatory changes that occurred or in the number of texts and reports published since then on the subject of CG.

Before the 1980s

The current debate on CG in French law cannot be understood without underlining that there has been an attempt to import and impose mechanisms and concepts from the Anglo-Saxon world in their original form or by adapting them. The terms of the debate come from the difference in the legal systems and the legal cultures between France and the Anglo-Saxon countries, notably the United States. The Anglo-Saxon countries have what is called "Common Law," whereas France is considered a country of "Civil Law." This means that in countries with "Common Law," statutory freedoms are much wider in scope than in "Civil Law" countries, thus creating an obstacle to the "uniformization" of the rules of company law. Consequently, CG legal provisions in the United States are logically part of stock market regulations or the adoption of codes of ethics or of good conduct, and not in the adoption of laws or regulations as in France, although the Sarbanes–Oxley Act (SOX), adopted by the American Congress in July 2002, is the perfect counter-example.

In the United States, questions linked to CG first concerned the small amount of time dedicated by directors to the company and the little effectiveness of the body that brings them together in the essential goal of preventing risks of engaging their responsibility. The results of studies carried out in the United States led to the adoption in 1993 by the American Law Institute of the "Principles of Corporate Governance Analysis and Recommendations," updated in 1999, points out directors passivity. Such a situation was confirmed in the United Kingdom, where similar questions have been brought up by the Bank of England and other reports.[1] It is interesting to observe that the studies published in the United States in the 1970s to resolve dissatisfaction with the performances of American corporations and dissipate the doubt surrounding the abilities of their management, took the German and French systems as references.

It was not until much later that the debate shifted toward the role of directors, before focusing on the relationship between shareholders and directors, thus shedding light on the divergence of interests at work. In 1931, it was already decided that shareholders and directors were responsible in events concerning their organization. The debate came to France, only later, in the 1970s, although the CG issue is much older, practice in the nineteenth century, for instance, had already censors with wide-ranging powers of control. Daigre (2004, p. 497 et seq.) observes:

> We like nothing better in France than to cloud the issue and to obscure business life as well as private life. In how companies operate, anyone who does not belong to the group of directors – which itself is made up of concentric circles – is the subject of mistrust, whether shareholders, employees, consumers or the State.

To this Guyon (1998) would add:

> Networks of influence, sometimes materialized by internal checks, (which) have enabled certain socio-professional groups to take over the boards of directors of large corporations, so that tolerance, complaisance or compromise have replaced the vigilance that we should expect among shareholder representatives.

The mid-1990s saw a deepening and an acceleration of the acceptance of the mechanisms of CG due to four main factors: the rapid globalization of financial markets, the internationalization of investors in the Paris stock market, privatizations and political-financial scandals concerning private corporations, as well as public corporations.

After the 1980s

We concentrate here on fours specific issues. The first is the importation of an economic system (United States system) based on financial markets supremacy and the unchallenged trust placed in them. The second is the crisis shaking up this system itself, as can be seen from financial scandals. French privatizations, especially starting in 1993, have encouraged an unprecedented influx of foreign investors to French exchanges due to the lack of domestic investment, demonstrating thus a weakness in the capitalization of the French market. Finally the aging of the French population has pushed for the creation of pension funds and alike.

The 1990s were also marked by an acceleration in corporate concentrations through the use of takeover bids, etc. The years 2002–2003 were, for example, marked by a wave of new financial scandals concerning large listed corporations (Rhodia, etc.), and record debt levels (Vivendi, France Télécom, etc.). But references to CG in France were even stronger, notably under the impetus of various bodies across the Atlantic, such as the American Law Institute. The year 2004 and the beginning of 2005 witnessed other listed companies in CG crisis: the Shell group, for example, was fined £17 million for having over-evaluated its oil reserves.

Moreover, the amplification of the use of CG concepts also results from the increasingly pressing activism of minority shareholders and associations of minority shareholders whose most recent illustrations in France include:

i The refusal of the demand from the Association de Défense des Action-naires Minoritaires (Minority Shareholder Defense Association – ADAM, a minority shareholder defense association led by Colette Neuville, acting against Vivendi Universal), on 7 June 2002, by the Commercial Court of Paris, tending toward designating an expert "in futurum" (Bull. Joly 2002, August–September 2002, p. 942 et seq., paragraph 212); and

ii the acceptance by the Commercial Court of Paris, in a ruling dated 3 December 2003, on the case filed by the Eurotunnel Shareholder Defense Association (ADACTE) tending toward calling a general shareholders' meeting in order to revoke the entire board of directors, even though in this case there was little chance that the minority shareholders could actually achieve the revocation of the entire board due to the small percentage of voting rights brought together (approximately 7.99 percent according to the bailiff's report) (JCP. E 2004, II, 71, note by A. Viandier).

But financial scandals and minority shareholder activism are not enough to explain the importance gained by CG in French law. It is also necessary to point out debates concerning compensation for executives,[2] notably when stock options are granted, despite their liabilities, or even their incompetence. Above and beyond these various factors, it can mainly be seen that the recent scandals are the result of the breakdown of audit systems, whether internal (shareholders, boards, committees, etc.) or external (auditors, accountants, etc.).

Overview of legal sources and studies

The introduction and transposition of CG and the resulting debates can be seen in the various studies and legal sources dedicated to subject, as well as to external legal borrowings and progress made in French law.

Reports and studies on CG

Company law has been the subject of many reports, either domestic or European, from professional organizations or from official institutions since the mid-1990s. The understanding of the evolution of French company law today cannot be made without understanding the influence of the European Union (EU). Internal reports dedicated to or targeting the concepts of CG, chronologically include:

  i Viénot report I, CNPF and Association Française des Entreprises Privées (French Association of Private Businesses – AFEP), July 1995, titles Le board of directors des sociétés cotées (The Board of Directors in Listed Companies);
 ii Marini report, 1996, on the modernization of company law;
iii Viénot report II, Mouvement des Entreprises de France (Movement of French Businesses – MEDEF) and AFEP, July 1999, titled Rapport du comité sur le corporate governance (Report by the Committee on Corporate Governance);
 iv Bouton report, MEDEF, AFEP, AGREF, September 2002, titled Pour un meilleur gouvernement des entreprises cotées (For Better Governance in Listed Companies);
  v The report by the Institut Montaigne, March 2003, titled Mieux gouverner l'entreprise (Governing Companies Better);
 vi The report by the Cercle des économistes, May 2003, titled Le gouvernement d'entreprise n'est pas du seul ressort du board of directors (Corporate Governance is not just the Board of Director's Business);
vii The report by Pascal Clément, MP, December 2003, which was the result of the work of a French National Assembly fact-finding mission on La réforme du droit des sociétés (Company Law Reform);
viii MEDEF, in May 2003 and May 2004, published a report from its Ethics Committee on Rémunération des dirigeants d'entreprise, mandataires sociaux (Compensation for Corporate Executive and Managing Agents);
 ix The "European Corporate Governance Service," an association of eight national organizations, including Proxinvest in France, published its "Corporate Governance Principles for Listed Companies" in 2004;

x The "Association Française de la Gestion Financière" published an updated version of its CG recommendations in March 2004.

Besides internal reports, international organizations have also published reports or documents focused on CG. We could mention as examples:

i A report in November 2000 from the Korn/Ferry International company titled Gouvernement d'Entreprise 2000 – Deux visions de la démocratie d'entreprise, la France et l'Allemagne (Corporate Governance 2000 – Two Views of Corporate Democracy, France and Germany);

ii The publication in January 2004 of the OECD's Principles of Corporate Governance, modernized version of the principles published in 1999;

iii The publication in December 2003 of a report on small, and medium-sized enterprises and corporate governance by Grant Thornton France.

Action by the EU, on the other hand, has only recently translated into various documents. It was not until November 2002 that European institutions integrated CG into their reflections on the future desirable evolution of company law.

i On 27 March 2002, the European Commission's Directorate for the Internal Market published a comparative study of Codes of Corporate Governance concerning the EU and its member states;

ii On 4 November 2002, the report from the High-Level Advisory Group on company law, created on 4 September 2001, titled "A modern regulatory framework for European company law concerning company law and corporate governance;"

iii On 21 May 2003, the European Commission published a communication to the Council and Parliament dated 21 May 2003 titled "Modernization of Company Law and Reinforcement of Corporate Governance in the European Union – A Plan for Progress;"

iv On 10 October 2003, the Commission published a communication to the Council and the European Parliament to reinforce legal control over accounts in the EU;

v On 23 February 2004, the Commission undertook consultations on executive compensation;

vi On 26 April 2004, the Commission launched consultations on the responsibilities of the board of directors and on improving information in financial and CG matters;

vii On 23 July 2004, the Directorate-General for the Internal Market published a working paper on strengthening the role of non-executive members of the board of directors and members of the supervisory board;

viii These two consultations, as well as the working paper, were recently the subject of two recommendations from the Commission (see No. 24);

ix On 16 September 2004, the Commission launched a public consultation on shareholder rights.

All of these reports and studies, whatever their origin may be, have led to a substantial modification of French company law in order to take into account, or even to comply with, the Anglo-Saxon world's precepts of CG.

Legal sources relative to CG

Reports and studies mentioned have influenced the evolution of French company law starting in the middle of the 1990s. In fact, either most of the time for ideological reasons, or for practical reasons, more rarely, French company law is "law in perpetual movement" whose legibility and comprehension are increasingly difficult, both for practitioners and for academics. The successive changes made to it have simply produced a successive stratification with no method of common reflection or common objectives. On this point, it can be asserted that the analysis of French company law requires researching the method of discourse before understanding "the discourse on method!"

The main legislative interventions taking CG into account have come about as follows:

  i Law No. 1996–597 of 2 July 1996 on the modernization of financial activities;
  ii Law No. 99–532 of 25 June 1999 relative to savings and financial security;
  iii Order No. 2000–912 of 18 September 2000 codifying the Legislative part of the Commercial Code;
  iv Order No. 2000–1233 of 14 December 2000 codifying the Legislative part of the Monetary and Financial Code;
  v Law No. 2001–152 of 19 February 2001 on save-as-you-earn schemes;
  vi Law No. 2001–420 of 15 May 2001 relative to new economic regulations;
  vii Law No. 2002–73 of 17 January 2002 on social modernization;
  viii Law No. 2002–1303 of 29 October 2002 modifying certain provisions of the Commercial Code relative to terms of corporate office;
  ix Law No. 2003–706 of 1 August 2003 relative to financial security;
  x Order No. 2004–604 of 24 June 2004 reforming the rules governing securities issued by commercial enterprises.

European texts concerning company law and CG include:

  i Commission Recommendation of 16 May 2002 titled "Statutory Auditors' Independence in the EU: A Set of Fundamental Principles;"
  ii The European Commission Action Plan of 21 May 2003 titled "Modernizing of Company Law and Enhancing Corporate Governance in the European Union – A Plan to Move Forward;"
  iii Directive 2003/58/EC of 15 July 2003 as regards disclosure requirements in respect of certain types of companies;
  iv Directive 2003/71/EC of 4 November 2003 on the prospectus to be published when securities are offered to the public or admitted to trading;

  v Directive 2004/25/EC of 21 April 2004 on takeover bids;
 vi Directive 2004/72/EC of 29 April 2004 implementing Directive 2003/6/EC
    of the European Parliament and of the Council as regards accepted market
    practices, the definition of inside information in relation to derivatives on
    commodities, the drawing up of lists of insiders, the notification of man-
    agers' transactions and the notification of suspicious transactions;
 vii Regulation (EC) 809/2004 of 29 April 2004 implementing Directive
    2003/71/EC of the European Parliament and of the Council as regards
    information contained in prospectuses as well as the format, incorporation
    by reference and publication of such prospectuses and dissemination of
    advertisements;
viii Commission Recommendation of 6 October 2004 on fostering an appropri-
    ate regime for the remuneration of directors of listed companies;
 ix Commission Recommendation of 6 October 2004 on the role of non-
    executive or supervisory directors and on the committees of the board of
    directors or supervisory board;
  x Directive 2004/109/EC of 15 December 2004 on the harmonization of
    transparency requirements in relation to information about issuers whose
    securities are admitted to trading on a regulated market.

From the viewpoint of French legal analysis, CG covers three basic themes:

   i the functioning of the board of directors;
  ii corporate management;
 iii the rights of shareholders and the role of general meetings.

But, in reality, these three themes must be extended to other concepts which will concern the operations of companies and financial markets: internal and external company audits, financial transparency and, more recently, corporate social responsibility.

Functioning of the board

While the reforms made to the board of directors have several causes, the essential cause is related to the spirit of the law of 24 July 1966. At the time, this law could not foresee, as is necessary today, the problems that would arise from the question of powers within corporations as well as the very strong link that has been formed over the years between the market and power structure(s). Along-side this general cause, there is a series of other criticisms all related to the problem of the ineffectiveness of the board of directors, which has been denounced since the beginning of the twentieth century:

   i The first of them is mainly based on the fact that boards are made up of the
    same people, which some people describe as "colonization" or "consan-
    guinity," this concentration having been made possible by the procedures

of reciprocal shareholding and cooptation, thus leading to a lack of critiques of managerial action.

ii   The second criticism of the board of directors is that it operates as a rubber stamp body for the chairman's decisions, which is the result of the board's closed character, for the reasons mentioned above. And today, one might wonder whether the board of directors has not become a rubber stamp body for the demands of the majority shareholders ... The most important consequence of this passivity of the board is the absence of any oversight over policy or the strategy implemented by the managers in charge of the everyday management of the corporation.

iii   The third criticism of the board of directors concerns information for board members. Indeed, even though the board of directors is first and foremost a collegial body, the legislator has not organized a mechanism for informing board members.

iv   The fourth criticism traditionally mentioned against the board of directors is that it tends to be more concerned with the interests of its members (=directors) and majority shareholders than with those of the company, a corporate entity with its own interests, or those of minority shareholders. On this point, the practices of "golden hellos" and "golden parachutes" are topical in this criticism.

As a remedy to these criticisms, several ideas for changes have been proposed. Some are the result of the intervention of "hard law" legislators; others come from recommendations for practices or organizations which have taken up the subject of CG, to the point of creating what is called "soft law." Without distinguishing between the legislator's intervention and non-intervention, it is possible to group together the changes made in several themes: the makeup of the board, how the board operates, multiple directorships and the creation of committees to assist the board in exercising its duties.

The question of the makeup of the board of directors is linked to the fact that it is accused of being a simple rubber stamp body and of being mainly made up of directors who know each other and help each other out because of reciprocal shareholdings between groups of companies, thus leading to consanguinity and, consequently, a lack of critical thinking and freedom of judgment.

The demands in this area have mainly consisted in opening up the board of directors, notably by reinforcing the interdiction of multiple directorships (see No. 66 et seq.), but especially by including independent directors and integrating employees into the structure.

The legislator, however, has also acted in another field to give meaning to the operations of the board of directors by reducing the maximum ceiling for directors from 24 to 18 members (NRE law, 15 May 2002). This provision was justified by the Minister of Justice at the time in order to forbid plethoric boards of directors in the future, to strengthen the supervisory role of the board of directors and to take into account the limitation on multiple directorships (see No. 66 et seq.).

The notion of director as evoked today in the French debate on CG in no way corresponds to that initially envisaged. Actually, the first demands for the presence of independent directors came from minority shareholders who wanted them to represent a certain category of shareholders. But this claim was rejected as it was considered dangerous for the company's operations. Indeed, there is a clearly identified risk that representing category interests might keep the company from operating correctly, such as conflicts of interest between majority and minority shareholders which can block, or make more difficult, the adoption of deliberations by the general shareholders' meeting.

The notion of independent director, furthermore, is often falsely presented as a way of transposing into French law the distinction that is prevalent in laws in the Anglo-Saxon world between "executive directors" (EDs) and "non-executive directors" (NEDs). In the model of the Anglo-Saxon world, the distinction between EDs and NEDs consists in distinguishing the members of the board of directors with executive functions from those who do not have any. But in French law, this justification poses a problem. These notions cannot be understood in the same way in France for the simple reason that French law distinguishes, in principle, between the functions of director and general manager. Moreover, a general manager is not necessarily a director and the directors are not necessarily general managers, so that the reference to this criterion of executive functions is not the most relevant.

The latest figures available in France[3] on this subject show that the majority of listed companies have appointed independent directors to their boards of directors. These appointments, however, are still considered to be largely insufficient, since it appears that the number of independent directors does not exceed one-third of all directors.

Another problem that is not taken into account by those in favor of a reinforcement of the presence of independent directors on boards of directors deals with the way in which they are appointed. In practice, no one knows whether there are several candidates for a position and how the official candidates are selected. This lack of transparency could, and does, lead us to imagine that directors are not all that independent. One way of remedying this lack of transparency would be to undertake the appointment of independent directors at the general shareholders' meeting after selection of the candidate(s) by a selection committee. Often in practice, this is made up of the chairman of the board of directors and other directors (three or four) and at least one independent director.

On 6 October 2004, the European Commission, in a follow-up to the action plan it published in May 2003, considered that the board of directors should include a fair proportion of executive and non-executive directors in order to avoid one person or a small group of people dominating the decision-making process within the board of directors. Including independent directors on the board of directors poses many other problems for companies from the viewpoint of French law. Employee representation already exists in corporations through two mechanisms:

i   The first, calls for optional employee representation (L. 225–27 of the Commercial Code), in that it is up to the articles of association, and, therefore, the general shareholders' meeting, to foresee that directors elected by all employees should sit on the board of directors with voting rights in a number which shall not exceed four (non-listed company) or five (listed company) nor exceed one-third of the number of other directors. The presence of employees was also called for in privatized companies (laws of 6 August 1986 and 25 July 1994).

ii   The second requires the convocation and presence of two members of the works committee, appointed by the works committee, at all meetings of the board of directors or supervisory board. But these two members of the works committee attend the meetings in an advisory capacity only (article L. 432–6, paragraph 1, of the Labor Code).

There was therefore no obligatory employee participation with voting rights. This was the contribution made by the laws of 19 February 2001 and 17 January 2002: obligatory salary participation on company boards with voting rights. The laws of 19 February 2001 and 17 January 2002 created a third regime of employee representation depending on the percentage of share capital held by the employees in the context of shareholder plans set at 3 percent of the share capital. The law of 19 February 2001 called for the optional appointment to the board of directors or the supervisory board of one or more shareholder employee representatives at the general shareholders' meeting.

Three other proposals for change have also been put forward concerning the composition of the board of directors: the feminization of the board of directors, the presence of creditors on the board of directors and the presence of minority shareholders on the board of directors.

Although the seating of creditors on the board of directors may seem to be an interesting solution given the financial and managerial skills of the banks, we should not underestimate the problems of possible conflicts of interest between the role of creditor and the obligation of loyalty related to the position of board member. Thus, contrary to Institut Montaigne, which decided not to take sides on this issue, it would seem preferable for the creditor bank not to be allowed to become a director due to the significant risk of its privileging its own interests as a creditor over the interests of the company and its shareholders. At most, the creditor bank could be a shareholder in the company. In this second case, the creditor bank would be faced with the other shareholders, who could either back its viewpoint, or block it by opposing its desires.

Traditional demand from minority shareholders and shareholder defense associations has not been enshrined in law by the legislator. In practice, however, some chairmen of listed companies have invited representatives of these shareholder defense associations to sit on the board of directors, such as Madame Colette Neuville, chairwoman of the Minority Shareholder Defense Association (ADAM – Association de Défense des Actionnaires Minoritaires). While this claim indeed takes into account the interests of minority shareholders, which are often in opposition to those of the majority shareholders, insofar as the board of directors collectively represents all shareholders, it is problematic since the risk of transferring to the board of directors the opposing interests which exist in the general shareholders' meetings, thus judicializing the operations of the board of directors.

If the inclusion of the principles of CG in French law has improved the composition of boards of directors, it has also changed and modernized the operations of the boards in depth. All of these changes were inspired by the concepts of CG. The legislator's efforts in this area have been concentrated on the strict separation of powers between the board of directors, the chairman of the board and the general manager, as well as the improvement of the board's operations. Before the law of 15 May 2001, the legislation in the law of 24 July 1966 called for the board of directors, the chairman of the board and the general manager to be vested with the widest powers to act in the company's name under all circumstances. This resulted in confusion in terms of powers and consequently legal insecurity for third parties seeking to contract with the company. The changes in fact clarified the missions of the board of directors while assigning it a function of discussion and supervision, thus trying to turn the board of directors into a body to oversee the actions of those who act in the company's name and to institute a better balance of power within the traditional corporation.

Improving the operations of the board of directors has translated into the attribution of new missions to the board of directors through a reform in the legal status of the agreements signed between the company and one of its managers, as well as by the insertion into company law of information and communication technologies (ICT). All of these changes, however, leave a certain malaise for some in terms of legal analysis because of excessively frequent changes and unclear concepts which are increasingly adopted by the legislator.

Following these various legal changes, the board of directors now has new general powers and special powers. The general powers deal with how the company is managed. They concern determining the orientations of the company's activities, the settling of questions affecting the company's smooth operation and any checks and verifications considered necessary. As for determining the orientations of the company's activities, the legislature certainly did not make the board of directors a competitor with the general management. Consequently, this should be understood simply as the power to set the general orientations that the general management should then carry out.

Concerning the settling of questions affecting the company's smooth operations, deliberating on such affairs does not make it a body which can act in the company's name. It is just the simple, logical consequence of being able to set strategic orientations for the company. What would be the point of setting strategic orientations if the board of directors then has no power over the general management? An example of possible deliberations by the board of directors on this point could be the revocation of a general manager who does not follow the objectives assigned to him. Another example could be the decision to undertake a capital increase to be able to finance a precise strategy. This is, therefore, the first part of a supervisory mission, and not a power of external company representation with third parties.

As for the useful checks and verifications that it undertakes, this new function is the clear manifestation of the supervisory mission it now has. It is a question of a "veritable counterweight" that has been created, which is sure to rebalance the exercise of power in the corporation and strengthen the effectiveness of its operations. The principal merit of this supervisory power is consequently to clearly indicate the rights and obligations of the directors who make up the board (see No. 60 et seq.).

Agreements signed with the company often deal with the existence of conflicts of interest which could be harmful to the company. On this point, it suffices to mention the practice which consists, for many managers reaching "retirement age," in having the company pay for their pensions or pension supplements. In this situation, there is a real risk of collusion between the remaining directors and the person retiring, the goal being to grant an undeserved pension supplement to the detriment of the company. To prevent this type of situation, and more generally to avoid having the company used for personal gain, the legislator created, in the law of 24 July 1966, a distinction between forbidden agreements (borrowing money from the company, for example), common agreements signed under normal conditions (not subject to any supervision) and regulated agreements which are covered by special procedures.

The law of 15 May 2001

The law of 15 May 2001 therefore widened the scope of application for the system implemented previously. Concretely, the changes deal with regulated agreements and common agreements signed under normal conditions.

i   Concerning regulated agreements and common agreements signed under normal conditions, the scope of application of the regulations applicable to these agreements was extended to shareholders holding more than 5 percent of the voting rights as well as to agreements signed between the company and the manager of another company.
ii Concerning common agreements signed under normal conditions, the legislator imposed an obligation, under the responsibility of the interested party (manager or director) for the notification of said agreements to the board of directors and the shareholders.

Although it really was a constraint, the system thus implemented, nonetheless, prevented conflicts of interest, a major theme of CG. Lobbying by professional organizations such as the MEDEF (Mouvement des Entreprises de France – Movement of French Businesses), enabled them to obtain more flexibility in the system of these agreements in the law of 1 August 2003, called the financial security law.

The law of 15 May 2001 allowed the board of directors to hold its meetings by videoconferencing if the company's articles of association so stipulate. Directors can therefore take part in and vote at board meetings without being physically present at the meeting place. This possibility is, however, limited to the least important decisions. It, therefore, excludes deliberations on closing the corporate accounts and consolidated accounts, the appointment and revocation of the chairman or of the general manager. In keeping with what is now possible for shareholders if they so accept, it is possible to include in the articles of association that the directors can be convoked by e-mail, which will make convocation itself easier. Here again, the use of ICT procedures is far from being contrary to the concepts of CG. The AFEP/MEDEF/ANSA report of October 2003[4] advocates leaving the possibility to the shareholders to "determine the means of remote transmission which may be used for meetings of the board of directors, as well as the decisions for which this method of meeting could be excluded."

The legislator has also changed the legal status of directors, and significantly so. To take CG into account, the interventions undertaken cover three areas: directors' rights and obligations, directors' responsibility and the internal rules of the board of directors accompanied by the directors' charter.

Directors' rights

Directors' rights changed following the modification of the board of directors' missions, notably their right to information. From now on, directors have a legally enshrined right to information. Before the law of 15 May 2001, directors' right to information was the result of jurisprudence (Cass. com., 2 July 1985, JCP E, II, 14758, A. Couret; Cass. com., 24 April 1990, Rev. Sociétés 1991, 347, P. Didier; Cass. com., 8 October 2002, Dr. Sociétés 2003, No. 36, H. Hovasse). The mechanism created by the judges called for an individual right to information whose nullity would lead to the nullity of any acts and deliberations adopted during the board meeting. This individual right to information was prior to the meeting of the board of directors and portable, that is to say that the information had to be supplied by the chairman of the board either by sending it or by making it available.

The law of 15 May 2001 enshrined this mechanism in article L. 225–25 of the Commercial Code, which called for "each director to receive all information necessary for fulfilling his mission and to have transmitted to him all documents he considers useful." This right to information therefore concerns all of his missions and not just his supervisory mission, and is twofold: it is spontaneous, as the director does not need to ask for the information; but it can also be the result of a request by the director to the chairman of the board of directors, who is free to assess the need for transmitting documents if the request has no other aim than to harm the company's interests or is abusive. The law of 15 May 2001, however, did not indicate who held the obligation to provide the information, although it was logical that this should not be the chairman of the board of directors, nor did it indicate the penalty if this obligation is not fulfilled. This solution was not without risk, however, since the information could also be held by other persons: the general manager, the auditors or the bodies representing the personnel.

The law of 1 August 2003, which was supposed to remedy the shortcomings of the text of 2001, actually restricted directors' individual right to information. While the person who holds this obligation is now identified (chairman of the board of directors or general manager), it eliminated the directors' right to request documents they consider useful. Furthermore, it still does not solve the problem of information held by persons other than those indicated in the legal text.

Directors' obligations

In the terms of the corporate governance doctrine, directors are responsible for a fourfold "requirement of diligence, competence, loyalty and good faith." These requirements, accordingly should not be considered in the same way in all companies.[5] Quite the contrary, whether or not the company is listed should be taken into account. The reinforcement of the directors' obligations translates in reality into an increased exigency in their responsibilities, at least in theory. According to the concepts of CG, director accountability entails several changes of different types depending on whether the proposal comes from the European Union (EU) or French legislators. The proposals are based on three essential ideas and come from the European Commission Action Plan (21 May 2003) integrating the recommendations from the High-Level Group of Company Law Experts (4 November 2002):

i   introduction of a right to special investigation, under which shareholders may ask a judge for a special investigation into company affairs (European Commission Action Plan);

ii   elaboration of a rule on punishable negligence for "wrongful trading" under which directors could be held personally responsible for the consequences of the company's fault if it was foreseeable that the company was no longer able to continue to cover its debts and if they, nonetheless, abstained from deciding to bring it back to viability or to undertake winding up of the company by a court ruling (European Commission Action Plan);

iii imposition of a ban on exercising the position of director in the EU as a penalty against supplying false financial or other information and other forms of harmful behavior by directors (European Commission Action Plan).

The various measures called for by the European Commission Action Plan are not unknown in French law, the right to investigation being similar to management consulting, punishable negligence, actions for the coverage of liabilities, the ban on holding the position of director for personal bankruptcy or the ban on managing.

The report by the High-Level Group of Company Law Experts included a new legal element, not taken up in the European Commission Action Plan, which, while not unknown in French company law, has a wider scope than what existed in France. According to the group's work, directors must be collectively responsible for everything concerning the annual and consolidated accounts, but also for all statements concerning the company's financial situation, including quarterly income statements, and non-financial information, notably the annual statement of CG. The new aspect of this collective responsibility relates not to the annual accounts, but to financial statements.

Internal rules of the board of directors

Internal rules are not imposed by the Commercial Code, although this question did come up during the debates that preceded the adoption of the law of 15 May 2001 on new economic regulations, for which the draft bill had called for imposing the drafting and publication of internal regulations of the board of directors. The law of 15 May 2001 merely mentioned it in several articles. The COB (Commission des Opérations de Bourse, the French equivalent of the US Securities and Exchange Commission), now called the Autorité des Marchés Financiers – Financial Markets Authority (AMF), however, filled in part of this legal vacuum in its 2001 instruction requiring that "particular provisions concerning directors (charter, internal regulations, etc.)" be mentioned in the reference document drawn up by listed companies. It should be immediately pointed out that only listed companies are covered by this requirement, which further widens the dissociation between listed companies and those which are not listed.

Formalizing regulations for the board of directors is also accepted and recommended by all organizations. It can be considered that, in the case of an accident, managers could be exposed to a civil liability suit. Another penalty could result from agencies' taking into account the "ethical" rating of this criterion as a particularly important characteristic in making the decision to invest in a given company. A market penalty is also possible, although it should not be overestimated.

It is up to the board of directors to draw up its own internal regulations. If the articles of association impose the drafting of such regulations, however, they may lay down their contents more or less precisely by listing the main headings that they cover. This is not without legal effects, contrary to what certain directors have sometimes thought. It is in fact binding for the board of directors and its members. Disclosure of the internal regulations is not dealt with by the Commercial Code. The COB instruction of December 2001, however, requires that the rules of operation governing the company's administrative, management and supervisory bodies be presented in the reference document drawn up by listed companies.

If the internal regulations are withheld, an appraisal of article 145 of the New Code of Civil Procedure (NCCP) will no doubt enable the shareholder to learn of its content, if necessary by obtaining a restraining order.

Legal analysis of the directors' charter poses a problem in that it could be considered that it is a contract signed by each director individually with the company and/or shareholders, or that it is just a simple unilateral commitment by each director, who can be sanctioned in case of breach due to tort liability or quasi-contractual liability. Above and beyond these questions, it is certain that, like internal regulations, it is binding to the directors alone and any breach is subject to civil sanctions. Along with the reform of the operations of the board of directors, the legislator, to take into account the consanguinity among boards of directors, has also reformed the rules for multiple directorships.

Multiple directorships

This reform was carried out in three stages, in such a way that it removed all logic and clarity from the provisions in place. A first change was undertaken in the law of 15 May 2001, which seriously restricted the possibility of multiple directorships and called for very strict penalties if this rule is not followed. A law of 29 October 2002 loosened the rules governing multiple directorships in the sole goal of responding to the pressing demands from professional organizations, such as MEDEF, AFEP (Association Française des Entreprises Privées – French Association of Private Businesses), etc. And, if that was not enough, the financial security law of 1 August 2003 also added to the perpetual movement in multiple directorships. While it is certain that, for the smooth operation of boards of directors, the possibilities for multiple directorships must be restricted, thus opening up the boards, the back-and-forth method used by the legislators, for purely political considerations, should be sharply condemned due to the legal insecurity that it causes and the complexity that it adds in the application and analysis of legal provisions.

Multiple directorships are the result of a desire to monopolize power as well as the absence of a social status for directors. Thus, if we want to reduce the possibilities for multiple directorships, should we not create a social status for directors? This would make the function of director more attractive. Along the same lines, should companies not plan for continuing education for directors to enable them to operate in a legal environment that is increasingly complex?

Most of the recommendations for CG call for the boards of directors to be assisted in making certain decisions by committees which are supposed to provide special enlightenment.

Board committees

The creation of specialized committees is one of the major objectives of the principles of CG. This creation could make the boards more effective, insofar as their decisions would be prepared in advance by the committees. With the existence of these specialized committees, investors would be reassured that decisions are made in the interest of company management and profitability. All recommendations call for the creation of an audit committee, a remuneration committee and an appointment committee. More recently, company managers appear to have rediscovered the usefulness of an advisory censor.

The principles taken from CG call for the creation of at least three committees: an audit committee, a remuneration committee and an appointment committee. Some companies have preferred to add a fourth committee: the strategy committee. It is therefore necessary first to examine the legal framework of these specialized committees before studying the powers of each of them and attempting to determine the responsibilities applicable to them. The creation of specialized committees does not pose any particular legal problem insofar as the decree of 23 March 1967 laid down the existence of some of them in article 90, paragraph 2, according to which: "The board of directors may decide to create committees in charge of studying questions submitted by itself or by its chairman for recommendations after their examination. It sets the composition and attributes of the committees, which perform their activity under its responsibility." Under French law, the legal framework may be set as follows:

i   specialized committees are not mandatory;

- their creation and their composition are under the responsibility of the board of directors;
- they only have an advisory role, article 90 paragraph 2 of the decree using the term opinion;

ii   the board of directors is responsible for their activities.

The composition of specialized committees is the subject of convergence for certain points and divergence for others. Opinions converge on the fact that they must be made up of directors and non-directors. Shareholders can therefore be included. Here again, the response to this possibility converges in that it is preferable not to include non-director shareholders, due to a break in the equality between member shareholders on these committees and non-member shareholders. Another question is that of desirability of the presence of the chairman of the board of directors. According to Professor Y. Guyon, it appears difficult for the chairman to accept that most important specialized committees are outside his control. But at the same time, once again according to Professor Guyon, the presence of the chairman reduces the independence and consequently the usefulness of these bodies.

For concision's sake, we will only examine the audit, remuneration and appointment committees.

Audit committees

Also called accounts committees, these have two basic missions: management control and verification of the reliability and clarity of the information to be supplied to the shareholders and markets. But their mission is "less to go into the details of the accounts than to appreciate the reliability of the devices used to draw them up." It is preferable for the accounts committees also to look into important operations from which conflicts of interest could occur. To truly carry out its mission, the accounts committees should be able to meet those who contribute to drawing up the accounts: statutory auditors, financial managers, etc. Lastly, after performing its mission, it must report to the board of directors.

In its composition, the principles of CG lay down that it should be made up in part by directors, but should also have a majority of independent directors.[6]

Remuneration committees

These are in charge of proposing remuneration for corporate officers. For the system to be effective, a wide concept of remuneration is needed, this wide acceptance of the notion of remuneration being used to take into account directors' fees, reimbursements of expenses, exceptional remunerations and share purchase or subscription plans (stock options).

Here again, to reinforce their legitimacy, the principles of CG recommend that the remuneration committees should be made up of a majority of independent directors and reciprocal directors should be avoided.

However, the Proxinvest 2004 report on management remuneration in listed companies is not optimistic as to the role of remuneration committees. Their rate of existence has not grown since 2003, their independence is still weak, although increasing, and the controls exercised by remuneration committees have not frankly improved in recent years (Proxinvest press release dated 1 December 2004).

Appointment committees

Also called selection committees, their mission is to propose to the board of directors the names of candidates that they have selected after examining a certain number of criteria, such as the makeup of the board, the possible representation of category interests, the search for and appreciation of possible candidates and opportunities for renewing mandates.

They should, therefore, implement a recruitment procedure to be able to give an informed opinion to the board of directors. It is even possible for these committees to use "headhunters" who will propose an initial selection of candidates, with it being up to them to choose potential candidates upon examination of the applications selected.

The principles of CG recommend that appointment committees be made up of at least one-third independent directors. In analogical application of a ruling handed down by the commercial chamber of the Cour de Cassation (France's court of last resort) on 4 July 1995, (JCP 1995, II, 22560, note Y. Guyon, Rev. Sociétés 1995, p. 504, note P. Le Cannu), these committees have only advisory authority. They cannot make any decisions in the board of directors' place. In the affair in question, an ad hoc commission had granted the chairman of the board of directors a pension supplement, which it did not have the right to do, since remuneration, including pension supplements, is part of the exclusive powers of the board of directors or comes under regulated agreement procedures.

The second consequence of this advisory authority is that the committees must obey the legal rules of devolution of powers within the company and thus follow the hierarchical system laid down by the Cour de Cassation in a ruling on 4 June 1946.

The recent principles of CG recommend the creation of a charter for these specialized committees; which should be included in the internal regulations of the board of directors and which would be relative to their operations and powers.

The responsibility of the specialized committees poses a problem in that the principles of CG require that they be made up of directors from the board and independent directors from outside the board. Do they have civil and penal liability? It is certain that the independent directors cannot be held responsible on the basis of the texts that apply to the directors as they are not themselves directors. Moreover, directors on a specialized committee exercise a mission outside the board of directors, so it is not possible to apply to them the general legal liability of directors. All of these questions need to be answered, and as there has been no litigation in this area, the jurist can do little more than prognosticate on the outcome.

Company management

One of the essential points of the corporate governance doctrine is the call for the dissociation of the functions of general manager and chairman of the board of directors. This dissociation of functions is not the equivalent of the situation in companies in the English-speaking world, which aims at dissociating the functions of "directors" and "officers." "Directors," under the direction of the "Chairman of the Board," have a supervisory function over the "officers" who, under the direction of the "Chief Executive Officer" (CEO), ensure the day-to-day administration of the company. In France, the objective of the dissociation is to separate, insofar as possible, the function of chairman of the board of directors and the function of general manager. And for certain authors, the dissociation of functions in France corresponds less to an objective of transparency and clarification than to an objective of freedom in the organization of the corporation. This dissociation has, however, provided a certain degree of clarification among functions and, more precisely, the missions of the general manager and the chairman of the board of directors. The second advance in the application of the concepts of CG concerns manager remuneration.

Long a taboo subject kept in the dark, managers' pay slips have been a source of heated debate. For companies experiencing difficulties, how can pay increases for the managers be justified when the employees are being laid off and minority shareholders are receiving reduced dividends. Thanks to the demands of trade unions and shareholder associations, legislators have finally made manager remuneration more transparent.

Redefinition of management functions

The redefinition of functions is clearly the result of French law's taking CG concepts into account. This holds true for all companies, without making a distinction between listed companies and non-listed companies. Now, the chairman of the board of directors directs and organizes the board's work, draws up a report included in the annual report, explaining the conditions behind the preparation and organization of the board's work and the internal audit procedures implemented by the company, and oversees the smooth operations of the company's management bodies. The general manager is the person who holds the widest powers to act under all circumstances in the company's name, a power that is nonetheless limited by the object of the company, by the powers granted to the shareholders' meetings and by the powers specifically reserved to the board of directors.

The law of 15 May 2001 made the chairman of the board the representative of the board of directors. But the article setting the powers of the board of directors stated that "in relations with third parties, the company is responsible even by the acts of the board of directors which are not part of the object of the company." There was thus a risk that the chairman of the board could oppose the general manager. Since the law of 1 August 2003, the chairman of the board of directors no longer represents the board of directors. From the point of view of legal analysis, however, this representation was not a bad idea: it stated that the chairman of the board of directors had a power of internal representation and the general manager a power of external representation. This dissociation between the power of internal and external representation further clarified the functions of the chairman of the board and the general manager. Along with dissociating management functions, the legislator, taking CG into account, also modified the rules concerning the disclosure of manager remuneration.

Disclosure of manager remuneration

Before the law of 15 May 2001, shareholders only had a right to limited notification for questions of manager remuneration. In fact, they could not obtain the overall amount of the remunerations paid to the five or ten people with the highest earnings. This information was partial and problematic in that the terms of remuneration and the persons concerned were not defined. Moreover, the overall amount held little meaning. This opacity in remuneration had been decried since the mid-1990s, notably in English-speaking countries and by the Greenbury report, titled "Director's Remuneration."

In France, the disclosure of remunerations does not concern the individual amount of remunerations as much as the remuneration policy followed by the company (see the OECD report, 2004, p. 22). The law of 15 May 2001, under pressure from foreign investors, as well as from shareholder associations, imposed the disclosure of manager remuneration in the annual company management reports (article L. 225–102–1 of the Commercial Code). These reports, presented by the board of directors or the executive board to the general meeting, are supposed to report on the total remuneration and benefits paid during the accounting period to each corporate officer. It should also indicate the amount of the remunerations and benefits that each of these officers received during the accounting period from controlled companies.

The New Economic Regulations (NRE) law was accused of aiming at listed companies, as well as non-listed companies, even though in practice there is a difference in terms of remuneration. This criticism, while founded, should not hide the fact that, in a certain number of family-owned corporations, the managers grant themselves their own remuneration and do not hesitate to give themselves benefits that are sometimes comparable to those of the managers of listed companies. The second criticism concerns the mechanisms of the NRE law, which did not apply to the remunerations paid by the parent company to a representative in one of its subsidiaries. On this point, the criticisms were founded, since disclosure was truncated.

The law of 1 August 2003 changed the mechanism from the NRE law on two points. First, now, only listed companies have this disclosure requirement, non-listed companies having been excluded from this system. Non-listed subsidiaries of listed companies, however, are considered. The second change lies in the fact that the remunerations paid by the parent company to a representative in one of its subsidiaries should be included in the annual report on company management. The legislator did not, however, call for penalties if the annual management report does not contain this information. It is possible that the members of the board of directors or the supervisory board could be held liable, or that shareholders could ask written questions to the managers since it is, in principle, a question of management operations.

The order issued on 24 June 2004 imposed on the mechanism, discussed above, that total remuneration and benefits paid to each corporate officer also be disclosed, even when in the form of "allocation of equity capital, debt securities or securities granting access to the capital or rights to the allocation of debt securities of the company or companies mentioned in articles L. 228–13 and L. 228–93" of the Commercial Code. Here again, it is a question of gaining an overall view of company manager remuneration and, therefore, of encouraging transparency. Thus, all securities that mangers may receive must be taken into account in order to avoid their adopting a bypass strategy granting securities that are not required to be disclosed. Article L. 225–184 of the Commercial Code calls for disclosure to the general shareholders' meeting of stock options or share purchases granted or exercised by drawing up a special report from the board of directors concerning the option plans implemented. Disclosure concerns each corporate officer who benefits from stock options.

Even if the legal nature of the remuneration is questionable and questioned, it, nonetheless, contributes to constituting the assets of the manager who benefits from the agreement. Moreover, if these compensation agreements are actually illegal – revocation normally came without compensation, and if a text calls for compensation, this only concerns the case in which the revocation is undertaken without valid reason – judges have stated the conditions of validity for these agreements. In practice, this compensation may be at the expense of the company, a majority shareholder or a subsidiary, even if the judge considers that the agreement signed with the company or majority shareholder is invalid. In fact, this compensation is the result of a transaction organized between the revoked manager and the company through their respective legal counsel. This transaction is a purely private agreement that is not intended to be published or disclosed.

Consequently, due to their importance, and to fight against a certain lack of transparency, these compensation agreements should be disclosed in the annual report. This would avoid having certain managers decide to relinquish them only under media pressure or because the minority shareholders decide to look into this point.

The recent abandonment of the "dual" formula in foreign groups: lessons for the French law?

Alongside the corporation with a board of directors, French company law provides for a corporation with an executive board and a supervisory board. This setup, from the point of view of the need to dissociate functions, corresponds to CG expectations. As Professor Le Cannu has pointed out, a corporation with an executive board and a supervisory board clearly distinguishes between tasks, although certain textual arrangements are needed. We should point out, however, that "dual" corporations are far from being the majority in France. This observation can be illustrated by a certain number of structures which, since 2004, have been abandoning this type of organization. Thus, two major foreign groups, Unilever and Royal Dutch Shell, have decided to abandon a "dual" structure, with two chairmen, for a non-operational chairman and a general manager. The justification for this simplification is clearly linked to CG, as stated by A. Burgmans, the non-operational chairman of Unilever: "Since the Enron and Worldcom scandals, shareholders and financial authorities have been exercising greater influence over corporate governance than before".[7]

For legal analysis, this situation is not going to significantly increase the number of corporations with executive boards and supervisory boards in the near future. In fact, in structures with a simple board of directors, and with no real counterbalancing power, as illustrated in certain recent affairs (Vivendi Universal, France Telecom), it appears more than necessary to set up audit procedures, whether internal or external, and to reinforce shareholder rights.

Oversight methods for company management and the board

One of the recurrent criticisms against the board of directors and company management has concerned the lack of oversight exercised over these bodies' actions. In practice, there are multiple controls over these bodies since, while the traditional company management control is in the hands of the shareholders, control is also exercised by the auditors and the works committee. Moreover, the change in the distribution of powers between the board of directors and the general management has transformed the board of directors into an oversight body for the general management.

The legislators have intervened in the methods of oversight of the management and administration. Concretely, legal oversight has been reformed and the auditors have been made a nearly counterbalancing power vis-à-vis the management bodies. The recognized aim of all of these changes was to increase transparency in company operations, i.e. to "ensure the truthfulness of information."

Reform of the legal oversight of the accounts

The reform of legal oversight had already begun with the law of 15 May 2001, which had undertaken the unification of the status of auditors without distinguishing between a corporation or any other kind of company (general partnerships, simplified joint stock companies or limited partnerships).

The law on financial security of 1 August 2003 brought about an in-dept change in the legal oversight of accounts to take into account the scandal caused by the Enron affair and the progress made in CG. These two subjects perfectly demonstrated the lack of independence among auditors and the non-separation of audit functions and advisory functions. To reinforce the auditors' action, the legislator decided to modify the organization of the profession with the creation of a High Council of Statutory Auditors.

Statutory auditors

Schematically, the High Council of Statutory Auditors is an appellate judge for decisions handed down on the regional level for questions of registration and discipline. Moreover, it is supposed to oversee the profession, identifying and promoting good professional practices and issuing opinions on the professional standards drawn up by the Compagnie Nationale des Commissaires aux Comptes (CNCC; National Auditors Corporation) and defining the orientations and the framework for the audits that professionals undergo.

Beyond the new organization of the profession of auditor, the financial security law of 1 August 2003 developed possibilities for cooperation between these two stakeholders in CG. This cooperation will take shape in the obligation for auditors to inform the AMF of any fact or decision leading to a refusal of certification, sending it the written document transmitted to the heads of the company if the warning procedure is triggered and transmitting the report that they plan to present indicating any misstatements and irregularities. On the other hand, the auditors may request information from the AMF for any question encountered in the exercise of their function and which could have an effect on the entity's financial reporting. Reinforced independence is linked to several rules laid down by the financial security law of 1 August 2003:

i   separation of audit and consulting missions by forbidding the statutory auditor from providing the entity who appointed him to certify its accounts from providing any advice or services which are not directly linked to the auditor's mission;

ii   an auditor may not take, receive or hold, directly or indirectly, a stake in the entity for which he is in charge of certifying the accounts or an entity which has control of or is controlled by said entity;

iii an auditor may not be appointed manager of a company that he audits less than five years after the end of his functions, the opposite rule being applied to managers or employees of a corporate entity who seeks to be named auditor;

iv   an auditor may not certify the accounts of a corporate entity making public offerings for more than six consecutive fiscal years.

All of these new provisions are essentially aimed at avoiding having any phenomenon of the Enron type occurring in France, although the French rules, contrary to the American rules, are much stricter and are designed to keep this kind of thing from happening. A certain degree of vigilance should be observed in the future, however, with the application of the new International Financial Reporting Standards (IFRSs), some of which are quite similar to American accounting mechanisms.

New auditor–general management relations

These new relations can be seen in two areas. The first area concerns the certification of accounts. Before the law of 1 August 2003, auditors had to certify, refuse to certify or certify with reserves the audited company's accounts. The innovation of the financial security law lies in the fact that the auditors must justify their appreciations before the general shareholders' meeting. The second area concerns the special report that the auditor must draw up for the internal audit procedure. The financial security law states that auditors are to present, in a special report, their observations on internal audit procedures concerning the elaboration and processing of accounting and financial information. The parliamentary debates and comments relative to this new mission for auditors gives rise to twofold reserves as to the existence or non-existence of an auditor's responsibility on this level, as well as the auditor's report, for which it is not clear whether he should make an assessment or simply present his opinion of the chairman of the board's report.

Shareholders' rights

Shareholders, who make up the general shareholders' meeting, are one of the pillars of "Corporate Governance." The CG doctrine argues for an increase in the individual rights of shareholders, as well as for an increase in the powers of the general meeting. It is not illogical for the shareholder to be one of the centers of interest of CG, since the corporation is designed as a democracy in which power lies with the shareholders brought together in the general meeting. In practice, this representation is false since in small structures, there is often a single shareholder and, in listed groups, a huge majority of the shareholders to not take an interest in the life of the company. This lack of interest leads to two simple facts: absenteeism from the general meetings and the use of blank proxies.

It appears, however, that since the late 1990s, there has been a renewal in the general shareholders' meetings through a twofold movement: the reinforcement of shareholders' rights and the judicialization of the protection of shareholders' rights. This twofold movement is proof of the increasing power of shareholders. The passive shareholders have become active, either individually or collectively. From this point of view, the creation of shareholder associations is one of the key elements that has helped to rebalance the power struggle within corporations. In the Vivendi affair, the minority shareholder defense association (ADAM) played a central role; in the Eurotunnel affair, the shareholder defense association (ADACTE) brought down the management and had it replaced with a new management team. But another, equally fundamental element for the renewal of the general shareholders' meeting is the massive arrival of foreign investors, those famous pension funds, which have brought about a change in management's attitudes toward shareholders.

The main texts that have led to the strengthening of shareholders' rights are the laws of 15 May 2001 and 1 August 2003 and the order of 24 June 2004 reforming the securities regime. Behind this reinforcement of shareholder rights lies the reinforcement of transparency in how companies operate, of which the shareholders must be the primary beneficiaries, because they have the right, each year, to examine, approve or refuse the company's management. The shareholders are therefore the first controllers of the company's management. It is now possible to question the reality of shareholder control in companies, notably when looking at Vivendi Universal and France Télécom, which reached record levels of indebtedness without no reaction from the majority shareholders. Is there an unacceptable collusion between the interests of the management and those of the majority shareholders?

Shareholders' rights have been reinforced in several areas: shareholders' right to information, shareholders' voting rights, the modernization of general shareholders' meetings and legal action taken by shareholders and shareholder associations.

Shareholders' right to information

Shareholders' right to information is a traditional shareholder right enshrined in the law of 24 July 1966. There has long been a well-identified criticism of shareholder information, however, while shareholder information is plethoric, it is not sufficient and the documents transmitted either come late or are not transmitted at all. And yet, shareholder information is essential to making informed decisions at general meetings on how the management has done its job or on capital increases that are essential to the company's survival.

The essential character of shareholder information allowed the Cour de Cassation, in a case dealing with a capital reduction (equals reduction of the share capital to zero immediately followed a capital increase), to consider that shareholders who refuse to vote for a capital increase are not committing minority abuse if they had not received the information necessary to give informed consent (Cass. com., 27 May 1997 and Cass. com., 5 May 1998). The novelty actually lies in the reinforcement of shareholder information through new fields: environmental and societal information and information on the company's internal operations.

Obligation for information in listed companies

The creation of an obligation for environmental and societal information originated in the law of 15 May 2001. It included article L. 225–102–1, paragraph 4, which states that the report presented annually to the general meeting by the board of directors "reports on employee participation in the share capital on the last day of the fiscal year (...)," "and also includes information on how the company takes into account the social and environmental consequences of its activity." This obligation, which is only imposed on those companies whose shares are listed on the stock exchange, is part of a new channel for CG as it integrates the topic into the corporate social responsibility (CSR) method. This social and environmental information should not be confused with the information required by the AMF, nor with the annual social report drawn up in compliance with the French Employment Code, nor with the information given in the report on sustainable development.

This obligation raises two questions. The first concerns the fact that this information is subject to controls by the auditors, a provision whose relevance can be legitimately questioned. Are auditors really competent in this area? There is also control by the works committee and the shareholders.

Critical appreciation of the obligation

Without going back over all of the elements developed on this subject, this obligation for information does appear to be praiseworthy, but it could raise problems in terms of company performances (the Nike Corporation, because of a court judgment, decided to stop publishing this kind of information in its annual report). Moreover, while there is a universal outcry against the information given to the shareholders as being too complex and too voluminous, this new obligation for information could in turn reinforce the excessively vast character of shareholder information. Lastly, it is too easy to ask whether this information is used as a simple communication or marketing tool, which would remove all relevance from this information.

The legislator also modified shareholder information on company operations by reinforcing it, this information often being assimilated with "one of the methods of organizing a possible counterweight within companies." For this, certain acts were depenalized, being replaced with a civil procedure for transmitting information and increasing the information due from the managers, notably for questions of internal audit procedures. At the same time, the management consulting procedure was reviewed.

The law of 24 July 1966 laid down a large number of penal sanctions in the shareholders' favor, but without providing the shareholders with the possibility of obtaining the forced transmission of certain documents. In practice, it was seen that these penal sanctions were rarely applied and that they were void of all effectiveness. Consequently, minority shareholders and shareholder defense associations demanded the possibility of obtaining the documents they felt they needed from the management.

The law of 15 May 2001 brought into French law a new procedure in favor of shareholders which stated that:

> When persons cannot obtain the production, communication or transmission of documents (…), they may ask the President of the Court to issue an injunction constraining the liquidator or board members, managers and directors, to transmit them, or to appoint an agent in charge of undertaking such transmission.
>
> (article L. 238–1 of the Commercial Code)

These procedures concern, among others, the transmission of a certain number of documents upon request by the shareholders, including the annual accounts, the management report, draft resolutions to be submitted to the general meetings, the transmission of the minutes of the general meetings and the attendance sheets from the general meetings for the last three fiscal years.

The order of 24 June 2004 strengthened the field of application of the "injunction to execute" procedure by creating two new reasons for injunctions to execute for the convocation of certain general or special meetings (L. 238–6 of the Commercial Code) and for the transcription of the minutes of the meetings of the administrative and managerial bodies on a special register kept at the head offices.

The purpose of creating these injunction procedures with penalties is to make information available that shareholders have a right to under the legal provisions, i.e. to enforce and reinforce shareholders' right to information by constraining the company managers who do not obey this elementary shareholder right.

To improve information for shareholders and transparency in company operations, the financial security law of 1 August 2003 created a new report joined to the annual management report on "the conditions for preparing and organizing the board's work and the procedures for internal auditing implemented by the company"[8] with the text indicating that the chairman of the board of directors "reports." This information concerns all corporations, whether they have public offerings or not. Moreover, by targeting the companies who do so, the legislator excluded simplified joint stock companies.

The information called for in the financial security law[9] therefore constitutes an interesting innovation for transparency in how the board of directors operates, all the more so in that the AMF has to draw up a report every year on the basis of the information supplied by companies making public offerings. One could consequently imagine that, for companies making public offerings, the report will mention the conditions for preparing and organizing the board's work. The objective of transparency will thus be met.

Content of the report on the board operations

Concretely, this report will have to contain information on the number of board of directors meetings, the length of the board of directors meetings, convocation periods, information given to the directors, the directors in attendance, absent, represented, the subjects dealt with, the distribution of directors' fees, any conflicts of interest arising from one or more directors, etc. It is, therefore, a question of giving the shareholders concrete, practical information enabling them to evaluate the efficacy and seriousness of the board of directors, notably enabling them to make sure that the major questions for the future of the company are properly debated and prepared. On the other hand, concrete application of the text could pose problems insofar as the legislator did not call for sanctions if this provision is not followed.

Information on internal audit procedures

This is an innovation of the financial security law of 1 August 2003. Under the terms of article L. 225–37, paragraph 6, of the Commercial Code, the chairman of the board of directors "reports, in a report joined to the annual management report (...), the conditions for preparing and organizing the board's work and the procedures for internal auditing implemented by the company." This concerns listed companies as well as non-listed companies. Simplified joint stock companies are, therefore, excluded.

Here again, the introduction of this provision was presented by the legislator as encouraging transparency in company operations and providing better information to shareholders enabling them to better understand the "evolutions and any progress in terms of control, audit or risk management." Thus, this obligation, which lies with the chairman of the board of directors, was strongly inspired by the Sarbanes–Oxley Act (SOX) which, in article 404, states that the management of listed companies sets up a system of internal audits and attests to its effectiveness in the annual report.

Information on internal audit procedures: content of the report on internal audit procedures

While the text clearly identifies who is responsible, the designer of the report, the praiseworthy goal of the provision should not make the reader of the article forget the essential problem: that of the information to be included in the report joined to the general annual report concerning internal audit procedures. To delimit the content of this report, different bodies have issued recommendations, including MEDEF and AFEP (17 December 2003), AMF (Rev. AMF March 2004, No. 1, p. 39) and CNCC (technical opinion of 23 March 2004).

Concretely, the report will include the following points: the company accounts, the economic and financial management of the company, the independence and behavior of the managers, the behavior of the shareholders, procedures for settling conflicts of interest, prevention of abuse, etc. At the initiative of MEDEF and AFEP, the information will not be limited to the financial sphere alone. The report should include information on security, quality and environmental protection.

First, the procedures cover accounting, financial and management information, but also, second the procedures cover environmental, social and, where necessary, security information, depending on the company's activity. One of the main questions on the information contained in the report concerns its descriptive or evaluative nature. No consensus has been reached on this point. For some, the information must be descriptive (MEDEF, ANSA, AFEP and the Ministry of Justice), for others the information must be evaluative (AMF and CNCC). In application of the principles of CG, it appears consistent for the chairman to describe and evaluate the procedures implemented.

Information on internal audit procedures: which procedures?

The legislator has never precisely indicated the procedures to be implemented; the legal text simply requires that the chairman of the board of directors submits a report on these procedures. Actually, the internal audit procedures partially cover risk management in the company. Consequently, each corporation is required to undertake an analysis of risks which could occur and to implement internal mechanisms to prevent them, or to deal with them if they occur. This analysis may and should take into account the size of the company, its business sector and whether it is international in scope or not. These procedures may take the form of internal procedure manuals, as exist in the banking industry or, for example, granting credits to a company to follow a precise process designed to limit litigations. They are, in a way, rules of conduct that the company imposes and that it imposes on everyone in it (managers, employees, shareholders, etc.) or who works with it.

Given the usefulness of these procedures in providing information to the shareholders, there is a consensus on the fact that either the general manager or the executive board is responsible for drawing up the procedures and the resources applied to make them work or to verify their application. The board of directors or the supervisory board is only responsible for verifying the procedures. The chairman of the board of directors is only responsible for the report attached to the general report on the company's management.

Despite the dispersion of responsibilities, the fact that the board of directors is considered responsible for verifying the procedures and the chairman of the board of directors is responsible for the report alone is in keeping with the principles of CG relative to the transformation of the board of directors into an oversight body monitoring the general management and the board of directors' accountability in precisely determining responsible parties. This increased accountability is illustrated by the fact that the responsibility of the directors will be easier to call into question if the procedures have not been implemented or if there is no internal audit.

The Financial Markets Authority made public its 2004 report on CG and internal audit procedures (press conference of 13 January 2005). It appeared that, overall, listed companies had fulfilled this obligation. Thus, 92 percent of companies indicated in their reports the objectives assigned to the internal audit procedures, and half of the companies selected had described or named their principal risks. A certain number of improvements are possible, however, in terms of the link between the risks and the procedures implemented, and the mention of the diligence "underlying" the preparation of the chairman's report. Lastly, the AMF proposes setting up a working group whose mission would be to establish a common position on a standard reference system on the national and European levels.

Management consulting was created by the law of 24 July 1966 and was called "expertise de minorité" (minority consulting). It was created in response to the improvement in shareholder information by constraining managers to be more transparent. Shareholder information is indeed improved by the report that the expert appointed by the courts presents to the shareholder plaintiff. Minority consulting has, however, been transformed into management consulting and its use has also been accepted in favor of shareholder associations. But, like all legal provisions, a practical trend toward the instrumentalization of management consulting has appeared. The law of 15 May 2001 was therefore adopted to remedy this situation. To do so, the legislator divided the management consulting procedure into two phases: the shareholders or shareholder associations submit written questions to the managers concerning a management operation in the company, or in a company that it controls; it is not until after this, if the manager does not respond or if the information transmitted is insufficient, that they can ask a judge to appoint a management consultant.

Management consulting is not, however, a miraculous cure-all. The conditions for appointment are strict, because of the "Cour de Cassation's jurisprudence" on this question. In fact, only management operations are targeted, in other words those originating in management bodies (board of directors). This, thus, excludes from the field of management consulting those operations which require a twofold intervention of a management body and the general shareholders' meeting. But a trend is appearing in the Courts of Appeal on this point, only to exclude operations which are the sole responsibility of the general shareholders' meeting. Thus, some Courts of Appeal accept the appointment of a management consultant in the context of regulated agreements, which require prior authorization by the board of directors and discussions by the general shareholders' meeting. Moreover, the judges demand that the plaintiff establish the suspicious character of the operation, which is often hard to do in practice when the shareholder(s) are not sufficiently informed.

Use of common law consulting

Consequently, shareholders turn to the consultants in article 145 of the new Code of Civil Procedure, which deals with common law consulting and is in direct competition with management consulting. Here again, this common law consulting is instrumentalized to get around the restrictive application of management consulting. Success has been variable depending on the case. Thus, in the Vivendi Universal affair (Commercial Court 27 June 2002, Bull. Joly 2002, paragraph 942, note A. Couret), a shareholder filed a request for an appraisal with the President of the Commercial Court. This request dealt with the board of directors' operations. The shareholder wanted to know the number of meetings held by the board of directors, how long the meetings lasted, the nature of the documents transmitted to the directors, the directors who were present and absent, and the procedures implemented by the board for its deliberations. Contrary to all expectations, the Commercial Court refused the request because it did not prove that the board of directors had not operated properly. Such a motivation cannot help but come as a surprise insofar as the shareholder was asking for information on the board's operations. Luckily, the financial security law intervened on this point by requiring the chairman of the board of directors to draw up a report on the conditions under which the board of directors' work is prepared and organized (see supra Nos. 138–139).

Shareholder voting rights

The right to vote is one of the essential prerogatives of all associates and it is directly attached to the right to participate in the general meetings. The principle of participation in the general meetings while not contested and perfectly clear in its application, has, nonetheless, been called into question by statutory or legal provisions restricting the possibility for associates to take part in the general meetings by requiring that a certain number of shares be held to gain access to the meetings. This has reached such a level that the Cour de Cassation, in a recent decision, pointed out that, "all associates have the right to participate in collective decisions and to vote, and the articles of association may not provide any exceptions to these provisions" (Cass. com., 9 February 1999, Bull. Joly 1999, paragraph 122, p. 566 et seq., note J.-J. Daigre). French law did not wait for the principles of CG to come along. The usefulness of shareholder voting rights is, however, contested for various reasons that are not unfounded: the absenteeism of shareholders from the general meetings, the low use of the right to vote by shareholders who act more like spectators than investors, the existence of legal setups used to concentrate power in the general meetings (shares with double voting rights, voting agreements), etc. This observation, however, is currently being questioned somewhat by the activism of foreign investment funds and shareholder defense associations, as well as by the renewed vitality of general shareholders' meetings.

Consequently, as a remedy to these criticisms, the legislator has intervened several times to ensure that the right to vote maintains all of its usefulness: this is the case of the elimination of restrictions on the access to shareholders' meetings and of the voting obligation for mutual funds. But this intervention has actually been ambiguous and partial, as can be seen in the problem of blank proxies and the creation of preferential shares, which characterize a certain limit on the renewed vitality of voting rights.

Modernization of general shareholders' meetings

The modernization of shareholders' meetings will only be studied here in light of the contributions of ICTs. The use of ICTs to make shareholders' rights more effective and to make the role of shareholders' meetings more efficient is a demand from many actors in CG, whether shareholders or shareholder associations, organizations or institutions having issued reports on CG.

The law of 15 May 2001 and its application decree of 3 May 2002 added the use of ICTs in shareholders' meetings to the Commercial Code. Are now accepted:

i   electronic convocation of shareholders;
ii   electronic requests for placing draft resolutions on the agenda;
iii exercise of shareholder communication rights;
iv   participation in shareholders' meetings by video conferencing or by other telecommunication means allowing their identification;
v   voting by electronic communication means, using electronic forms for remote voting.

Furthermore, it is stated that companies using electronic voting mechanisms will have to set up an Internet site designed exclusively for this purpose. Lastly, the possibility of electronic voting will have to be laid down in the company's articles of association and prior written agreement from the interested shareholders is required. On the European level, there is a certain desire to reinforce the use of ICTs in general meetings (2002 Report by the High-Level Advisory Group, European Commission Action Plan of May 2003). Proposals for using ICTs concern:

i   the publication, for listed companies, of all information relevant to their shareholders on their Internet site;
ii   the obligation for listed companies to offer all of their shareholders possibilities to vote without being present, using electronic supports;

iii the possibility for listed companies to authorize their shareholders who are not physically present to take part in general meetings using electronic access (Internet, satellite, etc.).

Overall, French law is hardly behind European recommendations, since the legal and regulatory provisions even go beyond these recommendations.

Employees consideration

The debate on the place of employee participation in company management has a long history. In fact, starting at the end of World War II, the question of employee participation in management was raised, then the Sudreau report (1975) proposed simple joint oversight by employees. In doing so, the initial idea of transposing the German system of co-management into French law was far from being achieved.

We must therefore recognize that, until recently, employees were mainly left out of company law, as is the case in questions of companies experiencing difficulties. This situation can be explained for a large part by the defiance that employees have always inspired among managers and shareholders, who feel that employee participation in company management could call into question the power sharing arrangements that they do not want to change or further share, and could lead to "demagogical demands." It can also be explained by an eclipse of employees which is linked to the traditional positions of the trade unions, which feel that employees are actually being excluded from real decision-making power.

The issue of the place of employees in company management existed before the concepts of CG appeared. And yet, it is thanks to CG, at least in part, that the question of the place of employees has been revived. This revival is the result of the definition given of CG which consists of considering that, while the interests of the corporate entity are important, it is just as important to take all stakeholders into account, including employees. It is furthermore symptomatic to observe that only the Principles of Corporate Governance published in January 2004 by the Organization of Economic Cooperation and Development (OECD) consider the employees as one of the important points in its recommendations. On the other hand, there is no trace of employees in the European Commission Action Plan of 21 May 2003. And again, it should be pointed out that the European Commission Action Plan mainly concentrates on the problem of company mobility within the EU. In fact and in law, to find a trace of employees in company law, we must look to the two European regulations that created the European company and the European cooperative society, each of which is accompanied by a directive concerning employee involvement in the company.

Employee participation in management is the result of the law of 15 May 2001, which improved shareholder information, the law of 19 February 2001 on save-as-you-earn schemes and the law of 17 January 2002 on social modernization. These three texts group together three main ideas: employee information, employee financial participation and employee representation on the board of directors or supervisory board.

Information in company law through the law of 15 May 2001

The law of 15 May 2001 included the works committee in commercial company law, and more precisely in corporations, giving it special attributions. The first states that the works committee can call a general shareholders' meeting by asking the courts to appoint an agent in charge of calling the meeting. This possibility was used in the Gemplus affair (Trib. Com. Marseille, 7 November 2001, Bull. Joly 2002, p. 106). The judge is required to verify whether there is an emergency situation and whether the corporate interest is respected. The second states that the works committee can call for the inclusion of draft resolutions on the agenda of the meetings. The third authorizes two members of the works committee to attend general meetings.

This third prerogative should, however, be put into perspective insofar as this new prerogative really only takes on meaning in non-listed companies.

Information in company law through the law of 17 January 2002

The law on social modernization of 17 January 2002 strengthened interventions by the works committee during the company's life for questions of dismissals (see No. 177). But it also strengthened the works committee's prerogatives in questions of public announcements of economic strategy by distinguishing whether or not the measures implemented might significantly affect work or employment conditions. If they do not affect employment conditions, the employer is not required to give prior notification to the works committee, which may, however, meet within 48 hours following the announcement. On the other hand, the head of the company is required to inform the works committee before making a public announcement.

Employee profit-sharing is an old mechanism. Just look at the employer's payment of a year-end bonus to the employees. Despite the adoption of legal provisions on 7 January 1959 instituting optional profit sharing and 17 August 1967 creating a mandatory profit-sharing system, save-as-you-earn schemes have long had a hard time developing, despite later legal texts. It took the laws of February 2001, May 2001 and January 2002 for the mechanisms of employee profit.

Conclusion

"Le gouvernement d'entreprise," an imperfect French translation of the English term "Corporate Governance," has managed to make a spectacular breakthrough in French law since the middle of the 1990s. This sudden appearance of CG in French law partially originated with financial scandals, both internationally (savings and loan bankruptcies in the United States, Maxwell affair in Great Britain, Polly Peck International affair, Bank of Credit and Commerce International (BCCI) bankruptcy, etc.) and in France (Crédit Lyonnais affair and various financial frauds, Elf, etc.) which have marked this period. Both French and EU actions have only recently translated into various documents.

It was not until November 2002 that European institutions integrated CG into their reflections on the future, desirable evolution of company law.

Reports and studies, whatever their origin may be, have led to a substantial modification of French company law in order to take into account, or even to comply with, the Anglo-Saxon approach of CG.

Notes

1 Enjeux – Les Échos, no. 145, March 1999, p. 24, "Administrateurs plus efficaces."
2 See, for example, the recent dispute over the "cloth cap" retirement of the chairman of the "Carrefour" group.
3 Proxynvest press release in February 2005.
4 Pour un Droit Moderne des Sociétés (For Modern Company Law), p. 27.
5 Professor Yves Guyon.
6 Vienot reports I and II.
7 Les Echos, 12–13 February 2005, p. 19.
8 Article L. 235–37, paragraph 6, of the Commercial Code.
9 Ibid.

7 The Japanese national system of corporate governance

M. Yoshimori

Introduction

Corporate governance (CG) has become one of the most popular management issues in Japan since the beginning of the 1990s when the economic bubble burst and Japan went into the decade of economic downfall. An endless series of corporate scandals, illegal behavior of top executives and bankruptcies of once well-reputed firms have suddenly made the Japanese keenly aware of the deep-rooted flaws of their CG system. CG is now not only an economic but a social issue. That Japan is a latecomer in this problem area is illustrated by the fact that the term "corporate governance" is usually used as a phonetic transcription of the English term. This chapter attempts to analyze the current CG system of large publicly held corporations, unless otherwise specified.

The historical setting

Japan's process of modernization started in 1868 to cope with the urgent need to maintain her national independence amid the colonization of her neighboring countries by Western powers. In her hasty attempts to achieve the national goal of a "rich country with strong soldiers," nearly all Japanese institutions – political, social, economic, military, educational and otherwise, which characterize a modern nation – were modeled after that of the Western European countries. Thus the first Japanese Commercial Code was enacted in 1899 based on the draft written by a German scholar, Hermann Roesler. The obvious German legacy was visible until the end of the World War II and traceable even today. For instance, Article 261–3 of the current Commercial Code stipulates that the authority of the Representative Director is to carry out all affairs of business in and out of court. This is a literal translation of the German provision in the Aktiengesetz Article 78.[1] After World War II, in 1950, the first major revision of the Code was made while Japan was still under control of the Allied Occupation forces dominated by the Americans. The primary architects were the five officials of the Supreme Commander for the Allied Powers (SCAP), the governing arm of the Allied Occupation forces. As a result the new code was a replica of the US model, more specifically, the Illinois Code, as three of the five officials were trial lawyers from

Illinois (Poe *et al.*, 2002). The Japanese Code is thus characterized as a mixture of the US and the German models.

Democracy and CG in Japan

One of the essential pillars of a modern state lies in the democracy which calls for the sovereign power residing with the people, and the checks and balances of the political governance system. Contrary to most Western nations where democracy was won by the grassroots through the painful process of centuries-old struggles, often violent, to free themselves from the feudal yokes, Japanese democracy was imposed from above after World War II by the Occupation forces.

What the Japanese have implemented, however, is not a democracy in spirit and reality but one that remains largely on paper. As a result there is a tremendous gap between the law and the reality of its application. A case in point is the Statutory Auditors, as discussed later. The law gives them an overwhelming power to suspend Board decisions that are illegal and counter to the corporate bylaws. Yet they are powerless against the Chief Executive Officer (CEO) and the Board dominated by him, because they are practically appointed by the very CEO whom they are legally obligated to monitor. This blatant contradiction has been left intact for a number of decades by law academics, lawyers, politicians and above all by the business community. At the national governance level, the most notorious article of the Japanese Constitution, imposed by the Americans during the Occupation period, is Article 9 which "forever renounces war as a sovereign right of the nation and the threat or use of force," and which vows that "land, sea, and air forces, as well as other war potential, will never be maintained." Yet the reality is that Japan has the biggest military "potential" in Asia supposedly reinforced by the US nuclear umbrella, though this potential has, fortunately, never been resorted to so far. Despite this discrepancy the Constitution has never been amended since it was proclaimed in 1947. Immature democracy is therefore the fundamental reason why Japan's CG has been grossly deficient. The latest reform of the Commercial Code that came into effect in April 2003 is just one step, though important, toward rectifying the flaws.

The conceptual framework

Perhaps the shortest and one of the most appropriate definitions of CG is that of Blair. For her, CG is about allocation of control and reward among stakeholders (Blair, 1995, pp. 19, 262, 273). As this is too abstract for the purpose of this chapter, CG is defined here as a set of responses to the following questions:

i   Who is the key stakeholder to whom the top priority is given in the allocation of rewards and control over the management? What are the criteria used to determine the key stakeholder?

ii   What should be the rules and organizational structure to oversee top management?
iii How should the management be motivated to give a full play to their entrepreneurial flair and talents?

There are three reasons why any discussion on CG must start with the definition of the central stakeholder which underlies the above first question. First, defining the key stakeholder is the fundamental factor that determines the CG system. Second, legitimacy of the key stakeholder is crucial for CG. Without a broad consensus on this issue among the stakeholders, the cohesion and cooperation among them are hard to be achieved in a corporation. Third, conventional discussions on CG are too concentrated on the policing system over the CEO. While this is an important component, CG should play a more active role in trying to give incentives to the CEO to do better in the form of monetary and psychological rewards.

One of the most often cited definitions of the stakeholder is that of Freeman who says: "A stakeholder in an organization is any group or individual who can affect and be affected by the achievement of the organization's objectives" (Freeman, 1984, pp. 31–32). This definition is too broad and does not easily lend itself to operationalization. This chapter takes the perspectives of top managements whose fundamental task is to define the key stakeholder in all major decision making. They are special stakeholders, since they themselves are one of the firm's stakeholders. From their perspectives, stakeholders are defined specifically as a group or individuals who are closely identified with the survival and prosperity of the firm, i.e. employees, management, long-term or block shareholders, as well as banks, suppliers and customers with which the firm is engaged in the bulk of transactions on a long-term basis. The defining characteristic of these stakeholders lies in the quantitatively important and long-term interdependence between them and the firm. For this reason, neither short-term shareholders such as day traders, investors and speculators, nor banks, suppliers and customers who do not depend on the firm for their survival and prosperity are excluded from the stakeholders, though, of course, their interests as stakeholders should not be neglected. This definition is similar to the primary stakeholders defined by Frederic and others, two other categories being secondary and tertiary stakeholders (Frederic *et al.*, 1992, pp. 3–27).

Unlike the United States and the UK where shareholder primacy is the prevailing ideology, Japan is still dominated by the employee-centered concept of the corporation. This conviction is exemplified by the provocative declaration by Okuda, CEO of Toyota. In an article titled "Managers! If you Dismiss Your Employees, Do Hara-kiri," he blasts the attitude of some of Japan's top executives who do not hesitate to get rid of employees in the name of shareholder value as "a short-sighted view dominated by the stock market logic" and champions the Japanese traditionalist emphasis on job security. The CEO of the largest car maker in Japan believes that long-term employment fits well into the Japanese mentality that puts a premium on job stability and team work. His people-oriented concept of the corporation is all the more significant, as he is the chairman of the Nippon Keidanren, Japan Federation of Economic Organizations, the most influential national organization that represents the interests of the largest corporations in public policy formulations. In the same issue of the monthly magazine, Miyauchi, the CEO of Orix, a major lease service company and one of the best known defenders of shareholder interests, refuted Okuda's view in an article titled "Job Security at All Cost is the Road to the Titanic." Miyauchi emphasizes that "if a company does not do anything with (redundant) employees, it will sink like the Titanic. How profitable it may be?" But his statement must be taken with caution, as he recruits, for his company, mostly young female employees who spare his trouble of redundant jobs; they leave the company at relatively younger ages for reasons of marriage, childbirth, and husband's relocation, etc. much earlier than male employees. He also suggests that Japanese CEOs should stay in their position for at least ten years instead of conventional four years, so that he may have a long-term view to allow his employees to make a maximum of two mistakes. In his view, management is about risk taking, but one can judge a good risk and a bad risk only after one has undertaken an innovation. For this reason, Miyauchi continues, "one should not discontinue a new business too soon and punish the person who has taken the risk." One wonders how this long-term outlook could be compatible with his attitude toward restructuring of personnel. In essence, therefore, what Miyauchi maintains is not so convincing and is identical to Okuda's viewpoint in that both place importance on long-term outlook which is only possible under long-term employment. There has been much debate in Japan, just as in France and Germany, over the issue of the key stakeholder. After the corporate scandals involving Enron and others in 2001, the fad over shareholder value has quickly subsided.

The legal framework: the revised Commercial Code of 2003

The legislation that has direct and most important bearing on CG is the Commercial Code. In an effort to bring about a radical reform, the latest amendments of the Code which came into effect on April 1, 2003 marks one major step, albeit overdue, toward the right direction for a more transparent and effective CG system. The Code brings it still closer to the US model, as illustrated later. The revised Code is applicable to about 10,000 large companies. This organization was merged into the Japan Federation of Economic Organizations at his initiative, where he is the chairman at the time of this writing in September 2003. The reforms have been preceded by several voluntary codes of CG, the most well known being the Corporate Governance Principles published by the Japan Corporate Governance Forum composed of top executives, managers, lawyers, consultants and academics. None of them, however, has found the same level of acceptance and compliance as the French Viénot Reports I and II, or the UK's Combined Codes integrating the foregoing Cadbury Report, Greenbury Report, Hampel Report and Mainers Report, or the latest German Government-sponsored Cromme Committee's Codes of Best Practices. The amendments to the Code is, to a large extent, a legal confirmation of the Board reform realized by Sony in 1997. Sony broke up its 38-strong Board into Directors and Executive Officers; ten Directors of which three are Outside Directors and 34 Officers including nine newly appointed. Seven Directors assumed concurrently Officer position. The move was quickly followed by hundreds of listed firms to become a de facto law. In 2001 Sony took another step in the same direction by introducing the Nominating Committee and Compensation Committee two years before the revised Code went into force. These Board reforms are the most significant contribution by the CEO Idei and the success of the reform is no doubt thanks to his strong commitment. Sony proved itself as an innovator not only in electronic products but also in CG. Probably this is the first case where a reform initiative taken by a private company was incorporated into the Code. This shows that the business community is ahead of the conservative law makers. The split of Inside Directors away as Officers from the Board of Directors also meant that the average size of large Japanese firms was reduced to a more manageable size. Before the Sony reforms, a typical public corporation had an oversized Board ranging from 30 to 60 Directors. Few firms had Outside Directors, and if any, they were not truly independent as they were former managers of the company, or those sent from the firms with which the company had business ties. According to the survey conducted by the Tokyo Stock Exchange on 2,103 listed firms of which 65 percent or 1,363 responded, a majority or 54 percent have now a Board size smaller than ten. Even Toyota has modified its conservative stance on Board size and structure. As of July 2002, Toyota had altogether 58 Board members or almost five times as many as that of GM with only 12 and three times DaimlerChrysler with 20. Typical of a Japanese firm, Toyota had seven different titles for the directors indicating fine gradations of a presumed hierarchical order of authority, responsibility and seniority. These are, in strictly following the Company's list which is supposed to reflect a descending order of the authority of the titles; one Honorary Chairman, one Chairman, two Vice Chairmen, one President and CEO, eight Executive Vice Presidents, five Senmu Senior Directors, 14 Jomu Directors, and finally 26 ordinary Directors. Six statutory auditors are supposed to monitor the Board. Toyota's board was undoubtedly one of the largest among listed companies in Japan, where the trend is toward a reduced Board size. In June 2003, Toyota slashed, by more than half, the Board size to 27 composed of Directors above Senmu level. Thirty-nine Executive Officers were appointed including, for the first time in company's history, three non-Japanese, who are executives of Toyota's subsidiaries in the United States and the UK. There are no Outside Directors. Large firms are defined as joint stock companies with a stated capital of ¥500 million and above, or with liabilities of ¥20 billion and above.

Three optional structures under the revised Commercial Code

The most salient characteristic is the discretion allowed to the large firms to opt for either of the two types of Board structure; the innovative type or the conventional type. The second novel aspect is that the former is basically modeled after the US system which is widely recognized as the de facto standard across industrialized nations. The conventional type, on the other hand, is basically identical with the traditional model, though there are some improvements which are largely marginal in significance. The legislators had only the first US-type model in mind. Vehement protests from the business community including Japan Keidanren successfully forced them to settle with the optional system.

The innovative Board – "firms with committees"

The defining aspect of the innovative structure, officially termed as "firms with committees" under the revised Code, lies in the substantially reinforced oversight authority of the Board of Directors through more clear-cut divisions of monitoring functions by Directors and management functions by Officers. The second thrust is the increased authority of the Board while the power of the General Meeting of Shareholders has been further diminished. As underlined by Figure 7.1, the following legal provisions have been made to ensure achievement of this purpose:

i   separation of Directors and Officers;
ii   mandatory setup of three major Board Committees;
iii more strict definition of Outside Directors;
iv   except for the Audit Committee, Officers may assume Directorship;
v   the term of office of the Director is shortened from 2 to 1 year;
vi   reinforced reporting duties of the Officers to the Board.

Senmu and Jomu are widely used position titles of Senior Directors in Japanese companies, large or small, with no legal foundation. The former is next to the Executive Vice President or, if there is no such title, to the President and CEO in terms of authority and responsibility, and therefore potential

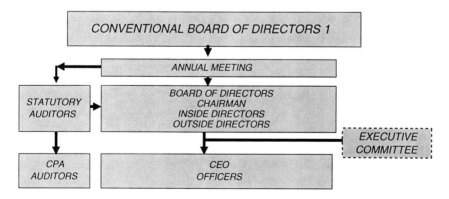

Figure 7.1 Conventional Board 1.

candidates as the President's successor. In some cases, these titles do not correspond to any specific function or authority, but are more or less honorary titles to express.

Separation of directors and officers

Prior to Sony's reforms in 1997, the Board of most Japanese companies was composed of Inside Directors. Hence there was little distinction between Directors and Officers, though this is common in the United States and the UK, and legally binding in Germany. The revised Code defines for the first time in Japanese history between Directors (Torishimariyaku) charged with oversight responsibility over the Officers and basic decision making, and Officers (Shikkoyaku) responsible for day-to-day managerial operations. This amendment is simply a legal recognition of the Sony reforms. The Board nominates and monitors officers but does not interfere with their activities. The separation is not strict, however, as Directors may concurrently assume the position of Officers. It is therefore possible for the CEO to combine the position of the Chairman of the Board, as in the case of Sony. Only the top echelon of Officers, however, such as the CEO and its closest collaborators are expected to be on the Board at the same time. Chances are, therefore, that the Board size will tend to be small and closer to the US average of about 12.

Mandatory setup of the three Board committees

This is the key provision of the revised Code. Indeed, Japan is the only country where the large firms, if they opt for this type of the Board, are legally obligated to establish all three major Board committees: Audit Committee, Nominating Committee and Compensation Committee. In the United States, only the Audit Committee is mandatory as a listing requirement for the New York Stock Exchange (NYSE). In the UK, Germany and France, Board committees are encouraged in voluntary codes of best practices but not a legal obligation. Another significant stipulation calls for at least three members for each of these Committees of which majority must be Outside Directors who may sit simultaneously at all three Committees. This reflects the intention of the legislators to increase Outside Directors on the Board and to assure neutrality of the Committees toward the CEO. The requirement of a majority of Outside Directors in any of the Committees with a minimum three members means that the Board must have at least two Outside Directors. But as a precaution against an accident or health problem, firms will generally end up with three Outside Directors. It is this provision for mandatory Outside Directors that provoked bitter resistance from the top executives of big businesses. Mitarai, CEO of Canon, for instance, declared that he would have Outside Directors on his Board "over his dead body." The detractors typically justified their opposition by alleged lack of expertise and information of Outside Directors on the business and industry of the company. Another ground is the difficulty of finding "qualified" Outside Directors in sufficient number. They also stress that the conventional Statutory Auditors would do very well the oversight responsibility, because they are well familiar with the company's businesses through many years of their working experience. General lack of experience of Japanese firms with Board Committees was also cited as another reason for their resistance. A real cause of the resistance may be that most CEOs would not like to see their hitherto almost unlimited authority restricted in nominating their successor and in all major decision making activities. Another cause would be the position title of the CEO which is changed from the "Representative Director and President" (Daihyo Torishimariyaku Shacho) to the "Representative Officer (Daihyo Shikkoyaku)." This latter title may not be attractive for most would-be CEOs, as President is much better known and perceived as more prestigious by the public. The Ministry of Justice had to accommodate these complaints of managers and allowed firms to make a choice between the two types of Boards.

The functions of the Board committees

The Committee members are nominated by the Board of Directors but are not subject to its instruction or orders in fulfilling their duties. Officers may assume directorship concurrently and sit on the three Committees. The amended Code specifies functions of each of the three Board Committees as outline below.

Audit Committee

Duties of the Audit Committee are:

i   to oversee Directors and Officers;
ii   to audit financial statements and report the results in the audit report for approval by the Board;
iii   to propose Chartered Public Accountant (CPA) auditor candidates to the General Meeting of Shareholders.
iv   to represent the company in derivative suits against Directors and Officers to ease their liabilities.

Authority of the Audit Committee is significant. The Committee may now approve financial statements including appropriation of earnings and report the decision to the General Meeting of Shareholders. These agendas were formerly subject to approval by the General Meeting of Shareholders. In this respect, the power of the Board is enhanced to the same level as the US counterpart. One minor difference from the US is that the Audit Committee assumes the functions of the US Litigation Committee, as the last item above suggests. No Officer of the company with Committees, and no Director or Officer of its subsidiary firms may be a member of the Audit Committee.

Nominating Committee

Duties of the Nominating Committee are:

i   to select and propose Director candidates to the General Meeting of Share-holders;
ii   to evaluate annually individual Board members including the CEO for re-election or removal.

Under the former Code, these prerogatives were assumed by the Board of Directors which was dominated by the CEO. Seventy-five to 90 percent of the respondents of two studies undertaken in 1991 and 1996 pointed out that the CEO's influence was decisive in the selection process of Director candidates and his successor.[2] This obviously provided the CEO with the most important source of influence and power. Since the Nominating Committee can propose director candidates directly to the General Meeting of Shareholders under the new Code, CEO influence is minimized, at least theoretically, in the selection process of Director candidates.

Compensation Committee

Major functions of the Compensation Committee are:

i   to determine compensations of all modalities for individual Directors and Officers;
ii   to propose stock option plans to the General Meeting for approval.

Compared with the United States, the UK and France where disclosure, legal or voluntary, of Director and Officer compensation is most advanced, Japan is at the other end of the spectrum. This situation is not improved by the revised legislation, as it does not devote a single word to the issue. Even the CEO of such an internationalized company as Sony declined to accommodate the demand of a shareholder at the 2002 General Meeting of Shareholders for an individual disclosure of remuneration, insisting that the total sum of remuneration should be sufficient for the shareholders. Most Japanese top executives say that their compensation is so low that they are "ashamed" to disclose it. It is well known and is documented that the compensation level for Japanese directors and managers is low by international comparison. This attitude against straightforward disclosure leads many observers to suspect that their compensation might not be as low as they tend to stress, if their perks, expenses and benefits are taken into account. So far only one firm announced to disclose individual compensation packages.

Suppression of Statutory Auditors

Firms that opt for the innovative Board need not have the Statutory Auditors, for the obvious reason that the said Committees, the Audit Committee in particular, can very well replace them. It is not an exaggeration to say that the innovative type has been legislated to do away with them. Indeed no institution of Japan's CG has been and still is so flawed and controversial as Statutory Auditors, as detailed later.

Shortened director tenure

The term of Office of Directors is reduced from two years to one year with the possibility of re-election. This makes it possible, at least theoretically, for the Board to remove quickly inappropriate or underachiever Directors including the CEO/Director based on an annual evaluation and recommendation of the Nominating Committee. This provision may lead to short-term outlook, according to some observers.

Independence of Outside Directors and the Committees

Independence of Outside Directors is crucial for the effectiveness of the Committee activities. Outside Directors are defined under the revised Code as Directors who are not currently and have never been engaged in managerial activities of the company or its subsidiaries. The previous criterion called for the absence of five years of such relations with the company. The new Code, however, does not prevent a parent company sending its Officers or managers to its subsidiaries as Committee members. A possible problem is that the subsidiary may be obliged to work in the interests of its parent and conflicts of interests between them may result. If the subsidiary is a listed company, which is not unusual, shareholders of the subsidiary may be dissatisfied under such circumstances.

Strengthened reporting duties of the Officers

The monitoring effectiveness of the Board depends on the timeliness and quality of the information provided by the CEO. For this reason, the CEO and Officers are now required under the revised Code to report every three months, to the Board, the performance of the company. They are also to report, when requested, any eventuality that might lead to serious damage to the company at Board or Committee meetings as well as to the Audit Committee.

Shorter tenure for Officers

The tenure of Officers is now shortened from two years to one year, as is the case with the Directors. This revision is intended to evaluate the performance Officers, particularly the CEO every year and if necessary to remove underperforming Officers more rapidly, keeping them on their toes.

Reaction towards the Innovative Board

As of March 1, 2003, the firms which have announced their decision to adopt the Innovative Board include; Sony, Hitachi and its 18 affiliated companies, Toshiba, Orix, Ion, Nomura Holdings, Palco and Konica-Minolta. These are still a small minority, as a large majority of 60 percent is still against it. Thus, a January 2003 survey on 100 large corporations reveal that 58 percent of the responding 90 firms would maintain the Conventional Board with Statutory Auditors, while only 2 percent replied that they were planning the introduction of the Innovative Board. For 38 percent the new Board structure is worth considering as they are in the process of examining whether to adopt it or not. Similar findings are reported by a survey on 2,103 corporations listed on the Tokyo Stock Exchange with 1,363 respondents. Sixty-six percent answered they would not adopt the new system, while 5 percent gave positive responses and 2 percent made decisions for it. It seems that the majority of firms are opposed to the Innovative Board as exemplified by Toyota and Canon, while others are taking the wait and see policy unable to determine which way to go.

The Conventional Board: firms with the Statutory Auditors

As already mentioned, and indicated by Figure 7.2, this type of Board is a result of compromise to satisfy those CEOs who were opposed to the innovative type of Board with compulsory Outside Directors and the three Committees. The defining characteristic of this Board is the preservation of the Statutory Auditors whose monitoring effectiveness has been highly controversial. The conventional type is not, therefore, substantially different from the traditional model. There are two varieties: the traditional type and the revised type, the choice being left to the discretion of the firm. Differences between these are minimal. The institution of Statutory Auditors is specific to Japan

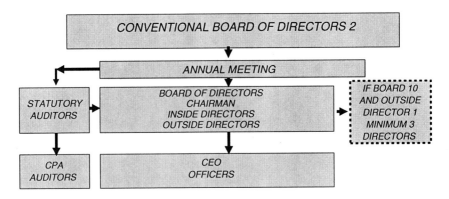

Figure 7.2 Conventional Board 2.

and exists neither in the United States nor in the UK, Germany nor France. They are elected at the General Meeting of Shareholders on the proposition of the Board of Directors. They are to represent shareholder interests by monitoring the Board so that its decisions comply with the laws and by-laws and at the same time being economically judicious. Their functions are, therefore, similar to those of the US Audit Committee. Despite their powerful and comprehensive authority including the right to suspend illegal Board decisions, their real monitoring power over the CEO and the Board was, and is, practically non-existent. The major cause for this serious flaw is that their candidates are selected by the CEO and are automatically approved at the General Meeting. The legislators tried to remedy their economic and psychological dependence on the CEO by allowing firms to continue with the existing Board structure on the condition that the following revisions be made on the Statutory Auditors:

Increased independence of the Statutory Auditors

There must be more than three Statutory Auditors the majority of whom are to be independent. They must have never been (previously in the preceding five years) an employee, or a Director of the company. This provision strengthens the neutrality of auditors who were practically selected by the CEO and for this reason their independence toward the CEO was seriously undermined.

The term of office

The term of office of the Statutory Auditors is lengthened from three to four years, double the tenure for Directors. This revision is supposed to increase independence of Statutory Auditors by allowing them increased job security.

Attendance at the Board meeting

They must be present at the Board meeting and express their opinions. Their authority and duty are increased as, before the amendment, the Commercial Code stipulated that they may attend the Board meeting.

Explanation of the reason for resignation

They can explain the reason for their resignation at the General Meeting of shareholders. This is yet another potential means to improve neutrality of Statutory Auditors, as the modification would make it harder for the CEO to remove them for arbitrary motives. It is rather doubtful how many Statutory Auditors would excise the right as they still are at least psychologically dependent on the CEO for having appointed them for the position.

The rights of consent and proposal

Auditors have the right to consent to and make a proposal for the appointment of a new Statutory Auditor. This clause enhances their authority over the CEO who has had, as mentioned above, the final say in the selection of candidates.

The Conventional Board with the Committee for Major Assets

As indicated by Figure 7.3, this is a variation of the Conventional Board and is different from the above Conventional Board in one respect: installation of the Committee for Major Assets. This Committee is the institutionalized organ of the traditional and informal Executive Committee (Jomukai, Keiei Iinnkai, etc.) set up in most firms for day-to-day decision making by the CEO and several of his closest Directors-Officers. Under the amended Code, the Committee is to be composed of at least three Directors.

With regard to Outside Directors, large companies with at least ten Directors are qualified to introduce the Committee. The Committee can decide on and implement the disposal and acquisition of important assets, as well as incurring large borrowings. These were decisions exclusively reserved for the Board of Directors before the revision of the Code. This provision enables speedy decision making by the Committee as deliberation and approval by the Board are not required. This advantage is considered to be an incentive for firms to introduce Outside Directors. This type of Board is the least meaningful of the three optional Board types, as the differences from the Conventional Board with Statutory Auditors are minimal. As of October 2003 only one firm, Honda Motors, has opted for it.

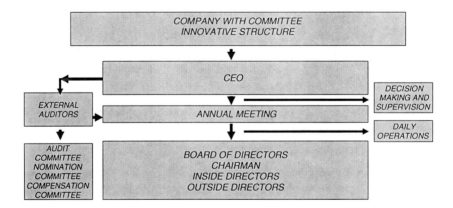

Figure 7.3 Company with committee innovative structure.

The Board Chairman and CEO (CEO duality)

There is no provision in the Code that prohibits CEO duality, i.e. the same person assuming both the CEO position and Board Chairmanship. In most listed corporations, however, it is almost an established rule to separate both positions. Sony, Sanyo and a few others form a minority of the CEO duality. This does not mean at all that the oversight by the Board Chairman over the CEO is effective. On the contrary, the reverse is the case. According to a survey on 761 CEOs, 235 Board Chairmen and 1,537 managers, close to 70 percent of the respondents reply that the Chairman is adviser to the CEO, followed by 55 percent who consider his actual role as the representation of the firm at economic and trade associations. 48 percent say the Chairman is involved in the selection process of Director and executive candidates, and 26 percent in the selection of Executives for subsidiaries and affiliated companies. Monitoring over the CEO does not, therefore, belong to the Chairman. Indeed, the prevailing norm dictates that the Board Chairman should not stand in the way of the CEO's job. Chairmanship is the last or second last step before the definitive retirement from active life and generally perceived as an honorary position. In any case a typical Chairman is over 70 years old and is unable to be involved in management details.

General Meeting of Shareholders

Effective April 1, 2002, shareholders may exercise voting rights through electronic means, for instance e-mail, with the authorization of the Board of Directors. With the consent of individual shareholders, firms may now communicate to them on the Internet or other electronic means information on the General Meeting of Shareholders. Mandatory disclosure of balance sheets and profit and loss statements may now be made on the company's website. The General Meeting of Shareholders must be held within 60 days after the end of the fiscal period. Since the majority of listed firms have their fiscal period from April 1 to March 31 of the following year, the last week of June is the busiest month for the General Meeting of Shareholders, followed by March. The ritualism of the General Meeting of Shareholders is not specific to Japan. In no other country as in Japan, however, is the tendency so pronounced. True, there are those that last for several hours where agendas are discussed seriously but such meetings are exceptions rather than the rule. The basic cause is that the majority of shares outstanding are held or "stabilized" by "friendly" hands or "stable shareholders." These are the main bank, non-financial corporations in manufacturing and service industries, and institutional shareholders such as pension funds. In principle, they do not sell them without a previous agreement by the portfolio company.

The bottom line is that nearly all decisions are made in line with the management among major stable shareholders before the General Meeting takes place. A mail survey carried out in June 1993 by Japan Association of Statutory Auditors on 1,106 public corporations revealed that nearly 80 percent of their

General Meeting of Shareholders ended in less than half an hour including recess time. A recent survey carried out in 2002 indicates that 38 percent of the firms finished the meeting in less than 30 minutes. They indicate that the General Meetings last substantially longer than before. This is a result of increased emphasis on investor relations activities, as well as the decline in number and influence of Sokaiya, or corporate extortionists. It has been a firmly established convention for most listed firms to hold their General Meetings on the same day at the end of June. The major objective is to keep off Sokaiya. But legitimate shareholders who hold shares of several companies are also deprived of their opportunity to participate in the Meeting. On this score, certain improvement was seen in 2002. In 1998, 91 percent of the listed firms held their General Meetings on June 26, while in 2002 the degree of concentration was reduced to 77 percent for the General Meetings of 2,047 forms held on June 27. Corporate racketeers above mentioned are linked to the business mafia. Typically they meet company executives and managers as small share-holders to hint at potentially embracing questions to the management at the forthcoming General Meeting.

Companies troubled with poor performance or hidden scandals are preferred targets. Anxious to finish the Meeting as quickly as possible, such companies give away a kind of hush money through various means to go around the regula-tions. Once "remunerated" they transform themselves into "cooperative" or "ruling party" shareholders and hamper questions by normal shareholders with intimidating jeering and booing, speeding up resolutions along the company lines (Shoji Homu, White Paper on General Meeting of Shareholders 2002, 2003 (in Japanese)). The situation is a testimony to the lack of courage of many other-wise respectable companies to face squarely their subtle blackmails and open challenges by their normal shareholders. Despite various legislations and stricter sanctions implemented since 1981 to crack down on such unorthodox sharehold-ers and firms involved in the payoff, the unhealthy relations are detected almost every year. In 2002 eight top executives of Nippon Shinpan, consumer credit company, were arrested and the CEO resigned after the company had been involved in a payoff scandal. In 1997 alone such respectable companies as Nomura Securities, Nikko Securities, DKB Bank, Mitsubishi Electric, Mit-subishi Motors, Toshiba, Hitachi, etc. were charged with a payoff to Sokaiya. Even after that, Japan Airlines, Kobe Steel, Kubota and others were prosecuted for the same illegal action.

Shareholders' derivative action

The Japanese legal provision on derivative actions is more stringent than that of the United States. Whereas in the latter, the legal reforms introduced in 1995 made it almost impossible for disgruntled shareholders to sue a company for poor profit performance, any shareholder under certain conditions may file law suits against the company by paying a mere ¥8,200 mandatory fee as a result of the 1993 amendment of the Commercial Code. There were frivolous shareholder litigations, but it was the astronomical amount of damages payment imposed by the court on the Directors of Daiwa Bank that raised the clamor from the alarmed business community to limit Director liability. In the well-known Daiwa Bank case, the Osaka District Court ordered the Bank's 11 Directors to pay a total compensation for the damages of $775,000 or about ¥82.9 billion. The amount was later reduced in an out-of-court settlement. Under the revised Commercial Code, the maximum liability is reduced to an amount equal to six years of remuneration, four years for other Directors and two years for Outside Directors and Statutory Auditors. At the moment the Shareholders' Derivative Action is the most powerful deterrent against management misconducts, as it may directly hit management's personal material well-being.

The Statutory Auditors – internal auditors

The Statutory Auditor, as illustrated already, is an internal audit organ responsible for ex ante and interim control, i.e. to forestall any decisions by the Directors to be taken or implemented, if they are judged to be in violation of laws, ordinances, articles of incorporation or otherwise detrimental to the company. Statutory Auditors thus perform both accounting and operating audits to protect the interest of the company and the stakeholders by preventing any adverse decisions and actions before it is too late. Their ineffectiveness as monitoring agents has been pointed out already in the Introduction. Major causes are discussed below.

Dysfunctions of Statutory Auditors

This is another typical illustration of a large gap between the legal provision and its application, a phenomenon so pervasive in Japanese society. Seemingly endless series of corporate wrongdoings indicate poor track records of the Statutory Auditors. Of course there are auditors who are determined to carry out their duty even at the risk of losing their job. There are also CEOs who are well aware of the importance of their functions and respect and facilitate their auditing task. But the general image of a Statutory Auditor is someone without much authority, with plenty of time (sarcastically dubbed as Kansanyaku meaning Directors without much to do, a pun on Kansayaku, auditor), who failed to be on the promotional mainstream to a higher executive position or to Board membership. This negative image has not changed much since the beginning of the last century when one of the prominent law academics wrote,

> An auditor in Germany would correspond, in status and power, to a Board member in Japan or a person in a still higher position, controlling Board members. In contrast, an auditor in Japan is someone without much to do in the company, a second-class person, or someone too old for any job but maintained in the position to be given some prestige.
>
> (Nihon Keizai Shimbun, 1993)

According to the survey carried out by the Japan Association of Auditors in 1993 on 2,427 auditors of listed firms, only 6.8 percent of them are former Chairman, Vice Chairman, President or Executive Vice President, who would carry substantial influence as auditors over the incumbent CEO. The bulk of the Statutory Auditors, 55.6 percent are less influential former Senior Executives (Senmu and Jomu) or ordinary Directors. Twenty-four and a half percent are division or department managers before being promoted to auditors (Hosoda, 1994). Yet, the Statutory Auditors are given a powerful and comprehensive set of supervisory authorities over management under the Commercial Code. Nominated by the General Meeting of Shareholders, the Statutory Auditors are legally independent of the Board of Directors dominated by the CEO. Theoretically, therefore, they are in the position to monitor the Board and the CEO. Though the Code does not precisely define the exact scope of their monitoring authority, the prevailing theory holds that monitoring is not only for verification of legal conformity, but also for economic judiciousness of managerial decisions. In other words, the Statutory Auditors are called upon to ensure that the activities by management are legal, and that they constitute good and sound business decisions. To perform this duty, the Statutory Auditors are empowered, among other things, to:

i   participate in the Board meetings to voice their opinions;
ii   report to the Board possible and actual deviation from the company's scope of activities, laws and bylaws;
iii if necessary, demand that a Board meeting be convened and, if not accepted, convene it anyway under their own authority;
iv   to require reports on business at all times from the Board members, management and employees and to inspect operations and assets of the company as well as of its subsidiary companies;
v   present the audit report to the General Meeting of Shareholders; and
vi   suspend any actions, illegal or outside of the company's main objectives or of the bylaws.

If the Statutory Auditors had properly fulfilled these roles, most of the notorious corporate scandals in recent years would have been prevented. The reality is that practically none of these functions are effectively discharged by them. For instance, actual use of the most powerful authority to suspend illegal actions by Directors is unheard of, according to Shin'ichi Suzuki, Executive Director of Japan Association of Statutory Auditors (Nihon Keizai Shimbunnsha, 1993, p. 74).

Causes of malfunctions

The root cause of the lack of monitoring by the Statutory Auditors is that they are practically selected by the President/CEO whom they are supposed to monitor, as indicated already. This situation is identical to the lack of independence of the

Inside Directors because they are appointed by the CEO. Whether their position will be renewed for another term depends on whether they have been quiet and obedient to the CEO. Human nature is such that persons with power do not normally want to have it reduced, let alone challenged. If they take their duty seriously, therefore, they must be always prepared to resign from the position.

Even if the Statutory Auditors were completely independent, another more serious obstacle for their effective audit is that they are at a definite disadvantage to top management in terms of the quality and quantity of the information on the firm's activities and situation. This informational asymmetry is caused by two factors. Statutory Auditors were typically excluded from the scene of top-level decision making. As is indicated already, real decisions are taken, not at a formal meeting of the Board of Directors, but at a small Executive Committee meeting called Jomukai attended by the CEO and his executive team. Rarely Statutory Auditors are invited to the meeting. They are therefore not in the position to obtain the same level of information about the company, while top management have a control over vital information. This is exactly what happened in the window-dressing case of Aipec, publisher of educational books whose shares were traded on the over the counter market. This company had two Outside auditors, a retired Public Prosecutor General and a former high-ranking officer of the National Tax Agency. Despite their background, qualified as almost ideal for auditors, they have been used as a sort of camouflage for the window-dressing which was reportedly so sophisticated as to defy detection (Mori, 1994). In order to boost the power of the Statutory Auditors, the Commercial Code was amended and came into force on October 1, 1993. Every large company was required to increase the number of Statutory Auditors from the previous minimum two to minimum three, one of which being an Outside Auditor. An Outside Auditor was defined as one who was not a Director, manager or employee of the company or its subsidiary for at least five years before appointment. This revision was a small step in the right direction but fell too short of the remedy, as long as the CEO continues to select them. A study on 1,314 listed firms revealed that 45 percent of them recruited their Outside Auditors from among former Executives or auditors of their parent company or affiliated/subsidiary companies. This lack of independence was quickly criticized by US institutional investors. One of the fundamental aims of the latest revision of the Commercial Code was precisely the abolishment of the Statutory Auditors through creating the Innovative Board with Committees.

Audits by external CPA auditors

Attempts to restore tarnished credibility

Independent audit is carried out by CPAs, professional accountants qualified to undertake audit activities after passing one of the most selective examinations administered by the Government. Less than 10 percent of the applicants succeed in the three-level examinations in a typical year. These professional accountants work individually or as members of an audit firm. Most of the audits for large listed corporations are performed by audit firms. Corporations with a capitalization exceeding ¥1,500 million, with total liabilities of over ¥120 billion and listed on a securities exchange are required to have their financial statements audited by CPAs or an audit corporation. If Statutory Auditors cannot be counted on to provide effective checks on management, the last legal resort is independent External Auditors. But they hardly function as such. The classical instance is Sanyo Special Steel Company which filed in 1965. For seven years the company had been overstating earnings and understating remunerations for the management. The company's External Auditor knowingly reported the fraudulent financial statements with "unqualified opinion," i.e. as "presenting fairly financial conditions and results of operations in conformity with accounting principles" (Ballon *et al.*, 1976, p. 163).

In 1991 some of the major securities houses including Nomura, Nikko, Yamaichi, etc. were found guilty of compensating a part of the losses incurred by their institutional clients in investments made through them. According to one of the Board members, himself a CPA with a long experience, of the Japanese Institute of Certified Public Accountants (JICPA), the CPAs in charge of auditing these securities firms were probably aware of this illegal expenditure. In the same year in a bankruptcy involving Maruko, a real estate company, the auditors reported no anomaly in the financial statements published only half a year before. In less than one year from this incident, LEC, one of the largest manufacturers of interior decoration products, listed on the Second Section of the Tokyo Stock Exchange, became insolvent. The auditing report on the company's financial statements published only four and half months before certified them with "unqualified opinion," despite the fact the company had doubtful loans far in excess of its capitalization (Ballon *et al.*, 1976, p. 163). The failure of Yamaichi Securities with almost one hundred years of tradition is another case in point. The CPA auditors could not detect large-scale illegal business operations which led to one of the most spectacular bankruptcies in Japan's business history since World War II. One of the major causes of inadequate CPA audits is the universal problem of informational asymmetry. There is always a possibility for the top executives to withhold or even manipulate information, so that the CPA cannot effectively carry out its audit. They are in most cases powerless against top management who are determined fraudsters, as the US cases such as Enron or WorldCom suggest. Two additional causes, probably specific to Japan, are illustrated below.

Causes of dysfunction

First, the relationship between External Auditors and their client firms are almost identical to those between the Statutory Auditors and the President/CEO. Clients do not want to deal with auditors who in their eyes are "too rigorous." If CPAs are true to their professional ethics, therefore, they must be prepared to lose their client and a sizable income, which is an unrealistic expectation. This potential risk is too large for most of the Japanese auditing firms which are small by international comparison and do not have enough resources. Apart from this weak bargaining position, CPAs must face a heavy psychological pressure when they have to qualify or disclaim their opinion, as this will certainly reduce the client's credibility with the banks, customers and suppliers, and might even lead to delisting. The outcome is that in most cases auditors tend to refrain themselves from such serious reservations. A case in point is Gajoen Kanko, a listed firm engaged in the hotel business, which discontinued its contract with its auditing firm. It is widely believed that the company's management did not like the auditor's adverse opinion which might well have led to its delisting. The company immediately hired another CPA who performed as an individual an audit reported with "unqualified opinion" with an unprecedented speed of about one week. Surprisingly neither the JICSA nor Ministry of Finance, the supervisory ministry of CPAs at that time, contested the validity of the dubious audit nor ordered the company to reinstate the discharged CPA. This notorious incident was claimed to reveal some fundamental flaws of the Japanese independent audit system (Toba, 1993).

Second, most auditors have long-standing business relations with their clients often extending to 20, 30 or even 40 years. Over this period of time many of them have become too identified with their clients through informal personal contacts on golf courses or restaurants with the Finance Director and other top Executives. The prohibition which the JICPA imposed on its members to retain shares of their clients companies evoked suspicion of widespread insider trading involving CPAs. In some cases, auditing firms accepted from their client companies their employees with the CPA qualification who will eventually audit their former employer. This reality indicates that most CPAs have become quasi-insiders of their client companies, losing their arm's length relation as fair and independent auditors. They end up protecting the client company's Directors and management rather than shareholders and other stakeholders. The result is lax assessment and control, and even occasional complicity with the client in window-dressing and other illegal practices, as noted already.

In an effort to restore public confidence in CPAs and accounting firms, sweeping changes have been made in the audit practices (Nihon Keizai Shimbunsha, 1993, pp. 114–116). Within fiscal 2001 auditing standards were completely reviewed and revised, including the auditing of going concerns, adoption of a risk approach, enhancement of fraud detection, a quality control practice review and a CPA Investigation Examination Board (CIEB). The most significant change in auditing standards is that auditors are now required to evaluate the viability of businesses. Their responsibility now goes beyond simply checking compliance of their client firms with the accounting rules. This requires their much higher independence and higher standard based on professional ethics. The most significant change since the 1970s was made on May 30, 2003 with the passing of the bill for amendment of the CPA Law. The revision is made under strong influences of the US Sarbanes–Oxley Act (SOX) of 2002, as illustrated below.

On the other hand, effective April 2004, the revised CPA Law prohibits audit firms to provide the following non-audit. The following descriptions on the CPA reforms draw heavily on JICPA, "Oversight and Independence of CPA Auditing in Japan, 2002" available on www.jicpa.or.jp/n–eng services to any clients that are required to be audited in accordance with the Securities and Exchange Law and certain large corporations subject to statutory audits under the Commercial Code. In addition to tax consulting services which are already prohibited under the present CPA Law, the banned non-audit services are:

i   services related to book keeping, financial documents and accounting books;
ii design of financial or accounting information systems;
iii services related to appraisal of the contribution-in-kind reports;
iv actuary services;
v   internal audit outsourcing services;
vi any service of dealing in, or being promoter of shares or other interests of audit clients;
vii any services that are equivalent to the above listed services which may involve management decisions or lead to self-audit of the financial documents the auditor examines.

Note also that current requirement for auditor partner rotation is seven years with two years of time-out period. This will be amended to rotate every certain period within seven years with time-out period to be prescribed later. In other words, more frequent rotation of audit partner will be provided for increased independence of audit work.

Current CPA Law does not, however, rule out for a client corporation to hire a retired partner of the audit firm as management. There will be a one-year period before the retired auditor may take on a management position in the company that was audited by him or her.

The Financial Services Agency is currently responsible for overseeing auditors and the JICPA. The amended CPA Law stipulates that a new CPA and Auditing Oversight Board (CPAAOB) will be established to reinforce monitoring over CPAs. The Board will have ten members to be nominated by the Prime Minister with the approval by the Diet. This nomination procedure reminds us of the US Security Exchange Commission's (SEC) commissioners who are directly appointed by the President of the United States. The revised Law provides for mandatory quality control review of auditors by JICPA.

Effective January 2006, the amended CPA Law will simplify the CPA examination process by changing the current three-step to single-step examination, followed by two years of practical training and other modality of training. This provision is designed to increase substantially the number of CPA's which is too small to cope with ever complicated accounting transactions of large firms. As of March 31, 2003 there were 13,721 CPAs, while in the United States the comparable number is about 330,000.

Currently every partner of an audit firm assumes unlimited and joint responsibility for liabilities. The revised CPA Law provides that only the auditors who performed audits will be jointly liable for misconduct and negligence, while other partners are liable up to the maximum of their equity position in the audit firm. This is an obvious defense measure against increased numbers of litigations by investors against CPAs.

Accounting and disclosure system

The accounting system of a country, as all economic institutions, is a product of history. The Japanese accounting system was based, until recently, on the German model with an overriding concern for creditor protection and conservative valuation standards based on historical costs. This is a natural consequence of the relatively underdeveloped equity market and conversely well developed banking sector in Japan and the Continental European countries. This system did not call for a high level disclosure of accounting information, as nearly all financial transactions were made among partners known to each other through long-term personal, equity and business relations. The Anglo-Saxon approach, on the other hand, reflects a long tradition of stock market capitalism and therefore protection of interests of a large number of anonymous investors takes precedence by providing them with as accurate and reliable information as possible on corporate performance and forecasts to facilitate their decision making. The valuation standard under this model is market value and consolidated financial statements to reveal the true value of the company. The level of disclosure is obviously higher.

The disclosure system under the triangular system

The Japanese accounting system is subject to three different laws: Commercial Code, Corporate Securities and Exchange Law and Income Tax Law. The Commercial Code requires joint stock companies to prepare an annual report on an individual basis, which is one of the major reasons why consolidated accounting was not a rule in Japan until recently. The Commercial Code requires the annual report to be approved at the General Meeting of Shareholders and to include the balance sheet, the income statement, the business report and the proposal on profit appropriation or loss disposition. For large corporations as defined in the Commercial Code, consolidated financial statements i.e. balance sheet and income statement must be included in the annual report for the accounting years ending in or after April 2004.

The Securities and Exchange Law provides for the issuing corporations of securities to file annual and semi-annual reports with the Prime Minister and copies thereof with the Stock Exchange(s) where the securities are listed. The financial statements in the said reports must include those required under the Commercial Code mentioned above, plus supporting schedules thereto, as well as consolidated balance sheet, income statement, statement of retained earnings, cash flows and supporting schedules thereto. The financial statements prepared under the Commercial Code and the Securities and Exchange Law are, for the most, compatible. The Corporate Tax Law defines the methods for calculating taxable income and requires revenues and expenses to be recorded in the books of account to be justified under the Law.

The latest accounting reforms – the financial "Big Bang"

For half a century, accounting standards were prepared by the Ministry of Finance (MOF) through its external body called the Business Accounting Deliberation Council. To comply with the urgent need for a private and independent standard setting body, the Financial Accounting Standards Foundation (FASF) was inaugurated in 2001 with the participation of ten leading private sector organizations including JICPA. Within the FASF, the Accounting Standards Board of Japan (ASBJ) was created as an entity directly responsible for setting accounting standards. These are reviewed and approved by the Business Accounting Council (BAC) of the Financial Services Agency (FSA) to become legally binding. In addition, Practical Guidelines are issued by JICPA. The Accounting "Big Bang" was declared by Prime Minister Hashimoto in 1996 to bring the Japanese financial market closer to the level of New York and London markets. This attempt was inspired by the UK experience of the 1980s. The Japanese reforms had three principles:

i   Free: Let the market determine the cost of service.
ii Fair: Formulate rules for improved disclosure and transparency.
iii Global: Harmonize with the international standards in laws, accounting and tax codes. Numerous accounting reforms have been implemented since then: introduction of consolidated financial statements in 1997, retirement-benefit accounting and tax-effect accounting in 1998, and in 1999 accounting for financial instruments and market-value accounting for financial instruments such as securities. As a result the Japanese accounting standards have been brought closer in line with the International Accounting Standards and US General Accounting Agreed on Principle (GAAP). Some of the major reforms are detailed below.

Consolidated accounting

The Consolidated Accounting Standards for Tax Purposes came into effect in April 2002 making them closer to the US Tax Code. Companies can now write off losses at their subsidiaries against income of the parent, effectively reducing total tax bills. Under the new system, it is no longer possible for a parent company to use its subsidiaries as a vehicle for accounting manipulation which was rampant before. Subsidiaries were used to inflate earnings of the parent company by fictitious sales of products and assets to them. Crucial factor of consolidated accounting is the definition of subsidiaries or affiliated companies that must be consolidated. A new criterion called for a company's extent of control or influence has been introduced rather than equity holdings, the only criterion previously prescribed. As a result of this accounting rule, companies cannot hide losses, non-performing assets and debt-ridden subsidiaries by excluding them from the consolidated assets statement. Consolidated cash flow statements became mandatory.

Market value accounting

One of the major shifts to the Anglo-Saxon accounting model was realized in April 2000 when the acquisition cost accounting was replaced by a market value system. Firms are now required to record their holdings of marketable assets and securities at current market value rather than at cost. Thus unrealized gains and losses must now be reported on the income statement for trading securities, and on the stockholders' equity of the balance sheet for marketable securities. One of the significant consequences is the increased unraveling of cross-shareholdings, as they are exposed to the downward share price volatility. A large number of companies, financial and non-financial, saw their earnings reduced to a loss when the current price of the shareholdings fell below the acquisition cost as a result of sluggish stock market performance in most of the 1990s and early 2000s.

Impairment accounting

Impairment accounting is due to be mandatory from fiscal 2005 on and firms must record on their balance sheet losses incurred when the market value of fixed assets such as landholdings, factories, office buildings, golf courses, etc. have fallen by 50 percent below the book value. This accounting system is also applicable to businesses whose operating profits or cash flows are expected to be negative for three consecutive fiscal years including the current year. Impairment accounting is expected to have a huge impact on profits, as prices of land acquired during the bubble period have been declining since the end of the bubble. It is possible for companies to proceed, on a voluntary basis, with applying this method of accounting to get rid of unrealized losses. One of the major issues confronting the implementation of impairment accounting is the determination of the accurate market value for certain assets whose market is not well developed.

Retirement benefit accounting

This accounting system came into effect in 2001 and requires companies to report on the financial statements' future liabilities for retirement benefit for employees consisting of pension payment and retirement allowance. A shortfall must be written off as operating expenses. The net liabilities are to be calculated using market value accounting for the securities and other assets by using present-value actuarial methods on the liabilities. Reflecting sluggish stock market, most companies have not been able to realize expected return on investment for their pension funds, which have lead to creating huge liabilities. Many otherwise profitable companies have seen their performance falling into a deficit simply because they had to finance under funded pension plans.

The regulatory framework and enforcement

FSA

The basic role of the FSA is to ensure the stability of the financial system, protection of depositors, insurance policy-holders and securities investors. The FSA is the most important organ responsible for regulating and supervising financial institutions of banks and insurance companies and other private-sector financial institutions as well as securities companies. It also has the authority to enforce Banking Law, Securities Exchange Law and laws relative to bankruptcies of financial institutions including the Deposit Insurance Law. The FSA works out rules for trading in securities markets, establishes business accounting standards, supervises CPAs and audit firms, and ensures compliance with rules governing securities markets through surveillance and inspection. The history of FSA shows regulatory soft-pedaling and lax enforcement of Japan's most influential regulatory and supervisory body, the MOF. The functions of today's FSA were previously assumed by the Ministry's Banking Bureau and Securities Bureau. By the end of the 1990s the MOF lost credibility with the public as a result of sloppy supervisory activities and even collusive relations with companies involved in financial scandals. Bad debts held by banks grew to an uncontrollable level and the Hokkaido Takushoku Bank failed, the first bank to do so since World War II. Then came the liquidation of Yamaichi Securities after its losses in off-book accounts were uncovered apparently with the knowledge of at least one MOF official. In 1998 another spectacular scandal involving MOF officials lead the Tokyo Prosecutor's Office to stage a massive raid involving 100 investigators on MOF premises for proof of accepting bribes in the form of lavish and dubious entertainment paid to MOF officials in charge of bank inspection. Two officials were arrested, a third committed suicide. Despite widespread functions of the FSA, its total staff members numbered only 1,100 as of March 2003. Consequently the said two bureaus were split. The descriptions on the FSA draw heavily on the information available on www.fsa.go.jp/info from the MOF and transferred to the FSA.

Securities and Exchange Surveillance Commission (SESC)

SESC is the market watchdog closest in its functions to the US SEC. The SESC is an organ established within the FSA and is responsible for ensuring compliance with the rules of securities markets, and financial future markets are complied with. A Chairperson and two Commissioners are directly appointed by the Prime Minister. No rules nor laws are of much value if they are not enforced in word and spirit. Legal obligations are generally more effective than voluntary rules or codes of best practices, since their violations are usually accompanied by sanctions such as fines or imprisonment. With its total staff of 217 its enforcement role, however, is no comparison with the US SEC with 3,000 experts and administrative staff, despite the fact that the Tokyo Stock Exchange is the world's second largest next to the New York Stock Exchange (NYSE) in terms of market capitalization. There are growing calls for its reinforcement to the SEC level.

Conclusion

As illustrated already with respect to the latest legal reforms of the Japanese Commercial Code as well as various accounting and institutional reforms, there is no doubt that the Japanese CG is converging on the US model. This is not specific to Japan, Germany and France share a similar trend as the German Code of Best Practices recommended by the Cromme Commission and the French New Economic Regulations (NRE) indicate. For Japan, however, the firms that have opted for the US style Board of Directors are either those with predominantly international business activities or those that have experienced serious losses or that have been involved in wrong doings. It remains to be seen if the optional US style Board structure will be adopted by a majority of firms, as the surveys reveal a consistently overwhelming majority of firms determined to maintain the traditional Board with Statutory Auditors. It should be stressed, however, that the convergence on the US model is confined to the Board structure and functions for increased oversight effectiveness.

Notes

1 "Der Vorstand vertritt die Gesellschaft gerichtlich und außergerichtlich" DTV-esellschaftsrecht.
2 "Report of the Survey on the Statutory Auditor System" (in Japanese), The Study Committee on the Auditing Environment, Faculty of Business Administration, Kobe University, 1991, p. 42, and the results of survey on 5700 Statutory Auditors of the Association of Statutory Auditors, Nihon Keizai Shimbun, April 16 1996.

8 Hong Kong system of corporate governance

S. S. M. Ho

Introduction

It is commonly agreed that the 1997 Asian financial crisis was mainly the result of structural weaknesses – i.e. a lack of effective corporate governance (CG) and transparency – in many of Asia's financial markets and institutions. Misinvestment, over borrowing, and low quality disclosures were blamed on the absence of proper checks and balances to monitor Asia's tycoons. Many banks were controlled by owner–managers, and the boards of directors played limited roles in much connected lending. Growth was more important than returns and liquidity, and risk management was usually poor. In fact, there was a tendency for the less transparent markets in the region (such as Thailand, Malaysia, Japan, and Indonesia) to be subject to more volatile shocks than the more transparent markets (such as Hong Kong, Taiwan, and Singapore) (Ho, 2000). Analysts agree that the reason for the relatively smaller effect of the crisis on Hong Kong's businesses was the territory's established CG regime. Thus, a solution to restore international investors' confidence in the Asian corporate sector and attract more capital inflow has been to strengthen its CG and disclosure. Over the last several years, most East Asian economies have been actively reviewing and improving their CG and transparency. However, only a few have made substantial progress.

The recent corporation collapses in the US and similar incidents have underscored the critical importance of structural reforms in the governance of large companies and financial institutions. These will undoubtedly result in stricter economic, financial, and accounting regulations for capital markets around the world. The CG issues transcend national boundaries. Although the West has been the home of the bulk of recent corporate controversy, certainly Hong Kong and other East Asian economies are not innocent. Recent corporate oversight or misgovernance cases in Hong Kong include Peregrine Investment, Shun Shing Group, Guangnan Group, Kit Wai International, and Euro-Asia Agriculture in Hong Kong. For instance, in Hong Kong, Peregrine Investment had virtually no practice of CG before its collapse in 1998 under the weight of a huge loan to an Indonesian taxi company. The Guangnan collapse also revealed how some red chip firms abuse corporate assets and manipulate their accounting records. The Kit Wai and Euro-Asia Agriculture scandals revealed how the controlling shareholders, the board, and all initial public offering (IPO) intermediaries did not fulfill their fiduciary duties. These incidents also suggest that there are shortcomings in the local legal and regulatory framework and their enforcement. Not only have many of these incidents hindered financial market development, but they have also substantially reduced investors' confidence in the market.

While the problems to be dealt with have a US focus, the Hong Kong market, banks, companies, and regulators will draw their own conclusions on how to prevent such incidents because Hong Kong often looks upon US financial regulatory frameworks as models to be emulated. In any case, improving CG practices should be an ongoing process rather than an ad hoc reaction to sudden events or failures. This chapter systematically surveys the key concepts, current practice, effectiveness, core problems, and future prospects of CG in Hong Kong.

Standards and core problems of CG

Good CG is certainly important to Hong Kong. From the perspective of globalization, it is the way that firms in Hong Kong are able to compete with well-governed overseas companies. The Hong Kong government has realized that good CG is necessary to improve corporate competitiveness and attract international capital. Former Financial Secretary, Donald Tsang, said in his budget speech in 1999 that high corporate standards were the hallmark of a first-class financial centre. According to Tsang,

> Our aim is to establish Hong Kong as a paragon of corporate governance, ensuring that those investments in Hong Kong are afforded the best protection and that our listed companies are managed with excellence, complying with the highest international standards including those related to risk management and disclosure of information.

In his 2000 budget he tasked the Standing Committee on Company Law Reform (SCCLR) with conducting an overall review of CG, particularly relating to proposed changes to the Companies Ordinance. CG reforms then take place through accelerated legal reforms, the enforcement of rules and regulations, industry awareness and training, school and public education, and market forces.

Most countries in East Asia are still a long way from conforming to the international rules of business, possibly with the exception of Singapore and Hong Kong. These two economies benefit from a colonial legacy of common law institutions, relatively strong judiciaries, good ethical standards, and low corruption.

While many Asian countries made significant improvements in their CG scores in 2002, Hong Kong's score was unchanged from the previous year. This was attributed to a number of setbacks, including the Boto and Pacific Century Cyberworks (PCCW) incidents, to be explained later. At the corporate level, several blue chip Hong Kong companies were selected by Euromoney in 2002 as the best companies in Asia. Three companies in Hong Kong were also ranked by CLSA as being among the best 30 CG Asian companies in 2003, and the top-ranked company was HSBC Holdings. (Singapore and India also had three companies each.) CLSA said that while Asian CG standards were improving, they still had a long way to go (South China Morning Post, 2003).

At country level, there is a good regulatory foundation of CG in Hong Kong. Standard and Poor's[1] (see Dallas, 2002) had five positive observations for Hong Kong as a whole: a stable common law legal system and independent judiciary, active advocacy of improved CG by regulators, international accounting standards, good overall standard on a global basis and a trend of improvement, and leadership in Asia. Other strengths of the Hong Kong investment infrastructure include being the freest economy in the world with a relatively low level of corruption. The overall infrastructural environment is conducive to achieving international governance standards. However, in Asia in general and Hong Kong in particular, Standard and Poor's also observed several governance weaknesses, such as family ownership being the norm, a high level of legal compliance but form being more significant than substance, and the limited independence of directors. The core problems or unique concerns of CG in Hong Kong can be summarized as follows:

i   Seventy-five percent of listed companies are domiciled outside of Hong Kong and are not subject to some relevant local laws.
ii High ownership concentration and low free floats of shares.
iii The manipulations of controlling shareholders via insider or connected party transactions.
iv The lack of truly independent board directors.
v   The lack of corporate transparency, particularly on connected party transactions and directors' remunerations.
vi The low quality of many listed firms which have recorded net losses and very low stock prices across several years.
vii Weak legal protection for minority investors and a relative lack of shareholder activism.
viii Weak enforcement of rules and the lack of a super-regulatory body with full investigative powers.
ix Insufficient legal status of listing and CG-related regulations.

One major goal of improving CG in Hong Kong is to reduce abuses and inefficiencies that are due to conflicts between controlling owner–directors and outside investors using various rules, standards, and mechanisms. The protection of minority shareholders has become the focal point of international investors. Effective CG in Hong Kong must incorporate a critical approach that covers all of these aspects that are required to enhance shareholder protection.

The more unique and critical issues of CG in Hong Kong are divided into the following areas for discussion: the legal and regulatory framework, conflicts between owner–directors and minority shareholders, directors' duties and board practices, the setting of accounting disclosure standards, auditor independence and accountability, market intermediaries and analysts, and shareholder empowerment and activism.

The legal and regulatory framework

Regulatory bodies establish and implement rules and regulations,[2] monitor compliance, and take part in enforcement activities. They monitor company shareholders, boards of directors, accountants, auditors, investment analysts, and the financial market and institutions. Rules and regulations are always needed to ensure that participants strike the right balance between self-interest and the interest of the majority public. It is generally agreed that sound legal regulation and enforcement are key pillars upon which good CG is built.

Regulatory requirements relating to CG rules are covered by a variety of sources in Hong Kong and administered by different authorities.[3] As Hong Kong was a British colony before July 1997, its legal and financial reporting system is largely influenced by British practices. Statutory rules on CG in Hong Kong are stipulated by the Hong Kong Companies Ordinance (with Cap 32 being a primary statute that applies only to Hong Kong companies) under the continuous revision of the Companies Registry and the SCCLR, and the new composite Securities and Futures Ordinance (SFO) enforced by the Securities and Futures Commission (SFC).

Non-statutory rules and standards include the Code on Takeovers and Mergers and Share Repurchase (the 'Takeover Code') enforced by the SFC; Listing Rules, Listing Agreements, and the Codes of Best Practice that are promulgated by the Stock Exchange of Hong Kong Ltd (SEHK), a subsidiary of Hong Kong Exchanges and Clearing (HKEx); and the Statements of Standard Accounting Practice (SSAPs) and Statements of Auditing Standards as issued by the Hong Kong Society of Accountants (HKSA).

Banks and authorized deposit-taking financial institutions are exempt dealers and are further regulated by the relevant Hong Kong Monetary Authority (HKMA) governance and disclosure rules, including their securities trading business. The HKMA issued a guideline on CG for locally incorporated authorized institutions in May 2000. It stipulates that the board of banks should have a minimum of three independent directors, and that there should be a separation of the board chairman from the chief executive officer (CEO).

Under the Companies Ordinance, directors and senior management are subject to criminal and civil liability in cases of misconduct. The relevant offences include fraudulent trading and other breaches in relation to insolvent companies. The SCCLR proposal on the Hong Kong Companies Ordinance aims to empower shareholders and to encourage them to stop "voting with their feet." Due to attractive tax incentives and less restrictive corporate control rules in countries such as Bermuda and the Cayman Islands, over 75 percent of listed firms in Hong Kong are domiciled or incorporated outside Hong Kong. These companies are not principally governed by the Hong Kong Companies Ordinance, but rather by the corporate laws of their home jurisdictions. This would cause the individual shareholders of different listed firms to be subject to different levels of legal protection. The lack of legal parity may lead some companies to change their domiciles in order to enjoy the greatest level of unchecked powers at the expense of minority shareholders.[4]

While the Companies Ordinance covers all companies incorporated in Hong Kong, the responsibility for regulating the conduct of listed companies (both locally and overseas incorporated) falls on HKEx, which is in turn supervised by the SFC. As the statutory securities regulator, the SFC is expected to ensure that investors have enough information to assess the difference in disclosure risks, enhance allocation efficiency, prevent fraudulent offerings and manipulative practices, and restrain opportunistic behavior by directors and controlling shareholders.

Until recently, besides the Companies Ordinance, several statutes regulated the activities of Hong Kong listed companies – and in particular their directors – which is essential for sound CG (Anonymous, 2001). The Securities (Disclosure of Interests) Ordinance (Cap 396) (SDIO) obliged directors, together with their spouses and children, and substantial shareholders of listed companies – i.e. those who hold more than 5 percent (was 10 percent before the SFO) of the company's voting share capital – to disclose to the stock exchange and the company their shares in the company or any associated companies, as well as any additional acquisition or disposal of their interests. The Securities (Insider Dealing) Ordinance (Cap 395) (SIDO) prohibited directors or other people connected with the company (widely defined as including a director, employee, substantial shareholder, or anyone who occupies a position that may reasonably be expected to offer them access to relevant information) from using price-sensitive information when dealing in or procuring the company's shares. In a case of suspected insider dealing, the SFC could refer the case to the Insider Dealing Tribunal (IDT), which can disqualify the defaulting director. These two securities ordinances, together with eight others, have been incorporated into the new composite SFO.

The Takeover Code regulates takeovers and mergers of public companies to protect shareholders' interests as a whole. To afford fair treatment for minority shareholders who are affected by a takeover, the Takeover Code sets standards to which offeror and offeree companies must comply. With the Takeover Code, all shareholders of the same class are treated similarly. Recently, the SFC has conducted an overview of the Code to bring it into line with international standards.

In Hong Kong, the first formal CG initiative took place in 1992, when the SEHK created a CG project to raise awareness of such issues. The governance regime in respect of listed companies is set out in the HKEx's Listing Rules. In fact, the Listing Rules had already covered some important elements of good CG (such as seeking independent minority shareholders' approval for connected transactions and recognizing the importance of directors' fiduciary duties) in the late 1980s, even before the term "corporate governance" became popular in the mid-1990s.

The Listing Rules prescribe the timely disclosure requirements for notifiable transactions and connected transactions. In terms of notifiable transactions, details of significant acquisitions or dispositions of assets have to be disclosed when the value of the transaction relative to the value of the issued share capital of the company exceeds a specified percentage. The company has the obligation to keep the market informed of all sensitive information. Should the stock exchange and the SFC be aware of any price-sensitive information that may have an effect on the market, the stock exchange may use its powers to suspend trading in the shares of the company until such information enters the public domain. Connected transactions between a listed company or its subsidiary and a connected person (including a director, chief executive, or substantial shareholder of the company or its subsidiaries, or an associate of any of these) are subject to disclosure to the stock exchange and shareholder approval in the general meeting while interested parties are prevented from voting. An opinion of an independent expert is required as to whether the transaction is fair and reasonable as far as the shareholders of the company are concerned. These connected transaction requirements are significant in the context of the predominance of family ownership and the control of listed companies.

As an integral part of the Listing Rules, in 1993 the HKEx introduced a Code of Best Practice for firms to follow.[5] The Code seeks to increase the accountability of directors and enhance transparency. As guidelines for directors of listed companies, the Code provides for the following:

i   Full board meetings to be held at least every six months with adequate notice.
ii Full minutes of meetings to be kept and to be open for inspection.
iii Full disclosure of directors' fees and dues payable to independent non-executive directors in the annual report and accounts.
iv Non-executive directors (NED) to be appointed for specific terms, and all appointments to be noted in the annual report and accounts.
v   A full board meeting to be held for matters that involve conflicts of interest for substantial shareholders and director resignations, and the removal of independent NEDs to be explained to the stock exchange.
vi The establishment of an audit committee consisting of a minimum of three NEDs (a majority of them should be independent).

Although compliance with the Code is voluntary, listed companies are required to disclose in their interim and annual reports whether they have so complied, and if not, the areas of and reasons for non-compliance. In the case of audit committees, firms have to report the establishment, or the reasons for non-establishment, for accounting periods beginning January 1, 1999.

Recent regulatory reforms

In order to improve CG and market quality, there have been a number of recent market and legal reforms in Hong Kong. Under a new ordinance, the SEHK, the Hong Kong Futures Exchange, and Hong Kong Securities Clearing Company Ltd (HKSCC) were merged to become a single listed holding company – HKEx – in

March 2000. While this change forced the HKEx to become more publicly accountable and subject to market forces and transparency requirements, there are also some potential conflicts of interests. HKEx is the primary regulator of the companies listed on the SEHK as well as the primary regulator of SEHK participants with respect to trading matters. Many people suggest it would be best if HKEx's listing and regulatory functions were assumed by the SFC.

Other legal reforms include the revision of the Companies Ordinance, the enactment of the SFO, and the continuous revisions of the Listing Rules. While the existing Companies Ordinance provides restrictions and disclosure requirements that are central to sound CG, in many respects it falls short of a satisfactory standard. Recognizing this, and with a view to bringing the Companies Ordinance and Hong Kong's existing CG regime more into line with the international trend, the Financial Services Bureau and the SCCLR put forward 62 recommendations in July 2001 for public consultation. These recommendations, to be legislated in different stages over three years, cover directors' duties and responsibilities, shareholders' rights, and corporate reporting. The key recommendations include abolishing corporate directors; making a director vicariously liable for the acts and omissions of his alternates; reducing the threshold for circulating shareholders' proposals from the existing 5 percent to 2.5 percent of the voting rights; giving every shareholder the personal right to sue to enforce the terms of a company's memorandum and articles of association; and allowing Hong Kong-incorporated listed companies to issue summary financial statements in place of full accounts.

With the similar objective of providing a regulatory regime that is on a par with international standards, and in view of local needs, the SFO, which was enacted in March 2002 and became effective in April 2003, is seen as another significant step in the direction of sound CG in Hong Kong. As a consolidation of existing laws governing the securities and futures markets currently spread over some ten statutes and parts of the Companies Ordinance, the SFO is expected to enhance the SFC's investigatory powers, prevent fraudulent behavior, increase the channels of adopting criminal prosecutions and strengthen market efficiency. Among the new measures that will improve CG, one is the promotion of the timely and accurate disclosure of price-sensitive information by lowering the initial shareholding disclosure threshold for persons other than directors and chief executives from 10 percent to 5 percent, and shortening the disclosure notification period from five to three business days. This proposed amendment is comparable to regulations in the US, Australia, Japan, and Singapore.

The new SFO also allows individual investors a statutory right to ask for loss compensation via civil procedures against company directors and management who release false and misleading information. As a matter of right, they can also claim compensation against those proven guilty by the courts or by the newly formed Market Misconduct Tribunal (MMT) without the need to seek redress under the common law. This will also reduce the onus of proof on the part of the victim. However, since the government wishes to keep regulations flexible enough, both to suit Hong Kong's unique circumstance and avoid rigid laws that might prove inefficient for business, some long-standing issues have not been handled in the new SFO – for example, class action and proof of burden on the defendant.

HKEx released its Consultation Paper on "Proposed Amendments to the Listing Rules Relating to Corporate Governance Issues" in January 2002 (HKEx, 2002). The paper promoted level-playing-field disclosure via the HKEx Price-sensitive Information Guide issued previously. It also suggested more frequent disclosure of profit warnings and more restrictions on rights issues; voting by poll for connected transactions and transactions requiring controlling or interested shareholders to abstain from voting, the introduction of "total assets tests;" increasing the required number of independent non-executive directors from two to three; directors' contracts and remuneration; the requirement of quarterly reporting; and a revision of the Code of Best Practice. However, there were certain areas on which diverse views were expressed. After one year of open consultation, the HKEx published its Consultation Conclusions on the proposals in January 2003. Unfortunately, only some of the proposed changes in the Consultation Paper were finally adopted, to be implemented to the Listing Rules or the Code of Best Practice by the middle of 2003. The HKEx Code of Best Practice will also be revised to contain two tiers of recommendations. The first tier will contain minimum standards of board practices, and the second will be the recommended good practices serving as guidelines for issuers' reference. The revised Listing Rules require issuers to include a report on CG practice in their annual reports, and to provide details of any deviation from the minimum standards set out in the Code of Best Practice.

Most of these current change proposals on rules and regulations will certainly advance board practice, increase the transparency of issuers, and improve the protection of shareholders' rights. However, given the vested interests of the different stakeholders and the complicated relationship between big family business groups and the government, plus other core problems discussed earlier, all regulatory reforms so far have been slow, as well as conducted in a piecemeal manner. Many critical proposals were dropped after a long lobbying process by the big market players. Since the Enron incident, many people in Hong Kong believe that the recommendations as proposed in the Companies Ordinance, the new SFO, and the HKEx consultation papers are far from sufficient.

Enforcement of rules

After several revisions in the past two decades, the regulatory structure of Hong Kong still has a number of weaknesses which need continuous improvement. According to the "Report of Security Review Committee" in 1987, Hong Kong has adopted the so-called "three-tier" market regulatory system: the government, the Securities and Futures Commission, and the stock exchange. The government is the overall policy maker, facilitator, and regulator of regulators, the SFC enforces the new SFO and the Takeover Code and is the statutory regulator of listed companies, and HKEx is the non-statutory frontline regulator of listed companies and enforcer of the Listing Rules.[6]

SEHK/HKEx

The profit-making HKEx has been criticized for allowing low-quality firms to list on its two boards for reasons of revenue and a lack of full-time experienced professional staff to assess listing applications. The Listing Rules set out the obligations of listed companies and attempted to address those areas not covered by corporate and securities laws in order to provide basic shareholder protection. It should be noted that the Listing Rules (and the Code of Best Practice) are non-statutory regulations and only form a contract between the stock exchange and the issuer and each director of the issuer wherein the parties are bound. The merit of non-legal rules and guidelines is that they can avoid the lengthy legislative process involved when the HKEx wishes to revise the Listing Rules to reflect the latest market changes. When a firm violates the rules, or when HKEx does not enforce the rules diligently, shareholders cannot sue the firm or the stock exchange as they are not party to the contract.

There has been public criticism that, as a front-line regulator of listed firms, HKEx's regulatory abilities are too weak and its enforcement record is too lenient. The record of leniency may be due partly to the fact that there are entrenched conflicts of interest in that HKEx serves both as a profit-making listed company and the front-line regulatory body of listed companies, and HKEx seeks part of its revenues from companies that list and trade with it.[7]

It is also commonly admitted that the non-legal status of the Listing Rules reduces their effectiveness. The PCCW incident mentioned earlier was a good example. This company drew negative attention in the CLSA 2003 report on Asian CG, which saw its CG score fall more than that of any other Hong Kong company. The giant Hong Kong telecommunications firm made a botched attempt in early February 2003 to take over Britain's Cable & Wireless, and then offered different statements to exchange officials in two jurisdictions – a move that prompted a huge outcry and a sharp fall in its share price. PCCW finally received a warning from HKEx in mid-2003, indicating that the firm had violated the Listing Rules. Under pressure from giant investment banks and other parties with vested interests, the Legal Department of the Hong Kong government agreed not to convert part of the Listing Rules into law. Whether non-statutory rules or codes can effectively regulate corporate behavior seems a major issue worthy of continuous review.

The SFC

To maintain an appropriate level of regulation and a fair, open, and reliable market is the most difficult target that a security regulatory body wishes to achieve. The SFC insists on a "disclosure-based" regulatory framework to avoid over-regulation. Except for commercial secrets, SFC encourages all firms to increase transparency by more voluntary disclosures.

Although there are occasional voices to be heard saying that the SFC over-regulates and abuses its power, the more common impression of the SFC is that it does not enforce its own rules diligently, and that it lacks the power and will to tackle big market players. There also appears to be an apparent reluctance on the part of the judiciary to impose tough punitive measures or sanctions against wrongdoers as provided for by law. However, some senior SFC officials deny that they are unable or unwilling to curb market abuses. The new SFO allows the SFC to choose between criminal, civil, or both channels to handle market misconduct cases. The IDT has also been expanded into the new MMT to facilitate the process of civil claims. The MMT is empowered to impose fines of up to HK$10 million, or ten years' imprisonment. However, whether this new set-up will increase the determination of the SFC to impose more appropriate penalties is not yet known.

The new SFO expressly gives the SFC the power to inquire into the circumstance and instructions relating to accounting entries. It also empowers the SFC to verify such findings with other sources not previously available to them. Such sources include the papers of the auditors, suppliers, customers, and even the banks of the listed company. However, there are still concerns about the degree of power afforded to the SFC when conducting such investigations. Since the new SFO still does not allow the SFC to regulate the banks' securities business, many people believe that the SFC can only act as a second-class regulator. As the SFC does not have a mandate from the government to impose bolder changes in legislation and law enforcement, it is very hard for it to change itself into a single super-governance body with full powers of investigation and prosecution.

HKEx has expressed openly the view that the SFC intervene too much in their listing operations, and the co-operation between them in policy development is also not particularly satisfactory. To improve the quality of newly listed companies, under the new SFO, the SFC launched the "dual filing" scheme in mid-2003. This new scheme requires all companies applying for listing to submit all prospectuses and other mandatory disclosures to both HKEx and the SFC. While the SFC will not investigate individual applications on its own initiative, it could use its veto to reject any applications where misleading information is found in the submitted materials. However, some market players believe such a mechanism will cause more duplication of effort and hence conflicts.

In late July 2002, the government unveiled a number of delisting proposals, the details of which were released by HKEx in a subsequent consultation paper. The paper suggested the delisting of firms that had suffered losses for several years, or those with insufficient assets. About 350 firms trading below HK50 cents might have needed to consolidate their shares, as the exchange planned to remove penny stocks. But when the proposal was announced, the market overreacted and numerous small investors dumped their penny stocks in a single day, with a loss of HK$5,800 million of capitalization. The government, the SFC, and HKEx officials apologized for the unexpected incident, and an independent inquiry was conducted into the matter. Due to market pressure and the sentiments of public investors, there is a high possibility that the proposal on delisting penny stocks will finally be dropped.

Even though Hong Kong may not want to move to a statutory regime like that of the US, it needs at least to streamline the existing regulatory structure and processes to avoid duplication and delays in the regulatory response to corporate misconduct. Currently, there are grey areas in the division of regulatory duties between the government, the SFC, and HKEx, and further clarification is needed to avoid potential conflicts. To achieve this and to improve further the quality of listed firms, many have argued that HKEx should hand over its listing and regulatory functions to the SFC. In the wake of the penny stock incident, the relationship between the government, the SFC, and HKEx was under substantial review in late 2002 by a team of three experts appointed by the Financial Secretary.

The Expert Group report

The Expert Group to Review the Operation of the Securities and Futures Market Regulatory Structure submitted its report to the government in late March 2003. Following the UK and Australian models, the report called the existing structure "fundamentally flawed," and the central recommendation was that HKEx should drop its regulation business, including the listing function. It was the group's view that HKEx could not both exist to make a profit and regulate in the public interest, no matter how many control mechanisms had been installed.

The report called for the SFC to establish the Hong Kong Listing Authority (HKLA),[8] which would take over the regulatory role from the existing Listing Division of HKEx. Furthermore, it recommended that the Listing Rules be given statutory backing without going through any legislative process. It would become a legal offence to violate the Listing Rules, and it would also allow for prosecution with more meaningful fines. Also, the enforcement of the Listing Rules would be conducted by full-time experienced professionals of HKLA, including the approval of listing applications. The report also recommends that government considers putting some Companies Ordinance rules under the SFO and allowing the SFC to enforce them.

On the day (21 March 2003) of the release of the report, the Financial Secretary endorsed the report and committed the government to implementing its recommendations as soon as possible. However, under the pressure from HKEx and a few other big market players, the Financial Secretary suddenly announced that, in view of the controversial nature of the proposals and their far-reaching implications, the proposals would be postponed for 12 to 18 months to allow for further public consultation before a final decision was made. The matter has unfortunately become a political battle, and is viewed by many people as a power struggle between the SFC and HKEx.

Although the main Expert Group report recommendation is correct in its direction and is feasible, it is not the only option. For reasons of history, the conflicting interests of different stakeholders, legal and ethical responsibilities toward HKEx shareholders, the unclear extra monitoring costs to be incurred, and political sensitivity of the issues, the author suggested to the government a compromise resolution for consideration. A new Listing Authority could be set up that is solely owned by HKEx or co-owned by HKEx and the government. Besides reforming the listing function, other regulatory measures must be implemented as soon as possible in order to improve the quality of the market. Among other measures, these include the tighter supervision of market intermediaries, greater legal protection for investors via derivative and class actions, freezing the shareholding of controlling shareholders for at least 12 months after IPO, and restricting the number of genuine outside shareholders to say not less than 300.

Class actions and burden of proof

Currently, given the high level of expense and difficulty involved in civil claims, it is almost impossible for an individual investor in Hong Kong to sue a suspected market player.[9] Therefore, a certain kind of class action seems necessary to provide the minimum basic protection for public minority investors. However, the SFC chairman put forward the view that, under Hong Kong's legal system, which is similar to that of British common law, if the plaintiff loses, he or she has to pay the defendant's legal fees, and legal fees are high in Hong Kong. Further, if all of the assets of the implicated firm had already been expropriated, merely winning a case would not help the victim gain monetary compensation. Class action suits also imply that any compensation after wining a case would be shared between the plaintiff and his or her lawyers, and some people think this will lead to a litigious society. Regarding the burden of proof, in the Blue Bill of the SFO, it was proposed to put the burden of proof on the defendant. However, under pressure from big market players, the White Bill shifted this burden of proof back to the prosecutors.[10]

Owner-directors and conflicts of minority shareholders

Ownership structure is always the foundation of CG mechanisms. On the basis of ownership structure and other governance attributes, the four most common generic CG models can be identified as: the US/UK Market Model, the Germany/Japan Main Bank Model, the East Asia Family Control Model, and the State Control Model.

In the 1980s, many of the debates on CG focused on the merit of the two major CG systems: US/UK versus Germany/Japan. The family control model has not garnered any attention over the last 30 years in Western literature. In contrast to the assumption of Berle and Means (1932) that all large companies will mature to an ultimate structure that will be characterized by the separation of ownership and control, recent evidence suggests that concentrated ownership by an individual or a family exists in many countries, particularly in those of East Asia (Shleifer and Vishny, 1997; Ho, 2000; Claessons *et al.*, 2000; Roe, 2000). According to La Porta *et al.* (1999a), Claessons *et al.* (2000), and Fan and Wong (1999), over 70 percent of the listed firms in East Asian countries (except Japan) have a dominant shareholder that is usually a family.

The first report of the HKSA's Corporate Governance Working Group (CGWG) confirmed that over 70 percent of Hong Kong listed companies were majority controlled by a family or an individual (Hong Kong Society of Accountants, 1996). The ten wealthiest families in Hong Kong owned over 47 percent of the total market capitalization of the SEHK in 2000. Fifty-three percent of all listed companies had one shareholder or one family group of shareholders that owned 50 percent or more of the entire issued capital (Hong Kong Society of Accountants, 1997). The average shareholdings of the board of directors were 43.5 percent of the total shares on the SEHK (Hong Kong Society of Accountants, 1997). In over 85 percent of listed firms, board directors owned at least one third of all shares (Ho *et al.*, 2002). The HSBC is apparently one of the very few firms that is traded on HKEx with no majority controlling interest by one group. Together, these controlling shareholders or families represent the most powerful groups in Hong Kong, their interests sometimes further promoted by political connections. The government has been often criticized for being too close to powerful vested business interests, and for not disentangling itself from such interests – the CyberPort Project is a good example of this.

Most of these controlling families secure their control via a complicated ownership structure (such as pyramid, cross-shareholding or interlocking directorships), and a large separation of voting from cash flow rights (Claessons *et al.*, 2000). A pyramid allows the controlling families to exercise a great deal of control for very little ownership. It works in the following manner: a family owns 51 percent of company A, which owns 51 percent of company B, which owns 51 percent of company C, which owns 25 percent of company D. Hence the family controls 25 percent of company D, but its ownership stake is only 3.3 percent: 51 percent of 51 percent of 51 percent of 25 percent. To enhance a family's control, other companies that own shares are mainly its own affiliated companies or private investment companies associated with controlling family members. Many families develop a business from its inception, and even when the company is growing bigger or has been publicly listed, the founding family still wishes to retain its tight control. In recognition of this situation, the SEHK only requires that 25 percent or more of the issued shares of listed companies be held by unconnected persons.

In general, Hong Kong-listed firms are owned and managed through blood and marriage ties. Many of these family members also actively participate in the daily operations of their firms by appointing themselves or trusted relatives and colleagues as senior executives or board directors. Ho and Wong (2001b) found that the average percentage of family members sitting on boards was 32.1 percent. In the case of family control of a company's board, the potential for a family patriarch to influence decisions is particularly strong. It is also assumed that every family owns and votes collectively. Although some people perceive family businesses as old-fashioned and slow to grow due to their relationship-based business networks, research shows that family-controlled companies are at least as successful as widely held multinational companies (see, for example, Lang and Young, 2001; Ho and Lam, 2003). Because of the close attention that is paid to the front-line business, family-controlled companies can always make efficient decisions. In Hong Kong, Li Ka-shing has blended some elements of international best practice with Chinese culture, though he still makes use of pyramid structures to maximize family control with minimal capital.[11]

However, there are inherent conflicts between the controlling and minority shareholders of firms due to the high incentives for controlling shareholders to extract private benefits through their control in connected party transactions. Through connected party transactions between affiliated companies controlled by a family, owners can effectively transfer wealth from one company to another by selling assets at lower-than-market prices. With pyramid and cross-shareholding structures, insiders can gain wealth by setting unfair terms for intra-group sales of goods and services and the transfer of assets and controlling stakes, at the expense of minority shareholders. One possible way of expropriation is that the listed company at the base of the pyramid sells its shares to the public and then passes the proceeds up the pyramid via numerous internal transactions. In return, less profitable assets are passed down the pyramid. Another example is that the holding firm receives very low interest loans from associated companies or takes on high-risk projects jointly with its associated company.

Other common forms of misbehavior among controlling shareholders in Hong Kong include directing corporate resources to themselves, the dilution of existing shareholders' holdings by share placement with outsiders or issuing shares to insiders, seeking outside loans that are secured through the assets of associated listed companies, the payment of excessive executive compensation despite poor firm performance, and unfair dividend policies. Currently some subsidiaries of a group make use of their shareholding in their parent company as collateral for huge borrowings from banks. They further use such funds for trading their parent company's stocks and other risky investments. Currently, there is no rules directly governing or restricting cross-shareholding in Hong Kong.

Directors' duties and board practices

The focus of many international guidelines on CG is the role of the board of directors in ensuring sound CG practices. The part of any organization that has the greatest control over governance is the board of directors, because it is the board's core responsibility to be accountable.

In the US, recent high-profile corporate scandals indicate that many directors' acts are not for the benefits of the company, but originate from a desire for personal benefit. In fact, this could happen in any country regardless of how strict its regulatory framework is. Establishing good director and board practices is intrinsic to ensuring that directors and their boards act responsibly in the governance of their companies, and that working outwards they are accountable to all shareholders for the assets and resources which are entrusted to them. Working inwards, boards should set corporate missions and objectives, and select, monitor, and compensate senior executives. The board should ensure timely and accurate financial and non-financial disclosure and present accounts to shareholders which reflect the true state of the company's financial position.

The Listing Rules of HKEx for the Main and Growth Enterprise Market (GEM) boards specify the duties and responsibilities of directors. Every director of a listed company must satisfy the HKEx that they have the character, experience, integrity, and ability to demonstrate a standard of competence that is commensurate with their position. Directors are expected to fulfill fiduciary duties and the duties of skill, care, and diligence as may reasonably be expected of a person with their knowledge and experience. They should avoid actual and potential conflicts of interest, and fully disclose their interests in contracts with the company. However, the Listing Rules do not specify that directors must act in the interests of the shareholders. Under the Companies Ordinance, directors should fulfill their fiduciary duties to the company, but not to the shareholders.

Although directors' duties are stipulated in the Listing Rules, they lack statutory force, which makes any breach of duty difficult (and therefore more costly) to enforce under common law. In any case, for listed companies, it is directors, not managers, who are ultimately liable if company actions lead to the breaching of listing rules or company law. For CG, directors also bear much more responsibility than managers.

According to a survey by the Hong Kong Institute of Company Secretaries (2002), less than 40 percent of directors in Hong Kong understand their fiduciary duties and legal responsibilities, and the rest give them low priority. In fact, many smaller company directors are ignorant of the concepts of CG and directors' duties. The role of a director is sometimes mixed up with that of a senior manager. This is a common problem of many directors in Hong Kong (Mobius, 2002).

Regarding qualifications and training for directors, Hong Kong is far behind nearby countries in terms of preparation training, professional certification, and mandatory continuous professional education. Malaysia adopted professional training and examination schemes for candidate directors, and China has started running certificate courses for would-be directors. Although it could be argued that it is easier for these transitional economies to start new things from scratch, it is hard to believe that nothing has been done so far in this respect in Hong Kong. Although Hong Kong has an Institute of Directors, it has done very little toward pursuing professional certification or a self-regulatory scheme. As an international financial center, Hong Kong should catch up in this dimension to make its corporate directors more knowledgeable and accountable.

Independent non-executive directors (INEDs)

As in many other countries, the existence of INEDs on boards in Hong Kong is seldom voluntary. Since 1993, the Listing Rules of HKEx, as part of its Code of Best Practice, have required that every listed firm must have at least two INEDs.

These INEDs must have no past or present financial or other interest in the business of the company or its subsidiaries, and no past or present connection with any connected person of the company who might affect the exercise of independent judgment. These conditions are critical due to the predominance of family ownership and control of firms in Hong Kong. However, other requirements of being an INED are not clear, such as the knowledge and experience that are needed, residency, number of directorships held, meeting attendance, and minimal time spent on firm business. The definitions of independence and the classification of directors as independent in some cases raise questions as to whether such people are truly independent.

Ho and Wong (2001b) found that the average proportion of INEDs on the boards of listed firms in Hong Kong was 34 percent, and the average number was 2.45. Therefore, INEDs are still a small minority. However, it is required by the Listing Rules that at the committee level some committees, such as audit and remuneration committees, must have a majority of INEDs and be chaired by an INED. Clearly, the quality of INEDs is as important as the number in ensuring better governance. However, it is always difficult to find experienced and devoted INEDs, and most new appointees do not usually know enough about the realities of business to effectively monitor inside executive directors (Tricker, 1995).

As most listed firms in Hong Kong are family-controlled, and in view of the low free float, it is generally perceived as being impossible to have truly independent directors. Real outsiders are usually not trusted, and friends or close contacts of the controlling family fill the independent director slots. In other words, these directors are less than fully independent. INEDs are often nominated by executive directors who represent controlling shareholders, who in turn hold the key votes at shareholders' general meetings on the election or re-election of those executive directors. Such INEDs can be replaced any time if they are not loyal to the controlling shareholders. Therefore, most INEDs are unable or unwilling to state the case of minority shareholders. Sometimes, when things go wrong, these INEDs simply resign early to avoid liability. Recently, there have been suggestions that independent directors should be elected directly by minority shareholders only.

The audit committee and other committees

The Code of Best Practice of HKEx recommends listed firms to establish and disclose the existence of audit committees (or to give reasons why they do not exist) in their annual reports since January 1999. The HKSA also issued guidelines on the formation and operation of an audit committee. The guidelines, which have been endorsed by the stock exchange, stipulate that an audit committee company should consist of a minimum of three INEDs with board business backgrounds (the majority of whom should be independent), with written terms of reference that deal clearly with the "four responsibilities:" financial and other reporting, internal control, internal and external audits, and the needs of management.

The revised Code of Best Practice will recommend the establishment of a remuneration committee and a nomination committee. Nomination committees make recommendations on the appointment or re-appointment of executive and non-executive directors by listed issuers. These committees should be composed mainly of INEDs.

Despite the fact that the oversight of the audit committee contributes significantly to corporate accountability, most countries around the world mandate the adoption of audit committees for all listed companies. In Hong Kong, it is surprising that neither the Companies Ordinance, the Listing Rules, nor the SFC requires this adoption. Under the terms of the HKEx Corporate Governance Consultation Paper, the establishment of an audit committee would be made a requirement for main board issuers (it is already a requirement for GEM companies). However, HKEx finally decided to leave it as a voluntary act. This leniency reflects how Hong Kong is still lagging behind international standards in the realm of CG.

Dominant personalities (CEO duality)

CEO duality is common in the US, although the world trend tends to decouple the two roles.[12] In 1998, this separation existed in 71 percent of listed companies in Hong Kong (Ho and Wong, 2001b). Currently most Chinese-owned banks in Hong Kong have no separation of the two roles. In early 2002, the HKMA recommended that these banks separate their board chairmen from their CEOs; some banks accepted the recommendation and made the separation. The HKEx Corporate Governance Consultation Paper recommends that the roles of the chairman and the CEO should be segregated, but HKEx concluded that it would be sufficient to include it in the Code of Best Practice rather than making it mandatory.

Directors' dealings

In the Enron incident, dealings by directors with linked and associated companies appear to have been one of the problems. One of the major areas that both the SCCLR and the HKEx Corporate Governance Consultation Paper have concentrated on is directors' dealings with their companies, subsidiaries, and associated companies. This is an area where it is likely that abuses could easily arise. The aim of any new rules will be to prevent directors from deriving unfair advantage from their positions. In formulating proposals, the SCCLR will resolve whether the regulation will be achieved by statute or Listing Rules. Further, the scope of the transactions that are covered needs careful consideration, as an "associated" company is an accounting term and is not defined in legislation. In the HKEx Corporate Governance Consultation Paper, various proposals were made to clarify the rules concerning directors' dealings and their disclosure. Stricter rules on the disclosure of securities transactions by directors were also proposed. Under HKEx's Consultation Conclusions, the Exchange will amend the Listing

Rules to require shareholders' approval for a service contract that is to be granted to a director of the issuers or its subsidiaries for a period not exceeding three years. Shareholders who are the directors with an interest in the services contracts and their associates will be required to abstain from voting at the general meetings approving the respective service contracts.

Directors' remuneration

In Hong Kong, the average pay of a listed firm director–CEO in 2000 was about HK$5.7 million, while the highest paid executive director in 2002–03 received HK$373 million. These payments include salaries, bonuses, stock options and other allowances. In the US, the average paid to CEOs in 2002 was less than 2001 by 10–15 percent, although the median pay was still increased by 6 percent. Internationally, the US is ranked the top and Hong Kong is ranked fifth in the world and first in Asia in terms of senior executives' pay. Reports in the media in recent years have woken Hong Kong investors to the issue of excessive pay packages for company executive directors. The issue has become especially controversial because, at the same time, company profits have dropped. In an often cited example, the directors at PCCW received a huge payment of HK$768 million in 2000 (at 50 times the amount of 1999), despite the company's record loss of HK$6.9 billion and a 72 percent fall in its share price (South China Morning Post, 2002). According to a South China Morning Post (SCMP) survey, the total directors' pay in 2001 among the 33 Heng Seng Index firms increased by 63 percent, despite a 33 percent fall in the combined net profit of these companies. Other Hong Kong firms paying high salaries despite poor performance include Dickson Concepts, Luk's Industry, Emperor International, Far East group, Century City, Sunday, and Sincere, etc. Certainly, a few companies are exceptions. For example, the directors of the Shui On Group cut their own pay by 10 percent in 2002.

In a recent Hong Kong study by Ho and Lam (2003), it was found that directors' ownership had a negative and moderating effect on the total amount of pay to the top five executives of a firm and the total cash bonus that is paid to executives. It seems that pay-for-performance compensation schemes are not major factors in setting top executive remuneration in Hong Kong. Moreover, board size, firm size, market to book assets, and the existence of a bonus plan have a positive and significant effect on the total amount of pay to top five executives. Among those few firms that link pay to performance, blue chip companies without controlling shareholders tend to pay the fairest. In family-controlled firms, pay for performance may not be important because the executives have contributed their own capital and personal reputation to the business. This union of ownership and management tends to lead to a difficulty in distinguishing between personal and company assets. However, company directors in family firms might use their control to manipulate the system and use compensation to benefit themselves and their associates at the expense of minority shareholders. In Hong Kong firms with controlling shareholders, the small shareholders have very little say about directors' pay because the board can make a proposal to the shareholders' general meetings and obtain approval quite easily.

While executive directors are over-paid, there is a common saying that INEDs are under-paid. There have been suggestions that the pay which is given to an INED should be commensurate with their quality, risk profile and performance. There are also arguments that each INED should hold a very small percentage of a firm's stock (say not more than 1 percent) in order to show their commitment to the firm. However, the issue of shareholding by an INED is still controversial although such practices are quite common in the US and the UK.

Hong Kong is also well-known for its opacity on executive compensations. Local companies usually disclose very little about their policies on compensating their directors and senior executives. They had resisted proposals to increase disclosure of directors' pay on the grounds of privacy. Disclosure requirements on executive pay in the US and the UK are much stricter and demanding than they are in Hong Kong. In recent years, steps have been taken to increase the disclosure of executive pay, in the hope that it would increase transparency and be more closely tied to firm health and performance of the company. The HKSA has proposed more detailed disclosure requirements of directors' incomes such as aggregate amount, analysis by components, analysis by bands, remuneration policy, fixed versus discretionary pay, the value of options realized, and amount by individual name.

The power and abuses of stock options

The principle underlying all the requirements of International Financial Reporting Standard (IFRS) 19 is that the cost of providing employee benefits should be recognized in the period in which the benefits are earned by the employee, rather than when it is paid or payable. However, there is no equivalent accounting standard in Hong Kong yet. Current requirements in this area under Hong Kong SSAP are restricted to disclosure requirements (particularly the Listing Rules and the GEM rules). In May 2001, the HKSA issued an Exposure Draft proposing a revised SSAP based on IFRS 19 but no official pronouncement yet, as of mid-2003.

This slow standard-setting process in Hong Kong is probably due to the difficulties in identifying a commonly-agreed and easily understood method of calculating the fair value of stock options granted. In the US, the major valuating method is the Black-Scholes option pricing model but this approach involves complicated estimations and computations. In any case, once such an accounting standard was released in Hong Kong, it would probably affect more the earnings of firms which are short of cash, less profitable or listed in the GEM board. The average drop in earnings is about 3 percent (individual firms could be up to 40 percent) and this extent is still far lower than in the US.

The less negative impact on earnings in Hong Kong is due to the fact that Hong Kong firms adopt far less executive stock options schemes than their counterparts in the US. Most listed firms in Hong Kong are controlled by a family or individuals, these controlling shareholders/directors have invested their own personal assets and reputations on the business, and therefore there is little need to give extra incentives for the owners/directors. In general, these firms also tend to grant cash bonus than stock options to employees as they believe accounting earnings or other performance indicators are more reliable than short-term stock prices. Ho and Lam (2003) found that the existence of a stock option plan in Hong Kong is not associated with the amount of pay, directors' ownership, dividend yields, P/E ratios, earnings and market value ratio, leverage ratio, market value and net fixed asset ratio, and capital expenditure. This could be explained by the fact that the adoption of stock options schemes is not common in Hong Kong.

Of course, in order to achieve the powerful incentive effects of stock options, the existing legal, financial, and accounting infrastructures should be further improved with bold steps, and executive compensation loopholes tightened up. Specifically, it is wise to reapportion the ratio of fixed to variable pay that executive directors receive so that the variable pay should not exceed, say, 60 percent. Moreover, rules can be introduced so that these options cannot be exercised within several years unless the performance of the firm exceeds the average of the stock prices in the market or only when these executives left the company for at least three years. Directors and executives should be excluded from selling their holdings of company shares while serving on the board. Some experts also suggest executives' net gain (after tax) after exercising their options should be held in the company stock until a certain number of days after they leave the company.

There is no magic formula for how much directors should be paid. However, there must be some theoretical linkage to show to outside investors that the amounts paid are not random or controlled by the directors themselves, that they are based on reasonable models and that they are transparent and acceptable to minority shareholders. From an outsider's point of view, if directors continue to enjoy higher levels of pay regardless of profitability of the company, this is clearly not in the interest of the investing public.

Accounting disclosure and standard setting and corporate reporting

The effective functioning of capital markets critically depends on effective information sharing among companies, securities analysts, and shareholders. One major element of good CG is transparency – the provision of timely, true, and relevant corporate information to stakeholders (especially investors) to enable them to make decisions. Improvements in information sharing should increase management credibility, analysts' understanding of the firm, investors' patience and confidence, and, potentially, share value (Eccles and Mavrinac, 1995). In a study by the Chief Financial Officer (CFO) of the 116 largest listed firms in Asia, those which disclosed more extensively were found to perform much better in earnings and stock prices than those which disclosed less extensively (Apple Daily, 2002). Among the top ten companies in terms of disclosure quality, three were from Hong Kong. Sufficient information disclosure is an effective mechanism to reduce information asymmetry and increase market efficiency.

The mandatory disclosure requirements in Hong Kong are mainly stipulated by the Hong Kong Company, the SFO, the Listing Rules (Appendix 7A), the SSAP, and the Industry Accounting Guidelines for certain special sectors. Besides shareholding and significant transaction disclosure requirements, some of the important disclosure requirements in the Listing Rules of the SEHK include principal activities and segmented information, directors' interests in shares, directors' service contracts and interests in contracts and emoluments, substantial shareholders, published forecasts of results, details of borrowings, details of properties, five-year financial summaries, emoluments of the five highest paid employees, principal suppliers and customers, management discussion and analysis, and the profile of directors and senior management. The new Code of Best Practice requires listed companies to disclose whether an audit committee is in existence, and all financial statements must be prepared under approved accounting standards. Overall, the scope of disclosure requirements in Hong Kong is much narrower and less specific than that in the US and the UK (Eccles and Mavrinac, 1995). For instance, until recently only interim (mid-year) and year-end reports were provided. There was no need for listed firms to disclose their balance sheets in their interim reports, and the cost of goods sold was not available in income statements. Disclosure rules governing ownership interests, notifiable and related party transactions, and directors' interests and remuneration are much less stringent than in the US.

Financial reporting standards and compliance

Much of the financial reporting information is prepared by management, endorsed by the audit committee, approved by the board, audited by the external auditors, and circulated widely via various channels. Each participant in this chain must play its role with high professional standards to ensure transparency, reliability, and integrity. It is also important to bear in mind that the quality of accounting and auditing standards and their enforcement have a direct bearing on the quality of the financial information that is disclosed.

Unfortunately, the manipulation of accounting standards, window-dressing, creative accounting, earnings management, and even fraudulent reporting have been the practice of some of the largest listed firms in the world. These practices include channel stuffing, recognizing exchanged-out network capacity as income, excluding executive stock options and other liabilities from balance sheets, and overemphasizing certain earning indicators, such as earnings before interest, taxes, depreciation, and amortization (EBITDA). As a former colony, Hong Kong's financial reporting or accounting system largely follows British accounting practices. The SSAP, the Accounting Industry Guidelines, the Statements of Audit Standards (SAS), and professional ethical standards are issued by a self-regulated professional body – the HKSA. Although non-statutory, compliance with these standards is required of all HKSA members. In terms of accounting standards, Hong Kong SSAP were in the main local adaptations of the UK SSAP in the early years. However, at the end of 1992, the HKSA switched to IFRS (formerly known as the International Accounting Standard (IAS)) that are issued by the International Accounting Standard Board (IASB) as models for the new Hong Kong SSAP.

Among some 35 IFRS, about half are compatible with local SSAP. If there is no Hong Kong SSAP on a particular issue (there were about seven such cases in 2002), the IFRS is usually followed. Many local standards have been converted to make them consistent with IFRS. The general policy is to produce totally original statements only if no equivalent IFRS exists. For this reason, local statements have been restricted to mainly Accounting Industry Guidelines. This symbolizes Hong Kong's commitment to the international harmonization of accounting practices. As Hong Kong SSAP are in line with IFRS, Hong Kong main board and GEM issuers with a primary listing can adopt IFRS (while overseas issuers with a secondary listing in Hong Kong can adopt US generally accepted accounting principles (GAAPs)). The international standards on which Hong Kong standards are modeled follow a principle-based approach as opposed to the rule-based approach that is adopted in the US. The principle-based approach, which emphasizes substance/spirit over form, is regarded as a more effective safeguard against abuse. In principle, the kind of off-balance sheet finance arrangements through special purpose entities (SPE) that were permitted under US GAAPs are not permitted under IFRS or Hong Kong SSAP.

Disclosure practice and effectiveness

Overall, conformity with the Listing Rules and accounting standards by Hong Kong firms is high (Tai *et al.*, 1990; Hong Kong Society of Accountants, 1997). The only area that has a comparatively low standard of compliance is the disclosure of related party transactions (Hong Kong Institute of Company Secretaries, 1998), which is most likely to be due to the high proportion of family-controlled listed firms. The Judges' Report of the Hong Kong Management Association Best Annual Report Award noted that many Hong Kong companies still made only the minimum disclosures that were required by the accounting standards and statutory provisions. In addition, over the years, the quality and quantity of information that is disclosed in annual reports has varied, even though the degree of difference has been decreasing and the quality of Hong Kong annual reports has improved (South China Morning Post, 1998b). Nevertheless, firms in Hong Kong still have to provide more in-depth analysis of their business and performance (e.g. management analysis and discussion). Mandatory disclosure rules ensure equal access to basic information (Lev, 1992), but this information has to be augmented by firms' voluntary disclosures and information production by intermediaries.

Gray (1988) suggested that although the "Asian–Colonial" cultural group to which Hong Kong belongs has a system of accounting that is characterized more by transparency than by secrecy, it consistently lags behind the "Anglo" cultural group. Williams and Tower (1998) found that Hong Kong companies appear to disclose more additional information than do companies in ASEAN countries including Singapore, the Philippines, Thailand, Indonesia, and Malaysia. In a recent survey by Standard and Poor's, Hong Kong was ranked the same as China, South Korea, Malaysia, and Thailand. Singapore was ranked top, and Indonesia, the Philippines, and Taiwan were rated the lowest (Ming, 2002b).

Many investors and auditors in Hong Kong have worried about company disclosure practices for related party transactions and other dealings, and they have called for greater financial disclosure for listed companies following the series of corporate fraud cases mentioned above (South China Morning Post, 1998a). Some audit firm partners have suggested that the Stock Exchange should increase its disclosure requirements, while others have suggested the voluntary disclosure of more information (South China Morning Post, 1998a). To avoid the danger of over-regulation, the HKEx hopes to encourage such a culture of voluntary disclosure. It believes that the quality of a company's disclosures will be reflected in its stock price and its future ability to raise share capital (Hong Kong Institute of Company Secretaries, 1998). Nevertheless, disclosure requirements in Hong Kong are reviewed and extended regularly. Besides seeking increased regulation, investors are increasingly concerned with the communication and disclosure processes of listed firms (South China Morning Post, 1998a).

As mentioned previously, the new SFO introduced additional disclosure requirements to combat market misconduct and empower investors further. It has put in place a disclosure regime that is more in line with international standards.

Auditor independence and accounting

Although the local statutory accounting body, the HKSA, has a set of ethical standards for auditors to follow – including guidance on independence, objectivity and integrity, practice promotion, fees, clients' monies, and confidentiality – some people believe that the auditor failure of the Guangnan Group (a red-chip trading firm with diverse investments) in 1998 is similar to the Enron case in the US. The firm faced serious unexpected financial difficulties even though all its recent audited financial statements did not show any red flags and was finally collapsed. Fraudulent activities in some red chip firms (firms registered and listed in Hong Kong but with controlling owners based in China) were exposed after the economic boom in China, but their accounts were all approved by their local auditors. This aroused people's suspicions about the quality of auditors in Hong Kong. A lot of market players wonder whether the HKSA has an effective enforcement regime to safeguard its members' adherence to the stated principles.

There have also been serious concerns about the role of auditors in the IPO process. Originally scheduled to be listed in July 2001, some information in Kitwei International's IPO prospectus was found to be untrue, even after the company was given the green light by its auditors, the regulators, the underwriters, and the listing committee of the HKEx. The company's auditor, Arthur

Andersen, withdrew its audit report from the prospectus after the incident was released but did not explain why the false information was not discovered in the auditing process earlier. Were there no reporting of such cases by anonymous people, public investors would be cheated. More recently, the fraudulent financial reporting case of Euro-Asia Agricultural (Holdings), a People's Republic of China (PRC) private enterprise listed in Hong Kong, was described as the "mini Enron" case of Hong Kong. The orchid grower was alleged in October 2002 to have inflated its revenue 20-fold when it applied for a Hong Kong listing. Its listing was subsequently suspended, and the firm and its founder, IPO sponsor, and auditors were investigated by relevant authorities both in Hong Kong and China. There have also been cases in which the earnings of newly listed firms have increased a thousand times after their IPOs, and this has caused further worries on the reliability of audited financial statements.

Auditor independence

Auditor independence has become the focus of much worldwide attention in the wake of the Enron collapse. The controversial independence issues that have arisen in the US are generally attributed to the dramatic growth in the size of some audit firms' consulting businesses relative to audits, and the widespread provision of management consulting services to audit clients. In contrast, audit and other traditional professional services – such as tax advisory – are still mainstream services that are provided by certified public accountants (CPAs) in Hong Kong. As most local family-controlled listed firms tend not to use independent consulting services, such conflicts exist to a lesser extent than in the US. Furthermore, as most of the consulting activities of audit firms in Hong Kong are conducted by independent divisions, auditors should face fewer independence issues than in the US. However, the HKSA has admitted that there are no statistics on how CPAs perform auditing and non-auditing services, and it has no idea about the potential for conflict of interest in the profession. In any case, many in Hong Kong still believe that auditing should be totally separate from management consulting activities. If an auditor also serves as a financial advisor to a client firm, they are less likely to report any fraud that is found in the audit process.

Another major issue of auditor independence is that although auditors are employed by a listed company and should be accountable to shareholders (especially minority shareholders) by conducting professional and independent audits on the company's accounts. However, in practice, only corporate management has direct contact with the auditors and these auditors are therefore inclined to be accountable to the management or the controlling shareholders/directors more than to outside minority shareholders. As such, conflicts of interest often exist.

Further, the Big-4 auditing firms monopolize the auditing market for listed firms in Hong Kong and thus control the structure and norms of the industry. These firms not only participate in relevant legislations and policy making indirectly for protecting the interests of practicing accountants, but the local professional body formed by such an industrial structure would find it difficult to perform the role of monitoring among each other. Currently, in Hong Kong the HKSA is allowed by statute to grant practicing licenses and to monitor the professional conducts of its members. It is therefore necessary to enhance the independence of the current regulatory system and ensure that auditors can perform their independent auditing duties to protect minority investors' rights.

Following the IFAC's recently released International Code of Ethics for Professional Accountants, the HKSA's current ethical standard recognizes the possible threat to independence that is created by a quantum of fees, and imposes a guideline that fees from any one client should not exceed 15 percent of the total fee income of the audit firm. It also deals in depth with other potential threats, such as personal relationships, financial involvement, and the provision of non-audit services such as management consulting. The standard requires audit firms to take care not to perform management functions. When the safeguards are insufficient to eliminate the threats to independence or reduce them to an acceptable level, the firm is expected to decline the work or withdraw from the assurance engagement. Although this principle-based approach has its merits, it also allows easy opportunities for some auditors to make use of the gray areas and discretions for abuses.

The new SFO allows the SFC to gain access to an auditor's working papers, and provides auditors of listed companies who choose to report any suspected fraud or misconduct to the SFC with statutory immunity from civil liability under client confidentiality rules. Unfortunately, the SFO does not compel auditors to report fraud (which is obviously a crime) to the regulators but makes this voluntary. Some auditors argue that it would be sufficient for them to report fraud to the client company's audit committee, but this view ignores the fact that many audit committees in Hong Kong are not truly independent. It is argued that the failure to impose a positive duty to report fraud is a significant omission in the SFO. Although auditors have no duty to detect or investigate fraud, they should be mandated to report irregularities to the audit committee of a client company and the regulatory body if any are detected in the auditing process. Auditors should care not only for their clients' interests but also the interests of the investing public.

Self-regulation versus independent public oversight

The HKSA's traditional self-regulation system relies on its own practicing members to monitor other members' professional conduct. This approach worked quite well for the last several decades. Naturally, in today's much more complicated business environment, more conflicts of interest tend to arise. The effectiveness of a self-regulatory system has been the subject of ever-increasing skepticism and challenges. Since 1998, the HKEx has submitted 11 suspected auditor misconduct cases to the HKSA for investigation. Other than the four cases which were withdrawn due to insufficient information, the HKSA has not so far been able to inform the public of its progress with regard to its investigations or any action taken in the remaining seven cases.

Currently, there are three committees under the HKSA Council which handle members' ethical and disciplinary matters: the professional ethics committee, the investigation committee, and the disciplinary committee. When the Council receives a complaint, it usually refers it to the professional ethics committee to ascertain whether further investigations are needed. The Council then decides whether to let the investigation panel carry out further investigations or the disciplinary committee makes disciplinary decisions. In the first case, the investigation panel gives its results to the Council, and the Council decides whether it will make its own disciplinary decisions or let the disciplinary committee do so. Under this arrangement, the disciplinary committee has no powers of investigation and cannot take the initiative to follow up any complaint.

Many market participants believe that, in the long run, Hong Kong needs an independent public oversight body (instead of an Independent Investigation Board (IIB)) which directly monitors the practice of the HKSA. It also has the right to follow up and investigate an independent complaint or a case noted from public sources. This should have full investigation, prosecution, and disciplinary powers and should also monitor the way that the HKSA handles public complaints and member disciplinary matters. It is generally believed that before the government makes a decision, the HKSA Council should allow the disciplinary committee to handle and investigate any complaints directly and make final disciplinary decisions. As an interim measure, this implies that the investigation and disciplinary panels can merge into a single committee.

Improving the independence of the regulation of the accounting profession by introducing more pubic participation is a worldwide trend. It is believed that if the local accounting profession does not take the initiative to form an independent oversight board, it is hard to regain lost confidence in public accountants and their audited reports. Ultimately, the government will have to take over the profession in the interest of the public if more accounting frauds and scandals occur.

Market intermediaries and analysts

Since the Kit-Wei International and Euro-Asia Agriculture scandals in the early 2000s, the independence and integrity of IPO sponsors and other intermediaries have been subject to public criticism. The performance of some newly listed firms dropped rapidly after IPO, and was significantly different from what was forecast in the IPO prospectuses. It was found that intermediaries had assisted these companies to apply for listing by decorating their accounts and "repackaging" their IPO materials. Collusion between the issuers and some intermediaries to exaggerate IPO earning figures has been the subject of attention by the regulatory bodies.

The responsibility of an IPO sponsor is to ensure that an issuer fulfills all of the listing requirements, and to employ relevant professionals to verify related information and documents so that investor interests can be protected. In theory, IPO sponsors are accountable to future shareholders, but in practice most sponsors are directly employed by the senior management of the issuer. Sometimes the sponsor also serves as the issuer's IPO underwriter, responsible for IPO packaging and promotions in order to get the best deals. This clearly leads to conflicts of interest. Even when these roles are separate, as long as IPO sponsors are directly employed by an issuer the independence problem cannot be completely resolved. To improve market quality in Hong Kong, both HKEx and the SFC need to ensure the quality of newly listed companies, and must also effectively monitor the market intermediaries. The government, HKEx, the SFC, and the HKSA have all made suggestions for improving the situation. The SFC currently supervises these intermediaries through the Code of Conduct on registered corporate finance advisors and their licensing rules. It can suspend or terminate the registration of an intermediary in case of misconduct, but this practice has been criticized as lacking flexibility since it would be difficult to find out whether the management or the sponsors violate rules. For this reason, since 1997 the SFC has condemned only 13 registered corporate finance advisors, seven of whom had their registrations temporarily suspended. One major difficulty, however, in regulating IPO intermediaries is that it is difficult to ascertain the specific responsibilities of the different intermediaries involved, such as sponsors, lawyers, accountants, and valuators. When a new issuer is caught, each of these bodies will try to point their figures at the other intermediaries. The regulators wish to ensure that each intermediary knows its responsibilities and is accountable to the investors.

In the financial markets, due to information asymmetry and complicated transactions, outside investors face difficulty in monitoring listed companies, relying usually on professional analysts for additional information, analyses, and advice when making investment decisions. These supplement other limited information sources and make the market more efficient. Unfortunately, most analysts cannot survive on an independent self-employed basis, and they are usually employed by a stockbroking firm or investment bank. These stockbrokers and banks have close business relationships with many issuers – serving as IPO sponsors or underwriters, for example – and this easily affects the independence of analysts. Many investment banks release research reports on new issuers before IPO activities, and as there is a close relationship between analysts and the investment bank, many analysts would be affected by the views of the bank's financing or marketing department when putting together pre-IPO reports. These reports always become PR documents for new issuers, even though many of them have no earnings records or even real business activities. Since these research reports, many of which contain forecasted earnings data, are technically not part of the IPO prospectus, they are not subject to the requirements of Listing Rules. Many of the analysts are compensated with bonuses and share options according to the earnings of the bank employing them and if they, through personal interest, provide misleading or inaccurate information in their reports, investors could be seriously misled about investment decisions.

In Hong Kong most individual investors are not able to obtain research reports from large investment banks. With the exception of a few independent press columnists, there are not enough independent voices to pressure regulators into making Hong Kong markets more transparent and improving CG. Some media analysts, with or without disclosing their identity, are employed by security firms or investment banks. According to a survey by the Democratic Party, over 70 percent of investors do not trust analysts' advice when making investment decisions. What is needed are independent analysts such as Terry Smith in the UK and Zhang Hua-qiao in China (both of UBS-Warburg), who assert their independence without fear of termination by their employers or legal action by the firms they criticize. The culture of accountability that values high quality and objective research and reporting holds the key to future confidence in analysts.

Empowering minority shareholders and activism

Overall, Hong Kong's minority shareholders are not properly represented, have very little influence, and are open to potential abuses by controlling shareholders who extract unfair gains from them. There are low free floats of the shares of listed companies, and the local media rarely investigates questionable corporate activities. The dominant voting power of insiders also easily neutralizes public shareholder activism and creates apathy. Individual investors in Hong Kong are usually inactive and vote with their feet. According to the CLSA, the country scores on the treatment of minorities are Singapore 100, Hong Kong 84, the Philippines 35, Taiwan 34, and Korea 33.3. La Porta *et al.* (1999c) found that common law countries (mainly the US, the UK, Canada, and Australia) appear to have the best legal protection of minority shareholders, while civil law countries – particularly the French civil law countries – have the weakest protection. The legal protection score of Hong Kong is five (six equals "excellent"), which is the same as the UK and the US, but many people doubt the accuracy of such a high ranking.

Although institutional investors count for 40 percent of the local market transactions, they mainly trade on blue chip stocks and are not active in monitoring the management of invested firms. Further, provident fund markets are just starting to develop in Hong Kong, which means that it will be a long time before the fund reaches a sufficient size to be able to behave like the California Public Employees' Retirement System (CalPERS), which is feared in boardrooms across America. Forms of market discipline such as takeovers are not effective mechanisms for monitoring managerial behavior and corporate performance in Hong Kong. This is because most family-owned firms are controlled by cross-shareholding, and corporate raiders or interested parties are not able to perform takeovers through open-market purchases.

In its consultation document of July 2001, the SCCLR proposed a number of amendments to improve shareholders' rights. These proposals included amending the law to provide outside shareholders with a more meaningful procedure by which to nominate and elect directors, and the introduction of statutory derivative actions whereby the SFC would be empowered to bring derivative actions against wrongdoers in relation to listed companies. There would also be an independent corporate accounts review committee. Measures to protect shareholders are also contained in the new SFO. As mentioned previously, the provisions in the SFO have enhanced the investigatory powers of the SFC, including the power to seek assistance from a listed company's bank, auditor, or business counterpart to verify information that is obtained from an investigation. Other measures include expressly providing for a private right of civil action for a person to seek compensation for a pecuniary loss that is suffered as a result of relying on any false or misleading public communication. Such compensation may be sought from the people who are responsible for disclosing the information, such as the directors or senior executives of a company. There is also a tighter voting mechanism for connected transactions by interested shareholders. However, civil suits involve large legal fees, and most individual investors would not be able to afford such fees to put up a case. Derivative actions, which involve suing those caught up in misconduct in the name of the company, would therefore be a useful channel for minority shareholders to realize their legal rights.

With regard to improving the right to derivative actions, the relevant local laws need to be revised. We can learn from the US and Canadian models. In the US, according to the Corporate Law, the decision as to whether to allow minority shareholders to adopt derivative actions is made by a group of corporate independent directors appointed by the court. These directors consider the cost-effectiveness by using corporate resources to sue those involved in misconduct (including controlling shareholders) for compensation. If the potential legal fees are higher than the incurred losses, these independent directors naturally will not opt for such rights or actions. Some experts suggest that the decision about adopting derivative rights should be made by the shareholders' general meeting instead of independent directors. In Canada, such decisions are made by the courts, as it considers that market misconduct involves the public interest. And, as mentioned earlier, the government should also consider the feasibility of class actions as soon as possible so that minor shareholders can sue collectively for compensation arising from misconduct.

Improved decision procedures at shareholders' general meetings

Stricter rules against the dilution of shareholders' interests through the placing of shares, rights issues, and share repurchases have been proposed by HKEx in its consultation paper. However, after consultations, the Exchange will retain the existing 20 percent limit on the issue of securities under the general mandate and will not impose any restriction on the number of refreshments of the general mandates, in light of the diverse views of respondents to the consultation exercise. The Exchange will amend the Main Board Rules to require independent shareholders' approval for any refreshments of the general mandate after the annual general meeting. To protect minority shareholders further, the Exchange will limit the placing of shares under a general mandate at a substantial discount (up to 20 percent unless otherwise approved by HKEx) to the market price. It is believed by many CG advocates that without restricting the number of times that a company can have a share placement in a certain period, other means would not be particularly effective in terms of minority shareholder protection. In view of the disappointing HKEx conclusions, independent market critic David Webb launched Project Vampire (Vote Against Mandate for Placing, Issues by Rights Excepted) in 2003. This campaign involved voting against the general placing mandate in its current form at all Hang Seng Index firms' general meetings.

After the HKEx Corporate Governance Consultation, since mid-2003 the Listing Rules require voting by way of a poll for connected transactions and transactions requiring controlling or interested shareholders to abstain from voting. However, a poll is not mandatory for "less important matters." This "half-baked cake" will certainly not be acceptable to many CG advocates. As independent critic David Webb pointed out in his Project Poll in 2003 (Webb, 2003), one share–one vote (OSOV) is an essential principle of shareholder participation in all decisions in a general meeting, and Hong Kong's traditional "showing by hands" system is incompatible with international best practice of CG. Although the controlling shareholders always dominate the decisions by whatever voting mechanism, a OSOV poll counting proxy votes could inform the public the extent of "for" and "against," regardless of the outcome. This would increase the transparency of the voting process and hold management accountable to shareholders.

Empowering minority shareholders

There are those who have focused on encouraging investors to take a greater responsibility in the monitoring of managerial behavior. This assumes that if minority shareholders grow increasingly active and knowledgeable and become the "first line of defence," more protection for minority shareholders will be put in place. For instance, disclosure requirements need investor vigilance to monitor actual practices, particularly in terms of related-party transaction disclosures. It is hoped that the introduction of the mandatory provident fund will lead to more institutional investors (particularly overseas investors) demanding a higher standard of CG from Hong Kong companies. These international institutional investors should become driving forces behind shareholder activism.

The SFC Shareholders Group has been upgraded to a standing committee, but its impact is still rather limited. Some people suggest the formation of a "shareholder support fund" to protect the interests of minority shareholders. The initial funding could be grants from the government, the SFC, HKEx, and private donations/subscriptions. A small percentage of the levy that is imposed on securities and futures transactions could be assigned to the fund, and its operations would be overseen by a board that would consist of a cross-section of the community. The fund could be used to provide advice or support in litigation against the company and/or its directors on a "sharing basis" (both costs and compensations awarded). In addition, investment in shares of companies can ensure the right of the fund to attend general meetings and ask questions of directors.

Following this idea, David Webb suggested establishing a shareholder activist group, the Hong Kong Association of Minority Shareholders (HAMS), in 2002, and it was hoped that the body would be funded by a levy on stock market transactions (about 0.005 percent each). HAMS will seek out companies that are guilty of misconduct, draw attention to their behavior, and, in the worst case, sue them on behalf of the group's members – similar to a class action – as long as one of the members holds that company's shares. The group will also develop a CG rating system for listed companies and publish its results to encourage good governance. It is expected that HAMS will be accountable to the Legislative Council. However, despite its merit and a number of supporters, the government and some industry leaders have deep reservations about the funding proposal. As a private association, they believe that the group should be funded by the investors themselves (both individual and institutional). Another problem is the conflict of interest for Hong Kong's large institutional investors, as many fund managers are attached to investment banks. Some market players also think that establishing an activist group like this will bring about more legal cases and make Hong Kong a litigious society, even without class actions.

While the government thinks that shareholder activism will occur naturally in time, some people believe that the government needs to catalyze this reaction, besides considering the possibility of class actions.

Conclusion

Good CG is the key to improving economic efficiency, enhancing the attraction of markets and investors' confidence, and maintaining the stability of financial systems. Enhancing Hong Kong's CG regime is a priority of the Hong Kong government, particularly in terms of protecting minority shareholders' interests. The government and all relevant sectors have attached much importance, and dedicated considerable efforts, to reforming our legislation, rules and guidelines to keep them up to date (Stephen Yip, Secretary for Financial Services, 2002). Despite some who prefer retaining the status quo because of vested interests, the ongoing efforts of different interested parties have made some good progress toward building a sound and solid CG foundation for Hong Kong.

Hong Kong still has a lot of work to do to improve CG, although it is ahead in the region. We cannot rely on stringent legislation and enforcement alone to enhance CG standards. The Enron case indicates that such incidents happen even in the US, notwithstanding its stringent legislation and advanced regulatory regime. Drawing from the experiences of other countries, this chapter suggested a number of ways to improve standards of CG in Hong Kong. It stresses that in the reform process, refining the regulatory framework, improving internal governance mechanisms, raising the ethical standards of market participants, securing top management's commitment and cultivating a healthy corporate culture are all important. Among the many suggested measures, we need to determine our priorities.

Good CG is the product of the concerted efforts and hard work of all market players and stakeholders, all of whom should be working toward the common objectives of creating values and wealth and furthering Hong Kong's status as a world class financial and business centre.

Notes

1 Standard and Poor's used four criteria when assigning a company a CG score: ownership and concentration, financial stakeholder rights and relations, transparency and disclosure, and board structure and process. There are also four elements in its country analytical structure: market infrastructure, legal infrastructure, regulatory environment, and information infrastructure.

2 When other foundation sources and means are not sufficient to maintain the market equilibrium, more laws and regulations are needed to ensure minimum fairness and market efficiency.

3 The Hong Kong government prefers a more market-oriented self-regulated system to reduce compliance and transaction costs.

4 To ensure fairness and a high consistency of CG standards, some market experts have suggested revising the local laws and rules so that they override those of the listed companies' home jurisdictions.

5 Several professional bodies have also introduced CG and disclosure guidelines beyond their professional standards.

6 However, there are some gray areas and the division of responsibilities is not particularly clear in certain areas.

7 Another possible reason is that although HKEx may have the will to enforce the rules, it does not have enough experienced professionals who know the market operations sufficiently well to enforce the rules effectively.

8 Objectives are to avoid a conflict of interests, to divide areas of responsibilities clearly, and to enhance market quality.

9 Unlike Hong Kong, the US legal system enables victim investors to sue over market misconduct through class action and contingency fee arrangements.

10 In the US, once the SEC initiates a hearing, the defendant has the burden of effectively rebutting the prosecutor's case. Most SEC cases are finally settled by civil suits, not by litigation (Lang, 2002).

11 Andrew Sheng, Chairman of the SFC, once noted, every successful business started as a family business.

12 Firms in which one individual serves as both chairman and CEO/managing director (i.e. in which there is CEO duality) are considered to be more managerially dominated (Molz, 1998).

9 The Chinese national system of corporate governance

S. S. M. Ho

Introduction

Corporate shareholding and corporate governance are new concepts in the People's Republic of China (hereafter PRC or China). The "corporatization" or "privatization" of state-owned enterprises in China has led to new agency problems generating conflicts of interest among different stakeholder groups. Recently, a number of efforts have been undertaken to improve China's business culture in the area of corporate governance. While large scale scandals in the Chinese business arena have recently been overshadowed by the bankruptcies of Enron and WorldCom in the United States, corporate governance (CG) remains a key area of economic reform in China.

The paucity of knowledge about CG in the East is a concern, particularly since foreign investment in China has increased significantly in the past decade. This growth brings with it an acute need to understand the dynamics of CG in the international context. An examination of international models of CG relations to Far Eastern economies such as China's could yield important insights into the topic and provide a fresh perspective on what has become an increasingly international debate. China is unique in many ways and therefore it provides a good case study for understanding alternative CG models.

This chapter outlines the background, practices, problems and effectiveness of CG of listed firms in China. Applying theories on property right, agency and economic behavior, it discusses how China can develop its own CG model in view of its political, economic, legal, cultural, ownership and market environments. On the basis of experience overseas, this chapter suggests a number of ways to further improve the standard of CG in China. It stresses that in the reform process, resolving many of the major issues concurrently is important. As China has a unique environment, not all overseas practices are directly applicable without modifications. It is vital that changes take place within the context of China's social and business institutions.

This chapter suggests a number of ways to further improve the governance standard. As China has a unique environment, not all overseas practices are directly applicable. It is vital that changes take place within the context of China's social and business institutions.

The three phases of CG

In a narrow sense, when the controlling rights are separated from the owning rights, CG is mainly concerned about how to balance the interests between investors and the company. In a broader sense, CG is concerned with the design of institutions that induce or force board directors and management to internalize and balance the welfare of the company, its shareholders and other stakeholders. A CG system delineates the rights and responsibilities of the owners, the board of directors, top management and other stakeholders of the business corporation (OECD, 1998). For a market to be efficient and effective, all stakeholders (or market players) must play their respective roles diligently and with integrity. Good CG also implies the need for an inter-related network of control and incentive mechanisms to ensure the accountability of the board/management to shareholders and other stakeholders.

Our knowledge of CG today is largely derived from the agency theory that was developed in the West. Governance problems in the West often originate from the problem of the separation of ownership and control within a business organization, which gives rise to information asymmetry and agency costs (Fama and Jensen, 1983a, 1983b). While the main agency problem in the United States and the United Kingdom is between managers and outside individual shareholders, the main agency problem in Southeast Asian family businesses is between majority shareholders (i.e. families) and minority shareholders. However, in China the main agency problem is multi-parties: major shareholders, directors/supervisors, managers and smaller shareholders.

Since China's economic reforms started in 1979, enterprises in China have undergone significant changes and CG has become a very heated topic of concern, particularly related to listed companies. In China, state-owned enterprises (SOEs) accounts for about half of the national gross domestic product (GDP). The inefficient and under-performed state sector continues to hinder China's economic development. Like some other transitional economies, improving and sustaining growth in the Chinese economy is likely to hinge on reforming the ailing state sector. Since 1980, China's economic system has been gradually changing from a planned economy to a market economy with socialist features. This requires Chinese enterprises to set up a modern enterprise system. Joint-stock limited company (JSLC) or corporation is an effective organizational form of business in a modern enterprise system, while CG is the core of the corporation concept. The development and changes of CG in China can be grouped into the following three phases: 1983–1992, 1993–1997, and 1998 to the present.

Phase 1: 1983–1992

China's first JSLC was incorporated in Beijing in 1984 and this started the building of a "market-style modern enterprise system." In 1990 China became the first socialist country to establish a stock exchange. Over 1,000 corporations have been listed and many of them were re-structured from traditional SOEs.

Listed firms with weak CG have repeatedly shown weak performance and have frequently been "expropriated" by their major shareholders and the management. Although many listed enterprises established the "3-committee system" (i.e. the shareholders' general meeting (SGM), the board of directors and the supervisory board), they were more in form than in substance. In many corporate boards of directors, the representation of the major owner (i.e. the government) was minimal, and there was not a mechanism for the state to realize as the major owner of the company. Top-level administrative agencies as owners still intervened in many business and personnel decisions of a company.

Phase 2: 1993–1997

The Company Law, which became effective in January 1993, contains the major legal requirements for PRC CG. It regulates the organization and behavior of companies, and specifies the functions and responsibilities of the three committees. The Chinese Security Regulatory Commission (CSRC) implemented a number of guidelines for CG and disclosure which further protect investors' interests. However, there were still inappropriate governance practices in listed companies. In many ownership structures, the major shareholder was in a dominant controlling position and its wishes will be honored every time in SGMs. Minority shareholders have many difficulties in influencing company policies. Since there were very close relationships between the major shareholders and the company, the independence of the listed companies was difficult to maintain. The agents of state shareholders occupied a majority of the seats on corporate boards. Boards of directors of many listed companies lacked internal checks and balances and supervisory boards were also not functioning as expected. With little incentive schemes, managers did not take up economic responsibilities for delivering economic returns. Many board chairmen and senior executives were still nominated or directly appointed by the government.

Phase 3: 1998 to now

The Securities Law was promulgated in 1998 which marked another milestone in the history of China's CG development. In late 1999, the Ministry of Finance revised the Accounting Law. In October 2000, the State Economic and Trade Committee issued the "Basic Rules on Establishing the Modern Enterprise System and Enhancing Management of Large and Medium SOEs." The CSRC issued the "Guidelines on Listed Companies' Establishment of Independent Directors System (Consultation Draft)" in 2000 and the "Code of Corporate Governance for Listed Companies" in 2001. All these regulations enhanced the regulatory framework significantly. Major problems that still remain are the insider control and the continuing expropriation of listed firms' assets by their holding parent companies via connected-party transaction. The 16th National Peoples' Congress Meeting held in 2002 resolved to further reform the national asset management scheme which provides a new route to the above problems.

Currently listed companies pay more attention to strengthen the functions of their boards, to increase the number of independent directors, to separate their board chairmen from general managers, to improve executives' incentive schemes by granting stocks or share options, to monitor their management more closely and to increase the quality of information disclosure. Smaller investors have started to sue listed firms and market intermediaries for misconduct.

The standard and core problems of CG

CG in Chinese listed companies continued to attract much international debate and interest in the late 1990s due to the many unique features of Chinese corporate ownership and governance practices. These debates are fuelled by a recent series of corporate failures, scandals and regulatory changes reflecting the problems of CG in China. For example, one beer manufacturer issued new shares, but used all the capital collected for securities investment in 1998. Some other firms borrowed from banks to invest in areas totally outside their core business. High-growth firms like "Zheng Bai Wen" and Euro-Asia Agricultural manipulated their accounting records causing its share prices to fall drastically. There have also been cases where directors and managers were not properly monitored and compensated, thereby encouraging some of them to engage in misappropriation, fraud and corruption.

These activities have led to financial distress, de-listing, and/or bankruptcy. The collapse of the Guangtong International Trust and Investment Corporation (GITIC) in 1999 due to huge loans and inefficient operations illustrate this. However, due to China's complicated procedures for filing for bankruptcy, many small investors received very little in the way of compensation. Not only have these incidents hindered economic development, but they have also damaged investors' confidence in the stock market. These have given rise to a heated debate about how companies in China should be directed and governed in the future.

One fundamental concern in China is the low ethical standard in business. Although honesty is one of the traditional virtues of the Chinese, it is mainly preserved in family circles and among one's close associates in mainland China. According to Professor Jiang Jin-Hua, the Vice Chairman of the National Peoples' Congress, the lack of credibility on market transactions in China is serious (Sing Tao Daily, 2003) "Fakes, refusing to pay debts, cheating, fraud, manipulation" are the five most common mal-practices in Chinese business, and such mal-practices have caused a total economic loss of over US$70,000 million.

According to a recent survey by the Political and Economic Risk Consultancy, among ten East-Asian countries, China is ranked the second last in terms of the quality of CG, just before Indonesia (The Economist, 2001; Ming, 2002a, 2002b) (see Table 9.1). The Chinese Government has realized that good CG is necessary to improve corporate competitiveness and to attract international capital (HKEJ, 2001).

Table 9.1 The political and economic risk consultancy, ranking of CG in Asia

Country	First quarter 2002	2001
Singapore	1	2
Hong Kong	2	3
Japan	3	6
Philippines	4	9
Taiwan	5	4
South Korea	6	7
Malaysia	7	1
India	8	5
Vietnam	9	12
Thailand	10	9
China	11	10
Indonesia	12	11

Source: Ming Pao, 2002a.

It is believed that with better CG, listed firms can reduce agency costs, become more competitive in global markets, and fulfill their social responsibilities. The "OECD Principles of Corporate Governance" (1999) emphasizes that good CG is important in building market confidence and encouraging more stable, long-term international investment flows. Empirical evidence collected by both the Mckinsey Group and the CLSA Group has shown that firms which practise good CG enjoy lower costs of capital and higher share values (The Economist, 2001; Gill, 2002). Recent research by Standard and Poor's (Dallas, 2002) indicates that investors are willing to pay a premium for shares in well-governed companies. These findings should provide the necessary impetus for regulators and companies to implement more measures to enhance the standard of CG.

It is argued that while governance practices in China are improving rapidly (see Table 9.A1) major problems and weaknesses exist. These major or core problems could be summarized as follows:

  i   intervention and expropriation of firm assets by controlling shareholders,
  ii insider control,
 iii weak regulatory enforcement,
  iv lack of independent board and effective controls,
   v lack of incentives and mature labor market for executives,
  vi low corporate transparency and disclosure quality,
 vii shortage of independent and quality auditors and other intermediaries,
viii insufficient protection of smaller investors' interests, and
  ix low business ethical standards.

Mrs Laura Cha, Vice-Chairwoman of CSRC and originally Vice Chairwoman of Hong Kong Securities and Futures Commission, remarked in an open speech that the key to handling various conflicts in China's capital market is "to improve corporate governance and quality of listed firms." She also emphasized after a national survey of CG practice of listed firms that "treating corporate governance as the core of the modern business system is the force to ensure sustained growth of listed companies" (Cha, 2003).

However, laws and regulations are only part of the whole CG system. Other institutions are needed to allow efficient private contracts (Coase, 1960). CG reforms take place through legal and jurisdiction reforms, stock exchange and other regulatory bodies' concerted efforts, the active monitoring of intermediaries and mass media, public education and market forces. As indicated by the chairwoman of CSRC in July 2001, in order to foster other social forces for making a collective effort in improving CG, it is necessary for the Chinese government to be involved (HKEJ, 2001). In this process, there should also be a balance between market efficiency and market fairness/credibility, incentives and controls, as well as economic benefits and social responsibilities.

The more unique and critical issues of CG in China are divided into the following eight areas for further discussion: the legal and regulatory framework, ownership structure, generic CG models, influence of major shareholders and insider control, the three-committee system, executive compensation and incentives and transparency and disclosure quality.

The legal and regulatory framework

There are four sources of forces regulating the market:

i   individual and corporate ethics and professionalism,
ii   internal control and incentive mechanisms,
iii   external monitoring by intermediaries and the market, and
iv   law and regulations and their enforcement.

When the first three sources are not sufficient to maintain the market equilibrium, more laws and regulations are needed to ensure minimum fairness and market efficiency. Regulatory bodies establish and implement rules and regulations, monitor compliance and take part in enforcement activities. They monitor company shareholders, boards of directors, accountants, auditors, investment analysts and financial markets and institutions. It is generally agreed that sound legal regulation and enforcement are key pillars upon which good CG is built. An ideal regulatory framework should be preventive (versus prohibitive) in nature (Ho *et al.*, 2003), protecting the interests of the majority of the public, and have clarity, transparency and market orientation. Since the Enron and WorldComm scandals, there has been a substantial increase in regulatory commitments and a growing emphasis on compliance. Stricter rules on accounting, disclosure and auditing have been implemented worldwide.

The Ch ese Government realizes that it is not sufficient just by simply relying on private contracts or voluntary acts to achieve the CG goals. It has been actively revising and improving the regulatory framework of CG. Table 9.A1 summarizes the major market-related laws, rules, regulations and guidelines[1] issued by various regulatory bodies including the State Council, the Ministry of Finance (MOF), the CSRC, the Chinese Institute of Certified Public Accountants (CICPA), the China Accounting Standards Committee (CASC), the State Economic and Trade Committee (SETC), the China National Audit Office (CNAO), and the two exchanges (Shanghai Stock Exchange (SHSE) and Shenzhen Stock Exchange (SZSE)).

In China, laws are classified into five levels. The Constitution is the supreme source of law (i.e. first-level). The second level is basic statutes enacted by the National People's Congress (NPC) and the third level is comprised of statutes enacted by the Standing Committee of NPC. The Accounting Law 1985, the CPA Law 1993, the Audit Law 1994, the Company Law 1993 and the Securities Law 1998 are all Level 2 and 3 statutes. Administrative laws are the fourth level of law which are administrative regulations made by the State Council and administrative rules made by ministries and commissions of the State Council. These include the CICPA Charter 1996, CSRC regulations, Accounting Standards for Business Enterprises 1992 and Revised Uniform Accounting System Regulations 1992. Local laws are the fifth and last level of law.

It can be seen that the legal development always lagged behind the market development. The Company Law was issued in 1993 and the Securities Law was enacted in 1998, years after the establishment of the first stock exchange. The Company Law contains 11 chapters:

- general provisions;
- incorporation and organizational structure and limited liability companies;
- incorporation and organizational structure of joint stock limited companies (incorporation, SGMs, board of directors and manager, supervisory board);
- issue and transfer of shares of joint stock limited companies (issue of shares, transfer of shares, listed companies);
- company bonds;
- financial affairs and accounting of companies;
- merger and division of companies;
- bankruptcy, dissolution and liquidation of companies;
- branches of foreign companies;
- legal liability; and
- supplementary provisions.

The Securities Law covers 16 chapters:

- general provisions;
- issues of securities;
- trading of securities;
- general regulations;
- listing of securities;
- continuing disclosure of information;

- prohibited trading acts;
- takeover of listed companies;
- stock exchanges;
- securities companies;
- securities registration and clearing institutions;
- securities trading service organizations;
- securities industry association;
- securities regulatory authority;
- legal liability; and
- supplementary provisions.

It is believed that the current Company Law and the Securities Law of China are outdated, and as China's economy develops and many new changes appear, new company and security laws are required. As yet, China has not issued a bankruptcy law which is desperately needed to protect individual shareholders. Further, many of these laws and regulations are broad in nature which makes them difficult to interpret and enforce in many situations.

The CSRC which was established in 1992, and whose functions are similar to the US Securities and Exchange Commission (SEC), is responsible for conducting supervision and regulation of the securities and futures markets in accordance with the law. The CSRC issued a number of rules and guidelines relating to CG and disclosures since 1994. In particular, on the basis of the Organization of Economic Cooperation and Development (OECD) Principles, the CSRC and the State Economic and Trade Committee jointly issued the "Code of Corporate Governance for Listed Companies in China" in January 2001. There are five parts to this new guideline:

- protecting legal rights of shareholders,
- strengthening integrity and fiduciary duties of directors,
- supervisory functions of the supervisory board,
- establish effective performance evaluation and incentive mechanisms, and
- protect the rights of different stakeholders.

The Codes allow civil compensations when an investor's interests were damaged. This is the first comprehensive and systematic document regulating the behavior of listed companies. All listed firms are expected to follow these principles in a few years' time. CSRC rules/guidelines on information disclosures and the Accounting Law and specific accounting standards will be discussed in the next section.

Regarding enforcement of rules, according to CSRC statistics, there were 10 companies de-listed so far. Since 1996, 42 companies were sanctioned by CSRC. In 2002, three Chief Executive Officers (CEOs) were jailed due to fraudulent financial reporting. However, there has been an impression of CSRC (and other enforcement agencies) that they do not enforce the relevant rules diligently and that they lack the power and/or will to do so. There also appears to be an apparent reluctance on the part of the judiciary to impose tough sanctions as provided for by the various laws and regulations. The sum of fine penalty imposed on firms violating rules is always immaterial when compared with firm asset size or the amount of return of the suspected misconduct. One commonly agreed cause of so many market misconducts is that the cost of committing dishonesty is too low but the potential return is very high. These practices send out the wrong message to the marketplace, and impede the establishment of a level-playing field. Further, under the current legal provisions, mainly criminal penalties could be imposed on market misconducts and no civil claims for compensating investors are usually allowed. The CSRC and other agencies have indicated to change these impressions by putting more effort into curbing market abuses.

In the United States, SEC is the single regulatory body that oversees almost all security law related to CG issues. Under the protection of the US Constitution, SEC has almost unrestricted investigative power to issue subpoenas nationwide against any person that is critical to the investigation of suspected misconduct cases (Lang, 2002). If a person refuses to comply with a subpoena, then SEC can apply to the federal district court to enforce it. However, in China, rules that are related to CG are rather dispersed, and enforced by different government agencies. Further, the CSRC lacks such extensive investigation and prosecution power.

The US legal system enables victim investors to sue over market misconducts through class action. Currently, given the high expense and complexities involved in civil claims, it is very difficult for an individual investor in China to sue a suspected market player. Therefore, certain kinds of class action seem necessary to provide the minimum basic protection or the public minority investors. In the US, once SEC initiates a hearing with preliminary evidence, the defendant has the burden of effectively rebutting the prosecutor's case. Most SEC cases are finally settled by civil suits, and not by litigation. In view of the consequences of the Enron incident, it is clear that such practices are worthy of serious consideration in China.

It should be noted that effective legislation, enforcement, judiciary process and level of sanctions are all important in building a regulatory framework. To maintain an appropriate level of regulation while maintaining an efficient and competitive market is the most difficult target that a regulatory body wishes to achieve. While excessive regulation leads to high transaction costs and discourages innovation, the main problem in China today seems to be more concerned with under-regulation, particularly in the enforcement and judiciary process. Regulatory bodies in China are still trying hard to strike the right balance and further improvements would be seen in the next several years.

Ownership structure

In China, most listed companies are either re-structured SOEs or founded by legal persons and the Company Law mandates the incorporator(s) to own no less than 35 percent of total share outstanding at initial public offering (IPO). The shareholders of listed firms include government (state shares), legal persons (non-bank financial institutions or non-financial-institutions shares), management and employees (employee shares), and public individual investors.[2] Only individual shares are tradable and by law they should not be less than 25 percent of total shares outstanding at IPO. The state and legal person shares are non-transferable or non-tradable except with domestic institutional investors upon approval by the CSRC.

Despite the fact that many SOEs are becoming public listed companies and private companies are contributing more to China's GDP, the government is still the largest shareholder on aggregate. Currently, approximately 30 percent of total shares are owned by the state, 30 percent by legal persons, 2 percent by employees, and the remaining 35 percent mainly by outside individual investors. There are very few foreign B (traded on the two domestic stock exchanges), H (traded in Hong Kong) or N (traded in New York) shares investors (see Table 9.2). About 60 percent of listed firms have state ownership, and over half of the firms having the state as its largest shareholder. Although the majority of shareholders are individual holders of tradable A shares, the personal ownership of each individual shareholder is very small. However, all categories of shareholders are entitled to equal dividend payment and voting rights (one share–one vote (OSOV)).

There is a high concentration of share ownership by the state or legal person blockholders in China. On average, over the past three years the largest five shareholders have held over half of issued shares, while the largest 10 shareholders have held over 60 percent of the issued shares (Fan *et al.*, 2000). Depending on the ratio of state shareholding, listed firms in China can be divided into three main categories:

- Traditional listed SOEs – Ownership: government >40 percent, legal persons 20 percent, employees and management 5 percent, public investors 25 percent.
- Modern listed SOEs – Ownership: government 20–40 percent, legal persons 30 percent, employees and management 15 percent, public investors 25 percent.
- Private listed companies – Ownership: government <20 percent, legal persons 20 percent, family 40 percent, public investors 25 percent.

Deng Xiaoping's "Three Benefits" (beneficial for developing production, beneficial for increasing comprehensive state power, and beneficial to raising the

Table 9.2 Percentage ownership of Chinese listed firms

	State	*Legal person*	*A shares*	*B shares*	*Employees*
Shanghai	34	28	29	0.5	6
Shenzhen	28	30	34	0.5	6

living standards of the people) speech given on his tour to the south in 1992 greatly accelerated the development of private enterprises. Private enterprises were gradually considered a "necessary, beneficial addition" to a socialist economy. In July 2001, President Jiang Ze-min stressed that private enterprise is an important part of the socialist market economy and his address was incorporated into the Communist Party's constitutions. This marked a milestone in the history of private enterprises in China.

Private or non-state-owned enterprises use non-governmental resources and means to operate. These include SOEs with its majority issued shares not owned by the state after they were reformed and restructured (i.e. the state no longer had a direct hand in their management except retaining ownership rights): wholly collective enterprises; mixed ownership group companies; privately-owned enterprises; individual enterprises; private Sino-foreign joint ventures; and wholly foreign-owned private enterprises. As at the end of 2001, 25.8 percent of private enterprises were re-structured from SOEs.

Statistics reveal that tax paid by private enterprises account for 45 percent of the national income in 1999. Some have argued that most of private firms' success has been due to their better internal CG. A detailed nationwide survey by the Chinese Academy of Social Sciences showed that 92.7 percent of private enterprise owners were also the general managers of the same enterprises, thereby combining ownership rights with control rights. However, the diverse of private enterprises and the rapid market changes during the transitional period of China's economic reform has made the classification of a private enterprise difficult and increased the complexity of the governance of private enterprises.

We can see that the development of CG in Chinese enterprises have followed two paths. The first path relates to SOEs that have vigorously shaken off the confines of the long-term planned economy and transformed themselves into legal person entities having distinct property rights, autonomous management and sole financial responsibilities. The second path relates to non-SOEs. On the one hand, village/township and collective enterprises which contribute in a significant way to national GDP need different ways to distinguish their property rights. At the same time they are similar to other fast-growing family-controlled private enterprises, moving toward modern management and governance systems. Corporate government mechanisms of non-SOEs can easily learn and benefit from the market economy. However, other apparent problems, as mentioned earlier, cannot be ignored. Since problems arising from the CG of transformed listed SOEs are more unique and significant, they become the major focus of this article.

Currently, the ownership structure in China is not optimal because state ownership is unreasonably high and concentrated. To optimize the ownership structure of firms, to increase the independence of the firm and reduce insider problems, the Chinese government planned to reduce the state shareholding, progressively. If China converts state shares into more legal person shares, it will allow more institutional investors (usually closely related business entities supplemented by pension funds and other non-bank institutions) to act as major shareholders and to actively monitor the management of a firm. This would help these firms to achieve more stable long-term growth and development. If a firm has a high level of legal person shares, it will also have a higher level of autonomy and will have more incentive to maximize profits. Since many legal person institutions in existence are also stated-owned, one may not be able to see significant performance improvement when more state shares are converted to legal person shares in the near future. However, when more legal person institutions become modern listed SOEs (i.e. less state ownership) or private enterprises, more significant improvement would be expected.

Traditional large- and medium-sized SOEs are unlikely to change to 100 percent private or family-controlled firms. The pace of change was slowed down in recent years in order to reduce individual investors' worries about market fluctuations. In fact, during the period from 1997 to 2000, the mean percentage of individual shares increased only slightly. This suggests that the process of privatizing state shares has been sluggish. The newly released proposal in 2001 on reducing state ownership by not more than 10 percent will, therefore, not change the controlling role of state shares in listed firms in the short term. However, since state and legal person shares are non-tradable and non-marketable, it is difficult to valuate their market price or optimize its true value. In these situations, collusion and corruption always appear and the owners are always the losers. In the long run, it is believed that as much state ownership as possible should be converted to individual shares, and all shares should be made tradable, ultimately. Currently, China lacks large institutional investors. As the Qualified Foreign Institutional Investor (QFII) scheme to be implemented soon, would further attract large international investors to China and would help enhance the CG standard in China.

Anyway, it would take a long time to reduce state ownership, and during this process China's listed firms need to adopt other means to improve its CG. The critical issue that China now faces is how to regulate the behavior of the representatives of the major state and legal person shareholders, so that they will not have a supermajority position to pursue "insider" interests. Restricting their representation on the board of directors to not more than their share proportion will certainly help in this respect.

Generic CG models

As Chinese firms undergo the transition from entities that are wholly state-owned to those that are partially owned by external shareholders, one would expect to see changes in the ownership structure and internal governance mechanisms. The question is whether different levels of state ownership necessarily lead to different practices of CG. Another key question is whether China should follow the US/UK market-oriented model, the Germany/Japan network-oriented model, or the Far East family-control model of CG, or develop its own.

The CG system of a country is determined by a number of interrelated factors, including political beliefs, culture, legal system, ownership structures, market environments and level of economic development. Because these vary across countries, there are also different CG systems. Each existing generic model has advantages and disadvantages and therefore, it is difficult to determine which is best. In fact, there is a trend that they learn from each other to make improvements.

Until now, our understanding of the concept of a "company" and "CG" has been based mainly on an Anglo-American model of "arms-length" contracting activities in which owners of a company are separated from the managers. Many common practices of CG in the US and the UK, today, have developed in socio-economic settings that have little in common with present-day China. The Chinese stock market is still in its infancy, and many firms still rely on financial institutions for intermediary financing. Under current Chinese laws and accounting standards, protection for investors has increased, but is still far from any international standards (La Porta *et al.*, 1998). China still lacks an active external corporate control market and other external monitoring, as well as internal monitoring mechanisms. Therefore, the full US/UK market model is not suitable for China given the current environmental constraints. Given the characteristics of the three existing models, some people argue that Chinese firms should adopt a mixed model of CG which is based primarily on the Germany/Japan network-oriented model, supplemented by some good practices of the other two models. This hybrid model emphasizes managers' self-realization of internal motivation and control, and therefore, should be more cost effective than the US/UK external monitoring mechanisms (i.e. the stock market and corporate control market). Since financial institutions in China are motivated to monitor firms, China's current institutional environments are more like those in Japan and Germany in the early days of their success than those in the United States or the United Kingdom. In the longer term, when the long privatization process is over and most shares are individually tradable, and when both the market and the individual investors become more sophisticated, then the US/UK model may be further experimented. However, in view of long-term development, it is desirable to develop a generic CG model that is applicable to the majority of listed firms in China.

According to Chinese economists He and Xu (2000), there are five conditions upon which China should base its choice of generic CG:

i   The model can cope with China's economic development and maturity of its capital market.
ii The model can assure that firms realize long-term stable growth and development.
iii The model can assure owners monitor managers effectively.
iv The model can assure managers have the autonomy to run the business independently.
v   The model can use incentive and control mechanisms effectively to motivate or regulate the behavior of owners, managers and employees.

Increasingly, there has been a global consensus on certain principles of good governance. Several codes of best practice or guidelines for CG have been developed by some international bodies (e.g. The Business Roundtable, 1997; CalPERS, 1998; European Corporate Governance Network, 1997; OECD, 1999; World Bank, 1999; PECC, 2002). China should be able to benefit from these international guidelines in building and improving its own system.

Influence of controlling shareholders and insider control problems

The ineffective governance of traditional SOEs can be understood using the agency theory perspective (Qian, 1996; Fama and Jensen, 1983b). As mentioned earlier, while the main agency problem in the West is between directors/managers of a company and its shareholders, the main agency problem in China is multi-parties: major shareholders, directors/supervisors, managers and minority shareholders.

Since most listed firms in China were originally SOEs, most of their senior executives were also former managers or party officials of the SOEs or their supervising agencies. The state (local government or communist party organizations), as a non-natural person, whose agencies are officially not allowed to get involved in business operations. Before 1993, in many corporate boards, the representation of the major owner (i.e. the government) was minimal, and there was no mechanism for the state to realize as the major owner of the company. However, top level administrative agencies as owners still intervened in many business decisions. These government agencies have to delegate control to state-appointed bureaucrats or representatives as agents. The mandate for them is to maintain or increase the value of state assets rather than maximizing market values of the ownership shares.

The party organization made final decisions on personnel matters without the effective monitoring by the board of directors or the supervisory board. Many of these state representatives also serve as directors, supervisors and senior management of the firms assigned to them (on average 70 percent of directors are appointed by the state). In a recent national survey among 5,000 enterprises (Yang, 2001), over 80 percent of managers of SOEs were appointed and about 30 percent of managers of non-SOEs were appointed. Since these positions are not open for public application in the job market, state-appointed directors and managers often attain their positions for reasons other than experience and qualifications. So even if their intentions are good, they may be incompetent.

These bureaucrats with fixed salary gain little in terms of personal benefits by improving corporate profits. Their positions are secure (i.e. iron rice bowls) even if they do not perform well (Mar and Yong, 2000). This also reduces the executives' appetite to taking strategic risk as they will tend to avoid initiatives and responsibilities. Furthermore, since there are multiple state representatives, the state lacks a clear system of accountability (Qian, 1996; Steinfeld, 1998). This leads to inefficiency and also gives rise to the abuse of company assets

Table 9.3 Distribution of the degree of insider control

Range (%)	Degree of insider control (%)
0–10	2.4
10–20	6.6
20–30	10.1
30–40	14.3
40–50	17.0
50–60	10.4
60–70	6.6
70–80	10.1
80–90	5.1
90–100	17.3
Total	100

Source: Chen *et al.*, 2000.

(i.e. leading to moral hazard). Very often managers and state-appointed representatives collude to jointly expropriate wealth from the firm (Lee, 1993).

Some SOEs remain the holding company even after they become listed companies. As the major shareholder of the listed company, the parent company always expropriates assets or funds at the expense of the minority investors. Further, the problem of "insider control" is very serious in China (see Table 9.3), as the internal controls are far less rigorous than in other countries and there is little protection for the rights of shareholders. In firms controlled by legal persons, the appointments of directors and top management are less politicized and their quality is usually higher. In these companies, the proportion of board directors appointed by the state is also much lower. In any case, minority individual shareholders are excluded from board participation. Even after the promulgation of the Company Law in 1992, the major shareholder of many listed companies was in a dominant controlling position.

The new three-committee system

An appropriate ownership structure merely provides a good foundation for building good CG. The next step is to develop a set of interrelated internal governance mechanisms that are compatible with the ownership structure of a firm. In other words, firms must develop appropriate decision, executive and supervisory mechanisms, and clearly delineate their compositions, roles and responsibilities. Since the SGM of SOEs in China cannot serve the monitoring role, a separate supervisory board is needed. Chinese Company Law requires that there are three governance bodies: SGMs, board of directors and supervisory board. Although it specifies the function and responsibilities of these committees in broad terms, there is a lack of detailed by-laws or operational rules for effective enforcement. This two-tier board structure is clearly different from the one-tier system in the United States, the United Kingdom and most

East Asian countries. Before 1998, although most listed committees established the "three-committee system," they were always more in form than in substance.

The SGM and investor relationship

According to Chinese Company Law, a shareholder's general meeting is the highest decision-making authority of a firm. The function of the SGM is to decide on the directions of the company's business and investment plans. However, in actual practice, shareholders always consult directors before making strategic decisions, which delays the implementation of some major plans.

In theory, all shareholders of a firm should attend the SGM. In practice, among those who attend the general meeting of shareholders, the majority are state representatives and representatives of legal persons, with only a few representing individual shareholders. Further, the state major shareholder is always in a dominant controlling position in the meetings and minority shareholders have many difficulties in influencing the company policies. Since in practice not all directors are elected at the shareholders' meeting and the board always violates the resolutions of the SGM, many people do not regard the SGM as the highest authority of the firm.

Board of directors

In China, the board of directors is responsible for making important tactical decisions. By law each board of directors must consist of five to 19 members to be elected by the SGM. In practice, over 70 percent of directors and board chairmen are appointed by the state and legal person shareholders, and over half are appointed by the major shareholder. There are rarely representatives of individual shareholders or independent outsiders. In most traditional SOEs, the party organization makes final decisions on personnel matters without the effective monitoring by the board. Boards of many listed firms lack appropriate checks and balances.

The Company Law does not clearly delineate the qualifications and duties of a director, which means that the quality of directors varies tremendously across firms. Most directors do not know the company's charter and their legal rights, obligations and responsibilities well. In most cases the chairman of the board representing the major shareholder was formerly a general manager in the state-owned factory or a party secretary, and hence they are used to being dominant in the board. In China, directors cannot be removed by the SGM "without good cause," which is not the case in the United States or the United Kingdom where such a resolution may be passed as long as the majority vote in favor of it. There is also no provision for shareholders to sue the directors for mismanagement.

Before 1998, due to the relatively low legal person and outside shareholdings, the practice of appointing external independent directors was not popular. The Guidelines for Listed Company Memorandum and Article issued by CSRC in 1997 specifies that "independent directors should not be taking up a company's shareholding or employees of a shareholder's business." On May 31, 2001 the

CSRC released the new "Guidelines for Introducing the Independent Directors Scheme in Listed Companies" which requires at least one-third of directors should be independent. Further, It emphasizes that independent directors should pay more attention to protect the interests of smaller investors. In many listed companies, there is still an absence of specialized board committees covering the main control functions, including audit, nomination and remuneration.

Since 1998, companies paid more attention to strengthening the functions of their boards, to increasing the number of independent directors, to separating their board chairmen from general managers, and to enhance directors' sense of responsibility toward shareholders. As of mid-2002, 1,124 listed companies have employed 2,414 independent directors (Cha, 2003). Among these companies, 20 percent have at least two independent directors, and 70 percent have at least one independent director with professional accounting background. Among the 2,414 independent directors, 50 percent of them are university professors and technical experts, 30 percent are information intermediaries (e.g. accountants, lawyers, investment advisors, etc.), 10 percent are business executives, and about 5 percent are retired government personnel.

The management

Although the Company Law stipulates that "a board can decide on appointing a board member to serve as a manager," most senior managers have been appointed by the state or party agencies. The management is subordinate to the board of directors and implements the latter's decisions. There should be a fiduciary relationship between the board and the management. In theory, although a manager can attend board meetings, he/she cannot vote as he/she is not a director. However, the Company Law does not specify clearly the relationship between a board of directors and the management of a firm. In practice, some CEOs and senior managers also serve as board members. Therefore, the capability on monitoring managers independently by the board is limited.

The functions of the management should be strengthened as managers spent more time handling their relationships with the government and their parent company. These managers were not able to spend more time on developing their firms' new markets, improving operational efficiency and accelerating technological development. Since 1998, companies paid more attention to monitoring managerial activities. After the promulgation of the Securities Law in 1998, investors can apply Rule 63 of the Law to sue listed companies and securities houses (and their directors, supervisors and executives) for releasing false or misleading information for compensations of losses in stock transactions.

Supervisory board

Chinese companies adopt the German concept of SGMs beneath a two-tier board structure. Reporting to the SGM, a supervisory board monitors the activities of directors and senior managers (except personnel matters), ensuring that they act in the interests of the company. As the law requires no separate audit committee, remuneration committee or nomination committee in listed firms, the supervisory board is expected to assume a wide range of monitoring responsibilities.

By law, the SGM should elect an appropriate proportion of shareholders' representatives and employees' representatives as defined in the company charter. In practice, supervisory board members or supervisors can be appointed at SGMs, by the board of directors or by the CEO. Many supervisory board members are state representatives, party officials or labor union leaders who lack experience in business and financial management. The Company Law specifies that members of a supervisory board can attend board meetings, but cannot serve as a board member or manager. Similarly, a director, manager or financial controller also cannot serve as a member of the supervisory board.

In theory, the board of supervisors should be able to call a SGM to exercise their veto power on certain critical decisions. Since members of a supervisory board are usually in a position lower than board members, they are always unable to monitor the directors. Also, most supervisors do not understand corporate law and finance and therefore their ability in monitoring is limited. Usually external supervisors are not stationed at the company's offices, and as a result, they cannot adequately monitor the board of directors or the CEO. Further, because the supervisory boards of some listed companies had close relationships with the major shareholders, these supervisors lacked monitoring skills and the environment for carrying their supervisory duties. Due to the limited effectiveness of supervisory boards in many firms, in July 1998, the central government promulgated the "State Council Audit Specialists Rules," which allow the government to assign auditors to check on a firm's activities. Currently, the supervisory board in China is more in form than in substance and its future is rather uncertain. Companies and regulatory bodies should enforce law tightly by holding any irresponsible supervisors legally liable so that the independent monitoring role of the supervisory board can be strengthened.

Board effectiveness

It can be seen that there is an agency relationship between the SGM (as the principal) and the board of directors as well as the supervisory board (as the agents). These three governance bodies check on and reinforce each other. This system is in co-existence with the "old three-committees" (i.e. employee representatives meeting, labor union and party committee) of a listed SOE, and is a unique feature of CG in China. However, this governance system (i.e. division of power among the new three committees) is difficult to implement effectively in real practice. It is commonly perceived that non-executive directors and external supervisors in China have limited independence.

Using most firms listed in Shanghai and Shenzhen Stock Exchanges for the period from 1997 to 1999, Fan *et al.* (2000) found the following internal governance mechanisms had significant impact on firm performance: proportion of top executives holding shares (+), the percentage of shares held by supervisors (+), the percentage of supervisors holding shares (+) and CEO/chairman turnover (–). Mechanisms such as percentage shareholding of major officers, CEO/chairman duality, and the ratio of inside directors were found to have no significant impact on firm performance.

Executive compensations and incentives

Since the markets for corporate control and executive labor are still developing in China, managers have little incentive to lower agency costs. There is also a lack of incentive payment schemes for Chinese executives. Executive incomes are rather low in China, and generally not linked to corporate performance. The remuneration of about 40 percent of directors is unaffected by the profit and loss of the company (Fan *et al.*, 2000), and many part-time directors do not receive incomes from the firms that they serve as they are paid by their appointing agencies. According to a recent national survey (Yang, 2001), almost 89 percent of managers received an annual income of less than 100,000 Yuan (US$1 = 8 Yuan). Among these managers, 41.7 percent (over half of them work in SOEs) received less than 20,000 Yuan. About 8.2 percent of managers earned 100,000 to 500,000 Yuan, and only 3.3 percent of managers earned more than 0.5 million (and all belong to non-SOEs) (see Table 9.4). The income gap between SOE managers and non-SOE managers has been growing. Certainly, one cannot determine the "actual income" of SOE managers in China simply by those figures as they receive a number of other non-monetary benefits (cars, meals, housing, etc.). However, it is believed that only until all incomes become monetary, managers will take up responsibilities in proportion to their actual incomes.

Relatively few firms issue bonuses and share options to managers along with their regular salaries (which usually are not high) as part of a performance-based incentive programme. According to CSRC in 2003, currently over 300 listed firms adopt some form of fixed yearly salary, and over 40 companies offer an executive stock option scheme.

According to Yang (2001), in China 80.6 percent of managers received monthly salary and cash bonuses, 22 percent share options and 18 percent annual salary. Non-SOEs issue share options 30 percent more than SOEs. There are 43.1 percent of senior executives holding less than 10 percent shares (mainly state-owned holding companies and listed companies), 23.7 percent holding 10–30 percent shares and 33.2 percent holding at least 30 percent shares (see Figure 9.1 and Table 9.4).

Currently all compensations are determined one-way by the firm without making reference to the market and executives have little bargaining power. Such practice hampers the formation of an efficient executive labor market. Again, this would lead to executives pursuing short-term profits at the cost of the long-term return of the firm. Fan *et al.* (2000) found that percentage shareholding of major officers is not related to firm performance, but the proportion of top

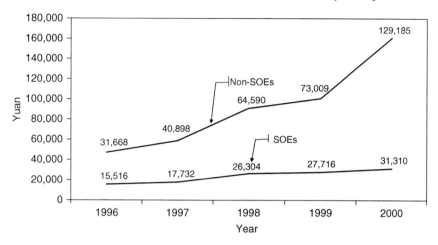

Figure 9.1 Incomes of Chinese managers in recent years (Yuan) (source: Yang, 2001).

Table 9.4 Employees' shareholding in joint-stock companies (%)

	Listed companies	Large companies	Smaller companies	State-owned holding companies	Total
Shareholding by top executives	46.0	13.1	14.5	6.5	14.3
Shareholding by middle executive and professionals	14.0	20.4	25.0	12.2	24.0
Shareholding by all staff	40.0	66.5	60.5	81.3	61.5

Source: Yang, 2001.

managers holding shares is positively related to firm performance. In addition, the higher the net profits, the higher the salary for top management (excluding supervisors). Furthermore, the higher the percentage of shares held by the CEO/chairman, the less likely that he/she will be replaced.

Since 1998, companies paid more attention to improving executives' incentive schemes. Except increasing executives' income levels, more companies choose to grant executives stocks or share options, so as to align their own interests with the shareholders' interest, and to link with the business's long-term goals. Currently China adopts a system which locks executives' shareholding. During an executive's employment period and within six months after leaving the company, he or she is not allowed to sell their shareholding, including those convertible shares bought after listing. It is hoped that CSRC will soon issue a guideline governing employee stock options schemes.

Corporate transparency and disclosure quality

The effective functioning of capital markets critically depends on effective information sharing among companies, securities analysts and shareholders. One major element of good CG is transparency – the provision of timely, true and relevant corporate information to stakeholders (especially investors) to enable them to make decisions. Besides traditional financial statements, this information should cover the overall company performance, future prospects and positioning, strategic planning and policies, risk management, remuneration policy and performance assessment criteria, both in financial and non-financial terms. Dipiazza (2002)[3] indicated that there were six objectives of corporate reporting: completeness, compliance, consistency, commentary, clarity and communication.

Improvements in information sharing should increase management credibility, analysts' understanding of the firm, investors' patience and confidence and, potentially, share value (Eccles and Mavrinac, 1995). In a study by CFO Asia of the 116 largest listed firms in Asia, those which disclosed more extensively were found to perform much better in earnings and stock prices than those which disclosed less extensively (Apple Daily, 2002). Sufficient information disclosure is an effective mechanism to reduce information asymmetry and increase market inefficiency. If enterprises (both SOEs and non-SOEs) wish to borrow from banks or obtain capital from the capital market, they have to show timely, accurate and independently audited financial reports in order to gain financier or investor confidence.

Disclosures are either mandatory, voluntary or provided by intermediaries, and they complement each other to enhance market transparency and efficiency. As additional disclosures involve extra costs and benefits, the management must always exercise its judgment carefully in voluntary disclosure decisions. Currently, the main disclosure issue in China is the low compliance of disclosure rules and the common existence of fraudulent accounting information.

With the development of the securities market, listed companies are required to publicly disclose certain financial and non-financial information. In the past 17 years, various regulations on the public disclosure of information by listed companies have been prepared and promulgated. In addition to Company Law, Security Law and Accounting Law, the specific regulations governing information disclosures of listed firms in China are "Issuance of Stock and Transactions Management Provisional Rules" released by the State Council in April 1993, the "Standards on the Contents and Format of Public Disclosure by Listed Firms" in 1994[4] and the "Notices on Enhancing the Quality of Financial Information Disclosure of Listed Companies" in 1999 issued by CSRC, various specific accounting standards issued by the MOF and the Listing Rules issue by the two stock exchanges in 2000.

According to Ball (1999), the primary role of accounting in CG is to provide independent accounting information that can be used to monitor the acts of managers and investors. These include the accounting for the assets under the managers' control and the evaluation of managerial performance. Much of the financial reporting information is prepared by management, endorsed by the audit committee (if one exists), approved by the board, audited by the external auditors, commented upon by independent analysts and circulated widely via various channels. Each participant in this chain should play his/her role with high professional ethics to ensure transparency, reliability and integrity. It is also important to bear in mind that the quality of our accounting and auditing standards and its enforcement have a direct bearing on the quality of the financial information that is disclosed.

In 1985, the first Accounting Law was enacted (and amended in 1999) which determines accounting responsibilities and procedures for SOEs. The first IAS-based Business Accounting Standard (No. 1 Fundamental Accounting Standards) was promulgated by the MOF in 1992 on advice from the CASC. Since 1997, there have been more than ten Specific Accounting Standards which guide accounting and financial reporting practices. Further, the "Uniform Accounting System" prescribes charts of account, reporting formats and detailed accounting instructions.

Since the first one was established in 1981, there are now around 5,000 accounting firms in China but only a few hundred of them can audit listed firms. Under the direct supervision of the MOF, the CICPA was established in 1988 and it now has 135,000 members. The CPA Law 1993 governs its activities. Since 1991, aspiring CICPA members must have an approved accounting degree, pass a uniform Chartered Public Accountant (CPA) examination, and demonstrate appropriate experience to gain membership. In 1997, a vigorous "Rectification Campaign" was conducted to improve professional practices and ethics. By the campaign's end in 1999, 12,700 individual CPAs and 580 CPA firms had been forced from the profession. Under the Sate Council and headed by the Audit General, the CNAO was established in 1983 to audit public sector organizations (including many SOEs) and to lead and supervise the auditing profession.

Many of these disclosure and accounting rules are loose and are difficult to interpret or to enforce, and this makes it difficult to obtain accurate accounting information from Chinese firms. This is also inherent conflict between an accounting system that emphasizes decision usefulness and one that is oriented toward profits-based tax collection. There has been a growing awareness within China that accurate financial reporting is an important basis for a healthy market economy. Along with steeper penalties for misleading information and false financial reports; there is a developing climate increasingly conducive to more accurate reporting. However, even with the best of intentions, the manipulation of accounting standards, window-dressing, creative accounting and even fraudulent financial reporting are still prevalent.

The Ministry of Finance released the findings on its recent study on accounting information quality of listed companies in early 2003. It found that the practice of disclosing unreliable information accounting is still very serious. Thirty-six companies (18.75 percent) were found with inaccurate reported asset, >5 percent; 103 companies with unreliable net income, >10 percent;

19 companies with net loss rather than reported net income; and 22 companies with accounts beyond their accounting system. The CNAO also found that 68 percent of SOEs were issuing seriously misleading or inaccurate financial statements (Sing Tao Daily, 2003). Overall, accounting activities are not well regulated and the overall accounting information quality is not high.

Seeing these deficiencies, the Accounting Law, which was revised in 1999 and effective in 2000, emphasizes the requirements for appointing qualified accounting personnel in order to reduce window-dressing and fraudulent accounting activities. It also further revised the requirements for identification, measurement and recording of accounting information in business firms. It holds the management of a firm legally responsible for the accuracy and completeness of the unit's accounting information. A firm should not authorize or instruct its accounting personnel to undertake unethical or unlawful accounting acts. If these regulations are not followed, disciplinary sanctions and criminal liabilities will be rendered according to the severity of the situation. These will undoubtedly improve accounting practices significantly and prevent management of firms from avoiding their responsibilities in offering falsifying information.

As managers in China have little incentive to reduce agency costs, and since the stock market, executive labour market and market for corporate control are not yet mature, the current financial reporting environment provides few benefits to firms for disclosing reliable and complete information. The information provided by intermediaries is also very limited, leading to very low transparency of firms in China. According to a survey by the SHSE, 80 percent of investors were not satisfied with the current corporate disclosure of list firms. However, very few of them brought up questions to the SGMs or management of these firms (HKEJ, 2001).

In the current stage of development, increasing both the quantity and quality of mandatory disclosure requirements is definitely necessary. In early 2001, the CSRC released another set of regulations governing corporate disclosures. It plans to establish a complete and systematic information disclosure regulatory system within a few years. Other requirements and relevant accounting standards are reviewed and extended regularly.

Furthermore, the quality, independence and liabilities of auditors and other intermediaries are still problems that need to be resolved in China. The Chinese audit profession vanished after 1949 and was only revived in the early 1990s. Currently less than half of CPAs in China are permitted to practise, and only a small proportion of audit firms are authorized to examine listed companies. In recent years, some audit firms were charged for professional negligence or collusion with firm management for producing fraudulent reporting. There have also been cases in which the earnings of newly-listed firms have increased a thousand times after their IPOs, and this has caused worries about the reliability of audited financial statements. The more recent fraudulent financial reporting case of Euro-Asia Agricultural (Holdings), a Chinese private enterprise listed in China and Hong Kong, was described as a "mini Enron" case. The orchid grower was alleged, in October 2002, to have inflated its revenue by 20-fold when it applied for a Hong Kong listing. Subsequently its listing was suspended, and the firm and its IPO sponsor and auditors were investigated by relevant regulatory bodies in both China and Hong Kong.

Auditor independence has become the focus of much worldwide attention, especially following the Enron collapse. The Chinese accounting profession has registered and taken seriously the public concerns that were expressed following the affairs locally and overseas. On the one hand, the threat of legal action is improving professional ethics and audit quality. On the other hand, conflicting laws and over-generous rulings are undermining the attractiveness of auditing. In 2002, the Ministry of Finance took over the monitoring duties of CPAs from the CICPA.

Since 1979, China has made tremendous strides in terms of developing an accounting infrastructure suitable to the needs of market economy. Many policy makers and academics in China gradually believe that there are many net benefits of transparency, although the current focus of companies is on compliance with rules rather than more voluntary disclosures to promote transparency. Therefore, adequate or full information disclosure has still a long way to go.

Direction for future improvement

According to a survey, about 35 percent of listed firms have problems related to CG (HKEJ, 2001). China faces international market environment and keen competition, and hence improvements of its CG are urgently needed for its future success. In a survey of 200 chief financial officers (CFOs) in the top 300 companies in China and southeast Asia, the Association of Chartered Certified Accountants (ACCA) found that awareness of CG continues to increase significantly in China, and that programs of reform are making some inroads into improving performance (ACCA, 2002).

According to a joint national survey of 1,124 listed companies (216 of them with detailed investigation), by CSRC and the State Economic and Trade Committee in mid-2002 on their progress of building a modern enterprise system, there has been much progress in terms of CG practice (Cha, 2003). It was found that there are many improvements in: the pace of diversification of ownership; independence of listed companies; the functioning of the independent director scheme; internal control mechanisms; and the quality of corporate disclosures. Seventy-seven percent of companies have set up internal audit departments, and 92 percent of them make mandated periodic disclosure on time and in compliance with the requirements.

The more serious and sustaining problem identified from this survey is that holding companies often expropriate the assets of their listed companies after restructuring from a SOE. This is done either through connected party transactions or receiving payments from a listed company as a loan or contributions. This practice is certainly at the expense of minority shareholders' interest, but also hampers the healthy development of the listed companies. The root of this problem has been the institutional framework that the state exercises its ownership rights. The CSRC has been taking a number of measures in tackling these inappropriate activities but with little effect.

Mrs Cha (2003) of CSRC stressed that the establishment of a modern enterprise system does not only involve listed companies and regulatory bodies, but also needs the fitting of the whole external environment. The whole society needs to cultivate a healthy culture of integrity, honesty and compliance, and there should be a set of comprehensive jurisdiction and legal procedures as a back-up. At the same time, all government agencies, intermediaries and mass media should play their respective roles diligently and make an influence together so that listed companies operate according to the rules of a modern enterprise system (Cha, 2003).

Among other suggestions given in earlier sections, to further improve its CG standard, it is suggested that China should take a bold position and take up the following high-priority changes.

To resolve the problem of dominant shareholders and insider control

"Absence of owner" has been a long-time problem disturbing listed SOEs and creates many other governance problems. Following the resolution of the 16th National Peoples' Congress Meeting in 2002 on the reform of the national asset management scheme, it is hoped that this problem and the insider control issue could be resolved ultimately. The new scheme should be able to regulate the holding company's behaviors and the relationship between the controlling shareholder and the listed company. These holding companies should not be allowed to exercise state ownership any more but to return their shareholding to the national assets management agency and separate itself from the listed company. If they do not return to the national asset management agency, then the agency should exercise the state ownership via the board of directors of the listed company. After restructuring, the board of a listed company can consider to acquire some or all assets of its previous holding company (so to avoid inside transactions). Alternatively, if the holding cannot survive after the return of the assets, then it should be dissolved or further re-structured. New legislation is needed to extend the fiduciary duties to controlling shareholders who are liable for compensations if they do not fulfill such duties.

Protecting shareholders' rights and enhancing investor relationships

Lessons can be drawn from other countries in preventing major shareholders from taking control of the SGMs, and there should be a balance of rights between large and small shareholders. Company Law should be revised to ensure that the board of directors and the supervisory board are elected at SGMs. Detailed codes of meeting for SGMs should be developed. A cumulative voting system should be introduced at SGMs so that smaller shareholders can select their own spokesperson who could represent their interests on the board of directors and the supervisory board. More investor education is needed to allow smaller shareholders to make more contributions at SGMs. Listed companies are encouraged to develop effective investor relationship management. Through the establishment of investor confidence on listed companies by protecting their information and other legal rights, then companies can seek investors' long-term support given to them.[5]

Further improving the composition and functioning of the board of directors

There is a need to further strengthen the composition of the board of directors, the independent director scheme, and the integrity and fiduciary duties of directors. There should be a system to search and appoint qualified persons to serve as executive directors and independent directors on the board. A major shareholder should not be allowed to take up more than one-third of the board seats. Most executive directors (including the chairman) and CEOs of listed state-owned firms should be recruited from the private sector. The Company Law should be revised to clearly spell out the rights, duties and legal liabilities of executive and non-executive directors. Board directorship should not be regarded as a benefit or an honorary or administrative appointment. Expert committees (e.g. audit, governance, budget, nomination, executive remuneration, human resources, strategic planning and social responsibility) should be established to clearly delineate the specific responsibilities of the board. All voting members of these committees should be outside independent directors.[6]

Ensuring reliable financial reporting and corporate transparency

The law and rules governing financial reporting and corporate disclosure should be further revised, expanded and enforced diligently. The regulatory framework should ensure that there should be accurate, complete and timely disclosure of information on all important company activities and decisions. More severe penalties should be given to firms and their management if there is violation of the rules, including criminal liabilities. Information intermediaries like audit firms should be dissolved if they are found to be involved in fraudulent reporting activities, especially involving IPO, acquisition and connected party transactions. However, enhancing disclosure requirements alone would not suffice to close the communication gap. An improvement in the quality of communication and disclosure processes is more important.

Safeguarding the benefits of other stakeholders and caring social responsibilities

Companies are not simply entities that exist for the sole pursuit of maximizing profits, they are the basic "cell" that fuels the social economy and various benefits are derived from it. Apart from benefits for various internal units of the company itself, companies also form a network linking all stakeholders. It is useful to permit representatives of employees, banks, clients, suppliers and other stakeholders to air their views and suggestions as non-voting members at board of directors meetings. Through the active participation of these stakeholders, it is expected that a high standard of CG can be realized. Companies should motivate all stakeholders, safeguard their legal rights, and strike a balance of interests among various stakeholders.

Conclusion

More than 20 years of economic reform in China has created a large number of joint stock limited companies characterized by separation of ownership and managerial control. As a result, this has created a new agency relationship, with the potential for conflicts of interest among different stakeholders, it is vital to understand the governance mechanisms of Chinese firms, particularly since virtually all SOEs in China are subject to different degrees of privatization and CG reform.

China saw a confluence of several forces in the 1990s and therefore experienced a serious challenge to the traditional structure of its economic system and CG. It was found that in this transitional process, the influence of the controlling shareholders and insider control are the key issues of CG in China. Other major problems are ineffective regulatory enforcement, lack of independent board and controls, lack of incentive for executives, low corporate transparency and unreliable financial disclosures, insufficient protection of smaller investors' interests and low business ethical standard.

Under such environments, decisions cannot be made effectively, contracts cannot be executed fairly and diligently, and shareholders' rights cannot be protected. Rather, state agents, other persons controlling resources or their associates, because of the "absence" of the real owner and their own vested interests, will take advantage of this non-mature system to expropriate interest from the company and other smaller shareholders via illegal or unethical means. In such an institutional environment, it is difficult for some market participants to uphold the traditional virtues of integrity and ethics as the one who practices integrity always loses. As the cost of violating rules is small and there is a high level of information asymmetry, coupled with weak control and motivational mechanisms, it induces many firms in China to commit fraudulent financial reporting and many other problems of CG appear.

China acted more decisively to improve CG since 1998. The CSRC had issued guidelines on independent directors, established a delisting mechanism for non-quality companies, and promulgated a systematic set of codes of CG for all listed companies, among other initiatives. Learning from the experiences of other countries, this chapter suggests a number of ways to improve the standard of CG in China. It stresses that in the reform process, resolving many of the major issues mentioned-above concurrently are important.

We do not believe that China, or any other country, will ultimately move to a full US/UK market model or a German/Japan bank-led model. Each country will seek its own system to accomplish the goals of effective CG, one that reflects its own institutions, values and traditions. China has to develop its own model in the long term in view of major thrust of change including market globalization, political and institutional changes. Moreover, the development of a new CG system understandably comes slowly, since there are many pieces that need to come together and the political and management changes involved take a considerable time. China will seek to retain its fundamental values and avoid some of the harshness it sees in other countries.

Table 9.A1 Major laws and regulations relating to governing CG in China

Date of issuance	Name of law/guidelines
1985	Accounting Law of PRC
1992	MOF: Basic Accounting Standard
1992	MOF: Revised Uniform Accounting System Regulations
1993	CPA Law, Accounting Law (Revised)
1993	Company Law of PRC
1993	Provisional Regulation Concerning the Issuance and Trading of Shares
1994	CSRC: Contents and Format of Public Disclosure by Listed Companies (Standard No. 2) – Contents and Format of Annual Reports
1995	MOF: Punishment of Crime for Financial Disorder
1996	CICPA Charter
1996	CSRC: Notice About Enhancing the Management of Directors, Supervisors and Managers Holding their Own Company's Shares
1996	SHSE: Guidelines on the Management of Shareholding by Company Directors, Supervisors and Senior Executives
1997	CSRC: Notice on Issuing Guidelines for Listed Company Prospectus
1998	CSRC: Opinions about Regulating Shareholders' General Meetings (Revised 2000)
1998	CSRC: Notice on Termination of Issuing Company Employee Shares
1998	CSRC: Contents and Format of Public Disclosure by Listed Companies (Standard No. 2) – Contents and Format of Annual Reports (Revised 1998)
1998	CSRC: Notice on Preparing the 1998 Annual Report Properly and Related Problems
1998	Securities Law of PRC
1998	MOF: Specific Accounting Standards for Business Enterprises
1999	CSRC: Measures on Further Promoting Standardized Operations and Deepening the Reform in Overseas-listed Companies
1999	CSRC: Notice on Prohibition of General Managers and Senior Executives of Listed Companies Taking up Part-time Jobs in Controlling Shareholder's Entities
1999	CSRC: Notice on Enhancing the Quality of Financial Information Disclosure of Listed Companies
1999	MOF: Accounting Law (Revised)
1999	CSRC: Notice on Preparing the 1999 Annual Report Properly and Related Problems
1999	CSRC: Contents and Format of Public Disclosure by Listed Companies (Standard No. 2) – Contents and Format of Annual Reports (Revised 1999)

continued

Table 9.A1 continued

Date of issuance	Name of law/guidelines
2000	SHSE: Listing Rules of the Shanghai Stock Exchange (Revised 2000)
2000	CSRC: Notice on Matters Related to Share Classifications of Listed Companies
2000	CSRC: Opinions About Regulating Shareholders' General Meetings (Revised 2000)
2000	CSRC: Guidelines for Introducing Independent Directors Scheme in Listed Companies
2000	SZSE: Listing Rules of the Shenzhen Stock Exchange
2000	CSRC: Notice on Preparing the 2000 Annual Report Properly and Related Problems
2001	CSRC and SETC: Code of Corporate Governance for Listed Companies in China
2001	CSRC: Notice on Issues related to Individual Domestic Residents Investing in Foreign Currency Stocks Listed in the Domestic Stock Markets (B-Share market)
2001	CSRC: The "Implementing Measures on the Suspension and Termination of Public Trading for Companies Suffering Losses" Applied to B-Share Companies
2001	CSRC: Steering Opinions on the Re-structuring of Companies Intended to be Listed (Consultation Draft)
2001	SHSE: Listing Rules of the Shanghai Stock Exchange (Revised 2001)
2001	CSRC: Securities Market Regulation in the Internet Age
2001	CSRC: Guidelines for Introducing Independent Directors to the Board of Directors of Listed Companies
2002	CSRC: Provisional Measures on Administration of Domestic Securities Investment of Qualified Foreign Institutional Investors (QFII)

Notes

1 Except specific accounting and auditing standards.
2 Domestic A shares and foreign B, H and N shares).
3 The CEO of Ernst & Young.
4 Revised in 1998 and 1999).
5 This could enhance listed companies' capital raising abilities in the securities market.
6 Other executives serving only as observers.

10 The Turkish national system of corporate governance

M. Ararat and M. Ugur

Introduction

Turkey is a rapidly growing emerging market and the largest economy lined up to join the European Union (EU). During its long march for integration with Europe, a high degree of volatility, underpinned by recurrent economic crises, has been a well documented aspect of Turkey's macroeconomic performance. Throughout the 1980s and 1990s, the Turkish corporate governance (CG) regime was characterised by opacity and was prone to corrupt practices. The capital market was characterised by low liquidity, high volatility, high cost of capital (low firm valuation) and limited new capital formation. Controlling shareholders maintained large stakes and have leveraged cash flow rights due to privileged shares and pyramidal ownership structures. Shortcomings in the legal and regulatory framework were contributing substantially to the risks of investing in equity markets in Turkey. These deficiencies affected adversely not only the flows of foreign direct investments but also the development of an equity market into which both foreign and domestic savings could be channelled.

In a follow up article (Ugur and Ararat, 2004) we argued economic policy reforms that followed the 2001 crisis can be expected to induce improvements in CG standards for two reasons. First, the transition to a rule-based economic policy would increase the credibility of the statutory CG reforms. Second, the macroeconomic stability that seemed to follow the economic policy reform would encourage voluntary improvements in CG standards as equity finance became a more viable option. Our research led us to conclude that the statutory CG standards in Turkey have improved, but highly concentrated ownership structures and the inadequacy of the enforcement framework would continue to constitute serious obstacles.

This chapter examines new evidence to ascertain the extent to which the quality of CG standards can be related to the emergence of a rule-based economic policy framework and the subsequent reduction in macroeconomic instability. The analysis below suggests that the positive impact of the change in the economic policy framework is still evident, but there is still significant resistance to change in a number of areas.

Setting the scene: economic policy in Turkey

During the last three decades in Turkey, macroeconomic instability went hand in hand with liberalisation, which started in 1980. Policy choices of populist and unstable coalition governments led to three financial crises (in 1994, 2000 and 2001). Inflation reached 106 per cent in 1994 and remained above 60 per cent until 2001. While macroeconomic instability undermined the credibility of the government as a rule setter and as an enforcer, corporations opted for low-quality CG practices in order to counterbalance the risks arising from macroeconomic instability and to secure an artificial competitive edge against their competitors. Disclosure remained limited, pyramidal structures proliferated, intra-group transactions and fund diversions became evident and boards remained dominated by insider owner/managers. These factors weakened the investors' confidence in the Turkish market and caused the share of foreign direct investments to remain low in relation to Turkey's economic fundamentals.

Macroeconomic instability and poor CG standards were related to the heavy involvement of the Turkish state in the economy, which led to two undesirable consequences. On the one hand, it fostered a political culture in which the legitimacy of the state was a function of the "rents" that the government could distribute rather than its ability to provide "public goods" such as a stable macroeconomic environment, a transparent regulatory system and social conflict resolution mechanisms, etc. On the other hand, the state's heavy involvement increased "private risks." Therefore, it induced private economic agents to pressure the government of the day to compensate at least part of their risks – irrespective of whether or not such risks have been due to government action or the private actors' own actions. This second tendency combined with the first and led to persistent favouritism, corruption practices, opacity, etc. (Ugur, 1999, chapter 3).

It is important to note here that macroeconomic instability in the 1990s was observed during a period when the role of external anchors such as the EU or the International Monetary Fund (IMF) was limited. The EU did not emerge as an effective anchor in the 1990s because it was not prepared to provide Turkey with a membership prospect. In fact, while the Central and Eastern European Countries (CEECs) have upgraded their relations with the EU and signalled firm commitment to policy reforms, as well as macroeconomic stability, Turkey's relations with the EU deteriorated since the rejection of its membership bid in 1989. The deterioration was evident up until the Helsinki Council decision of 1999, which granted Turkey an official candidate status. The EU's reluctance to take Turkey in was largely due to lack of commitment to integration on the part of Turkish governments. However, in the absence of an EU anchor in the form Copenhagen criteria tied to an eventual membership prospect, the Turkish policy-makers' attempts at reforms and stabilisation remained largely non-credible – hence the anchor/credibility dilemma analysed in Ugur (1999).

Similarly, the IMF did not emerge as an effective anchor either. The IMF intervened twice (in 1994 and 1999) with a package of credits in return for structural reforms and stabilisation. However, Turkish policy-makers made only half-hearted attempts to comply with the IMF conditionality. This lack of commitment has been underpinned by Turkish policy-makers' preference for discretion, which was necessary for maintaining clientelistic/populist policies. It was only after the crisis in 2001 that the IMF was able to secure firm commitment to stabilisation and economic reforms. The weakness of the external anchors until the end of the 1990s has contributed to the persistence of macroeconomic instability in Turkey and, thereby, reduced the probability of introducing CG reforms in Turkey (Ugur and Ararat, 2004).

The Public Sector Reforms focused on accountability and transparency leading to improvements in the audit capacity and framework, and in the efficiency of tax regulations. In addition, important markets such as electricity, telecommunications, sugar and tobacco and alcohol were liberalised, leading to gradual disappearance of administrated prices and subsidies. The third stand-by agreement with the IMF, still pending signature, foresees further improvements in the public sector by:

i   deepening of structural reforms;
ii implementing public expenditure management; and
iii strengthening public sector governance including implementation of the national anti-corruption strategy.

Rule-based economic policy and improved CG standard I: regulatory framework after 2002

Despite its long history and large-scale securities trading in the past (see Tanor, 2000, Volume I, pp. 18–28), the modern capital market of Turkey has only 20 years of history. From the 1980s onwards, there was a continuous increase in the number and size of joint stock companies that opened up their equity to the public. The Capital Markets Law (CML) was enacted in 1981 and the Capital Markets Board (CMB) was established as the sole independent regulatory authority at the end of 1985. Secondary market operations, initially limited to equity trading, started in 1986 with the foundation of the Istanbul Stock Exchange (ISE). In 1992, with amendments to the relevant legislation, the CMB's powers were increased to allow it to define new instruments in response to rapid market developments. The small- and medium-sized enterprises (SME) market, gold exchange and options and derivatives market were opened later in 2003 and 2004.

After a decade of successful performance until 2000, market activity declined with the economic crises. The decline started in 2000 with a loss of 31.8 per cent of market value in 2001. Market capitalisation went down to 20 per cent of the gross domestic product (GDP) from 35 per cent in 2000. Based on the closing values of the last trading day of 2001, the total market capitalisation went down to US$47.69 billion compared to year-end figure of US$69.5 billion in 2000. There were almost no initial public offerings after 2000 – when a record of US$2.8 billion of funds was raised through initial public offerings (IPOs) of

35 firms. A weak primary market was conducive to a combination of high trading and high price volatility. This, in return, was conducive to gains on speculative trading evidenced by high numbers of occurrences of capital market abuses.

From 2003 onwards, the picture started to improve significantly in line with the progress in achieving macroeconomic stability. While the "public sector" was putting its house in order and implementing a strategy to fight corruption, which was frequently blamed by the private sector as the main obstacle for CG reforms, the CMB of Turkey issued a number of significant directives and recommended a Corporate Governance Code in July 2003. The "Corporate Governance Principles" are presented as the road map for future regulations by the CMB. In the preface to the Principles, which are based on the Organization of Economic Cooperation and Development (OECD) guidelines, the CMB states very clearly that the voluntary nature of the Principles should not be taken lightly. The CMB is keen to ensure that explanations concerning implementation or non-implementation, conflicts arising from incomplete implementation, statements on future plans for the company's governance practices, etc. "should all be included in the annual report and disclosed to public" (Ugur and Ararat 2004).

At the end of 2004, market capitalisation recovered to US$98.3 billion and reached 37 per cent of the GDP with the inclusion of 12 IPOs. Average free float was around 35 per cent as of the end of the year, up from 22 per cent in 2001. Also, the share of 25 most heavily traded companies in total trading fell from 72 per cent in 2002 to 66 per cent at the end of 2004 – reflecting a moderate increase in the trading of other stocks. Balance of securities traded by foreign institutional investors increased from US$12.9 million in 2002 to US$18.9 million in January 2005 and the total transaction volume by foreign institutional investors increased from US$1.96 billion to US$3.6 billion. At the end of 2003, there were more than one million individual equity investors and two million mutual funds investors. In addition, 288 mutual funds and 81 audit firms were registered with the CMB. As of March 2005, the total market capitalisation of ISE had reached US$115 billion with an average daily trading volume of US$913 million. Nevertheless, the market is still shallow, as the total number of companies remains low (307 companies, 22 of which are investment partnerships) and the activities are still concentrated around financial institutions. In addition, the market capitalisation of the ten largest companies (3.3 per cent) represented 58 per cent of the total market capitalisation.[1]

The CMB, the ISE and Takasbank[2] are the major institutions involved in Turkey's capital market. The CMB regulates the operations of the ISE. Transactions are carried out on the basis of continuous action trading by an electronic system. As a body, the CMB is appointed by the Council of Ministers for six years and it is capable of directly imposing penalties – including suspension and cancellation of licences and putting the companies on a "watch list" for non-compliance. Securities of such companies can only be traded for 30 minutes in a day and transactions are closely monitored. However, the CMB could not directly take cases to court as this right is granted to public prosecutors only. Latest amendments in 1999 strengthened the powers of the CMB and enhanced the institutional infrastructure for the market by establishing new institutions under the CML, such as the Association for Securities Dealers, the Securities Investor Protection Fund and the Accounting Standards Board. The ISE's board and its chairman are appointed by the government from among the nominees submitted by the CMB for a five-year term. It is governed by a general assembly attended by its trading members licensed by CMB. The recent history shows that both the CMB and ISE have been responsive to market needs and that their structural fundamentals do not impose any problems for performing an effective role.

The primary sources of CG regulations are the Turkish Commercial Code (CC) of 1956, CML as amended in 1999 and regulations issued by the CMB. Currently, the CC is undergoing a radical amendment – with the explicit objective of aligning it with European directives on company and capital market laws. The CMB also announced a major review of the CML in March 2005 and invited market participants for consultation. A new Banking Law is in the process of being enacted after a few months of public consultation with substantial provisions regarding the governance of credit lending institutions. All these changes will substantially improve the legal and regulatory framework for CG, but most important, improvements will be brought in by the changes in the CC.

The draft Banking Law which was expected to be enacted by the Parliament at the beginning of 2005 set the grounds for dissolving the financial and industrial arms of family owned conglomerates by ensuing reduction in connected lending and limiting shareholding of banks in non-financial institutions to a maximum of 15 per cent of its own funds. The draft gives ample powers to the Banking Regulatory and Supervisory Agency and holds the board and senior managers liable, jointly and severally, for the repayment of credits extended in violation of the act. In addition to general technical requirements for prudent banking (in areas such as accounting, risk management, internal control, bad loan provisions, capital adequacy, elimination of full state guarantee on deposits, etc.) the draft Banking Law provides for alignment with international best practices and sets strict criteria concerning the personal integrity of general managers, assistant general managers and board members. It authorises issuance to issue mandatory Corporate Governance Rules which includes a strong component of independence in the Board assured by statutory approval of independent member nominations.

In addition to laws and regulations, Corporate Governance Principles issued by the CMB in July 2003 and amended in 2004, provides further guidelines for listed companies' governance on a "comply or explain" basis. They are based on OECD's Corporate Governance Principles and consist of four parts. Part one includes the principles on shareholders' rights and their equal treatment. In part two the principles for disclosure and transparency concepts are covered in detail. Part three is mainly concerned with stakeholders defined as company's shareholders and its workers, creditors, customers, suppliers, various non-governmental organizations, the government and potential investors that may decide to make investments in the company. Part four includes issues such as the functions, duties and obligations, operations and structure of the board of directors and the committees to be established for supporting the board operations. All listed companies are mandated to report their compliance with these principles in their annual report starting from 2004. According to CMB's announcements, to encourage companies to adopt high standards of CG, a separate CG index will be set up in the ISE. To qualify, companies should get six out ten points as a minimum in an independent rating of their compliance with CMB's CG guidelines. According to a press release issued by the ISE in March 2005, the index will be calculated as soon as five companies meet the minimum requirements. The ISE has also announced that listing fees for companies qualified to be included in the CG index will be discounted by 50 per cent. A new decree regarding rating agencies regulates the credit rating and CG rating activities. Rating companies can only be set up as joint stock companies with adequate capital; they are subject to the new regulation with respect to their independence and competence separately for credit and CG ratings.

Given the evidence above, we can state that the post-2002 reforms and changes expected in the near future in the legal and regulatory framework constitute significant steps towards the establishment of good CG standards in Turkey. In that sense, they are steps in the right direction and may contribute to the emergence of an effective capital market. In this process, the CMB emerges as a significant actor, who is committed to ensure full compliance with EU and International Organization of Security Commissions (IOSCO) principles by the end of 2005.[3] From an analytical perspective, these developments imply that the transition to a rule-based economic policy framework and the macroeconomic stability that followed have induced CG reforms in Turkey. The improvement in regulatory standards in the last few years either followed or was contemporaneous with economic policy reform and macroeconomic stability. As the government adopted a rule-based approach to economic policy, the statutory rules of the game in the area of CG are now being redefined. In addition, the corporate sector is now more willing to upgrade its CG practices as equity finance becomes a relatively more feasible option under macroeconomic stability.

Rule-based economic policy and improved CG standard II: improvements in the disclosure standards

The disclosure infrastructure for listed firms has been strengthened in the last few years through new decrees issued by the CMB on auditing and accounting standards and as a result of improvements in the technological infrastructure. A major missing component of international standards, namely inflation adjusted consolidated reporting was adopted in 2004. A vast majority of ISE-30 companies had been voluntarily issuing annual reports and quarterly statements, based on International Accounting Standards (IASs), for some time. In 2004 the International Financial Reporting Standard (IFRS) was an optional standard accepted by the CMB and finally it became the mandatory standard as of 2005 putting Turkey ahead of many EU countries in adopting international standards.

New regulations have also been adopted in harmony with international audit standards. Listed companies have to establish "Audit Committees" headed by a non-executive director and officers have to sign off the financial reports with the statement that the information reflects the financial position and operating results of the company and that the reports do not include unfair, misleading or deficient explanation. External audit standards have been substantially improved in the process by strengthening the regulatory oversight of audit companies, requesting rotation of auditors every five years and mandating the separation of consulting and auditing activities. Audit companies are approved by CMB and they are subject to civil actions if their letter misleads the investors. However the quality of majority of the audit firms is questionable. The Independent Audit Association founded in 1988 does not have statutory position to self-regulate the profession.

Public disclosure is facilitated by means of Prospectus and Circulars, Financial Statements and Reports and Public Disclosure of Material Events. As a general rule public companies are required to disclose any changes that may affect a company's market value. Specially mentioned by the CMB are changes in ownership and management, fixed assets through sales or purchases, business activities, investments and financial situation of the company. In case of subsidiaries, changes in the parent company are also required to be disclosed. Irregularities and non-compliance can be subject to criminal law.

The CMB's information infrastructure is currently being upgraded to a high standard in order to combat capital market abuses and ensure effective surveillance of market transactions, as well as timely disclosure. The Public Disclosure System will employ digital certificates and electronic signatures. All public disclosure will be disseminated electronically via the internet. Testing of the system started in November 2004 and the system was expected to be live and in full operation before the end of 2005, eliminating paper-based reporting completely.

Although the picture for listed companies looks rather rosy, it is much darker for unlisted firms. Furthermore unregistered economy and corruption are still posing serious threats for the efficient functioning of the market. There is no set of generally accepted accounting principles that applies equally to all companies operating in Turkey – other than general rules that govern the aspects of accounting in the Tax Procedures Code and the Uniform Chart of Accounts which prescribe a code of accounts and a format for presentation of financial statements. The new CC is expected to change the situation by adopting IAS for all joint stock companies and mandating annual external audit.

During the crises years the role played by the civil society against corruption and in monitoring corporations was extremely limited. First of all, restrictions imposed upon the civil society organizations coupled with a highly monopolised media and the tradition of opacity exacerbated the information asymmetry between society on the one hand and the state and the private sector on the other. Second corruption was legitimised in the eyes of the civil society due to the moral void (Ugur and Ararat, 2004). With the ongoing democratisation reforms this picture is expected to change but the monopolistic structure of media will continue to pose a problem.

A S&P/CGFT T&D Survey recently conducted by Sabanci University's Corporate Governance Forum and S&P evaluated disclosure practices of 52 companies listed on the ISE. The survey also compared these companies with companies in other markets, which are surveyed by S&P/IFC with the same methodology. Survey results (Table 10.1) reveal that Turkey compares with Emerging Asia, is better than Latin America and slightly worse than Asia Pacific (S&P and CGFT, 2005).

The survey indicates that Turkish companies score higher in financial transparency but the disclosure on board and management structure and processes are significantly worse than the rest of the world. This evidence, as it was the case above with respect to the regulatory framework, suggests that the transition to a rule-based economic policy has been followed by some improvements in Turkish CG standards concerning transparency and disclosure. However, the evidence also indicates that Turkey is still at the beginning of a lengthy catching up process – as can be seen from the difference between Turkish and developed-country standards.

Resistance to change

Despite the positive trends examined above, there are still significant obstacles to sustained improvement in Turkish CG standards. These obstacles are evident in the following areas: enforcement/implementation; shareholder rights and investor protection; board structures and processes; and corporate ownership structures. In what follows, we will examine the nature of resistance to change in these areas.

Enforcement

Throughout the 1990s, there were severe operational problems with the legal process and law enforcement in Turkey. First of all, ministers and members of

Table 10.1 Comparison of transparency and disclosure scores

	Composite score	Ownership structure	Financial disclosure	Board structure and processes	Number of companies
UK	70	54	81	70	124
Europe	51	41	69	41	227
US	70	52	77	78	500
Japan	61	70	76	37	150
Asia-Pacific	48	41	60	42	99
Latin America	31	28	58	18	89
Emerging Asia	40	39	54	27	253
Turkey	41	39	64	20	52

Sources: S&P's Transparency and Disclosure Study, 2002 and S&P/CGFT Transparency and Disclosure Survey – Turkey.

parliament enjoyed extensive immunity against corrupt practices, which included permissive supervision, lenient law enforcement and distribution of rents in return for political support (see Ugur, 1999, pp. 68–75). Second, the process was complicated, slow and costly; or it was unpredictable due to heavy reliance on decrees. Third, the general inefficiency of the legal process and the weaknesses in law enforcement compromised the institutions that were introduced to supervise listed corporations. Since 2000, the CMB has filed complaints to the office of public prosecutors for around 100 violations of CML every year. Only one case in each year has reached decree absolute, with the rest resulting in dismissals and adjournments. The average time between the CMB's appeal and the first verdict (excluding decisions on adjournment and dismissal) was 12 months. The public prosecutor had not reacted to files concerning 26 cases in 2001 and half of the cases in 2002. The result is that only 1 per cent of all complaints ended up with any punishment (www.spk.gov.tr). However, in line with our argument that macroeconomic stability provided incentives for improvements in CG, we observe some improvement in compliance. This is reflected in a decrease in the number of cases taken to the public prosecutors by the CMB. The number fell from 165 in 2003 to 50 for the first eight months of 2004. In addition, the enforcement and rule of law are now considered as the most important issues by corporate actors – as reflected in a conference organized by the Istanbul Chamber of Commerce in May 2004.

Shareholders' rights and investor protection

In Turkey the CML applies to all joint stock companies with more than 250 shareholders whether listed or not listed. In 2004 there were approximately 700 companies subject to CML; however the regulatory regimes are different for each group. For example cumulative voting is mandatory for unlisted joint stock companies with more than 500 shareholders. In general, fundamental rights of shareholders include participation and voting in general assemblies, electing the board, receiving dividends, requesting information from the corporation, haveing the company audited, challenging resolutions of the general assembly and filing civil actions against directors who failed to perform their duties. Minority rights start with 5 per cent in public companies and 10 per cent in non-public companies. Minority shareholders can veto the release of management, demand that the company or statutory auditors take legal action against the directors who have violated CC, demand special statutory auditors to be appointed, call an extraordinary general meeting or add items to the agenda and demand postponement of discussions on the balance sheet for one month. Recent addition to this list is the right to elect directors by the use of "cumulative voting" provided that the articles of association have provisions to this effect. Corporate Governance Principles have additional provisions that are voluntary. Cumulative voting is recognised and commended by CMB but implementation requires change in Articles of Association of the company.

With the exception of mandatory public announcement of the agenda and venue and making the documents available for shareholders at company premises 15 days before the assembly, provisions regarding general assemblies are vague. CC provisions regarding the rights to participate in discussions are also unclear and subject to board discretion. Unless required for quorum purposes, institutional shareholders are requested to abstain from voting.

Transfer of shares may be problematic; shareowners are required to register their ownership in the share register maintained by the board in case of transfer of nominee shares that are not traded in the stock market despite the decree that sets Takasbank records as the primary source for ownership of shares registered by the CMB. In addition, 23 per cent of companies listed in ISE are reported to have provisions imposing limitations on transfer of shares in their articles of association (CMB 2004). This is probably associated with the controlling shareholders' desires to maintain control.

Privileged shares are allowed subject to shareholder approval but CC requires all shares to have at least one vote. A unique exemption is usufruct shares (or dividend right certificates) that give additional cash flow rights to founders without voting rights. Usufruct shares are not included in the share capital and they can also be issued to the public after the incorporation. CG principles recommends one share–one vote (OSOV) but allows non-voting shares if provisions exist in the Articles of Association. Preferred shares are different than privileged shares and give rights to the owners to receive dividends before the shareholders of common stocks. Common stocks can be classified and assigned different privileges. Most common privilege is nomination rights. CMB notes that 42 per cent of the listed companies have privilege shares with nomination rights (2004). This may be understandable since board nomination is a right given only to the shareholders and to be used only during the general assembly. Uses of shares with nomination rights or keeping control rights are alternative means used by corporations to prevent chaotic assemblies. Other common privileges include multiple voting rights, pre-determined dividend rate or priority in the allocations in case of liquidation.

The CMB issues mandatory minimum dividend rates every year but there is no requirement to disclose the dividend policy. Shareholders are granted pre-emptive rights, but the CC allows shareholders to restrict those rights by a majority vote. Authority to restrict pre-emptive rights can be delegated to the board, but in any case restrictions can only be applied equally to all shareholders. In practice this authority is used for new issues. Share buybacks or treasury stocks are not allowed, although the amendments to the CC are expected to change this situation.

Insider trading is a criminal offence punishable with fines and imprisonment. The CMB is responsible to monitoring and investigating cases and application to the public prosecutors, however provisions are not very clear and monitoring capabilities are limited. The CML also regulates "disguised profit transfers" in the case of related party transactions, and requires disclosure of related parties.

Tunnelling and transfer pricing are unlawful and carry criminal liabilities although detecting and monitoring such transactions have not been very efficient in the past. Taboglu (2002) reports that 362 real persons or legal entities were prohibited from trading in stock markets in 2002 and notes that a high percentage of suspected cases are not prosecuted because of the difficulties in providing the prima facie case in the absence of effective surveillance and technical capacity. While the penalties are clear, the procedure to follow and the disclosure requirements are not. There is no definition of "related parties" in law. In most cases CMB instructs the company to remedy the situation within 30 days.

Neither class action nor derivative action exists under Turkish law, however the shareholders who opposed the decisions or who approved the decisions but were misinformed, may ask the courts to nullify the decision if the decision is proven to be contrary to the law. They may further take civil action against the directors and statutory auditors under certain conditions.

Shareholders' rights are uniformly applicable to both foreign and local shareholders. Procedures concerning the incorporation of foreign companies have been changed and most of the red tape has been eliminated with recent amendments in the foreign investment law.

A survey of websites of ISE-50 companies surprisingly shows that only 11 companies have their Articles of Association, the most important document on shareholders' rights, on their website. Only nine companies disclose any information at all about the backgrounds of their directors and only five companies disclose their Code of Ethics (Danışmanlık, 2005).

Board structure and processes

Boards usually consist of representatives of controlling shareholders which are in most cases members of a family. Day to day operations are delegated to a professional manager and usually one member of the board is designated to be in charge of execution with the oversight of the general manager on behalf of the board. Even when the manager is included and given the title "CEO," her authority is limited. Designated director who is usually a family member (murahhas aza) represents the board with extensive powers.

In a survey conducted by the CMB, listed companies are asked to report on their level of compliance with the Corporate Governance Guidelines (CMB, 2004). According to the survey only 9 per cent of the companies had established a CG committee. 78 per cent of the boards include non-executive members (CMB, 2004) but in most cases they are either the members of the controlling family or they are not independent. The CMB reports no acknowledgement of truly independent members as it would require a change in the articles of association of companies and hence filing with the CMB.

CMB (2004) reports that only 4 per cent of the boards are compensated on the basis of company performance. Anecdotal evidence suggests that in many cases boards are not compensated since members are also the owners. The CC allows the board to receive up to 5 per cent of the profits with the approval of the general assembly provided that the company pays dividends to all shareholders. A directorship fee for board attendance is also defined in CC but is rarely used.

In the S&P/CGFT T&D survey, preliminary results reveal that the disclosure about the functioning of the board is significantly poorer than financial disclosure or ownership disclosure. This may be considered as less important since the traditional agency problems are less significant in "insider" systems, but it may be an indication of informality/lack of professionalism in the functioning of the board. The fact that only 50 per cent of the listed companies have a mission or vision statement disclosed to the public (CMB 2004) may be indicative of this lack of formalism. Indeed, Aksu and Kosedag (2005) report using the S&P/CGFT T&D survey data that between the extreme quartiles of lowest and highest scores, companies with higher scores especially in the category of board structure and management processes disclosures, have higher returns and accounting measures of profitability.

The board does not have to meet physically unless it is deemed necessary and in most cases discussion matters are circulated among the members together with the proposed text of the resolutions. The decisions become binding once they are written in the minutes and duly signed by the members. Anecdotal evidence suggests that board meetings are rather short and important decisions are made by the controlling families. Employees of parent companies frequently sit in the boards of subsidiaries mainly for financial oversight. Often these employees are trusted members of the extended family and the number of boards they sit on may be in excess of 20.

Ownership structure

The fourth area where inertia is evident relates to corporate ownership structure and consequences. In his work on corporate ownership structures and corporate performance of 305 listed Turkish companies owned and controlled primarily by families under a pyramidal ownership structure Yurtoglu (2000, 2004) classifies Turkey as an "insider" country, with insiders being the country's richest families. Yurtoglu's research shows that companies with deviation of control rights from cash flow rights are systematically under valued by the market.

Families directly or indirectly control 80 per cent of all companies (242 of 305 companies). In a substantial majority of the companies, ownership and management overlap. Holding companies own the largest stake in 121 companies at a mean of 47 per cent of outstanding shares. Financial and non-financial companies own 39 and 57 companies at stakes close to 50 per cent. Overall the five largest shareholders owned about 64 per cent of the equity in ISE in 2001 (Yurtoglu, 2004). This figure is not expected to be very different based on the scarcity of new issues since then. The CMB survey (2004) notes that only 36 per cent of the companies disclose their ultimate ownership structure.

Investment companies or funds are closed-end partnerships based on contract law. Trust model or open-ended company model are not allowed in

Turkish law. The consequence of this situation is that outside investors have no voting rights – leading into increased volatility since the only option available to investors is to exit. Most funds including pension funds are managed by portfolio management companies belonging to a family owned group. Portfolios are populated by companies cross invested by groups in friendly terms. The "relationship based" nature of Turkish financial markets even in the case of equity investments makes new entries difficult.

Conclusion

Our findings above suggest that Turkey's legal and institutional framework for CG has improved over the past few years. In addition, transparency and disclosure standards are comparable to those in other emerging markets and recent legislation can be expected to have further positive effects. In terms of structural reform, the most notable change has taken place in the financial sector reforms and in improved supervision of the banking sector. This is followed by the CMB's Corporate Governance Principles, which provide a reference point for voluntary improvements.

These findings are in line with those of the research indicating that country characteristics are highly significant in shaping the CG system in less developed countries. If we focus on economic and financial development and the prospect for economic growth as two country characteristics, we can indicate with some confidence that the change in these characteristics have been positive and had a positive effect on Turkey's CG standards. However, country characteristics also include ownership structures of the firms and legal systems of the country in which the firms operate. When these characteristics are taken into account, we can see that there is still significant resistance to change. Therefore, the recent improvements in Turkish CG standards are still serving as a basis to fill the gap between the law and the desired corporate behaviour. This state of affairs is clearly visible in a number of areas (such as implementation, investor protection, ownership structures, etc.) where the effectiveness of recent reforms remains highly limited.

We see two obstacles to further improvement in Turkish CG practices. The first is related to the trends in capital flows favouring developed Anglo-Saxon markets and consequential decrease in significance of emerging market companies in strategic portfolio investments. In fact, when these companies are included in foreign investors' portfolios, liquidity tends to be the most significant selection criterion even though liquidity is not known to be a proxy for performance. One explanation for the relative lack of investor interest in emerging markets could be the lack of information on CG quality where it matters the most. In developed markets the indicators of CG quality is relatively better established and the data is more readily available from public disclosures. In emerging markets with lower standards of public disclosure, disclosure data may be non-credible. In this context, the findings by Aksu and Kosedag (2005) for the ISE provides sober reading: disclosure, widely excepted as the leading indicator of CG quality, does not have an explanatory power in explaining firm value since the variation is small between companies.

The second obstacle is highly concentrated ownership and low floatation rates, both of which deter investors from entering the Turkish market. The CMB's new regulations requiring at least 25 per cent floatation in the IPOs is a positive step in the right direction but is not sufficient to make a significant difference in the near future. The most important injection of capital to the stock market was expected to be realised by privatisations, but privatisation remains to be one of the areas that the current government seriously underperforms. Hence with 120 brokerage houses and only 307 listed companies with an average floatation of around 25 per cent, the Turkish market remains to be prone to excessive volatility.

Most research on CG treats ownership structure as exogenous with the exception of early work by Demsetz *et al.* (1985). However, recent empirical research on emerging markets and business groups suggest that ownership structures may be an equilibrium outcome of private benefits expected from group control (Khanna and Palepu, 2000, Chang, 2003, Dyck and Zingales, 2004, Kim *et al.*, 2004). Korean experience in dismantling the business groups through regulatory enforcement provides useful insights about how ownership structures can be influenced with policy choices. The draft banking code is expected to play a similar role in Turkey although to a lesser extent. We also expect the predicted acquisitions of Turkish banks to help further dilutions and dismantling of group structures.

Notes

1 Data: ISE and CMB web-site, www.ise.gov.tr, www.spk.gov.tr.
2 Settlement and Custody Bank.
3 President's speech in March 2005, www.spk.gov.tr.

11 The transition economies systems of corporate governance

R. Leban and T. Pasechnyk

Introduction

Countries where economies are said to be "in transition" are the Commonwealth of Independent States (CIS) and the Central and Eastern European Countries (CEEC).[1] As regards the CIS, this chapter will focus on its European part, i.e. Russia, Ukraine and Belarus and, within on its Eastern part, Kazakhstan and Georgia. Those countries went through multiphase partial privatization processes that influenced the inception of corporate models within these countries and induced an implicit somewhat specific and evolving over time "stakeholder model" of corporate governance (CG). In the CEEC CG standards are significantly at western level today, while in the CIS countries they are well behind and submitted to a specific stakeholder model. The main evolution driver toward improved CG resides in few dynamic companies in search of international financing.

This chapter discusses CG systems in economies in transition (EiT), emphasizing the confusion and hesitation characterizing recent actions and advocating long-term actions convincing enough to drain the so needed international capital to the region.

The development of CG models in economies in transition

There has been an interaction between privatization and the development of corporate structure and governance models in economies in EiT, and the study of CG in the region, goes inevitably through the study of its privatization movement. Corporate sector structure was significantly impacted by privatizations, since it was fundamentally built through appropriation of state ownership. The chaotic character of appropriation has, however, induced an early implicit CG model based upon a complicated nontransparent framework of relationships between corporate insiders and outsiders. It is only at the end of the 1990s, when privatization was over and ownership concentration reached its maximum, did CG become an explicit issue for companies, regulators and academics in EiT. Three phases of privatization can be distinguished according to the tools used to achieve appropriation by private interest of state property:

  i   the mass privatization phase;
 ii   the privatization in exchange of cash phase; and
iii   the strategic companies' privatization phase.

Actually a specific corporate model was progressively built and has evolved over these three privatization phases. Mass privatization allowed the transfer of a large number of publicly held small- and medium-sized enterprises (SMEs) to private ownership. Very few strategic companies were affected by this phase of privatizations. Privatization in exchange of cash covered big companies and the rest of SMEs. Finally, strategic companies' privatization focuses on strategic companies. Government priorities have, however, varied tremendously from country to country, and this created much confusion and hesitation. Consequently, this phase witnessed which privatizations but also re-nationalization, re-privatization, continuation of already initiated privatizations, etc.

Mass privatization and CG

Mass privatization, known also as voucher privatization, occurs when firms are sold at zero or nominal price. This method is considered to provide all citizens with equal opportunities in the appropriation of state-owned properties. Only three Eastern European countries avoided such a "fair" privatization method, namely, Russia, Hungary and Macedonia. Russia was one of the first EiT where mass privatization took place (1991–1995). The federal government issued non-registered privatization certificates/vouchers the price of which was calculated by dividing the total value of state property by the number of citizens.[2] This *privatization* policy was supposed to be inductive and determinant for the creation of capital markets in Russia. It was also supposed to help privatized companies so they can meet their future financing needs. Unfortunately, *mass privatization* has rather generated millions of poorly informed shareholders, and no efficient markets to trade their shares in. This lack of financial markets has created perfect conditions for diverse fraudulent actions and has facilitated the misappropriation of the newly privatized corporations' assets.

The main instrument of allocating and collecting privatization certificates/vouchers was the closed-end mutual fund formula. Always under control of the managers of companies to be privatized, such funds collected vouchers, either by buying them on the black market or by issuing investment certificates in exchange. This approach allowed managers to appropriate blocks of shares of companies under their management and even shares of other companies whose managers were considered to be less skilfull. On a foot print of the Russian experience and while and trying to avoid its setbacks, the Ukrainian government started in 1995 a three-year mass privatization program, by issuing registered privatization certificates/vouchers. The idea was to eliminate the possibility of trading vouchers on black markets. In absence of institutional mechanisms and appropriate state regulations, closed-end mutual funds managers were here again able to transform vouchers into anonymous investment certificates and to use them to acquire, anonymously, companies' shares. This kind of conduct has weighted heavily on the fate and the structure of the first corporate wave, characterized by the strategic position in the center conceded to the privatized production company, which is surrounded by trading firms and financial institutions of all kinds. In such a structure, each party in the group seems to have been assigned a specific role: asset-stripping and tax optimization for trading firms, appropriation of state ownership for mutual funds, transaction and financing for banks, money laundering and out-flowing abroad for insurance companies.

The only country in the former Soviet Union that still is in the process of privatization is Belarus. Although its privatization program started in 1993, only 60 percent of citizens have received privatization vouchers as of now. The situation can be explained by the insufficiency of the share supply and the limited extent of the privatization program itself. Indeed many companies in Belarus are still today state-owned enterprises. On the other hand, the restrictions imposed on acquired through vouchers share transactions constitute a real break in their circulation. For this reason, in an effort to give more chance to mass privatization, the government was promising legal money compensation to citizens whose vouchers would not be invested in shares by the end of the program. The value of vouchers not invested in stocks is currently very high and it is feared that the Belarusian government will not have enough resources to honor its promise.

Several objectives were assigned to mass privatization. Management regeneration is one of them, but there was also corporate restructuring in the sake of more competitiveness, external funds attraction, outsider control creation, and finally asset-stripping prevention. Those objectives were not met, neither in countries where mass privatization was conducted to the benefit of dispersed outsiders, like in the Czech Republic, nor in countries where mass privatization was conducted to the benefit of insiders, like in Russia or Ukraine. This result is confirmed by a number of studies: Shkurupiy (2000), Goldberg and Watkins (2000), Nellis (1999), Birdsall and Nellis (2003) and the World Bank (2002). On the contrary, countries that chose top-down sales to outsiders, like East Germany, or gradual bottom-up sales to outsiders, like Hungary, experienced fast replacement of management, partial corporate restructuring and significant prevention of asset-stripping, as well as important attraction of foreign investments.

The announced goal of mass privatization was to create effective shareholdings and efficient managers who would collaborate toward value creation. The dispersed ownership model was privileged and the existence of an efficiently operating secondary stock market was assumed. It was also expected that the feared lack of management direct monitoring and control would be compensated by the overall disciplining market mechanisms and the higher level of transparency they entitle. The unexpected has, however, happened in practice and mass privatization has actually resulted in the establishment of a specific or "modified" stakeholder model, inducing the supremacy of banks and governments.

An appropriate CG model entitles the respect of all stakeholders interests. In EiT, companies were commonly run in the sole interest of major shareholders, with little care for minority shareholders or employees. Actually, the trade unions role was limited and employees' interests were neglected. During the whole transition period, for instance, companies refused to pay or postponed salary owed to workers. Suppliers and customers were in a much better position mainly because of the lack of legal protection against contract violations, which allowed them to put an end to their engagement. Banks, on the other hand, were the most influential stakeholders.

Whereas, in Central and Eastern Europe inflow of foreign capital was not restricted and foreign acquired domestic companies received investment from their new owners, CIS corporations suffered serious scarcity of financing. CIS governments did not open the financial markets to foreigners and banks became powerful domestic stakeholders. They became the only financial suppliers, given the poorly developed stock exchanges. Power of the banks was even increased by the legal limitation imposed on customers to shift banks. In the mid-1990s, for instance, a company could have only one bank account. Banks seemed to have contributed actively to the development of the privatization shadow markets through trust services and bankruptcy mechanisms.

Simultaneously, the role of government agencies in the modified stakeholder model was crucial. Every business activity was subjected to central and/or regional governments' approval and submitted to tax administrations requirements and was in this way, forced to negotiate any business move with government officials, and this has led to much fraudulent behavior and lack of integrity. The inability to create appropriate CG conditions is considered a major impediment in EiT toward their move to market economy during the post soviet era. World Bank (WB) statistics seem to confirm this alarming conclusion; by showing a drastic drop in the GDP, during the period 1988–1998 (Stiglitz, 1999b, pp. 26, 42), in all countries of the former soviet block, except for Slovenia and Slovakia (Figure 11.1). Although, Eastern European and Central Asia countries started the transition period with some of the lowest levels of inequality in the world, ten years later the situation has worsened. Instead of decreasing, inequality has, in fact, increased steadily in all countries. As a result, countries like Armenia, the Kyrgyz Republic, Moldova or Russia are now among the most unequal societies in the world. Poverty has spread from 4 to 45 percent of the population, to 53 percent for Baltic Republics, or even to 65 percent for Central Asia (Stiglitz, 1999b, pp. 26, 42).

Mass privatization outcomes have certainly diverted greatly from their original goals and objectives, as underscored by the following:

> A decade after the beginning of the transition in Eastern Europe and the Former Soviet Union, and two decades after the beginning of the transition in China the picture is mixed. Each country started the course of transition with a different history, and a different set of human and physical endowments. The contrast between the strategies – and results – of the two largest

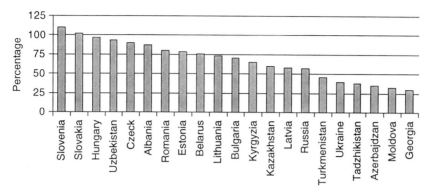

Figure 11.1 The level of GDP in 1998 compared to 1989.

countries, Russia and China, may be instructive. [...] over the decade beginning in 1989, while China's GDP nearly doubled, Russia's GDP almost halved; so that while at the beginning of the period, Russia's GDP was more than twice that of China's, at the end, it was a third smaller.

(Stiglitz, 1999a)

Kornai (1990) has explained that the reasons for those reform failures in EiT lay in opting for the wrong strategy. The author has proposed at the beginning of the 1990s two different strategies for ownership reform and development of the private sector. The first strategy, which he called Strategy A, assumed government to perform the following tasks:

i   create conditions for bottom-up development of the private sector;
ii   sell companies to outside-strategic investors; and
iii create a stable legal environment.

The second strategy, he named Strategy B, supposes that government would:

i   eliminate state ownership as fast as possible;
ii   distribute rights in state-owned companies for free and equally among the country's citizens; and
iii develop "people's capitalism."

Kornai was definitely against Strategy B, which he criticized and warned against. Ten years later he wrote: "I am reassured that strategy A was the correct position to take. However, in 90s, the majority of academic economists accepted and popularized the strategy of rapid privatization." One may wonder why Strategy B was promoted so quickly, eventually leading transitional economies into a ten-year period of economic crisis. It is possible that the main motivation may have resided in the eagerness and the strong desire of eliminating every chance of coming back to a planned economy. One may also wonder why governments of EiT did support the application of voucher privatization. According to the WB "Privatization to diffuse owners and worker-owners was appealing on equity grounds and in several countries this was the only way to make private ownership politically acceptable" (World Bank, 2002). Reasons for believing so can be one of the following:

i   Replacement of the management in place in order to increase the companies' efficiency: the most obvious way to achieve such an objective was to take enterprises out of the hands of the government and sell them to those who were assumed able to run them more effectively.

ii   Prevention of asset-stripping: if company's managers did not see the possibility to privatize a company for themselves, there was a risk that they would choose to sell the most profitable and liquid assets.

iii   Prevention of foreign capital domination: restricting foreign investors' participation in voucher privatization created advantages for affiliated to governments domestic investors and public authorities tolerated these unfair practices to allow cash-strapped domestic investors to rapidly gain control (World Bank, 2002).

iv   Defensive restructuring: governments were not able to restructure companies to make them competitive in a new market environment; yet, new owners could force the existing management to make necessary changes, thus allowing for increasing productivity and profitability (Djankov and Murrell, 2000). In an examination of 31 empirical studies on how private ownership affects economic restructuring Djankov and Murrell (2000) conclude that "private ownership produces more enterprise restructuring than does state ownership" in the post-Soviet area. However, evidences vary between geographical regions and are mixed for the CIS.

Privatization for cash and CG

The alternative to mass privatization was the so-called "privatization for cash," which involves the transfer of funds from private investors to the government through the sale of state-held shares. This can be reached using two different methods. The first method is called "full privatization" and it entitles the sale of stated-owned corporations to outsiders for a fair price. The second method called "mixed privatization" and it entitles the sale of state-owned corporations at a preferential price and this covers all the privatizations that were not already covered by mass and/or full privatization. This also includes manager–employee buyouts and shadow privatization.

Although it is easy to find common features in transitional economies' privatization programs in their phase 1, more differences can be observed, however, between Central and East European (CEE) and the CIS countries in phase 2 privatization programs. Differences in phase 1 programs were mostly due to initial conditions, such as the degree of industrialization, the traditional routes of trade, the extent of initial macroeconomic imbalances and the legacy of central planning. While in phase 2 programs differences were deepened by reform pattern choices. CEE countries made the choice of liberalizing markets in favor of openness to foreign investors. On the contrary, the CIS endeavored to protect their corporate control markets against foreign intruders. Besides, government policies in CIS countries was focused on promoting the interests of large financial-industrial groups (FIG),[3] despite announced state support to SMEs. SMEs were instead hardly pressed by taxation and regulations of all kinds. As a result, the share of the SME sector in the GDP is representing currently 13–17 percent in the CIS, while in countries like Poland, Hungary or Latvia, this share amounts to over 50 per cent of the GDP (Yablonovskaya and Zaderey, 2006).

Full privatization was supposed to have encouraged outsider ownership since it was conducted through auctions where the only valid criterion that enabled access to state properties was the willingness to pay the highest price. In the CIS, (mostly) small-scale privatization was also based on the auction system and has included not only municipal enterprises, but also production units which were part of state enterprises submitted to oversight of federal or republic ministry departments. Small stores, enterprises and service companies were auctioned to the public. Although, privatization of SMEs in Russia was impressive in absolute values, it certainly lags behind similar programs in other countries, like the Czech Republic, Estonia, Hungary or Poland, where a much larger percentage of the entire small-scale base has been divested.

The privatization of large companies was organized by means of a flexible combination of mixed privatization methods. The beginning of the second phase of privatization was realized in Russia through transactions of loans-for-shares type. Banks provided the government with badly needed cash, based on the collateral of enterprise shares. It was always stipulated under the terms of these deals that if the state government did not repay the loans by September 1996, the bank would automatically become owner of the shares, that can resell or keep for itself. Auctions were conducted in the fall of 1995 and, during the last two months of the same year, shares of the largest Russian companies were transferred to the limited number of existing banks and at extremely low prices. Norilsk Nickel, for instance, with $5 billion annual revenue was sold for the trifling sum of $170 million (see Table 11.1 for more details). Ten years later in 2006, all the largest Russian companies (except Yukos) acquired in this way were in the top list of market capitalization in Russia and most of their private owners are in the Forbes list of World's Richest People.

As should have been expected, the limitation placed on foreign investors' access to privatization in the CIS countries resulted in an insiders strong CG system and even if companies were privatized through auctions, most of them were bought by pseudo "outsiders" located in offshore zones. Actually local managers had prepared themselves earlier, by depositing offshore cash extracted in advance from companies to be privatized. Insiders were actually composed of companies' managers, affiliated offshore companies, trading companies (serving trade and cash flow inside of FIG) and they used the so-called "shadow" or

Table 11.1 Companies privatized through loans-for-shares scheme in Russia

Date	Company	Share (%)	Loans to Russian Government ($m)	Winners of auction	1995 Annual revenue ($ bn)	2006 market cap ($ bn)
17.11.95	Norilsk Nickel	51	170.1	ONEXIMbank	5.0	29.5
8.12.95	YUKOS	45	159	MENATEP bank affiliates	2.9	–
7.12.95	LUKOIL	5	141	LUKOIL-imperial	6.4	73.7
7.12.95	Sidanko (now TNK-BP)	51	130	MFKbank	4.8	40.9
28.12.95	Sibneft	51	100.3	Oil Finance Company Ltd	–	21.6
28.12.95	Surgutneftegas	40.12	88.9	ONEXIMbank	4.5	54.3
7.12.95	Novolipetsk Steel	14.87	31	MFKbank	2.2	14.4
17.11.95	Mechel	15	13	Rabicom Ltd	0.9	3.4

Source: Pappe, 2000.

Notes

* Expert 1995[a], 2006[b].

a Expert Ranking, Report, 1995.

b Expert Ranking, Report, 2006.

"dirty" privatization tools[4] (Paskhaver and Verhovodova, 2006; Black *et al.*, 2000). According to Paskhaver *et al.* (2003) and Bloom *et al.* (2003), by the end of the 1990s, the most popular methods of shadow privatization follow the this pattern:

i   The use of state block shares as a collateral, the formula is close to the loan-for-shares, however, in this case, the borrower is a government-owned company, not the government.

ii   The issue of new shares resulting in a reduction of government's ownership. Government's representative would vote in shareholder meetings for an additional issuing of stocks in order to raise funds for the company's future development; since the state never had funds to buy additional issued shares, government ownership would be automatically reduced. In many cases and after several new issues government participation in some companies was reduced, as low as 5 per cent.

iii   The nomination of the Bank as trustee. Government would assign banks to manage its block of shares, supplying concerned banks with yet more voting power at the general shareholders' meeting, particularly in the cases where new share issues or restructuring with the sale of the most liquid assets are on the agenda.

iv   The sale through state holding companies. Government-owned companies were united in holding companies by industries; the parent company was then able to sell any production units without permission from the government.

v   The bankruptcy. Creditors of the government-owned company used bankruptcy procedures to become the managers of debt restructuring and consequently acquired assets at preferential prices (Radygin *et al.*, 2006).

vi   The restructuring. On former government-owned company ashes, new companies were established which later were sold to new owners without participation of the government.

The insider model of corporate control was also enhanced in the CIS by putting in place various threats against outsiders like:

i   Threats of re-privatization, which is rendered even more credible by the absence of clear legislation on the issue;

ii   The lack of transparency in privatization transactions which allows all unimaginable misconducts.

iii   The discrimination against outsiders in the competition for investing in privatized companies with "special investment commitments." In 2000, for instance, conditions for competing on a 9 percent share of Lukoil were different and more restrictive for outsiders: the stock price including investment commitments was $6 for outsiders, while only 3$ for insiders; and

iv   Unequal and higher penalties for outsiders than for insiders in the case of violation of privatization commitments.

The privatization of strategic companies

The beginning of phase 2 of privatization is easy to determine in all former soviet countries, because all legislations on the issue provided for precise program for mass privatization the shift to phase 3, however, cannot be precisely identified on the time scale. The reason is that it was caused by changes in economic and political conditions and actually phase 3 was performed only in the CIS, and not in CEE countries. The first impulse for changes in corporate structure was induced by the 1998 world stock market crisis, having impacted drastically on CIS countries. The rapid outflow of speculative capital away from CIS markets led to governments defaulting on the numerous bonds they had issued to cover their budget deficit and this in turn has caused a major banking crisis. At the time banks were investing as much as 17 percent of their assets in state bonds and they suffered a huge loss when governments defaulted in paying their debts, initiating a general panic among the populations requiring the return of their deposits. The main reason, however, for this new privatization phase, could be the 2000 presidential election in Russia, which entered Vladimir Putin's era. Most CIS countries followed Putin's approach with regard to building a corporate sector and enhancing the role of government as a corporate owner for strategic development.

In the wake of this new orientation, nationalizations were again on the menu. Nationalizations in Russia, for instance, hit companies that had been privatized in earlier times, primarily because of their strategic position, like energy or industries related to weapon production.[5] Whenever a previously privatized company had qualified for takeover, the government would use one or a combination of the following "de-privatization" methods:

i   The negotiated return of the privatized company under government ownership because of given violation of privatization commitments.[6]
ii   The conversion of debt to government shares.[7]
iii   The initiation of tax investigations that usually ended by imposing huge fines and leading inevitable big firms like Youkos to go bankrupt.

Only two CIS countries, namely Georgia and Ukraine, chose an alternative way to Putin's by opening their market of corporate control to foreign investors after the 2003 and 2004 presidential elections. In the wake of the Orange revolution, the Ukrainian government announced the revision of the outcome of the privatization and re-privatization of more than 100 of the largest Ukrainian enterprises. In fact, it only re-privatized one company, Krivorozhstal, which produced 20 percent of domestic metal products and was first in the list of top Ukrainian exporters. Krivorozhstal had been sold, through an auction with limited investor access, for $800 million in 2003, before the presidential election and was resold, through a transparent auction, to Mittal Steel in 2005 for $4.8 billion. Although it was the only case of re-privatization, it had the merit of underscoring the scale of shadow privatization at preferential prices. The Krivorozhstal case has pushed governments of Ukraine and Georgia to make companies auctions more transparent for those strategic companies that remained to be privatized.

Corporate structure and CG in motion

Privatization phases in EiT have induced corresponding phases in the development of corporate structure and governance. Mass privatization allowed transferring government ownership to private interests on a relatively very short period of time and has given rise to a governance system, led by banks and government. This way of appropriation transfer has proven to be chaotic, leading to "segmented ownership" that has systematically discriminated against different shareholders at different stages of value chains. In the former USSR for instance, enterprises operating at those various stages in one "oblast" (region) were under the control of different Republic Ministries. With their privatization at the beginning of the 1990s, they passed under the control of groups of people "close" to these different Ministries. As can be seen, such ownership structure can only contain seeds of future corporate conflicts.

On another front, mass privatization has been resulting in multiple and dispersed ownerships. Assets were sold at plant level, giving rise to a lot of "medium size" companies, and managers of those companies were able to control them with less than 25 percent holding. Mainly by putting pressure on employees, who own the rest of the shares. This was usually done through threats of dismissal, salary reduction and other harassing means. Such forms of ownership structure made such corporations ideal prey for future hostile takeovers.

Mass privatization was conducted during a crisis period, when companies were making an extensive use of debt used to finance operations, due to the generalized lack of cash. This gave managers efficient tools to enhance their power inside their companies, since they were the only ones who knew and could negotiate complicated debt formula with the outside environment. They have also set the basis on which future raiders would organize those companies' takeover during the severe corporate struggle at the end of 1990 when raiders then bought out indebted companies' operational debts and forced them to go bankrupt by requiring reimbursement.

After initial appropriations of government properties had been realized, the second phase of privatization witnessed ownership concentration and industrial groups restructuring into conglomerates. As theory suggests and world practice shows (see, for instance, Weston *et al.*, 2001, p. 187), the first wave of integration was horizontal integration. Transition economies went to this at the beginning of 1990s when managers of the privatized companies tried to take control of other companies from the same industry thanks to the easy access they enjoyed through their membership of "nomenklatura groups." The next step was a vertical integration over value chains (from raw materials to end-use products) into financial-industrial groups.

Once FIGs were constituted, the fight between them for growth through acquisitions started and concentration of ownership inside each one of them was a defensive mechanism against hostile takeovers. It happened within an apparently dispersed industry structure and to describe this resulting corporate model we can use the oxymoron of a "concentrated ownership with dispersed structure." Indeed, the real (hidden) owner of a financial-industrial group, was represented by several types of opaque shareholding companies (offshore, trading and private equity companies), in each of which he owned from 10 to 25 percent of the shares. These shareholding companies had in turn crossed participations in industrial (plant-level) companies. A hostile takeover of one shareholding company of the group would then not lead to loosing the control over the group's industrial (plant-level) companies. As they do not account for these hidden owners. For this reason, many of the surveys conducted on ownership structure in EiT do not give a real insight into the actual level of concentration. Examining for instance the two largest Ukrainian financial-industrial groups, Private and System Capital Management[8] (Figure 11.2), on the basis of Ukrainian companies' official annual financial statements, Ukraine State Security and Exchange Commission's reports and information reported in mass-media, leads to the conclusion that the average level of concentration in each group was much higher than the maximum share of one shareholding company in the industrial companies of the group.

During the period 1999–2002, those groups further increased their corporate control by issuing new shares and pushing out minority shareholders, consolidating equity and buying up shares of other shareholders. This approach was

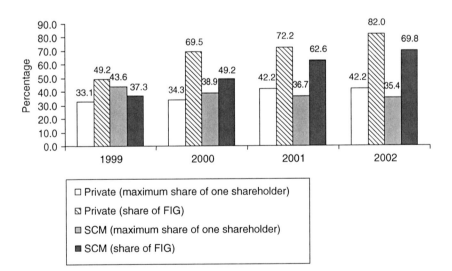

Figure 11.2 Apparent and actual ownership structure of the largest Ukrainian financial-industrial groups, private and system capital management, 1999–2002 (source: Pasechnyk, 2004).

used by all financial-industrial groups in the CIS, with Russia being the first mover and other CIS countries following with a 2–3-year delay.

In developed countries, the wave of integration of the 1960s into conglomerates was a defensive diversification that was aimed at fighting sales and profit instability, adverse growth developments, adverse competitive shifts, technological obsolescence and the uncertainties associated with industries. Conglomerate integration in transitional economies was also defensive diversification, but mainly aimed at avoiding hostile takeovers, damaging re-nationalization of some of the group's key enterprises, outflow of cash out of the group and reducing the uncertainties associated with their industries.

Financial-industrial groups in EiT were built from a number of financial institutions, enterprises and trading companies and transformed into conglomerates, able to perform internally all financial functions (banking, insurance, etc.). They are also present at all stages of value chains in several industries, with a key positioning mostly in the raw materials sector. They were purposely built as "industrially and financially autonomous" groups. Unsurprisingly, however, it became clear that conglomerates based on so non-transparent and complicated ownership structure could not be managed effectively. The ownership structure of actual conglomerates proves to be even more complicated than the "dispersed holding" pattern and this situation has paved the way for a new phase in corporate development.

Phase 3 of corporate sector development started at the dawn of the new century. As in the case of privatization, it can be observed only in CIS countries. This phase is characterized by a financial-industrial groups' search for foreign financing. During the first ten years of transition, they had not modernized their equipment and they keep using those built in the USSR era. For this reason their production means urgently needed renovation. Foreign markets can provide long-term financing with low interest rates, contrary to domestic CIS markets where the average term of loans does not exceed 3–5 years and interest rates in domestic currency is about 12–16 percent (10–12 percent in dollars), and the size of a loan is limited by the value of banks' capital, Eurobonds issues allow attracting cheaper long-term and larger funds. They, however, require from companies transparency and reliable financial and information disclosure. Such requirements and the desire to go for the international financial market have pushed "dispersed holdings" to restructure into "classic holdings" with more transparent ownership structure, with regard to participations and subsidiaries. Subsidiaries were established as joint-stock companies in the previous privatization periods, and now each one of them is an element of a production chain. To eliminate the possibility of a hostile takeover, parent companies were forced to hold more than 50 percent of their stocks and they have had no interest in their public trading (Pasechnyk, 2004a). Parent companies were decision-making centers, existing as private equity firms, but with no freely tradable shares. This situation is seen as the most important reason for stock markets under-developed in the CIS.

Regional stock markets in EiT can really exist only if financial-industrial groups agree to shift from the "classic holding" pattern to that of a "modern business corporation." Currently, only the biggest Russian companies seem to have reached such a level of development. Lukoil (number two after Gazprom) was the first company in Russia which eliminated stocks of its subsidiaries and made public its own shares.

The described fundamentals of holding and corporation development represent the main features of the Stakeholder model of corporate structure and governance in place in the CIS at the end of 1990s and at the beginning of twenty-first century, which we summarize below:

First, ownership is characterized by: (i) the high percentage of citizens share ownership. Indeed, thanks to mass privatization, the majority of the population became shareholders and more than 20 percent of them are still owners of stocks; (ii) the high level of ownership concentration, where parent companies try to control directly or through other companies over 50 percent of the equity of their industrial subsidiaries (Yakovlev, 2003); (iii) Ownership dominated by insiders, composed mainly of non financial companies, offshore companies, managers and employees; and (iv) Dispersed ownership and concentrated control: where major owners concentrate control indirectly to avoid hostile takeovers and nationalization.

Second, with regard to management, we can underline the following: (i) the domination of large companies. In fact, small and medium business only produces about 10 percent of GDP; (ii) the domination of "dispersed holdings." "Classic holdings" with non-transparent structure of decision making along with poor control of separate subsidiaries are the rule, but with a tendency toward restructuring (Pappe and Galukhina, 2006; Radygin, 2004); and (iii) finally the dominance of the two-tier board structure.

Third, concerning financing sources the following facts can be underscored: (i) bank loans represent more than 20 percent of GDP and this share is increasing; and (ii) largest companies go for cheaper sources of international financing, issuing Eurobonds and entering into Initial Public Offerings (IPOs).

Fourth, with regard to stock markets, the following can be underlined: (i) Market capitalization is close to the corresponding level of the so-called "stakeholder model" in Western Europe. In 1997 the book, published by PriceWaterhouseCoopers and entitled "Shareholder value" divided countries into two groups according to their level of market capitalization relative to GDP: countries that showed a ratio over 70 percent belonged to the "shareholder model" category, characterized by dispersed ownership and liquid markets; countries with a ratio under 70 percent belonged to a stakeholder model category. This approach still works in developed countries but cannot be applied to Russia: as Figure 11.3 shows, market capitalization has exceeded 80 percent of GDP in Russia in 2005, but the increase is mainly due to oil and gas price surges (50 percent of Russian market capitalization comes from the three largest oil and gas companies; one of them is Gasprom, which represents over 30 percent of the country's market capitalization; on the contrary, the level of Russia's GDP increases slowly).

The stakeholder model of the CIS differs from the one adopted by CEE countries. These countries opened their markets to foreign investors and this has led

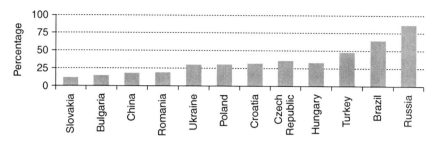

Figure 11.3 Market capitalization to GDP in 2005.[1]

Note
1 Investing in Ukraine, Dragon Capital, Kiev, October 2006.

to what we could call an "outsider stakeholder model." Moreover, foreign investors required modern corporate laws and more transparent company management. Striving to enter the EU, these countries implemented Western Europe standards of CG and thus contributed to deepened differences between them and the rest of the post-Soviet area in this matter.

CG legal framework in economies in transition today

In economies in transition, the legal framework depends on whose interest governments are willing to privilege. In the "modified" stakeholder model, government is one of the most powerful stakeholders and it goes hand-in-hand with an equally powerful stakeholder – the major shareholder. The regulatory framework and government regulations are also in line with the corporate structure and governance model. Stock market regulations are also influenced by the level of development of domestic institutional investors, pension funds notably, and the presence of foreign investors on the market.

Legal framework and regulation

The objective here is to identify the factors that influence the legal frameworks within EiT. Striving to join the EU, CEE countries adopted corporate legislations in accordance with EU standards. Simultaneously, however, some elements of Anglo-American origin were also implemented, due to mass privatization. For instance, board of directors in CEE countries, includes independent foreign directors[9] and the rights of minority shareholders are highly protected by the law. This, however, does not prevent boards of directors in CEE countries from acting in their own interest or the interest of major shareholders.

In the CIS, the improvement of CG via legal framework enhancement was always and still is a declaration of intention, as long as the largest financial-industrial groups are not interested. Moreover, corporate laws are usually defined at state level in the CIS, including in the Russian Federation, and their implementation is monitored by state securities regulators. Russia seems to have the most advanced corporate law in the CIS region. This is actually explained by its more developed corporate structure and more advanced governance model. The Russian legislation is, however, far from being unified: different laws and regulatory acts were usually approved to resolve short-term problems and they often contradict each other, often leading to corporate conflicts.[10] In this situation we can encounter legal issues like mergers and acquisitions, companies' reorganization, relationships between major and minor shareholders, dividend policy and use of insider information, affiliation and transactions with related parties. Moreover, even issues covered by the law can become the subject of conflict, because of the lack of court independence leading to varied interpretations of the same legal provision (Shastitko, 2004).

Under these conditions, the principle-based approach to CG adopted in CIS countries looks just like an effort of pleasing the international community. Rules are typically thought to be simpler to follow than principles, demarcating a clear line between acceptable and unacceptable behavior. Adopting a CG code that uses a principle-based approach cannot guarantee its implementation. Romania was one of the first countries that adopted a CG code in 2000; other countries in transition like the Czech Republic, Hungary, Poland, Slovakia, Lithuania, Macedonia, Ukraine, Slovenia, Latvia, Russia and Kazakhstan, did the same during the period 2001–2005.[11,12] Although, former soviet countries used different approaches in adopting their corporate codes, most CEE countries applied the so-called "comply or explain non-compliance" approach, where listed companies are obliged to comply with the CG code or explain reasons for non-compliance to the regulator. On the contrary, the CIS adopted voluntary-based codes with lower requirements regarding, notably, board independence[13] and the composition of audit committees. The consequences of such an approach is illustrated by the "survey of awareness" conducted on the Code of Corporate Conduct in Russia. In 2003, one year after the code's adoption, about 70 percent of the surveyed companies were not familiar with the code at all (Guriev, et al., 2003). In 2006 the proportion of non-aware companies had reduced to 33 percent, but the share of companies desiring to implement the code did not exceed 44 percent.

State and market regulation

The importance of the state regulation in CG is currently commonly recognized. CG was actually identified as a serious issue since the 1990s, when institutional investors like pension funds underlined the importance of "agency" phenomena, i.e. of the lack of control over managers by shareholders. It received much public and government attention after recent corporate frauds. Interest in CG rose in transitional economies for other reasons. As already mentioned, CEE countries modernized their regulation system according to European standards because they strived to enter the EU. In the CIS, however, governments still play more of a stakeholder role than a regulator role. As few large companies hold strong economic positions. The share of most private financial-industrial groups in the country's GDP exceeds 5 percent. In Ukraine in 2006 System Capital

Management represented more than 7 percent of the GDP; Industrial Union of Donbass, Privat and Interpipe represented, respectively, 5, 5 and 7 percent of the same GDP. In Kazakhstan, Kazakhmys's share in the GDP is 7 percent, Eurasian Natural Resources Group's share is 7 percent. In comparison, Nokia's share in Finland's GDP was about 3.7 percent in 2005. They have a notable influence on internal politics and governments tend to closely monitor their activity. Although governments usually promote their interests, they do not hesitate to take "corrective action" against them if their behavior is judged contrary to national interests[14] (export/import restrictions, tax investigation, etc.).

Stock exchanges traditionally play an important role in setting and ensuring good governance practices. Capital markets are accessible under certain conditions, good practices are rewarded and bad ones are penalized. The appearance of stock exchanges in EiT was mainly owed to privatization. Big companies were forced to be listed in order to be auctioned via stock exchanges. Most of them, however, left the market immediately, because they often were members of a same value chain and owners were wishing to eliminate the risk of hostile takeover via stocks purchases.

While in developed countries pension funds constitute the most powerful institutional investors, in EiT this kind of investor was quasi absent until the end of 1990s because pension systems were state government-administered. Joining the EU encouraged CEE countries to implement a three-pillar pension system where the second and third pillars, individual and/or occupational and voluntary funds, are private players. The countries that have reformed their pension systems are Bulgaria, Hungary, Latvia, Lithuania, Poland, Romania, Slovakia, Croatia and Estonia. From the beginning, these funds faced strong restrictions on international investments. Consequently, they had no choice but to invest heavily in the local market. Consequently, they quickly became determinant relative to the overall size of the market (e.g. in 2003, the equity investment of pension funds already represented 38 percent of all equity under free float on the Warsaw Stock Exchange (WSE)).[15] Researches show that the intensive investment of pension funds in local markets had a strong short-term effect on stock exchanges. The CIS countries like Ukraine, Kazakhstan and Russia have adopted a new pension system. However, pension funds are still weak players. Yet, the Russian stock market is among the leaders at the transactional level in CEE countries. In Russia, as well as in other CIS countries, there are about ten stock exchanges and trade floors but most of the volume of trading is concentrated in 2–4 stock exchanges. It is, however, difficult to raise funds in excess of $500 million in most EiT countries, including Russia. The largest Russian companies go for IPO in foreign exchanges and the smaller companies use Russian stock exchanges (MICEX, RTS, SPCEX and SPBEX), or the WSE.

The WSE is today an internationally recognized market within CEE countries for small capitalizations. Companies' shares from Poland, the Czech Republic, Slovakia, Hungary, the Netherlands, Israel, Ukraine, Germany and the United States are listed on the WSE. Consequently, market capitalization of Poland has doubled during the period 2004–2006, while the Russian market capitalization has increased by 4.5 times during the period 2003–2007. The quality of listing requirements is an important factor of attractiveness to the WSE and to other local exchanges in the former soviet area. Listing requirements can be an efficient incentive for CG improvement but even this tool of market regulation is impacted greatly by government interventions. Indeed governments define the quality (liquidity, outstanding character of shares) of the securities in which domestic institutional investors can invest.

Corporate ownership

How CG is achieved in a company depends among other things on the nature of corporate ownership structure. When, for instance, company owners intend to hide their real identity and/or strip assets, there is little chance that they will be interested in implementing constraining CG practices. On the other hand, when company owners are rather sustainable development oriented, they will strive for enhancing the quality of CG practices. This in turn will allow quality management and external resources easy attraction. This section will discuss private ownership, public ownership and market for corporate control and their effects on CG in EiT.

Private ownership, corporate strategies and CG

Currently, corporate strategic orientations in the EiT are defined by majority shareholders. On the other hand, three non-exclusive categories of management orientations can be distinguished, favoring, to a certain point, all of them CG improvement: (i) defense strategies (defense against hostile takeovers, raider attacks and re-nationalization), deployed by medium-size and big financial-industrial groups; and (ii) strategic development (diversification and expansion in international markets), implemented by the largest and most advanced companies. These three management orientations will be discussed.

Defense strategies

Although defense against hostile takeovers and re-nationalization is not the main strategic orientation in many EiT companies, because of unfair and corrupted privatization, it became an important element of the corporate strategy. Most governments in the EiT always face a non-negligible risk that privatization transactions might be cancelled or reconsidered at some point in time, with government support. The case of Yukos in Russia shows how the state can use such power in renationalizing previously privatized assets.

Established in 1993, Yukos was one of the world's largest non-governmental oil companies, producing 20 percent of Russian oil, i.e. about 2 percent of world production in 2003. In October 2003, Yukos announced its intention to merge with another petroleum company, Sibneft. A merger that would have lead Yukos to control 30 percent of the Russian oil production. The appearance of such an independent oil empire did not fit the plans of the Russian government, which decided to block the deal. Yukos was then subjected to the Russian tax administration control and charged in July 2004 with tax evasion, for an amount of over $7.6 billion. Additional back-tax payments of more than $10 billion, were required from Yukos in November 2004, bringing the company's total tax liabilities to above $17.6 billion for the period from 1999–2003. For comparison, Yukos's annual revenue in 2003 was about $15 billion. On August 1, 2006, a Russian court declared Yukos bankrupt and its president sentenced to nine years imprisonment. This gave rise to the third largest state-owned petroleum company, Rosneft; it was built on Yukos's assets under the control of Gazprom.

Yukos's re-nationalization has pushed Russian companies to develop defensive strategies. One of the main tools of protection is to act in an international legislation environment. Although IPOs and Mergers and Acquisitions (M&A) activities entail information disclosure, accounting and reporting in compliance with the International Accounting Standards (IASs; International Federation of Accountants (IFRS))/General Accounting Agreed on Principle (GAAP) and changing of ownership structure, they, however, reduce significantly the risk of state pressure inside any country of the EiT and contribute to the improvement of CG.

Strategic development

Strategy design is usually accompanied by the search of resources to finance development. IPO is only one way among others to attract investments and it is workable for the largest companies. Another way to finance development is to attract strategic investors by selling them wholly or partially private company equity. On the other hand, companies that show interest in implementing the best practices of CG are those that have reached the state of transnational corporations and to be competitive at the international market, they need to improve the corporate whole management style and governance. The Hungarian OTP Bank is an example of such strong corporate strategy and CG improvement.

OTP Bank has passed through all stages of development in the last decades, from a state bank, at the beginning of the 1990s, to one of the Eastern European banking leaders, assets wise, in 2006. In 1995, it was auctioned by fractions in order to prevent domination of foreign capital in the ownership structure. It was also required that more than 60 percent of the shares must remain in the hands of domestic investors. During the period 1990–2000, OTP Bank lost about 43 percent of its retail banking market, although remaining the leader, but the situation started to change as foreign investment was allowed to increase.

Banks expanding on new markets in CEE countries usually choose one of the following strategies:[16]

i "niche" strategy (small share of market in several countries);
ii "focus" strategy (large share on one or two narrow market segments);

iii   "discovery" strategy (very small share – just presence in a market – but in many markets);

iv   "expansion" strategy (large share in many markets).

About 85 percent of banks prefer a "niche" strategy, and only a limited number of banks are able to implement an "expansion" strategy. OTP Bank is the only Eastern European bank present among the champions of "expansion" strategy, as UniCredit, Erste Bank, Raiffeisen International, Intesa Sanpaolo. Indeed, only in 2006 did OTP buy five banks for 1.4 billion euro in CCE countries: Raiffeisen Bank of Ukraine for 650 million euro, Investsberbank of Russia for 477.5 million euro, Kulska banka of Serbia for 118 million euro, Crnogorska komercjalna banka of Montenegro for 105 million euro and Zepter Banka of Serbia for 34.2 million euro (Golovin and Taran, 2006). OTP has become a multinational bank with presence in nine countries (Bulgaria, Croatia, Montenegro, Romania, Russia, Serbia, Slovakia and Ukraine, besides Hungary).

OTP Bank has developed a special CG model for its foreign subsidiaries. Besides the local managers, one OTP Bank manager is responsible (as chairman of the supervisory board or of the board of directors) for the ownership control of each subsidiary in each country. In addition, each division of the bank is held responsible for the performance and professional control in its field for the whole group.[17]

Strategies oriented toward expansion into more developed markets push companies to modernize previously their management system. Russian companies show the highest speed of the growth because of huge increases in the prices of oil, gas and metals. Between 2000 and 2006, the number of companies with $1 billion annual revenue has increased by five times and is now close to 100. Besides raw materials companies, new industries like those of financing, retail trade, telecommunications, building and food are represented in the list of top companies. This intensive growth reflects the fundamental shift that has occurred within those companies from financial-industrial groups with conglomerate content to business corporations focused on one industry or "core business." Some of these companies were established separately from any financial-industrial group, but most of them were created as divisions inside such groups with a high level of autonomy. This new tendency in industrial specialization and expansion influences the CG models of the concerned companies. Usually the process of change has taken this form:

1   Corporate restructuring: financial-industrial groups will sell their non-profile assets and concentrate on one or two industries. These specialized companies become independent businesses with independent strategies but strong ownership control through representatives on boards of directors.

2   Integration of new companies: M&As will be followed by a successful integration of bought companies into a business. Especially cross-border mergers require improvement of CG so as to become more transparent

for new partners, to be permitted to expand by regional authorities (anti-monopoly authorities notably). At the same time, newly acquired foreign companies can bring better practices of CG, which are worth implementing in the parent company.

3   CG: integration of foreign assets requires the implementation of accounting and reporting systems in compliance with IAS (IFRS)/GAAP. Besides, internalization of the businesses must be reflected in the internationalization of boards of directors. In the largest companies from countries in transition, independent directors are invited from leading world companies who have an experience in the same field. It allows implementing the best western practices and makes the company more attractive for foreign investors.

4   Corporate strategy: the accent on corporate strategy will have to shift from a management of enterprises/assets relating to the different links of a value chain to the management of a (integrated) business that comprises all elements of the value chain. This is followed by the creation of a company's brand and the introduction of value-based management. The success of a new strategy is correlated with the level of transparency and effectiveness of CG in a company.

Public ownership and CG

All EiT, including Belarus, reduce the state ownership in their companies. Only Russia shows an active policy of nationalization. The starting point of the nationalization movement in Russia is often considered to be Rosneft's acquisition of Yukos's assets in 2004. The real first step was in fact taken much earlier, in 2000, with the establishment of the state-owned company Rosoboronexport, on the bases of three state weapons trading companies. At that time, Rosoboronexport competed with a number of private weapons trading companies. But during the following two years, it doubled its export and now this company is a world leader in weapons trading. Weapons trading is, however, only one item of Rosoboronexport business, in 2002, for instance, the company started expansion in the helicopter production industry. The state government gave Rosoboronexport all state shares in all companies producing helicopters. In parallel, the state increased the control of the industry using such means as annulations of state orders or tax administration pressures. Rosoboronexport continued its expansion in new industries like car production in 2005, titanium production in 2006 and special steel production in 2007 (Verner, 2007). Simultaneously, it expands in the EiT markets by acquiring plants in Ukraine or Kazakhstan.

Gazprom is another state-owned company but it is a public company with 50 percent government-owned shares and the rest is dispersed. The market capitalization of Gazprom is one-third of the whole Russian market of capitalization and it provides half of the annual growth of the Russian stock market. This market is one the fastest growing markets in developing and transitional countries. It has increased by 33 times during the period 1998–2006. Gazprom is in the top ten of the Financial Times Global 500. Such performance is not as much the result of management quality or CG improvement than the oil and gas booming prices and the active government support. Gazprom's business strategy can be summarized in three points, as posted on its website: (i) capitalization build-up; (ii) increase of gas production and strengthening of the mineral resource base, including M&A activities; and (iii) realizing large-scale international projects.

The opening of Gazprom's capital to foreign investors has been increasing, together with the enhancement of state control: the limit of 20 percent maximum ownership by foreign interests has been removed after the concentration of 50 percent of the shares in the hands of the state has been achieved. Gazprom is not interested by small companies; it focuses on the largest market players. In 2005, Gazprom took over Sibneft, the sixth largest oil and gas company in Russia for fossil fuel exploration and production. Now, second among the five leaders in this industry, Gazprom and Rosneft, are under state control. The fourth company, TNK-BP, is considered as a target for merger or acquisition by Gazprom's and Rosneft's boards of directors.

One of the largest strategic cross-border acquisitions of Gazprom is an agreement to get control of over 50 percent of Beltransgaz – which owns and operates the whole gas transportation system of Belarus – from 2007 to 2010 (buying up of 12.5 percent of Beltransgaz each year for $2.5 billion[18]). Since energy supply to Europe is one of Gazprom's strategic priorities, the group tries not only to build new gas pipelines but also to takeover national gas transportation systems in neighbor-countries. Gazprom has become one of the leaders by market capitalization thanks to M&A deals and fast expansion. From this point of view, the design and implementation of state-owned companies' corporate strategies appear quite successful. There are nevertheless problems of CG in these companies:

i   the state's interests and the company's interests can often diverge, especially in the field of energy supply (S&P, 2007);
ii   defending the company's minor shareholders may be difficult to realize;
iii boards of directors often play a nominal role of transmitter of the state government's decisions to the company's executives (S&P, 2007);
iv   the strong state protection of the company against bankruptcy and hostile takeovers is not an incentive for efficiency;
v   the use of non-market tools against competitors in their struggle with the company decreases the incentives to implement innovations within the company.

Markets for ownership control

During the 15 years following the USSR's collapse, markets for ownership control in the EiT were closed for foreign investors and reasons for ultimately liberalizing those markets are the same in all EiT. Many companies have reached a development level that requires long-term and cheap investments, non-available local markets and additional reasons may have to do with political changes. During the period 1992–2006, foreign inflows in new EU members have been increased from about $5 billion up to $62 billion, and with steady annual growth, an annual rate of more than 10 percent (except in 2003) (UNCTAD,[19] Kalotay, 2006). Foreign investments have been increasing in those countries that are rich in natural resources. The share of foreign investors in equity of the CEE companies now exceeds 50 percent and in banking this proportion reaches 70 percent in Poland, 90 percent in Hungary, the Czech Republic and Bulgaria. The wave of M&A in the CEE countries declines, but the new players are now in place. In CIS countries like Ukraine and Russia, the volume of M&A deals has been multiplied by four and the share of those countries in the Eastern European M&A market has doubled. In Ukraine, for instance, acquisitions by foreigners represent almost 85 percent of the whole of Ukrainian M&A transactions, while they do not exceed 25 percent in Russia.

The most attractive sectors for foreign investors are represented by banking, telecommunication and raw materials sectors and the possibility of selling companies at market prices has acted as a good impulse for implementing new practices of CG and in some cases to go public. The strategy used by CIS's companies preparing for IPO or M&A is:

i dividend policy: increase of dividend pay-out ratio and dividends payments' frequency;
ii transparency: accounting and reporting in compliance with IAS (IFRS)/GAAP;
iii information disclosure: press-release publishing, free access to information for analytical agencies and institutional investors, conferences given by top managers;
iv strategy statement and disclosure: internal and external sources for strategic development;
v performance: increase of financial performance (ROA, ROE, EPS, EV, EBITDA, etc.);
vi CG: structuring of boards of directors, specification of their duties and responsibilities, appointment of independent directors;
vii corporate culture: corporate value systems, human resource management;
viii going public: IPO or increase of the liquidity and marketability of stocks issuing in the privatization period, publishing of information on corporate events.

Ways for becoming public were different in the former soviet bloc, during the early privatization period. When companies had become public under legislation requirements without economic prerequisites, plant-level companies were progressively restructured into private companies. In CEE countries, big companies went through compulsory listing during privatization but left the market soon, since they were not able to withdraw financing from it, due to undeveloped exchange. In Bulgaria, for instance, the number of listed companies declined by a factor of 3, during the period 1997–2002. After privatization new owners did not actually see any advantage of staying public. Privatization through IPO was not, however, popular in CEE countries either and as a result, the total number of IPOs conducted in the period of privatization was 60 in Poland, 20 in Estonia and even less in Hungary.

The story is different when, pushed by strategic considerations, companies go public. Among the CIS, Russia is a leader in IPO implementation, while other countries are only at the entry stage. In 2006, with $18 billion Russia has occupied third place in the world, based on volume of financial transactions. The reasons for the popularity of IPOs in EiT are:

i   Increased capital. A public offering allows a company to raise capital for various corporate purposes and can also bring cash into the company for expansion.
ii Liquidity. Once a company shares are traded on a public exchange, they have a market value and can be resold. This also means the possibility to use stock incentive plans to attract and retain key employees. It also increases the liquidity of ownership shares of the company and gives greater access to capital markets by increasing the success of future stock offerings.
iii Increased prestige and performances. Public companies are often better known and more visible than private companies; this enables them to obtain a larger market for their goods or services and increased equity capital allows them to use more debt financing at less risk.
iv Valuation. The stock market defines the "real" price of the company, which in many cases is higher than before the IPO. This is helpful for a company that is looking for a merger or an acquisition. It also allows the shareholders to know the value of the shares.
v   Takeover advantages. IPO gives the company the possibility to acquire other companies by share exchanges.
vi Defense against nationalization and raider attacks. Presence of foreign investors in the ownership structure and listing in foreign stock exchanges protects the company against re-privatization and nationalization. Moreover, raiders supported by regional governments cannot use their raid tools in an international legal environment.

Although large EiT companies work to attract international investors and consequently endeavor to implement international standards of CG, the "modified stakeholder model" remains dominant in the former soviet area. The possibility of attracting financial resources from international markets through Eurobond issuing and IPO undoubtedly reduces the power of banks as stakeholders, but other stakeholders like the governments remain the second most powerful group and this still impacts significantly on boards of directors functioning.

Executive and supervisory boards

The approach to structuring boards of directors is influenced by the ownership structure. In CEE countries, where foreign shareholders dominate, top management is appointed according to Western standards and as in Continental Europe, one of the core problems of CG in CEE countries is how to balance correctly majority and minority shareholders' interests. The agency problem, met when managers run the company in their own interests, is less common, but it certainly poses itself when boards of directors play only a nominal role. In the CIS, however, the executive manager and the owner used to be the same person, until the beginning of the twenty-first century (Dolgopyatova, 2000). This was the result of the privatization process, which witnessed companies' managers becoming owners. To some extent, the agency problem did not exist as was the case in the West at the beginning of the twentieth century. When structuring of the corporate sector occurred in such a way that not only managers built financial-industrial groups and managed them personally, and that an agency problem of a special kind de facto arose. What happened in CIS is more serious than what was experienced in the West, mainly because of the extreme opacity on which financial-industrial groups were built.

The concentration of ownership and management in the same hand or small groups of people has resulted in companies hardly showing profits in CIS. At the end of 1990s and at the beginning of the twenty-first century, almost all companies in the CIS demonstrated losses or at best very low profit. One explanation is that all profits were deviated or withdrawn by owner-managers through dubious means, taking the form of offshore or limited liabilities firms (Yakovlev, 2003; Pappe and Galukhina, 2006). To exclude any profit sharing owner-managers even recorted to manipulating the numbers. An extreme example of sharp shifting from "non-profit" to "high-profit" business within a period of two years can be found in the banking system of Ukraine. Before the "orange revolution," namely in 2003, the banking system return on assets (ROA) was only 1.04 percent. When, however, most banks became targets for cross-border M&A, they had to show fast growth profits in order to appear attractive this resulted in their ROA reaching 1.61 percent by early 2005, inducing an increase in value. Similarly, while their average net income annual growth was between 20 and 30 percent per year before the "orange revolution," it reached 100 percent per year immediately after.

The relations between owners and managers have undergone similar evolution as the corporate sector. Early in the 1990s, successful "red directors" (owners-directors who were learning by doing) were those who had strong entrepreneurship skills and close relations with regional and state governments. Until 1998, foreign managers were not represented in companies' executive committees in the CIS. On the other hand boards of directors were formed according to personal loyalty to owners. The 1998 crisis has the advantage of unveiling the weaknesses of this post-soviet management style. Beginning 2000, with companies growing fast and increasing competition, owners-managers could no more manage conglomerates by themselves. They were forced to recourse to delegating some of their managerial functions to professional executives, particularly when:

i   owners-managers had no time for strategic management because of operating activities;
ii   owners-managers chose a new type of business or political activity as a priority;
iii   the company targeted international capital and product markets; and
iv   other major shareholders obtained more power to remove old management.

The lack of professional managers inside countries in transition reflected in invitations to managers from the leading international companies from abroad to manage domestic companies. This was fortunate since they brought the best managerial practices, new contacts and increased the company's reputation among foreign investors.

Almost all countries of the former Soviet Union have adopted a two-tier system of board of directors. A supervisory board must be established for all joint-stock companies and limited liability companies above a certain size. Only few countries like Macedonia, Lithuania, Slovenia or Hungary (from 2006) and Kazakhstan have implemented a mixed system. In Macedonia, the governance structure of the company may be organized as a one-tier system (board of directors) or a two-tier system (management board or manager and supervisory board). The general meeting of shareholders passes resolutions by a majority vote of the represented share capital, except in certain cases when a qualified majority is required. If the company has a one-tier management system, the general meeting is responsible for appointing the three to 15 members of the board of directors. In Romania, while the basic framework is a one-tier system, in practice the board of directors can take on some of the functions of a two-tier-style management board.

In Russian legislation, as in other EiT, the supervisory board is equivalent to the board of directors and it is composed in large companies of five members elected by the shareholders and according to International Finance Corporation (IFC) data for the largest Russian public companies, the average number of members is about 6.5.[20] The efficiency of the supervisory board depends on two key issues: its structure and its duties/responsibilities.

The structure of the supervisory board is defined by the relations between owners and managers. If an owner manages a company by himself, as a director, the supervisory board plays a nominal role and is composed mainly of affiliated persons. On the contrary, if an owner delegates managerial functions to executives, he/she appoints himself or devoted professional managers to the supervisory board. But in both cases, the insider boards' structure dominates.

An independent external director is considered to be "a billet to the club of foreign investors." Only companies interested in foreign debt or equity markets think seriously about independent directors. For this purpose, EiT companies are

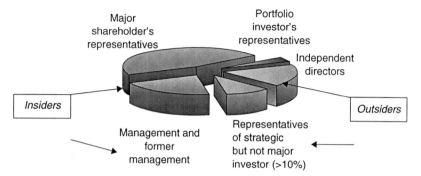

Figure 11.4 Structure of the board of directors of the largest Russian companies, 2006 (for 70 largest Russian companies covering 90 percent of market cap).[1]

Note

1 Portrait of Board of Directors of Russian Companies as a Mirror of Concentrate Ownership and Obstacles for Corporate Governance Development, Report, S&P's, Russia, 2007.

inviting and hiring foreign top-executives although highly expensive. They are currently playing more important roles in strategy development. In the top Russian companies by market capitalization, the average remuneration is about $1–2 hundred thousand per year. Actually, it costs a lot more to hire a foreign top-executive, because the remuneration in Russia is paid from a net profit and companies' foreign top-executives are also hired as advisors which allows for an extra salary. This, of course, has shed some doubt with regard to the independence of foreign external directors.

In countries like Poland, Slovakia, the Czech Republic, Hungary and the Slovak Republic, one-third of the members of the supervisory board are assumed to be elected by employees. In practice, employee representatives in the supervisory board are non other than local trade union leaders and/or the chair of the (central) labor council, or their deputies. In Poland, for instance, employee representatives are nominated by the company's labor council or central labor council, but prior to nomination, the labor council is obliged "to listen to the opinion" of company trade unions. The shareholders' meeting is required to appoint the labor council's nominees if they meet the established legal criteria.

In theory, the supervisory board is intended to play a monitoring and strategic governance role. In EiT, the duties and responsibilities of the board of directors are clearly defined by law only in Russia and even there supervisory boards carry out functions of strategic and sometimes operating management – the duties of executives. At the same time, boards are not structured by committees, except in a few of the most advanced companies. If, in EiT board committee's establishment has become a general rule, the proportion of boards in the countries that have committees is about 10 percent (IFC data). Among the EiT again, Russia is more advanced in creating board committees. All companies that have established board committees also have an audit committee, 82 percent of them have a remuneration committee, 78 percent have created a strategic committee and 40 percent have a CG committee. Other committees like investment or risk committees exist in less than 20 percent of companies that structured boards in committees (Filatov, 2006).

Conclusion

The development of corporate structure and governance in countries in transition went through three phases, summarized in Appendix 11.A1. "Mass Privatization" resulted in the establishment of an implicit "modified" stakeholder model with dispersed ownership and domination of several parties other than shareholders: managers, governments and banks. Corporate models in CEE countries and the CIS diverged in the "Privatization for cash," with CEE countries calling massively for foreign shareholding while the CIS protected their economies from foreign influence. The power in the "modified" stakeholder model then shifted to major shareholders, who took under their control all production chains via highly-concentrated but hidden ownership. The phase 3 of privatization has had less impact on. corporate models' development but showed different governments' priorities, ranking from the privatization of the largest strategic companies to the nationalization of previously privatized units. To stay in command new shareholders-managers groups in EiT made their organization evolve from a dispersed holding structure to a classic holding structure and finally to genuine corporate form.

Corporate structure and governance evolution in the EiT is driven by need for long-term and cheap external financing. International investors will not, however, accept diverse approaches to CG in different countries, companies looking for international capital will have to adapt their corporate models and CG systems to international standards. On the other hand, as government is a major stakeholder in this "modified" model, it is hoped that it will have incentives for improving legal and regulatory frameworks. All this is auspicious for the future of CG in economies in transition.

Table 11.A1 Modified stakeholder model of governance

Corporate model	*"Modified" stakeholder model of governance*
Phase 1 Mass privatization • Rapid transfer of state property • Segmented and dispersed ownership	Citizens became owners, but – as minor shareholders – had no real power The most powerful stakeholders were: • banks • state • managers-executives • customers, suppliers • foreign investors – major shareholders (only in CEE countries)

Corporate model	"Modified" stakeholder model of governance
Phase 2 Privatization for cash	
• Concentration of ownership	• State power did not change
• Vertical integration	• Major shareholders got dominating power
• Establishment of conglomerates	• Bank's power decreased
	• Consumers and suppliers had also less power because they were included in conglomerates and were under control of major shareholders
	• Major foreign investors-shareholders enhanced their power (only in CEE countries)
Phase 3 Privatizing strategic companies and revisiting early privatization	
• Corporate model depends on the level of a company development:	• Major shareholder leads the game
	• Executives' and boards' roles strongly depend on the corporate model and strategy
Step 1. Dispersed holding	
Step 2. Classic holding	
Step 3. Business corporation	• Foreign institutional investors become strong stakeholders when a company looks for external finance
• Development based on corporate strategy not on short-term plans	• State power does not change and increases in state-owned companies
• Search for foreign investments	

Notes

1 The CIS includes 11 republics of the former USSR: Armenia, Azerbaijan, Belarus, Georgia, Kazakhstan, Kyrgyzstan, Moldova, Russia, Tajikistan, Turkmenistan, Ukraine and Uzbekistan. From 2005, Turkmenistan is an associate member of the CIS, since it stopped its permanent membership. The CEE countries include the Baltic States – Latvia, Lithuania, Estonia – and other European post-soviet countries such as Bosnia, Bulgaria, Croatia, the Czech Republic, Hungary, Macedonia, Montenegro, Poland, Romania, Slovakia and Slovenia.

2 The State Property Fund, a body of the federal government, set up the value of all companies (except "strategic" companies) at the book value of their equity.

3 A kind of legacy of the economic thinking of the Soviet era.

4 The Ukrainian government used the term "shadow" privatization in its development program "Toward People" from February 10, 2005. That is a fact of official recognition of the existence of shadow privatization.

5 Helicopters, tanks and trucks.

6 Investment commitments included keeping employees for a certain period, increasing employees' salary, investing a certain amount of resources, etc.

7 This applied in particular to the companies' debts for gas to Gazprom.

8 Each of them provides about 7 percent of Ukraine's GDP.

9 They represent about 70 percent of board members of public companies in CEE countries, against 30–35 percent in Continental Europe.

10 This fact is recognized by Russian State officials like Zhukov (2006, p. 7), vice prime-minister of Russia.

11 European CG Institute, Index of codes, www.ecgi.org/codes/all_codes.php.

12 "Corporate Governance in Emerging Market Banks," Special Report, Fitch Rating, August 2006.
13 One-third or one-fourth of the members of the board of directors should be independent in the CIS, against at least half of them in CEE countries.
14 To realize the extent of states' determination in this matter, see the example of Yukos, pp. 25–26.
15 Zalewska, A. "Is locking domestic funds into the local market beneficial? Evidence from the Polish pension reforms," CMPO Working Paper Series, No. 06/153.
16 Central and Eastern European Banking Study, 2007.
17 Main Elements of OTP Bank's New Structural, Operational System, Effective from January 1, 2007. www.otpbank.hu/OTP_Portal/online/CE02050000000000.jsp.
18 The Belarus government estimated its gas transportation system at $10 billion, it accepted a price decrease since it has obtained below-market price conditions for gas supply in the short term.
19 UNCTAD, World Investment Report 2006.
20 "Corporate Governance Practice Survey in Russia," Report, IFC, 2006.

12 The MENA countries national systems of corporate governance

A. Naciri

Introduction

Corporate governance is also becoming an important issue in the Middle East and North Africa. The region called Middle East and North Africa, or MENA is a very disparate region, culturally unified however. It is composed, by alphabetical order, of Algeria, Bahrain, Egypt, Iraq, Jordan, Kuwait, Lebanon, Libya, Morocco, Oman, Qatar, Saudi Arabia, Sudan, Syria, Tunisia, United Arab Emirates (UAE), the West Bank–Gaza and Yemen, 18 countries[1] all together. The MENA region population as it is specifically defined here counts about 6 percent of the total world population (more than 300 million), almost equivalent to the population of the European Union (EU), and significantly larger than the population of the United States. MENA is also an economically diverse region that includes both oil-rich economies like the Gulf States or Algeria and also countries that are relatively resource-scarce such as Egypt, Jordan or Tunisia. Many MENA countries suffer from well-known economic illnesses, due significantly to factors expressing some weaknesses in corporate governance (CG).

The MENA region is indeed in urgent need of policy reforms, typically in the area of CG, and MENA countries have recently initiated a number of reforms and restructuring on legislative and infrastructure grounds, with the help of international organizations. CG issues have gained unprecedented awareness in most MENA countries today and economic legislations and institutions that provide the foundation for CG[2] are currently updated. The efforts made in this area start producing positive results and constitute one important aspect of market oriented reforms.

This chapter will attempt to synthesize CG efforts and advances in MENA countries, specifically; using the Organization of Economic Cooperation and Development (OECD) CG principles of 2004 (OECD-2004 principles) as benchmarks. The chapter is based on diverse reports prepared by various authors very familiar with the Middle East and North Africa. The reports were prepared as participation for a series of workshops on CG and the Global Corporate Governance Forum meetings organized in different MENA countries. The chapter uses Reports on the Observance of Standards and Codes (ROSC) issued by the International Monetary Fund (IMF) and the World Bank (WB) to gain some insight with regard to CG gains.

CG framework, an overview

MENA countries, as the product of specific historical evolution; are associated with a distinct set of cultural, social, economic and political institutions and practices which shape their current economic and social advance. The proliferation of family-owned firms, the dominance of state-owned enterprises, and the plurality of small- and medium-sized enterprises characterized indeed the business environment of MENA countries. At the same time, most MENA modern economic activity has been deeply impacted by oil price and the strong leading role of the government, but above all by the constant misallocation of oil-wealth. The result is that the region is suffering today from severe economic illness which is making about 23 percent of its huge population to live below the poverty level (WB reports). To break this poverty cycle MENA countries need to restructure their economic and financial activities and do seem willing.

The need of reform complying with CG international principles have finally emerged, even if only relatively recently. Awareness is advancing rather quickly in most MENA countries and is increasing due to consultation reports issued by international organizations like the IMF and the WB and focus group discussions, workshops and Global Corporate Governance forum meetings are flourishing and are organized in countries like Egypt, Jordan, Morocco, Lebanon, Saudi Arabia, etc. Most MENA countries have also taken part in the ROSC initiative, which summarizes the extent to which countries observe certain internationally recognized standards and codes, typically in the area of corporate governance.

Concerning the ROSC[3] initiative, 12 areas are identified and associated standards considered useful for the IMF operational work as for the WB. And both used them "to help sharpen the institutions policy discussions with national authorities and in the private sector." Precisely, the WB is charged with evaluating OECD Principles of Corporate Governance implementation and such assessments are considered main components of the ROSC program, whose objective is to identify weaknesses that may contribute to a country's economic and financial vulnerability. Each CG ROSC assessment is performed in three steps:

i   first, it reviews the country's legal and regulatory framework;
ii second, it reviews practices and compliance of country's listed companies; and
iii third, it assesses the framework relative to an internationally accepted benchmark.

Toward this objective, the WB has established a tailored program to assist its MENA member countries[4] in strengthening their frameworks. The objectives of this program are (AlYafi, 2005):

i   First, arising awareness of good CG practices among MENA countries public and private sector stakeholders;

ii Second, comparing MENA countries CG frameworks and MENA companies' practices against the OECD Principles for Corporate Governance; these Principles have been advanced in five main areas: Ensuring the Basis for an Effective Corporate Governance Framework; The Rights of Shareholders and Key Ownership Functions; The Equitable Treatment of Shareholders; Disclosure and Transparency; and The Responsibilities of the Board; and

iii Third, assisting MENA countries in developing and implementing their action plans for improving institutional capacity, with a view to strengthening their CG frameworks.

Many MENA governments, facing global market economy challenges, are turning to the private sector to foster economic growth and are becoming less inclined engaging themselves in the direct production and/or supply of goods and services (AlYafi, 2005). They are at the same time becoming more active in creating supporting institutions, protecting investors' rights and developing markets. They are progressively aware of the necessity of sound CG practices for the promotion of economic growth and the attraction of the much needed foreign investment and financing. Efforts in the area of CG in MENA countries are believed to foster business partnerships, improve overall business performance and ultimately enhance competitiveness throughout the region. In fact, it is commonly admitted that appropriate legal environment and enforcement of good corporate laws and regulations guaranteeing disclosure can help discourage fraudulent behavior and conflicts of interest. On the other hand, effective legal systems and monitoring can contribute to minimizing agency problems by providing shareholders the means to limit the divergence of the manager's interest (AlYafi, 2005).

The MENA region and its main financial markets are regulated by CG rules and legislations that are either recently updated or even recently promulgated and as usual, a gap between enforcement effectiveness and legislations availability is always expected. The seriousness of the gap may vary, however, across the region. For instance, most rules and regulations, laws and by-laws of stock exchanges of the MENA region, contain specific provisions that are supposed to preserve shareholders rights and such provisions are also clearly stated in company's by-laws (Sourial, 2003). They usually emphasize:

i the basic rights of shareholders;
ii the ownership registration;
iii the participation and voting in general shareholders meetings; and
iv the involvement in decisions concerning fundamental corporate changes.

Despite all that, MENA markets are still considered not to be responsive to minority shareholders needs. The reason for this situation is that investors' culture is still dominated by family investments and banks. The lack of equity culture seems to characterize all MENA countries financial markets and it generally leads to the defying of investors' rights. This situation may explain shareholders lack of interest in corporate affairs in the MENA region. This major financial market weakness seems to be exacerbated by the strong state intervention, which has been particularly strongly resistant to change. Consequently, private sector development in most MENA countries seems to have great difficulty materializing. This situation underlines the urgent need for more efficient structural reforms in most MENA countries.

With the help of international organizations, MENA countries are finally coming to the conclusion that good governance significantly matters for economic development and are progressively discovering the economic power of high-quality institutions in improving living conditions of the population by rising per capita incomes and promoting social welfare and economic development. It seems that it is in this perspective that most MENA countries[5] have accepted to undergo the ROSC exercise of the WB and the IMF.[6] Some MENA countries like Egypt, Jordan Morocco, Saudi Arabia and Bahrain are even represented in the S&P/IFC indices. Egypt, Jordan and Morocco are also presented in the MSCI EMF indices (Sourial, 2003). Obviously, things appear to be moving in the right direction. According to the IFC-Hawkamah CG survey of listed companies and banks of 11 MENA countries, conducted in March 2007 (IFC-Hawkamah, 2007),[7] 49.3 percent of respondents considered CG as important or very important. Respondents seem, however, to have mixed views of CG itself, given that 40.8 percent of them think that CG is "a set of tools to help management run the day-to-day activities of the company," and 19.7 percent think of CG as the company internal structure that will allow it to comply with drastic laws and regulations, etc.

The preponderant group of MENA companies, as we know, is represented by family-owned non-listed companies,[8] with small numbers of shareholders, whose shares are not sold in any free market, and majority shareholders actively participating in the management of the company, although relying on family and bank financing for expansion and growth.[9] These companies, which do not fit in a single mould, also employ different legal business forms to structure their organization, varying from partnership forms to limited liability companies and joint stock companies. All of them, however, miss the opportunity of easy access to capital market financing and ending up in pushing the whole economies in much allocation inefficiencies. As expected, CG internal and external mechanisms of MENA family-owned non-listed companies are shaped by the legal form of business they are submitted to. Moreover, given there is no market for corporate control for this kind of company; more effective and appropriate external and internal CG mechanisms are in need. Such systems will have to explore and propose appropriate mechanisms that are sufficiently responsive to the governance problems that occur in the MENA region.[10]

Shareholders, ownership and shareholders' treatment

Governance systems across the world can be classified in two major categories, mainly as a result of different legal origins (Sourial, 2003). The first category is based on market governance systems or external mechanism systems, which are characterized by:

i   dispersed equity holding,
ii   a portfolio orientation among equity holders,
iii a broad delegation and large discretion given to management in operating the company, and
iv   a separation of ownership and control.

The second category of governance systems is based on block-holder governance systems, which are characterized by majority or near-majority holdings of stocks concentrated in the hands of one, two, or a small group of large investors. In this kind of system the separation of ownership and control does not have its place.

As can be seen from the analysis of Table 12.1 (Shaker, 2004), most CG systems in the MENA region are rather block-holder governance systems and the controlling shareholders are either banks, individuals or influential institutions or families, most of the time related to the ruling class.

Such CG systems encourage conflict of interest between strong family or institutional shareholders and weak minority shareholders. In such cases also, and very often, a single family can have controlling shareholdings in a number of companies whether directly or indirectly. Moreover, according to Table 12.2, ownership in MENA countries is also highly concentrated. In fact, in some

Table 12.1 Company ownership composition, 2000 (%)

	Jordan	*Lebanon*	*Kuwait*	*Saudi Arabia*	*UAE*
Non-financial companies	15	12	20	15	13
Banks	25	40	35	40	45
Financial companies	8	13	15	11	9
Individuals	16	14	20	17	16
Others (Government, etc.)	36	21	10	17	16

Table 12.2 Company ownership concentration, outstanding shares, publicly listed companies (%)

Country	*Largest shareholder*	*Top five shareholders*	*As end of the year*	*Company coverage*
Jordan	20	35	2000	All PLC
Lebanon	25	55	2001	Non-financial PLC
Kuwait	60	80	1999	All PLC
Saudi Arabia	70	80	1998	Non-financial PLC
UAE	75	85	2000	All PLC

MENA countries, the top five shareholders may own up to 85 percent of the total outstanding shares.

Despite the fact that some MENA exchanges were created in the eighteenth century, the largest 20 companies in Bahrain, Lebanon, Egypt, Kuwait, Morocco, Oman, Saudi Arabia and the United Arab Emirates (UAE), are not listed on the stock exchange, except for the Jordanian exchange that has 17 listed companies among the largest 20 in the country and the government owns, however, about 24 percent of the shares of these largest listed companies (Anonymous, 2005). As a general rule, non-listed companies seem to dominate the MENA economic field.

A non-listed company is generally defined (Hansmann, 1996) as "a closely held company whose shares, unlike those of a publicly held company, do not trade freely in impersonal markets," either because shares are subject to restrictions that limit their transferability or because they are the property of a small number of persons, often members of founder families. Given the specific character of corporate ownership in the MENA region some are recommending

> that corporate governance principles address this issue and be geared to suit non-listed companies. They also feel that corporate governance principles should not be an obstacle for the establishment and development of family companies as they represent the backbone of MENA economies.
>
> (Corporate Governance Workshop, 2003)

Participants to an International Experts Meeting on Corporate Governance of Non-listed Companies (OECD, 2005), share also the previous view. They have rightly remarked that the classical debate on CG has mostly focused on listed companies. Unlike, however, non-listed firms shareholders, of those listed firms can be protected by market mechanisms (external CG mechanisms), while shareholders of non-listed companies cannot. As a rule, although legislations protecting shareholders' rights do exist in most MENA countries, minority shareholder rights do not seem to be protected enough in practice. Usually, minority shareholders are commonly denied basic access to information or even participating effectively in General Meeting's debate.[11] Minority shareholders in most MENA countries also pay little or no adequate attention to CG issues and they are far from requiring equitable treatment, with regard to any CG issue (IFC-Hawkamah, 2007). Most small shareholders hold share for strictly speculation reasons and they are far from being concerned by companies' management.

Consequently, In MENA countries controlling shareholders can easily monitor closely the company and its management and, of course, they always do and very often, their interest conflicts with the interest of minority shareholders. They do not, for instance, hesitate in abusing the company's resources and withdraw personal benefits at the expense of other shareholders. In some MENA countries controlling shareholders even consider their misconduct as legal and rightful. In some cases, they do not hesitate to use shares with special voting rights or indirect ownership to influence decisions favoring their private interests. MENA family investors also often recourse to indirect ownership in which members of big families have a number of controlling ownerships in a number of holding companies as well as in subsidiaries (Sourial, 2003). The resulting CG system is naturally a block-holder system. In such a system the availability and channels of financing are dependent mainly on banks.[12] In this respect, a healthy banking system would impose itself as of a necessity for improving CG. Unfortunately, some MENA countries' banking sectors seem to be a family banking system, which burdens them with non-performing loans, "mostly resulting from an excessive related lending, coupled with intentional fraud and/or inflated value of the collaterals" (Sourial, 2003). A number of Egyptian banks, for instance, were involved in this kind of lending activity having resulted in high levels of non-performing loans. Only one company out of several companies defaulted on their debts was listed on the Exchange. Similar cases were observed in Lebanon, Jordan and elsewhere.

The dark situation previously pictured has contributed significantly in the immaturity of security exchanges in the MENA region and has induced a mass inefficiency in the whole of its financial system. It seems that efficient CG is the shortest way to attracting both capital and most able executives, but also attracting new technologies and achieving efficiency alliances (Saidi, 2004). Establishing effective disclosure systems can only be of a necessity for the MENA countries, in need for capital, new ideas and modern generations of entrepreneurs, to break the circle of insufficiency. Thus the development of capital markets will allow new sources of liquidity notably risk and venture capital to enter the economy and hence create new wealth.

Financial reporting and disclosure

It is widely admitted today that the disclosure system is one of the central aspects to CG. It is also argued that financial disclosure should be as timely as accurate, and adequate, by being based on sound and recognized accounting and auditing standards, whose application requires certification by completely independent auditors. It seems that efficient disclosure is the shortest way of increasing efficiency in the market, thus creating more wealth.

As part of the ROSC initiative, the WB has established a program to assist its MENA region members in implementing international accounting and auditing standards for strengthening their financial reporting regimes. The objectives of this program are two-fold:

First, to analyze comparability of national accounting and auditing standards with international standards, determining the degree with which applicable accounting and auditing standards are complied, and assessing strengths and weaknesses of the institutional framework in supporting high-quality financial reporting.

Second, to assist MENA countries to develop and implement appropriate country action plans for improving their institutional capacities. The objective is to strengthen the country's corporate financial reporting system.

We will try to assess the quality of financial reporting, auditing in MENA countries, based on the WB tool, especially at the following levels:[13]

i   accounting and auditing environment,
ii   the comparison of national accounting standards and International Account-
     ing Standards (IAS)/International Federation of Accountants (IFRS), and
iii actual accounting auditing practices.

With regard to the accounting and auditing environment, as of the year 2007, most, if not all MENA countries, have national accounting associations and national accounting standards, as reported in Table 12.3.

Moreover, Bahrain, Egypt, Iraq, Jordan, Kuwait, Lebanon, Morocco, Saudi Arabia and Tunisia are also affiliated to the IFAC.[14] On the other hand, the majority of MENA countries requires all listed companies to prepare annual audited financial statements.[15] Some MENA countries, like Tunisia, have even their own accounting conceptual framework, inspired from the International Accounting Standards Board (IASB) model (ROSC Tunisia, 2006). There are also, in some MENA countries, oversight boards regulating and monitoring the profession and supposedly guaranteeing auditor independence.[16]

The quality of accounting and auditing education requires a lot of improvement in most MENA countries. The lack of modern curricula along with the scarcity of qualified instructors, are usually encountered in most MENA countries. At the undergraduate level, for instance, accounting and auditing courses seem to focus on bookkeeping only, neglecting financial reporting issues and

Table 12.3 MENA countries using or converting to IFRS, as of April 2007

Countries	Accounting principles	Notes
Algeria	National GAAP	IFRS permitted
Bahrain	IFRS	
Egypt	IFRS	
Iraq	No information	
Jordan	IFRS	
Kuwait	IFRS	
Lebanon	IFRS	
Libya	National GAAP	IFRS permitted
Morocco	National GAAP	IFRS permitted
Oman	IFRS	
Qatar	IFRS	
Saudi Arabia	IFRS	
Syria	National GAAP	IFRS not permitted
Tunisia	National GAAP	IFRS permitted
UAE	IFRS	
West Bank and Gaza	IFRS	
Yemen	No information	

Source: From Deloitte, IAS Plus, as of April 27, 2007.

implications. At the graduate level, however, the quality of accounting education is relatively in better shape and seems to be constantly improving (ROSC Jordan 2004). Very few, if any MENA countries, however, have comprehensive standard setting processes and often accounting standards and rules are promulgated by government agencies, commonly the Ministry of Finance. MENA countries seem to lean toward international accounting standards. Around 73.9 percent of respondents disclose financials in the annual report, and post, financials often based on IAS/IFRS (IFC-Hawkamah, 2007). Used IFRS are, however, very often lacking updates. According to the 2007 survey, 75.7 percent of the respondents cited that they prepare their accounts in accordance with IFRS and the other are working on converging them toward it.[17] Table 12.4 gives the list of MENA countries using or converting to IFRS.

It seems that the overall trend is toward convergence with IFRS. In Saudi Arabia, for instance, the national standards are consistent with the IAS (Sourial, 2003). Similarly the Egyptian Accounting Standards are continuously updated to be consistent with the IAS. In Lebanon a ministerial order of 1996, requires conformity with IAS for most companies. Generally, however, convergence with IFRSs may pose a certain cultural problem. Haidar (2006) advocates the right for MENA states, along with others, regardless of their representation status on the IASB, to bring up their concerns and discuss them with the IASB.[18]

Despite the obvious fact that culture particularities and family ownerships, make it more challenging for the MENA accountants to adopt international standards, their quality may not be subject to any concern (Sourial 2003). Most countries are working on upgrading progressively their standards in compliance with the IFRS. Usually, the quality of disclosed information is a function of sound accounting and auditing practices and the adequacy of a regulatory framework for the profession.

With regard to auditing, the appointment of a statutory auditor, elected by the shareholders at the general shareholders' meeting and to be reported on the annual financial statements of the company, is required from corporations by most MENA countries' legislations. The statutory auditor is granted all discretion in delimiting the scope of the statutory audit and the form and content of the report. Currently, however, audit assignments are frequently restricted to the certification of the financial statements, based on their concordance to the accounting records, even in the case of large companies. The review also assesses the compliance with existing national accounting standards and/or with IFRS. The auditor's report itself may vary from a short statement to a lengthy commentary on the financial statements. It contains, in some cases, critical analysis of the accounts and a sample of accounting records. Companies may also, from time to time, call upon the statutory auditor to issuing reports relating to exceptional events, affecting a company's chart and/or activities like, for instance, increases or decreases in capital, mergers, change in corporate name, objective, entity, etc. In addition to the statutory auditor, many corporations may have a professional accounting firm conducting an independent examination of the financial statements and to render an opinion as to their fairness.

Table 12.4 MENA exchanges

Exchange	Location	Founded	Listings	Link
Bourse d'Alger (Algeria)	Algiers			(French) Wikipedia article
Bahrain Stock Exchange (Bahrain)			50	BSE
Cairo and Alexandria Stock Exchange (Egypt)	Cairo Alexandria	1888	840	CASE
Iraq Stock Exchange (Iraq)	Baghdad			ISX
Amman Stock Exchange (Jordan)	Amman			ASE
Kuwait Stock Exchange (Kuwait)	Safat			KSE
Beirut Stock Exchange (Lebanon)	Beirut			BSE
Libyan Stock Exchange* (Libya)	Benghazi	Proposed		August 2006 – Article at Libyaninvestment.com
Casablanca Stock Exchange (Morocco)	Casablanca	1929	66	CSE
Muscat Securities Market (Oman)	Muscat			MSM
Palestine Securities Exchange (Palestinian National Authority)	Nablus			PSE
Doha Securities Market (Qatar)	Doha			DSM
Tadawul (Saudi Arabia)	Riyadh			Tadawul
Khartoum Stock Exchange (Sudan)	Khartoum			KhSE
Damascus Stock Exchange (Syria)	Damascus	Proposed		DSE article
Abu Dhabi Securities Market (UAE)	Abu Dhabi			ADSM
Dubai Financial Market	Dubai			DFM
Dubai International Financial Exchange	Dubai			DIFX

Disclosure of audited listed companies' financial and non-financial information, at least annually, is also required by all MENA exchanges' laws and regulations. In Egypt, for instance (Sourial 2003), listed companies are required by law to disclose all financial and non-financial information on a semi-annual basis and publish the information in two well-known newspapers.[19] The same requirement is in effect in most MENA countries. Furthermore, the new Listing and Delisting rules require listed companies to disclose information on a quarterly basis and to disclose any information about a transaction done by an insider and of any extraordinary event that might affect the company's status. Similarly, the 2003 Bahrain Monetary Agency, in a comprehensive Disclosure Standards, requires listed companies to disclose their information on a semi-annual basis, with regard to the disclosure of offerings and initial listings, periodic reporting, guidelines for transactions by insiders and other related practices. The Tunisian regulations require also from listed companies to submit semi-annual financial statements (www.bvmt.com.tn/, accessed 1 August 2007). In Oman, disclosure and transparency are regulated in both Capital Market Law and Code of Corporate Governance, and require publication of annual financial statements (www.msm.gov.om/, accessed 24 July 2007). Almost all MENA countries' regulations require the same level of transparency on the part of their listed companies.

Despite the amount of regulations, still the success of achieving objectives of timely disclosed information and transparency has not been fully observed in some MENA exchange markets. They still suffer from major delays in information disclosure and the information itself is not comprehensive enough and does not seem to guarantee enough efficient markets, for two main reasons: one concerns the quality of accounting and auditing standards adopted and the second has to do with the quality of the accounting and auditing profession. Indeed the standard setting process and the accounting profession need to be empowered and revitalized in most MENA countries and the questionable integrity has to be dealt with. It often hinders the development of the profession in accordance with the international practices.

Given the weaknesses of internal CG, MENA countries will have to turn to external governance mechanisms or market-based mechanisms, designed to reinforce the internal governance structure of the firm.[20] According to the OECD, the market for corporate control

> furnishes shareholders of listed companies with an increased possibility to tender to a hostile offer or when the company under-performs. The threat of hostile acquisitions of the shares in under-performing companies can influence managers' incentives to forego actions that have a detrimental effect on the performance of companies. Below-market performance may facilitate equity transactions that are large enough to change control and replace management.
>
> (OECD, 2006)

The MENA region has in fact some of the oldest exchanges in the world; the Cairo and Alexandria Stock Exchanges in Egypt, for instance, established in 1883 and 1903 respectively, and the Casablanca Exchange was created in the 1930s. However, MENA exchanges have experienced stagnation for more than half of century. As is obvious from Table 12.5[21] currently realizing their economic importance, most of the Arab countries have established stock markets and those that do not have them yet are in the process of establishing them.

Table 12.5 MENA countries exchange corporate models

Country	Governance model
Dubai	In Dubai, Exchange is an independent private company owned by its members and not for profit. The Dubai International Financial Center (DIFC) is established as a private entity governed according to the international practices. An independent sole regulator The Dubai Financial Services Authority regulates the Center.
Oman	The Minister of Commerce and Industry is chairman, and the executive president is responsible for operations.
Morocco	Morocco's ethical council for securities board (CDVM – the regulator) is chaired by the Minister of Finance and the board includes representatives from the Central Bank and other authorities.
Egypt	The Chairman of the Egyptian Capital Market Authority is assigned by the President and affiliated to the Minister of Foreign Trade. The board is assigned by a Prime Minister decree.
UAE	Chaired by the Minister of Commerce.
Bahrain	The Bahrain Monetary Agency is the country's Central Bank and sole regulator for the financial sector.
Saudi Arabia	Saudi Securities and Exchange Commission is governed by five commissioners appointed by a Royal Decree.
Jordan	In Jordan the Board is composed of five full time commissioners appointed by a Royal Decree. The ASE was established in March 1999 as a non-profit, private institution with administrative and financial autonomy. It is authorized to function as an exchange for the trading of securities. The exchange is governed by a seven-member board of directors. A chief executive officer oversees day-to-day responsibilities and reports to the board. The ASE membership is comprised of Jordan's 52 brokerage firms (http://en.wikipedia.org/wiki/Amman_Stock_Exchange).
Lebanon	The regulator is a committee established within the Exchanges, maintaining both the regulatory and the operational functions.
Kuwait	The regulator is a committee established within the Exchanges, maintaining both the regulatory and the operational functions.

Source: http://en.wikipedia.org/wiki/List_of_Mideast_stock_exchanges, as accessed 26 July 2007.

Most MENA exchanges are recovering, by registering significant increases during the last two decades. The importance of the Saudi market as a proportion of Gross Domestic Product (GDP), for instance, has increased from about 36.7 percent in 1990, to more than 73 percent in 2003. Total Value of Shares Traded reached over SR5.26 trillion, or US$1.40 trillion for the year 2006, compared to 0.23 trillion in 1995 (Saudi Arabia Stock Exchange "Tadawul" 2006 Annual Report).[22] The market capitalization of the Egyptian markets as a proportion of GDP also increased from 4.1 percent in 1990 to about 32.8 percent in 2003. Similarly, the Jordanian market's ratio increased from 49.7 percent to about 111.2 percent (Sourial 2003). Market capitalization remains small, however, for most MENA countries, in terms of GDP. In 2003, for example, this ratio was equal to 7.9 percent, 30.1 percent, 19.7 percent, 9.8 percent and 11.4 percent in the Lebanon, Morocco, Oman, Tunisia and UAE, respectively.

Weak market capitalizations are due to a limited number of listed companies in MENA exchanges. For example, the largest ten companies in the Jordanian capital market constitutes more than 60 percent of the capitalization of the whole market. In other words, Arab stock markets seem to be concentrated in terms of the market value of their listed companies. MENA markets are also opening up to foreign investors. Saudi Arabia allows foreign investors to participate in the securities market through investing in open-end mutual funds.[23] In 1997, the first special purpose vehicle or SPV was established to facilitate foreign portfolio investment in equities. Qatar, recently, allowed Gulf Cooperation Council (GCC) citizens and expatriates to invest in the Doha Securities Market and in September 2005 the Dubai International Financial Exchange (DIFX) opened. It aims to play the role of an international stock exchange between Western Europe and East Asia and its standards are comparable to those of leading international exchanges (New York, London and Hong Kong). (http://www.difx.ae/Public/home/home.htm, accessed 31 July 2007). The DIFX is gaining very quickly in international notoriety.

The number of listed companies is still very small in most MENA stock exchanges, with the exception of Jordan, other MENA countries largest companies[24] are not even listed on the stock exchange.[25] For instance, among the largest, only two companies are listed on the Saudi market, only three are listed on the Kuwaiti market, only one is listed on the Omani market,[26] and only two in Lebanon. In the UAE, most of the largest corporations are not listed as state-owned. Most of the large companies in Bahrain are, however, listed government companies. Few of the largest Moroccan companies are listed on the Casablanca stock exchange. As a consequence, boards of directors of some of the largest companies in the MENA region are mostly composed of government officials and/or rich family members (Sourial 2003).

Most MENA economies are dominated either by state-owned enterprises and/or by family-owned enterprises and this situation highlights the importance of CG in terms of its private and public sides. Indeed, if MENA economic performance was to improve, the issue of CG in its widest sense must be seriously addressed.

Boards of directors and committees

Efficient boards of directors are considered to be a fundamental internal CG mechanism, especially when external ones such as legal environment, enforcement and market discipline are not operating efficiently enough, for ensuring improved CG. We can commonly distinguish two fundamentally distinct board systems. The most common is the one-tier board which includes both executive and non-executive directors and the two-tier board, through which the tasks of management and supervision are split up by mandatory law.

Board power and responsibilities have been explicitly addressed in all rules and regulations that govern MENA companies, whether listed or not on stock exchanges. The board structure among MENA countries is definitely dominated by the one-tier structure; although some exceptions exist. The Moroccan model, for instance, is a two-tier board structure. In MENA countries, boards of directors are often dominated by controlling shareholders, often representing the interests of family and/or groups of families and close relatives. Board members are often controlling shareholders' relatives, or former high ranking government employees, who would not oppose managers, usually appointed by large blockholders who often have a strong or even dominant control over corporate fate and decisions. The separation of boards of directors from management is rarely encountered in most MENA countries, as boards of directors lack non-executive or independent directors representation (Shaker 2004). Very often the chairman of the board of directors is also the Chief Executive Officer (CEO) or a member of the top management team. On the other hand, given that outside directors are hardly accepted as members of the board, directors' remunerations are, therefore, determined by the board itself. Finally, Most MENA companies do not seem to have statutory rule preventing board members and managers from participating in decision making where conflict of interest may arise.[27]

Here also, however, things seem to move ahead, in Saudi Arabia, for instance, like in many MENA countries, there exists legislation providing guidance for the criteria of membership in Audit Committee. The definition of an independent non-executive director seems to pose a certain problem in certain MENA countries, especially environments where rich families play an important role in developing businesses (Sourial, 2003). Recently, much legislation starts dealing with the issue of committees of the board. The Bahrain Monetary Agency recently regulated board committees and senior management responsibilities. The Omani Corporate Governance Code regulates the structure and the responsibilities of the board, ensures fair representation and organizes the function of subcommittees especially the Audit Committee. The Egyptian Company Law[28] regulates board structure, responsibilities and the new Listing and Delisting Rules elaborates practices within the framework of CG. The Audit Committee has to be formed from three independent non-executive directors appointed by the board. Similar provisions exist in most MENA countries' legislation. The Lebanese Code of Commerce regulating the board of directors does not, however, make it explicitly mandatory for the establishment of an Audit Committee.[29]

Currently, the provision that allows minority shareholders to protect their interest by electing some board members such as cumulative voting does not exist and the separation of chairman and CEO functions is not an easy task in an environment dominated by family companies.[30] According to the Lebanese Code of Commerce, for instance, the chairman of the board of directors shall execute the duties of general manager unless he appointed a person as a general manager to act on his behalf. In Oman, however, it has been clearly stated in the Code of Corporate Governance[31] that the role of the CEO/General Manager and chairman shall not be combined.

The Majority of MENA boards consist of non-executive and independent elements representing 68 percent, have one or no independent directors and 54.7 per cent have one or no executive directors (IFC-Hawkamah, 2007). In MENA companies, being a shareholder seems to be the key criteria for a board seat

(68.8 percent), over integrity, qualification, etc. While 79.1 percent of boards have an Audit Committee, only 22.4 percent is independent (IFC-Hawkamah, 2007).

The position of the CEO and chairman are often combined in MENA countries and the board is unable to provide an independent oversight because of the lack of an outside perspective in terms of strategic guidance. Boards are seldom evaluated. In fact, more than 80 percent of respondents do not perform any board evaluation. Consequently, "strengthening the functions and duties of the boards of directors is requiring special attention in all MENA countries" (IFC-Hawkamah, 2007).

MENA countries regulatory frameworks and CG codes

The regulatory framework analysis, may allow unearthing several fundamental elements with regard to CG. No doubt, there have recently been serious efforts to improve CG in MENA countries and attempts to converge on the OECD principles are gaining amplitude and efficiency. The result is that most MENA countries are experiencing deep transformations in their national CG systems The OECD Principles were originally endorsed by OECD Ministers in 1999 and updated in 2004. They have since become an international benchmark for policy makers, investors, corporations and other stakeholders worldwide. Also, in recent years many MENA countries were seeking the restoration and the promotion of investor confidence in their financial markets and three governance models can be observed (Sourial, 2003):

i   a governmental entity with representation of members of the exchange in the board;
ii non-profit privately owned exchange; and
iii a for-profit privately owned corporation exchange model.

The MENA newly formed regulatory bodies adopted some combinations of the governance models cited, as indicated by Table 12.6.[32,33]

Table 12.6 Minority shareholder protection in MENA countries (on a scale of 1 to 5, with 5 means fully compliant)

	Bahrain	*Kuwait*	*Oman*	*Qatar*	*Saudi Arabia*	*UAE*
Minority shareholder protection	2.0	4.0	3.0	2.5	3.5	2.5
Voting rights	1.5	3.5	3.5	2.5	2.0	3.5
Company capital structure	1.5	4.5	1.0	2.0	5.0	2.0
Shareholder meetings/ other rights	3.0	3.5	3.5	3.0	3.0	2.5

Implementing CG in the MENA region faces, however, two major impediments (Saidi, 2004). First, governments and policy makers tend to consider that legislation is the only way out. Second, there is as well an excessive import of the so called "best practices" without adaptation to local conditions and institutions. Third, the majority of the legal systems in MENA countries follow the civil code and it is believed that such a code may prevent reform (Sourial, 2003). The judiciary system may have a determinant role to play in enforcing CG and MENA judiciary regimes are in need of a profound restructuring. In most MENA countries the government exchange corporate model seems to be the dominating model. Regardless, however, of the regulatory governance model adopted, it is usually stated explicitly in laws and exchange charts that the regulatory body is an independent entity. It is, for instance, formerly stated that the Dubai International Foreign Exchange (DIFX) is a company limited by shares. The Kuwait Stock Exchange also enjoys an independent judicial personality and so to the Amman Stock Exchange (ASE). Indeed, the ASE was established from the beginning (March 1999) as a non-profit, private institution with administrative and financial autonomy (www.ase.com.jo/, as accessed 2 August 2007). However, complete independence "à la SEC" is far from being fully encountered in MENA countries, like elsewhere. Some MENA countries are, however, starting to have unified regulatory agencies for their financial sectors.

Like in most developing countries, MENA countries face the major problem of legal enforcement and accountability. Companies and securities laws have, of course, to be updated and modernized, but more importantly, enforcement of existing laws has to be strengthened. Most MENA countries have, for instance, laws prohibiting corruption and giving and/or receiving bribes are subject to potential harsh penalties, and yet, such laws have, in fact, hardly been enforced. MENA countries have, however, recently engaged themselves in ambitious CG reforms. Most MENA countries, while submitting themselves to ROSC, have also developed their own respective CG code with technical support from the International Finance Corporation (IFC) the Global Corporate Governance Forum and the OECD.

All MENA CG codes use the OECD principles[34] as benchmarks and when compared to world average CG indicators, some MENA countries score well above with regard to the respect of OECD principles (Tarif, 2005).

The MENA region's CG systems, an evaluation

The MENA region, as a specific environment, historically, culturally and economically speaking, faces, nowadays, many challenges in the field of CG. The situation is, however, changing and rather rapidly. The following results from IFC-Hawkamah 2007 survey of 11 MENA countries with stock exchanges (Morocco, Tunisia, Egypt, Jordan, Lebanon, West Bank, Bahrain, Kuwait, Oman, Saudi Arabia and the UAE) confirm this wind of change. Minority shareholders seem to be normally protected in most countries in the sample (IFC-Hawkamah, 2007) (see Table 12.7).

Table 12.7 Structure and responsibilities of the board of directors in MENA countries (on a scale of 1 to 5, with 5 means fully compliant)

	Bahrain	Kuwait	Oman	Qatar	Saudi Arabia	UAE
Structure and responsibilities of the board of directors	2.0	1.5	3.5	1.5	2.0	1.5
Board structure	1.0	1.5	3.5	1.5	1.0	1.0
Disclosure	4.0	3.5	5.0	1.5	4.0	3.5
Others	1.0	0.5	2.5	0.5	2.5	0.0

Table 12.8 Accounting and auditing in MENA countries (on a scale of 1 to 5, with 5 means fully compliant)

	Bahrain	Kuwait	Oman	Qatar	Saudi Arabia	UAE
Accounting and auditing	2.0	2.5	4.0	2.0	2.5	2.0
Standards	3.0	3.5	3.5	3.0	3.5	2.5
Audit committee	0.5	0.0	5.0	0.0	0.0	0.0

Table 12.9 Transparency of ownership and control in MENA countries (on a scale of 1 to 5, with 5 means fully compliant)

	Bahrain	Kuwait	Oman	Qatar	Saudi Arabia	UAE
Transparency of ownership and control	2.5	3.5	3.5	1.0	4.5	2.5

Concerning the structure and responsibilities of the boards of directors in MENA countries, Table 12.7 indicates that most countries of the sample perform poorly at this level, except for disclosure activity.

With regard to accounting and auditing, Table 12.8 indicates that countries of the survey score rather well with regard to accounting and auditing standards, and poorly with regard to the Audit Committee efficiency.

Concerning transparency of ownership and control, Table 12.9 indicates an acceptable score for all countries surveyed, except for Qatar, accusing a score of 1 out of 5.

With regard to the regulatory framework, Table 12.10 indicates that the regulatory environment is less than performing, except for Oman.

Table 12.10 Regulatory environment in MENA countries (on a scale of 1 to 5, with 5 means fully compliant)

	Bahrain	Kuwait	Oman	Qatar	Saudi Arabia	UAE
Regulatory environment	2.0	2.0	4.5	2.5	2.5	2.0

Table 12.11 Overall assessment of CG in MENA countries (on a scale of 1 to 5, with 5 means fully compliant)

	Bahrain	Kuwait	Oman	Qatar	Saudi Arabia	UAE
Overall assessment	2	3	3.5	2	3	2

The overall assessment is given by Table 12.11. Three countries out of six surveyed have CG in the average, while the other three locate well under the average.

The top three barriers to CG, the lack of a qualified specialist to help with implementation is advance by 53.6 percent of the respondents; the lack of information or know-how is pointed out by 37.7 percent and the lower priority of CG in relation to other operate tasks is cited by 24.6 percent of the respondents.

This weak CG situation was corroborated by the 2003 WB report on CG in the MENA region and also confirmed by the Union of Arab Banks, in a 2003 study entitled "Corporate Governance in Public Listed Companies in some MENA Countries," namely Jordan, Lebanon, Kuwait, Saudi Arabia and the UAE. The main findings are:[35] first, the high concentration in corporate ownership undermines good CG principles. Second, substantial family corporate holdings are composing the bulk of company ownership and control, mainly banks and financial institutions. Third, boards of directors are dominated by controlling shareholders, while friends and relatives constitute the board of directors in many instances. Four, there is rarely any separation between ownership and management and it is rare to find independent directors among board members. In most companies the chairman of the board is also the CEO. Fifth, CG is not a priority in most companies, which are lacking transparency and disclosure. The situation results in nepotism and corruption.

Strengthening the functions and duties of the boards of directors, is one priority and implementing market-based CG is yet another. Available capital in the MENA region is huge but mainly committed to real state or invested abroad. Family ownership is the dominant form and major shareholders and related parties have often, in the past, exercised the greatest resistance to change, in spite of the benefits, which can be brought about by well-functioning markets and governing bodies and improvement of the framework regarding director qualifications and independence; and establishing specialized board committees.

Conclusion

MENA countries' economies are undergoing a number of CG reforms and the restructuring of legislature and infrastructure. The CG debate has mostly focused on listed companies, although in MENA countries market discipline, with its various tools, is still not yet developed to an extent that improves CG practices. MENA stock markets[36] are either inefficient or weakly efficient (World Bank, 2006b). Instead family businesses are still the backbone of the MENA countries' economies and will be so for a long period of time.

The challenges of MENA CG reside in extending the debate to non-listed companies and less developed equity markets (OECD, 2006). Indeed, the major challenge of MENA CG reform is to craft CG principles that reinforce corporate mechanisms without impeding the development of family businesses. Regardless, however, of the model chosen, CG practices will be reached only when people are convinced of their rightness and capitalize on trusts, confidence and general well-being.

Notes

1 According to the IMF classification of the MENA region comprises of 24 countries; adding Mauritania, Somalia, Afghanistan and Pakistan. Other definitions would include Iran and Israel.
2 Recent research documents that common law countries have stronger investor protection laws and more developed financial markets than civil law countries (La Porta *et al.*, 1997b, 1998).
3 Corporate Governance: Observance of Standards and Codes http://rru.worldbank.org/GovernanceReports/.
4 All WB member countries are eligible for ROSC.
5 Algeria, Egypt, Jordan, Morocco, Tunisia and the UAE.
6 The International Finance Corporation is the private sector arm of the World Bank Group.
7 Morocco, Tunisia, Egypt, Jordan, Lebanon, West Bank, Bahrain, Kuwait, Oman, Saudi Arabia and UAE.
8 We can distinguish a variety of non-listed companies, such as family-owned companies, state-owned companies, group-owned companies, private investor-owned companies, joint ventures and mass-privatized companies.
9 Nevertheless, MENA family-owned non-listed companies do not fit into a single mould.
10 Other mechanisms may include trust and reputation concerns.
11 Shareholder participation is passive, and legal protection for shareholders is inadequate.
12 Corporations usually build long-lasting close relations with banks and the recourse to securities markets as an alternate channel of financing is not even considered.
13 WB tool.
14 www.ifac.org/About/MemberBodies.tmpl.
15 Egypt Company Law 159/1981, the Companies Law 22/1997, etc.
16 Ibid.
17 Most MENA countries are also members of the IFAC.
18 One of his concerns is IAS 24, requiring all the transactions with "close family members of a related party" to be disclosed.
19 Few of them require the disclosure on quarterly basis.
20 The road, however, is at risk of being full of ambushes.

21 http://en.wikipedia.org/wiki/List_of_Mideast_stock_exchanges (accessed 30 June 2007).
22 www.tadawul.com.sa/ (accessed 31 July 2007).
23 Ibid.
24 Which includes Bahrain, Lebanon, Egypt, Kuwait, Morocco, Oman, Saudi Arabia and the UAE.
25 ASE has 17 listed companies which are among the largest 20 in the country.
26 The largest companies in these countries include the Arabian Oil Co. (Aramco), Saudi Basic Industries (Sabic), the Kuwait Petroleum Corporation (KPC) and the Oman Oil Company. The net worth of some of the privately held family businesses is totaling billions of dollars.
27 According to the Lebanese 2003 survey, 51 percent of the Lebanese companies fall in this category.
28 Egyptian Law # 159/198157.
29 The Lebanese Code allows the chairman of the board to appoint a consultative committee.
30 In some cases laws might prohibit the concept of separation such as in Lebanon
31 Article No. 3.
32 Ibid.
33 The Kuwait Stock Exchange shall enjoy an independent judicial personality with the right of litigation in a mode facilitating the performance of its functions for the purpose of realizing the objectives of its organization in the best manner within the scope of regulations and laws governing the Stock Exchange operations. www.kuwaitse.com/PORTAL/KSE/About.aspx.
34 www.eldis.org/static/DOC15957.htm.
35 Union of Arab Banks Report 2003.
36 Stock exchanges have been the focal point for CG reform in many developed economies.

13 EU corporate governance system

A. Naciri

Introduction

Good corporate governance (CG) is certainly important to the European Union (EU) from the perspective of both internal efficiency and globalization. European firms, submitted to different legal CG systems, should be able to compete with well-governed international companies. For this reason the European Council has set up as a priority the improvement of CG of European corporations, as a means of attracting to Europe, the so precious international capital.

The recent collapse, due to a lack of CG, of large companies, both US and non-US, has fuelled the European worries about CG. Financial markets, on the other hand, are pushing European companies, more than anybody else, to give priority to a governance approach based on shareholder supremacy. Proponents of such governance approach is advocating that corporations applying a CG model focusing on the "market," as the leading mechanism of CG, have a clear competitive advantage. CG is, therefore, of increasing importance for investment decisions in Europe. The EU has, therefore, launched on 21 May 2003, an Action Plan "Modernizing Company Law and Enhancing Corporate Governance in the European Union – A Plan to Move Forward"[1] (Action Plan). Although the EU does not see the need for a European Corporate Governance Code it is hardly working for the development of a strong and reliable European model of CG and which should essentially be enshrined in European and national legislation.

The EU CG initiative is mainly inspired by the US legislation which, in fact, sets the scene for the most important national CG systems in the world. The Sarbanes–Oxley Act (SOX)[2] has particularly set a pace against which Community legislation has found a proper response for promoting its own CG system. This chapter discusses such CG systems.

European CG framework

The EU has shown recently a strong determination in playing a major role in CG. Especially since its study of the 27 March 2002: "Comparative Study of

Corporate Governance Codes relevant to the European Union and its Member States," which underlines:

> the need to improve the corporate governance framework in the European Union. A series of corporate governance codes have indeed been adopted over the past decade with the aim of better protecting the interests of share-holders and/or stakeholders. Although these codes seemed to have some basic principles in common [...] they spring from long-standing legal and socio-economic national traditions.
>
> (EU, 2007b)

The EU is currently requiring from its Member States, through its multiple legislations, the improvement of CG by making appropriated changes in their respective company laws, securities laws or codes of CG. Such co-ordination is expected to facilitate the convergent Member States governance initiatives, or, at least, to avoid unnecessary divergences and such co-ordination is extended to monitoring and enforcement procedures. Although the European Commission (the Commission) believes that good and transparent CG are essential for enhancing competitiveness and efficiency of businesses, as well as strengthening shareholders rights in the EU, it was not until September 2001 that a European high level group of company law experts was set up to make recommendations on a modern regulatory framework for company law. This expert mandate was further extended to a number of CG issues. The group comprises twenty non-governmental individuals from various professional backgrounds (issuers, investors, employees' representatives, academics, regulated professions, etc.) with particular experience and knowledge of the subject. On May 2003 and based on the group of experts work (report of 4 November 2002), the Commission adopted its Action Plan entitled "Modernising Company Law and Enhancing Corporate Governance in the European Union – A Plan to Move Forward."

The Action Plan identified a series of actions that have to be undertaken for modernizing and simplifying the regulatory framework and CG in the EU. Among a range of proposals we can underline the strengthening of shareholders' rights, the modernization of the board of directors, the regulation of directors' remuneration and the creation of a European Corporate Governance Forum. This forum would serve as a body for exchange of information and best practices existing in Member States in order to enhance the convergence of national codes of CG. It would as well serve as a body for reflection, debate and advice to the Commission in the field of CG. The Action Plan received the ascent of the European Parliament, in its Resolution of 21 April 2004, where it expressed strong support for most of the initiatives announced and also called on the Commission to propose rules to eliminate and prevent conflicts of interest. The European Parliament stressed in particular the need for listed companies to have an audit committee whose function should include overseeing the external auditor's independence, objectivity and effectiveness.

Since the adoption of the Action Plan in May 2003, the commission has issued a number of directives, recommendations, regulations and studies to promote CG within the EU. Table 13.A1 gives the list of some European legal sources, regarding CG. These sources constitute real European framework for an effective EU CG system, which seems to be based on the following theoretical foundations:

i   "Consensus," always seeking agreement among Member States.
ii "Principle-based approach," EU CG initiative rejects adoption of detailed binding rules, given the complexity of the issue.
iii "Comply or explain," where companies are invited to disclose whether they comply with any national code and to explain any material departures from it.[3]

By opting for a principle-based approach of developing CG guidelines, the EU model departs seemingly from the American system but gets close to other Anglo-Saxon systems like the Canadian or the Australian. Full transparency, efficient disclosure, distinction between executive and non-executive, independence of board members and auditors, etc. are all part of the menu and also borrowed from the SOX. The EU seems also having opted for an approach of CG based on market primacy, also known as the CG shareholder model, usually contrasted with stakeholder models. The distinguishing criterion here, according to some, is not whether or not ultimate control lies with the shareholders, but rather what was needed to enable a company to maximize its profits in the long run and perform optimally while respecting its social and economic obligations alike.

Market primacy approach, however, requires conditions that can only be met in very few economic environments even in Anglo-Saxon environments (if not, in only the American environment) and such an approach to CG is questionable. According to Aoki (2000a, 2001) and Rajan and Zingales (1998b), it "is neither a necessary condition, nor a sufficient one."

The EU, however, seems to send a mixed signal. Indeed, in a communication from the Commission on 22 March 2006 to the European Parliament, the Council and the European Economic and Social Committee, proposed to promote corporate social responsibility (CSR) in the EU and globally.

> The Communication sends a message to businesses to play a part in the partnership for growth and jobs. It gives its political support to the creation of a European Alliance on CSR. It also sets priorities with regard to CSR and announces a series of measures to achieve them, including cooperation with Member States, support for multi-stakeholder initiatives, research, SMEs and global action.
>
> (Council and the European Economic and Social
> Committee (COM, 2006, p. 136))[4]

Most CG codes adopted recently in Member States tend to rely on disclosure to encourage compliance, based on the "comply or explain" approach where companies are invited to disclose whether they comply with the code and to explain any material departures from it. The EU believes the adoption of detailed binding rules is not desirable due to the complexity of CG issues and disparity of Member States. The European CG Forum recently confirms the EU "comply or explain" orientation for CG. For this approach, however, to be effective the forum underlines that there has to be: a real obligation to comply or explain.[5]

Shareholders rights and equitable treatment

In an appropriate system of CG, shareholders are supposed to have the upper hand and effective means to actively exercise their influence over the company's fate. The 2003 Action Plan proposed to carry out a study on the deviations from the principle of proportionality between capital and control existing in the Member States of the EU. Stakeholders confirmed the need for such a study in their response to the spring 2006 consultation conducted on the future priorities of the Action Plan,[6] commissioned by the EU and entitled "Proportionality[7] between ownership and control in EU listed companies." The study shows that numerous irritants are still preventing European shareholders from exercising efficiently their rights.

The quite diverse legal systems of the jurisdictions within Europe constitute one reason preventing European shareholders from exercising efficiently their rights. CEMs or "Control Enhancing Mechanisms" always appear to be at the juncture of two principles: the comparatively new proportionality principle, or "one share, one vote" principle (OSOV) and the traditional freedom of contract principle, The proportionality principle is defined by the Commission as the "proportionate allocation between ownership and control" and in this context, "Ownership,"[8] is defined as "cash flow rights." On the other hand, while most of the countries in the sample provide companies with relative freedom to implement certain CEMs if they so desire, not all companies choose to exercise such freedom.

The other irritant preventing European shareholders from exercising efficiently their rights may be found in Table 13.1, based on the 2007 EU commissioned study. This table provides the availability and actual utilization rates of the CEMs, as well as their ranking.

The study confirms the extensive use of CEMs within Member States. It indicates that pyramid structure (Legally permitted) is used in 75 percent of all the countries participating in the survey, and so non-voting shares implemented in 12 percent of these countries. Multiple voting right shares are also legally available in 53 percent of the countries and effectively implemented in 50 percent of them. Voting right ceilings are available in 58 percent of the countries and so ownership ceilings, one of the most ancient mechanisms providing for the decoupling of ownership and control is available in 42 percent of the countries. Cross-shareholdings are legally available in 100 percent of all the countries that participated in this study and actually implemented in

Table 13.1 Ranking of CEMs in Europe – summary

	Ranking	Available CEMs (%)	Actually CEMs (%)
Pyramid structure	1	100	75
Shareholders' agreements	1	100	69
Supermajority provisions	1	87	NA
Cross-shareholdings	2	100	31
Non voting preference shares	3	81	44
Voting right ceilings	4	69	56
Priority shares	5	56	12
Multiple voting rights shares	6	50	44
Golden shares	7	44	31
Partnerships limited by shares	7	44	0
Depository certificates	7	44	6
Ownership ceilings	8	37	25
Non voting shares	9	31	6

Source: Shearman & Sterling LLP (2007), "Proportionality between ownership and control in EU listed companies: External study commissioned by the European Commission."

only 31 percent of all those countries. Golden shares are legally available in 42 percent of all the countries studied and actually implemented in only 10 percent of all the analyzed companies. Shareholders' agreements are legally available in 100 percent of all of the countries and are present in 69 percent of the countries. Finally, depository certificates are only legally available in 26 percent of the countries and are only significantly present in the Dutch companies.

The previous picture invites for action on the part of EU. The latter, after it carried out two public consultations, proposed on 5 January 2006 a Directive which was formally adopted in June 2007. The Directive aims at ensuring that shareholders have timely access to the complete information relevant to general meetings and facilitates the exercise of voting rights by proxy. Furthermore, the directive provides for the replacement of share blocking and related practices through a record date system (EU site, accessed July 2007). Member States differ significantly, however, with respect to the regulation of shareholder rights, due, at least in part, to differences in markets, culture and shareholder behavior. Unfortunately, EU efforts on shareholders empowerment and protection, have concentrated on selected issues and in areas like communication, general meetings, cross-border voting, responsibilities of institutional investors and the right to apply for investigation and neglect shareholders awareness and responsibility, for instance.

In the area of communication, the new European legislation requires the following from all European listed companies:

i   the publication of all information relevant to their shareholders on their Internet site;

ii the obligation to offer all of their shareholders possibilities to vote without being present, using electronic supports;
iii the possibility to authorize their shareholders who are not physically present to take part in general meetings using electronic access (Internet, satellite, etc.);
iv effective communication between a company and its shareholders prior to a general meeting, including sending notices of such a meeting;
v   the preparation of a registered share system.

Listed companies can maintain a specific section on their website where they can publish all information they are required to file and publish.

With regard to the general meeting, as a physical gathering of shareholders who discuss and decide the future of their company, the EU CG system takes a number of initiatives to reinforce shareholders in their right and decision-making role. Vote in absentia by direct vote or proxies and the use of electronic support are but a few of the avenues explored by the EU to achieve shareholders' effective participation in corporate decision making.

Investors in European listed companies may face additional problems if they reside in countries other than where the company is registered. In these cross-border situations, where shares are held through chains of intermediaries, cross-border voting issues arise and the EU is searching for appropriate solutions.

Where commonly, in companies with dispersed ownership, shareholders can present little countervailing power against management, the rise of institutional investment may have changed the situation significantly. They are increasingly inclined to actively engage in internal control within corporations and this creates a new agency problem for the EU CG system. Regulation of institutional investors is suggested and it is assumed to include disclosure obligations with regard to investment policy, voting policy, beneficial holders and on request voting records.

Responsible shareholders are expected to take time to study issues debated in general meetings and carefully weigh the relevant information before deciding how to vote. Informed shareholders are, of course, desirable from a social point of view, it is not clear, however, that individuals will find it personally desirable to become business-like informed and the reason has to do with cost. Many corporate issues are complicated, and a great deal of technical knowledge and information is necessary to make an informed judgment on them and this is the cost that each shareholder has to pay personally for the benefits of being corporately informed, and many are not ready to pay it. This is what has come to be known as "rational apathy." Some believe that when the cost of acquiring information is greater than the benefits to be derived from the information, it might be rational to stay ignorant.

Consequently, despite all efforts of facilitating participation in shareholders meetings and voting, many shareholders will still refrain from doing so,[9] because of so-called "rational apathy," a kind of rational ignorance preventing many shareholders from exercising their votes.

Disclosure and transparency

The EU is striving toward improving public confidence in financial statements. Financial statements must be comparable across the EU to benefit integration of European capital markets. Financial statements quality is indeed at the heart of the concerns raised by corporate scandals. Most regulatory responses are focused on ensuring that financial statements correctly reflect the financial position of the company and are not manipulated, whether or not to the personal benefits of directors or block-holders. The Commission is convinced that "transparency about publicly traded companies is essential for the functioning of capital markets, enhancing their overall efficiency and liquidity" (Directive 2001/34/EC). Basis for transparency and adequate financial reporting in Europe were originally laid down by the Fourth Council Directive 78/660/EEC of 25 July 1978 and the Seventh Council Directive 83/349/EEC of 13 June 1983. Both directives were based on Article 54 (3) (g) of the European Treaty,

The Fourth Directive entitled "The Annual Accounts of Certain Types of Companies" states that:

> annual accounts must give a true and fair view of a company's assets and liabilities, financial position and profit or loss; whereas to this end a mandatory layout must be prescribed for the balance sheet and the profit and loss account and whereas the minimum content of the notes on the accounts and the annual report must be laid down.
>
> (78/660/EEC)

Whereas the Seventh Directive entitled "Consolidated Accounts Deals with Disclosure of Transactions between a Company and the Company's Affiliated Undertakings," dealing with consolidated financial statements, specifies that:

> Consolidated accounts must give a true and fair view of the assets and liabilities, the financial position and the profit and loss of all the undertakings consolidated taken as whole.

Also,

> a number of principles relating to the preparation of consolidated accounts and valuation in the context of such accounts must be laid down in order to ensure that items are disclosed consistently, and may readily be compared not only as regards the methods used in their valuation but also as regards the periods covered by the accounts.
>
> (83/349/EEC)

Additionally, the Directive of the European Parliament of the Council of 26 March 2003 entitled: "Harmonization of Transparency Requirements with Regard to Information about Issuers whose Securities are Admitted to Trading on a Regulated Market" and amending Directive 2001/34/EC, Imposes a new level of information transparency commensurate with the aims of sound investor protection and market efficiency. Its broad objective is enhancing EU requirements in the form of standardized interim, annual information or on ongoing basis information. It calls, for instance, for:

i   the improvement of periodic disclosure of share issuers over a financial year;
ii the introduction of half-yearly financial reporting to issuers who are currently not subject to any interim reporting requirement;
iii the on-going disclosure of changes to important shareholdings;
iv the adoption of capital market thinking.

On the other hand, the 27 October 2004 Directive of the European Parliament and Council, amending the Fourth and Seventh Directives calls for further enhancement of transparency and therefore confidence in the financial statements and annual reports published by European companies. Specifically by:

i   establishing collective responsibility of board members;
ii enhancing transparency about related parties' transactions;
iii enhancing transparency about off-balance arrangements; and
iv introducing a CG statement.

In line with what is currently prevailing in most national CG systems the responsibility of financial statements quality in the European Community (EC) rests collectively with all board members.[10] More precisely in a one-tier structure, this is a collective responsibility of both executive and non-executive directors, and in a two-tier structure, this is the collective responsibility of both the managing directors and the supervisory directors. Such responsibility also covered all statements regarding the company's financial position and covered other financial information such as "a description of the group's internal control and risk management systems in relation to the process for preparing consolidated accounts" (2004/0250). More important, Member States are responsible for laying down penalties and criminal sanctions to insure the implementation. As a rule the Commission proposes collective board responsibility and more disclosure on transactions, off-balance sheet vehicles and CG.

For further improvement of transparency and reporting quality, the EU has opted for International Financial Reporting Standards (IFRS). From 2005 onward all European listed companies, including banks and insurance are required to submit to IFRS financial statements.[11]

In order to contribute to a better functioning of the internal market, publicly traded companies must be required to apply a single set of high quality international accounting standards for the preparation of their consolidated financial statements. Furthermore, it is important that the financial reporting standards applied by Community companies participating in financial markets are accepted internationally and are truly global standards. This implies an increasing convergence of accounting standards currently used internationally with the ultimate objective of achieving a single set of global accounting standards.

(Regulation (EC) No 1606/2002)

The EU, however, may be facing some challenges at the level of IFRS application. It seems to have decided to rely on IFRS, conditional that the International Accounting Standards Board (IASB) will be more attentive to its specific needs. The EU is loudly expressing its desire of recovering more influence within the IASB decision-making process. Europeans appear to be especially frustrated by the IASB refusal to give them enough seats within its actual 14 member board. Such demand is met, till now, with skeptical refusal. The IASB is advocating, for motivating its refusal, that financial information should never be considered on political grounds, but rather on economic grounds, especially on the criteria of investor information needs. The IASB always estimates that the only way of defending its rational accounting policies is by keeping away from political pressures and it is convinced that taking into account geographical or sectarian differences would harm its international vocation.

Auditing practices

Recent financial scandals have revealed that a proper audit of financial statements of the company is a fundamental element of a CG system. Audit, in an appropriate form, is also an important safeguard in non-financial reporting. A proper audit depends on the role and performance of the external auditor, as well as the internal audit process of the company. The EU directives call for new levels of auditor efficiency and require certification of internal audit work by external auditors.

In fact, the European Commission has always put a tremendous emphasis on the quality of consolidated financial statements or consolidated accounts, published by European companies and that must be audited by qualified persons. The EC efforts toward the attainment of such objectives were as consistent as continuous. As mentioned before, starting in 1978, the EC dealt with the issue of certain companies accounts (the Fourth Council Directive 78/660/EEC). In 1983 it dealt with the issue of consolidated accounts (the Seventh Council Directive 83/349/EEC). Conditions for approving persons responsible for carrying out the statutory audit were laid down in 1984 (in the Eighth Council Directive 84/253/EEC). The issue of the annual accounts and consolidated accounts of banks and other financial institutions was dealt with in 1986 (Council Directive 86/635/EEC) and so consolidated accounts of insurances in 1991 (Council Directive 91/674/EEC).

It was, however, not until 1998 that, faced with the absence of a European harmonized approach to statutory auditing, the Commission recommended the creation of the "Committee on Auditing" responsible for developing further action in close co-operation with the accounting profession and Member States.[12] The Commission took charge again in 2000, by issuing its Recommendation on "Quality Assurance for the Statutory Audit in the European Union: Minimum Requirements" and again in 2002, by issuing its Recommendation on "Statutory Auditors' Independence in the EU: A Set of Fundamental Principles." Not yet fully satisfied the harmonization level of statutory audit requirements with Europe, the Commission, reacted again in 2006, by adopting its Directive on "Statutory Audits of Annual Accounts and Consolidated Accounts" (Directive 2006/43/EC), amending previous directives on the issue, notably Council Directives 78/660/EEC and 83/349/EEC and repealing Council Directive 84/253/EEC. It aims at a high-level harmonization of statutory audit requirements in Europe. This recent Directive deals with issues like:

 i audit qualification and approbation of statutory auditors (Article 6);
 ii adequate knowledge of statutory auditors and test (Article 7);
 iii registration of statutory auditors (Article 8);
 iv statutory auditors adhesion to the highest ethical standards[13] (Article 9);
 v strict rules on confidentiality and professional secrecy (Article 10);
 vi independent requirement for statutory auditors and audit firms (Article 11);
 vii international auditing standard adoption (Article 14);
 viii statutory auditors and audit firms responsibilities and liabilities (Article 19);
 ix effective system of public oversight for statutory auditors and audit firms on the basis of home country control (Article 20);
 x appointment by the general meeting of shareholders or members of the audited entity (Article 22).

The reinforcement of auditors' independence is indeed a major concern to the European CG system. The Commission's Recommendation of 17 May 2006 deals with such subjects as the independence of statutory auditor. In this regard, statutory auditors cannot provide to issuing companies while serving as its auditor any advice or services which are not directly linked to the auditor's mission (separation of audit and consulting missions). These include:

 i bookkeeping or other services relating to the accounting records or financial statements of the audit client;
 ii financial information systems design and implementation;
 iii appraisal or evaluation services, fairness opinions or contribution-in-kind reports;
 iv actuarial services;
 v internal audit outsourcing services;
 vi management functions or human resources;
 vii broker or dealer, investment advisor, or investment banking services;
 viii legal services and expert services unrelated to the audit; and
 ix any other service that the Public Accounting Oversight Board (PACOB) determines, by regulation, is impermissible.

Statutory auditor is also forbidden from taking, receiving or holding, directly or indirectly, a share in the entity or controlled affiliate for which he is certifying accounts and he cannot be appointed manager for such a company less than five years after the end of his audit functions. The maximum mandate for a statutory auditor is six consecutive fiscal years.

Moreover in the Commission Decision of 14 December 2005, the European Commission set up a group of experts to advise the Commission and to facilitate co-operation between public oversight systems for statutory auditors and audit firms. The expert group is called the "European Group of Auditors' Oversight Bodies" (Article 1). Composed of high level representatives drawn from the public oversight systems for statutory auditors and audit firms in Member States, the "European Group of Auditors' Oversight Bodies" may be consulted by the Commission and may also discuss any matter relating to co-operation between public oversight systems for statutory auditors and audit firms. The group's tasks (2005/909/EC) are mainly to:

i   facilitate co-operation between public oversight systems of Member States and to bring about an exchange of good practice concerning the establishment and ongoing co-operation of such systems;
ii contribute to the technical assessment of public oversight systems of third countries and to the international co-operation between Member States and third countries in this area;
iii contribute to the technical examination of international auditing standards, including the processes for their elaboration, with a view to their adoption at the community level.

All discussed EC provisions are essentially aimed at avoiding having any phenomenon of the Enron type occurring, and are reinforced by the EU adoption of IFRS. In most national CG systems, the Audit Committee is usually set up for purposes of reinforcing the audit process and auditor independence, has a key role to play. The audit committee's roles and responsibilities cover the following areas: financial reporting, internal audit, external audit, and appointment of external auditors.

The board of directors

Board reform is at the core of EU CG initiative. Indeed, good CG requires a strong and balanced board as a monitoring body for the executive management of the company. According to the Combined Corporate Code on CG, published by the Institute of Chartered Accountants in England and Wales (ICAEW) in 2003,

> the board's role is to provide entrepreneurial leadership of the company within a framework of prudent and effective controls which enables risk to be assessed and managed. The board should set the company's strategic

aims, ensure that the necessary financial and human resources are in place for the company to meet its objectives and review management performance. The board should set the company's values and standards and ensure that its obligations to its shareholders and others are understood and met.

On the other hand a corporate director can be defined as an officer in charge with the corporation management and the conduct of its operations. Taken collectively corporate directors form the board of directors. In principle the board of directors holds its power from shareholders' general meeting. In companies with dispersed ownership, however, shareholders are usually unable to closely monitor management, its strategies and its performance for lack of information and resources. The role of non-executive directors is to fill this gap between the uninformed shareholders as principals and the fully informed executive managers as agents by monitoring the agents more closely.

The European Commission recommendation of 15 February 2005 specifies that:

> supervisory directors are recruited by companies for a variety of purposes. Of particular importance is their role in overseeing executive or managing directors and dealing with situations involving conflicts of interests.
>
> (2005/162/EC)

Recent corporate scandals have highlighted also in Europe issues related to board members' misconduct and thereby the need for the Commission to pursue its Action Plan and establish an EU-framework of collective responsibility for board members, including appropriate liability and sanctions. It is hence proposed to make sure that Member States guarantee that board members are collectively responsible at least toward the company. This should not prevent Member States from extending such collective responsibility for board members directly to shareholders and other stakeholders. Collective responsibility is also reinforced by EU legislation which calls Member States to have appropriate sanctions and civil liability rules for non-respect of the accounting rules for the purpose of underpinning the collective responsibility (Directives 78/660/EEC and 83/349/EEC).

With respect to the qualifications of directors, the EU system, like most national CG systems, insists on the importance of having qualified individuals sitting on the board, but at the same time recognize that the definition of what constitutes appropriate qualifications should be left with the company itself, because such qualifications depend on each company's conditions. There is, nevertheless, one issue which is of common concern to all organizations, namely the required competence of Audit Committee members where some of them should possess specific knowledge in financial information analysis. Most national CG systems also seek to make sure that directors devote sufficient time to their duties. In this regard all Member States company laws include general rules on the competence expected of directors. In order to align the interests of executive directors with the interests of shareholders, modern systems of remuneration usually include performance-related remuneration,[14] often through grants of shares, share options or other rights to acquire shares, or by payments which vary with the share price. The result is that the remuneration of executive directors to a certain extent is dependent on the share price.

Sound CG would require, however, that:

i   the board takes up a position that is independent, so as not to become a plaything of stock market forces;
ii the company's executives are subject to expert, independent supervision by non-executives and/or supervisors, who constitute a buffer between the management and shareholders;
iii these non-executives and/or supervisors are appointed in a manner that guarantees their expertise and independence from management and keeps them at arms' length from the stakeholders;

In most European countries, workers should also be given a clear role in the company's decision-making system.

With regard to risk management and effectiveness of internal controls, two major components of modern CG, first introduced by Section 404 of the SOX of 2002, the Forum recognizes that the general purpose of risk management and internal control, which is to manage the risks associated with the successful conduct of business, can be reached by different means: laws, regulations or corporate codes

> that there should be an adequate balance between the benefits of any additional requirements and the costs and other burdens for companies. Therefore, the Forum while confirming that companies' boards are responsible for monitoring the effectiveness of internal control systems considers that there is no need to introduce a legal obligation for boards to certify the effectiveness of internal controls at EU level.[15]
>
> (European CG Forum on Risk Management and Internal Control)

Independent directors and board committees

The presence of independent representatives on the board, capable of challenging the decisions of the management, is widely considered as a means of protecting the interests of shareholders and, where appropriate, other stakeholders. The Commission's Action Plan to modernize company law and enhance CG in the EU (May 2003) announced the adoption in the short term of a Commission Recommendation on the role in listed companies of (independent) non-executive or supervisory directors. EC recommendation of 6 October 2004 urges Member States to ensure a strong role for independent directors.

Directors' remuneration

The Commission Action Plan recognized the need for shareholders to be able to appreciate fully the relationship between the performance of the company and the level of remuneration of directors, both ex ante and ex post, and to make decisions on the remuneration items linked to the share price. The Commission recommended the adoption in the short term of a Commission recommendation which should promote the swift application of an appropriate regulatory regime for directors' remuneration.

Commission Recommendation of 14 December 2004 "Fostering an Appropriate Regime for the Remuneration of Directors of Listed Companies" (2004/913/EC) calls for a transparent and efficient disclosure of directors remuneration and compensation plans. The commission considers, indeed, that remuneration is one of the key areas where executive directors may have a conflict of interest. Remuneration systems should therefore be subjected to appropriate governance controls, based on adequate information rights. Such control may build sustained investor confidence and constitutes an important tool for promoting sound CG throughout the Community. To that end, it is important that listed companies display appropriate transparency in dealings with investors, so as to enable them to express their views. Shareholders should be provided with a clear and comprehensive overview of the company's remuneration policy. Such disclosure would enable shareholders to assess a company's approach to remuneration and strengthen a company's accountability to shareholders. It should include elements related to compensation. Adequate transparency should also be ensured in the policy regarding directors' contracts. The EC requires that:

> In order to give shareholders an effective chance to express their views and an opportunity to debate the remuneration policy on the basis of a comprehensive disclosure, without having to initiate the process of tabling a shareholders' resolution, the remuneration policy should be an explicit item on the agenda of the annual general meeting.
>
> (2004/913/EC)

Executive and non-executive directors

On 6 October 2004, the Commission, in a follow-up to the action plan it published in May 2003, considered that the board of directors should include a fair proportion of executive and non-executive directors in order to avoid one person or a small group of people could dominate the decision-making process within the board of directors. The provisions are based on three essential ideas:

i   introduction of a right to special investigation, under which shareholders may ask a judge for a special investigation into company affairs (European Commission Action Plan);

ii elaboration of a rule on punishable negligence for "wrongful trading" under which directors could be held personally responsible for the consequences of the fault of the company if it was foreseeable that the company was no longer able to continue to cover its debts and if they nonetheless abstained from deciding to bring it back to viability or to undertake winding up of the company by a court ruling (European Commission Action Plan);

iii imposition of a ban on exercising the position of director in the EU as a penalty against supplying false financial or other information and other forms of harmful behavior by directors (European Commission Action Plan).

Apart from these, the Commission plan identifies five areas where there is a specific need for effective monitoring by the board of directors: an Audit Committee, a Remuneration Committee, an Appointment Committee and Finance Committee. Some companies have preferred to add a fourth committee: the Strategy Committee.

Boards should be organized in such a way that a sufficient number of independent non-executive or supervisory directors play an effective role in key areas where the potential for conflict of interest is particularly high and several committees are mandatory for this purpose.

Board committees

Listed companies in most parts of Europe are often controlled by one or a small group of large block-holders and this is generally seen as an advantage of controlling shareholder-structures. It is believed that large block-holders can be well informed about the company's operations and able to closely monitor its executive management team. The existence of the controlling shareholder(s) may give rise, however, to potential conflicts of interests with minority shareholders who often lack sufficient information and resources to monitor management and the controlling shareholders. In this type of controlled company, there is obviously a need for monitoring by non-executive directors, on behalf of minority shareholders.

Non-executive directors, who are not involved in the daily operations of the company, normally have a role of oversight of the executive managers in major decisions affecting its strategy and future. To this end, EU legislations call for the creation within the board of nomination, remuneration and Audit Committees. Those committees should make recommendations aiming at preparing the decisions to be taken by the board itself. The primary purpose of committees is the increase of the efficiency of the board by making sure that decisions are based on rational considerations. In companies where the board is small, it allowed that the functions assigned to the three committees may be performed by the board as a whole, provided that it meets the composition requirements advocated for the committees and that adequate information is provided in this respect.

It is also commonly admitted within the EU that nomination and remuneration of executive directors and the external auditors must be decided upon by exclusively non-executive directors and this can be achieved by creating both nomination and remuneration, but also an audit committee. All committees must be composed of non-executive directors. The primary responsibility of the Audit Committee is to oversee the company's financial reporting processes on behalf of the board and report the results of its activities to the board. In carrying out its responsibilities the Audit Committee should be allowed to take appropriate actions to set the overall corporate strategy for quality financial reporting. The Audit Committee should review the annual financial statements and assess whether they are complete and consistent with the information known to committee members. With regard to internal audit, the committee should discuss with management and the external auditors, the adequacy and effectiveness of the accounting and financial controls. Any opinion obtained from the external auditors on the company's choice of accounting policies or methods should include an opinion on the appropriateness and not just the acceptability of that choice or method. Concerning the external audit, the committee should be able to discuss with the external auditors the overall scope of the external audit, including identified risk areas and any additional agreed-upon procedures. The committee should also review the external auditor's compensation to ensure that an effective, comprehensive and complete audit can be conducted for the agreed compensation level. Concerning, finally, the appointment of external auditors, the audit committee should directly be responsible for making recommendations to the board of directors on the appointment, reappointment or replacement, remuneration, monitoring of the effectiveness, and independence of the external auditors, including resolution of disagreements between management and the auditor regarding financial reporting.

Employees representation

In many European countries it is mandatory for the workers' voice to be included in the national system of CG. Indeed, in European companies, employee participation has deep roots and it operates in different ways. In 12 out of 28 EU and European Economic Area (EEA) Member States (including Norway), workers have a mandatory, legally binding right to be represented on company boards and to influence management decisions in both state-owned and private companies. Co-determination in these countries is a fact, diverse in structure, but deeply-rooted in different cultural and historically developed environments. Worker participation seems to work well in both single and two-tier board environments, making a positive contribution to companies' performance. In other countries participation is the result of bargaining practices and also guarantees an influence on the strategic choices of the company. In any case, all the different participation models allow for different interests in the company to develop in full autonomy. European trade unions have no preference regarding these two models. They merely insist on respecting each of these historically developed structures. There is no evidence of an economic need to change or adapt systems in Europe to copy the US style of company management. On the contrary, an examination of micro and macro indicators indicates better performance by national economies with strong, widespread worker representation at board level, as recent studies conducted by the World Bank (ILO and ETUI-REHS).

European unions usually underline the fact that employees normally spend most of their time in the company and completely depend financially on it, and should have a say in its management and this is recognized by Member States' laws. In the unions view it is important that the process of enhancing CG in the Member States does not lead to a dilution of their rights. In reaction others are warning against the possible risks of including employees or other stakeholders into the CG debate. According to them, in some cases, employees defense is used by the management as excuse for acting contrary to the interests of the shareholders and this can be detrimental for the employees. The Forum is currently looking for avenues of approaching this issue, at least under a corporate social responsibility perspective.[16]

Conclusion

The European Commission Action Plan on Modernising Company Law and Enhancing CG, adopted in May 2003 laid down actions that are required in order "to modernise, complete and simplify the regulatory framework for company law and CG" (Action Plan) within the EU. The Action Plan underlines that a dynamic and flexible company law and CG framework is essential for a modern economy. Good CG practices throughout the EU will enhance the real economy:

i   An effective approach will foster the global efficiency and competitiveness of businesses in the EU. Well-managed companies, with strong CG records and sensitive social and environmental performance, outperform their competitors. Europe needs more of them to generate employment and higher long-term sustainable growth.

ii An effective approach will help to strengthen shareholders rights and third parties protection. In particular, it will contribute to rebuilding European investor confidence in the wake of a wave of recent CG scandals. The livelihood of millions of Europeans, their pensions and their investments are tied up in the proper, responsible performance and governance of listed companies in which they invest.

The Action Plan also setup the roadmap for achieving a pan-European appropriate CG. It calls mainly for shareholders' right protection, board modernization, directors' remuneration, the creation of a European CG Forum, and sound auditing procedures.

The Commission is already exploring channels for simplification. It adopted toward this end, on 10 July 2007, a communication "setting out proposals for possible measures to simplify the EU acquis in the areas of company law, accounting and auditing."[17] Interested parties are invited to comment on the communication and the proposals by mid-October 2007.

Although, a significant current within the EU State Members believing that good CG initiatives should come from the market and market participants,[18] knowing best what rules enhancing corporate reputation. The development of CG codes consequently, should be left to those who have an own interest in them, and that is "a certain regulatory fatigue [is appearing] in the EU due to the relatively important changes that have been made in the field of company law and CG during the last few years." There is, according to the Forum "still interest on the side of the stakeholders in enabling legislation that offers company additional options for organizing their business." Concerning the idea of codification, i.e. to consolidate and simplify the existing EU law in the field of company law in one legal act, the majority feeling is that for companies the implementing measures at Member State level are of much higher relevance in their daily work so that a codification exercise at EU level would not have much effect in practice.[19] In this regard, the Commission has set up a Scoreboard system to monitor the advance of implementation of its directives by Member States and as of July 2007, several Member States are subject of the Commission infringement procedures for failure to implement in national law one or more of eight different Internal Market Directives. They are referred to the Court of Justice over non-communication of national measures implementing certain directives (Czech Republic, Estonia, France and Luxembourg).

Despite the challenged orientation, serious and constant efforts were made by the Commission toward the development of a strong, reliable European model of CG which should essentially be enshrined in European and national legislation. The catch up is impressive, success was the result in most areas and benefits are yet to emerge.

Table 13.A1 Company law and CG sources[1]

Number	Title	OJL
31978L0660	Fourth Council Directive 78/660/EEC of 25 July 1978 based on Article 54 (3) (g) of the Treaty on the annual accounts of certain types of companies	(OJ L 222, 14.8.1978, pp. 11–31)
31983L0349	Seventh Council Directive 83/349/EEC of 13 June 1983 based on the Article 54 (3) (g) of the Treaty on consolidated accounts	(OJ L 193, 18.7.1983, pp. 1–17)
32001H0256	Commission Recommendation of 15 November 2000 on quality assurance for the statutory audit in the EU: minimum requirements (text with EEA relevance) (notified under document number C(2000) 3304)	(OJ L 91, 31.3.2001, pp. 91–97)
32001L0086	Council Directive 2001/86/EC of 8 October 2001 supplementing the Statute for a European company with regard to the involvement of employees	(OJ L 294, 10.11.2001, pp. 22–32)
32001R2157	Council Regulation (EC) No 2157/2001 of 8 October 2001 on the Statute for a European company (SE)	(OJ L 294, 10.11.2001, pp. 1–21)
32002H0590	Commission Recommendation of 16 May 2002 – Statutory Auditors' Independence in the EU: A Set of Fundamental Principles (text with EEA relevance) (notified under document number C(2002) 1873)	(OJ L 191, 19.7.2002, pp. 22–57)
32002R1606	Regulation (EC) No 1606/2002 of the European Parliament and of the Council of 19 July 2002 on the application of international accounting standards	(OJ L 243, 11.9.2002, pp. 1–4)
32003L0072	Council Directive 2003/72/EC of 22 July 2003 supplementing the Statute for a European Cooperative Society with regard to the involvement of employees	(OJ L 207, 18.8.2003, pp. 25–36)
32003R1725	Commission Regulation (EC) No 1725/2003 of 29 September 2003 adopting certain international accounting standards in accordance with Regulation (EC) No 1606/2002 of the European Parliament and of the Council (Text with EEA relevance.)	(OJ L 261, 13.10.2003, pp. 1–420)

continued

Table 13.A1 continued

Number	Title	OJL
32004D0706	2004/706/EC: Commission Decision of 15 October 2004 establishing the European Corporate Governance Forum	(OJ L 321, 22.10.2004, pp. 53–54)
32004H0913	2004/913/EC: Commission Recommendation of 14 December 2004 fostering an appropriate regime for the remuneration of directors of listed companies (text with EEA relevance)	(OJ L 385, 29.12.2004, pp. 55–59)
32004L0025	Directive 2004/25/EC of the European Parliament and of the Council of 21 April 2004 on takeover bids (text with EEA relevance)	(OJ L 142, 30.4.2004, pp. 12–23)
32005D0380	2005/380/EC: Commission Decision of 28 April 2005 establishing a group of non-governmental experts on CG and company law	(OJ L 126, 19.5.2005, pp. 40–42)
32005D0909	2005/909/EC: Commission Decision of 14 December 2005 setting up a group of experts to advise the Commission and to facilitate cooperation between public oversight systems for statutory auditors and audit firms	(OJ L 329, 16.12.2005, pp. 38–39)
32005H0162	EC: Commission Recommendation of 15 February 2005 on the role of non-executive or supervisory directors of listed companies and on the committees of the (supervisory) board (text with EEA relevance)	(OJ L 52, 25.2.2005, pp. 51–63)
32006L0043	Directive 2006/43/EC of the European Parliament and of the Council of 17 May 2006 on statutory audits of annual accounts and consolidated accounts, amending Council Directives 78/660/EEC and 83/349/EEC and repealing Council Directive 84/253/EEC (text with EEA relevance)	(OJ L 157, 9.6.2006, pp. 87–107)

Note
1 http://eur-lex.europa.eu/en/repert/1710.htm.

Notes

1 The plan received the strong support of the European Parliament in its resolution of 21 of April 2004.
2 Adopted in July 2002.
3 Commission Recommendation of 15 February 2005 on the role of non-executive or supervisory directors of listed companies and on the committees of the (supervisory) board (2005/162/EC) (4).
4 Communication from the Commission of 22 March 2006 to the European Parliament, the Council and the European Economic and Social Committee – Implementing the partnership for growth and jobs: making Europe a pole of excellence on corporate social responsibility (COM(2006) 136 final – Not published in the official journal).
5 22 February 2006, Statement of the European CG Forum on the comply-or-explain principle.
6 Proportionality between Ownership and Control in EU Listed Companies: External Study Commissioned by the European Commission, Shearman & Sterling LLP.
7 The "proportionality principle," also referred to as the "one share–one vote" principle.
8 Regarding the term "ownership," it should be noted that, in many jurisdictions, shareholders will not be viewed as "owners" from a legal standpoint.
9 Responsible shareholders are, of course, expected to take time to study issues debated in general meetings and carefully weigh the relevant information before deciding how to vote.
10 Proposal for a Directive of the European Parliament and of the Council, amending Council Directives 78/660/EEC and 83/349/EEC concerning the annual accounts of certain types of companies and consolidated accounts.
11 Regulation (EC) No 1606/2002 of the European Parliament and of the Council of 19 July 2002 on the application of international accounting standards.
12 Committee of Auditing Communication on the statutory audit in the EU: the way forward.
13 In this regard the EC privileges the principles contained in the IFAC Code of Ethics.
14 Remuneration is one of the key areas where executive directors have a conflict of interests.
15 Statement of the European CG Forum on "Risk Management and Internal Control," Brussels, June 2006.
16 European CG Forum Minutes of the meeting of 1 June 2006.
17 Communication of 12 July 2007 on a simplified business environment for companies in the areas of company law, accounting and auditing.
18 Report of the High Level Group of Company Law Experts on a Modern Regulatory Framework for Company Law in Europe, Brussels, 4 November 2002.
19 European CG Forum minutes of the meeting of 1 June 2006.

14 Concluding remarks

A. Naciri

Organizations in modern economies were granted extraordinary privileges allowing them to participate effectively in social and economic human advances. Unfortunately, abuses were quickly emerging and becoming more and more unbearable and subject to many citizens virulent denunciations and desperate protests. They also proved to be extremely detrimental to economic growth and social development. Not only were they of a doubtful morality, but they also seemed to be questioning the free enterprise system basis. The most notable abuse resides in weak corporate governance (CG) initiated under the cover of false transparency and misused regulated financial reporting. We would obviously like to think that the majority of our corporations aspire to a faultless behavior and that their advisers, lawyers, etc. do not see themselves as simple legality traders for payment, allowing the respect of the letter of the law, but disregarding its spirit. Unfortunately, in the field, little is already too much and it was thus necessary to act and quickly, given that recent corporate misconducts have proven to be extremely dangerous for all.

It is commonly believed that the 1997 Asian financial crisis was mainly the consequence of a lack of effective CG and transparency within most of Asia's financial markets and institutions and so the recent collapse of the Enron Corporation and similar frauds in other developed countries. These events have underlined the critical importance of structural reforms in the governance of large companies, particularly, and the financial system in general. For sure the CG issue transcends national boundaries, but CG responsibility within the organizations always remains shareholders' own, via their elected boards of directors. In this respect the board and its various committees must work for sowing germs of good governance, by addressing problem causes and not limiting themselves to symptom treatments. In others words, they must stay tuned to corporate operations, so that internal tensions or external events will not affect organization immunizing capacity against non ethical behaviors. Board members should be encouraged and oriented toward corporate problem solving; it is only a simple question of common sense and good governance.

This book reports some of the most notable national CG reforms throughout the world and recognizes the tremendous influence of the American vision of CG, as institutionalized by the Sarbanes–Oxley Act (SOX). It concludes that any internationalization of the American model risks proving detrimental to most national systems of governance. It suggests instead a more flexible system for the international arena, capable of marring itself to different socio-cultural environments and economic advance, sharing, however, fundamental principles of justice, transparency, honesty and corporative democracy. This is something the Organization of Economic Cooperation and Development (OECD) governance guidelines may have tried to achieve. Unfortunately such guidelines were tailored for listed companies of developing countries and still neglect other environments realities.

CG benefits

There still subsists a general feeling of incomprehension with regard to the potential benefits which can be withdrawn from CG improvement. CG opponents often, however, try to justify their opposition based on the Smithsonian notion of the "invisible hand." Adam Smith claims that, in capitalism, an individual pursuing his own good tends also to promote the good of his community, through a principle that he called "the invisible hand" of the market. Such a hand ensures that those activities most beneficial and efficient will naturally be those that are most profitable (Smith, 1776). Free enterprise systems can certainly emphasize the best part of each individual, by developing his creativity, his energy while increasing his aspiration to a better life. But such a system can function without a minimum of good governance and such governance would be realizable, given the multiple challenges which confront it?

Recent financial audacious frauds were surprising by both their impact and ingeniousness, they draw attention, not only on the dramatic consequences of weak CG, but they also give the CG issue urgent priority. Such frauds have underscored the critical importance of structural reforms in the governance of companies and financial institutions. They also show that CG issues transcend national boundaries. Although the Western corporations have been the home of the bulk of recent corporate controversies, no doubt other economies of the world are not innocent either (Ho, Chapter 9).

Weak CG has always borrowed the vehicle of financial information opacity. Information transparency, as we know, occurs only when there is no obstacle to the harmonious flow of quality information which is also relevant and credible. Similarly, information opacity occurs whenever irritants are deliberately placed on its harmonious flow, preventing users its free access. Weak transparency and uncertainty are, however, financial information inherent characteristics. The main reason is that financial markets are constantly engaged in a timeless and dubious trade, not only in monetary terms, but especially in informational terms. Information collected and treated by the market relates mainly to project selections and performance monitoring and follow-up. Interest for good governance (or concern as for its absence) comes mainly from its triple action, particularly its impact on organization effectiveness on market effectiveness, and on social harmony.[1]

i   With regard to organization effectiveness, it is easy to understand, at least at the theoretical level, that a transparency culture would have many benefits to any organization. Although the primary objective of corporations remains the maximization of their shareholders wealth, it becomes progressively obvious that if a wealth maximization objective has to be achieved it must go through the respect of other corporate stakeholders interests, including community interests. These diverse interests must, not only be assured, but also harmonized. Indeed, one organization is likely to create more wealth, for itself and for the whole society, by an ethical strategy, and this will gain the corporation an integrity reputation. As shareholders agents, members of the board of directors play a crucial and determinant role in organization governance. They should themselves be transparent and such transparency must be reflected in the first place, in their own selection criteria. For example, board transparency can also facilitate the separation of management from the capital and avoiding the negligence of shareholders interests and non respect of other stakeholders' rights. Such a situation, as we know, is capable of weakening employees' corporate commitment and leading to much skepticism by customers and suppliers. The board then becomes value creator. One can only deplore (until recently) the absence of interest at this level.

ii   Concerning the financial market, financial literature abounds with arguments suggesting the positive impact of good CG on scarce resources allocation, capital movement and general economic effectiveness, since CG's main component – financial transparency – makes direct investment more productive and this in turn leads to more efficiency and growth. But the highest cost of CG absence resides in the excess of corruption and frauds it leads to, along with the misallocation of resources it ends up to.

iii   At the social level, good CG makes it possible for honest individuals to be consolidated in their honesty and to those which are less convinced, to think seriously before committing themselves to transforming their job into a one-man business, for the sole purpose of maximizing their own utility, even at the price of fraudulent acts, creating a harmful corporate atmosphere of injustice and frustration.

These are but a few advantages of CG. In spite, however, of the multiple advantages of CG and efforts provided toward its generalization, as seen in this book, desire to reduce its scope remains very alive in the majority of modern economies and one can only wonder why. In fact, CG constraints are of different kinds. Some are purely philosophical, like the confidentiality right, others are of a practical nature:

•   First, the relatively high cost of implementing CG rules may constitute one main cause, and it is hence believed that CG improvement measures are taken only when benefit exceeds their costs.

•   Second, weak CG may also seem to be paying in the short term, especially, at its information transparency dimension, when, for example, companies are in strategic interaction and that some information disclosure may result in a loss of competitive advantage and thus in a lower profitability.

- Third, the value of some companies are related to each other, in such a manner that information on one of them can be used to evaluate the others. In such cases, managers may refrain from being all transparent.
- Fourth, financial literature states the possibility of risk increase for companies having opted for improved CG standards. It is believed that improved governance practices attract short-term strategy investors, mainly speculators. They seem to allocate more value to more transparent firms, and this leads to more variability in the share prices of transparent companies.
- Fifth, information asymmetry stating that managers of companies will always have better quality information than shareholders and other investors.
- Sixth, some managers may advocate the fact that the free enterprise system is based on what Adam Smith has described as "sympathy" principle, i.e. a kind of canalizing force of egoistic individuals' passions. Such a principle, however, does not seem to have held in the past, since it did not prevent corporate fraudulent conducts.

A whole market to blame, but who dares?

It is commonly admitted that from early 2001 until the collapse of Enron in October of the same year, all major investment banks' analysts in the US were still strongly recommending buying Enron's securities, stocks and bonds alike.[2] Some of these analysts admitted in their private emails that many of the shares they were recommending to clients were actually "junk stocks." After the collapse of Enron, some analysts, linked to investment banks or funds houses, were even condemned for conflicts of interests.[3] Obviously weak governance, as a major evil, has more extent and ramifications than first expected, it is actually a systemic crisis. Indeed, CG seems to be missing in many organizations because of the favorable environment gradually encouraged and instituted. For some time, for instance, it was believed that because of its efficiency, the market was capable of separating "wheat from the chaff." Quite naturally, interest was shifted toward market value instead of accounting value. No one, however, has yet successfully defined what market value exactly means or how it is computed.[4] Consequently, it should be no surprise that having lost its benchmarks, the evaluation process was confused and weakened and had ended up letting financial analysts and rating agencies, armed with approximation and a lack of rigor, to have precedence in security evaluation. Gradually, their control over security evaluation activity became without partition. Since then only one law prevails on the market – analysts' law, a law that promises punishment for corporations unable to meet analysts' profit anticipations and blessing for those that conform to it. With the help of the last stock exchange euphoria, conforming corporations had been indeed largely but unduly rewarded for their assiduity, by exorbitant and abnormal market returns, while others, although economically viable were ruined, quite simply because they prove to be unable to conform to the irrational analysts' desires.

As underlined previously, analysts' decision models were never, neither proved nor demonstrated, nor even commonly agreed on. Some analysts were, for instance, recommending strong purchases of companies' securities on the verge of collapsing and some rating agencies did not, at certain times, hesitate to low down Japan quotation to Malawi level. Often, inexperienced or unprofessional analysts make subjective earnings forecasts on the basis of simple data that is supplied by listed firms. Despite their illegitimate process, they can become market forces that drive concerned firms to adjust their strategies. Many people are convinced that the business relationship between an analyst's investment bank and a client firm affects the independence of the analyst to the point that they tend not to disclose, or delay disclosing, any negative news about the client firm. It is, for instance, mentioned (*The Economist*, 2007) that some well-known international credit rating agencies had intentionally, and for generous fees, delayed their announcements of negative rating reports on Enron and certainly on other listed firms. Christopher Cox, as chairman of the Security Exchange Commission (SEC) since 2005, keen for regaining the lead, has made fighting insider traders a priority. According to Walter Ricciardi from the SEC, the commission must prevent any "buzz in the markets that you can get away with it." He adds: "Nothing paints a picture as well as people being led away in handcuffs." It is believed the SEC will act even when it has no one to put the cuffs on. Very recently, indeed, the SEC filed a suit against unknown investors who had profited in the options market before the announcement of a takeover of TXU (Texan utility)[5] (SEC). To match analysts' predicted earnings and restraining their stock prices from collapsing, some companies, unable to meet the challenge honestly, learned how to use creative accounting methods to "fix" their account books and this opened the door to all corporate abuses and scandals.

Theoretically, managers can be discouraged from undertaking suboptimal decisions, privileging their own interests at the expense of the shareholders, quite simply by conceding them generous employment conditions. Some managers had quickly, however, invented the "magic potion" which will allow them to unduly inflate options value included in compensation plans and which deflate only in future purchasers' hands. Large shareholding dispersion makes it possible for managements to control without sharing company destinies. The extent of their hegemony is so strong it allows them to treat all shareholders as minority interests.

In these conditions voluntary governance would seem difficult to achieve and public intervention becomes desirable and unavoidable. Thinking must, however, precede legal action, Intervention has to deal with relevance, cost benefit and market transparency. Especially that those most eminent CG failures emanated from companies most respectful of standards. Following Max Weber,[6] we can assume individual actions to be initiated by anticipating others' reactions. Management fraudulent behavior can thus be explained by the anticipation of investors' behavior on the market, and CG weaknesses can only be the consequence of a favorable environment to fraud, one which was gradually encouraged by the market.

Interest for CG did not really wait for the recent corporate crisis to impose itself. Actually, major accounting legislations throughout the world were concerned, very early, with the issue, to the point where most of their accounting conceptual frameworks were based on it. Although such early awareness and the various accounting standards have contributed to CG improvement, they did not prove to be sufficient in avoiding resounding accounting frauds. In any case perfect CG would prove difficult to realize, as long as the financial market is not ready to adopt it, to require it and to remunerate for it. Instead the market was always requiring non realizable higher returns coupled with lower risks, and some corporations, looking for an alternative, have discovered that it was possible to please the market by simply manipulating the numbers. It was often stated that the market because of its supposed "efficiency" was able to operate without accounting information. More seriously, it was loudly announced that in the event of accounting method choices, any accounting method will make it. The market was supposed to have the ability to go to the heart of the problem.

Market operators were always keen on getting freed from accounting numbers burden, despite the fact that accounting information constitutes the only measurable data that exists. Quite naturally interest was moved toward the subjective and uneasy to handle concept of the "fair value," neglecting at the same token the much more objective concept of "historical value," which of course accuses its won limits, except non-measurability. Analysts' insistence was so strong as to bring the standard setter to require measuring assets and liabilities in fair value terms, knowing that no one can yet explain what such notion means and nobody has ever been able to test its usefulness.

Consequently, having lost its references, the evaluation process was weakened and so auditing activities, information transparency and financial reporting quality, in a word CG.

SOX, a specific paradigm

SOX is based on shareholder supremacy paradigm and this is not something everybody would agree on, not even Americans. According to a 1996 opinion poll (Louis Harris Associates, 1996), only 5 percent of American citizens would agree that the only purpose of the American corporations is to maximize shareholders' wealth. Actually 95 percent of them were of opinion that the corporation should have additional objectives.[7] Shareholder paradigm is actually the product of the highly developed equity market of the United States, backed by financial institutions whose business is to enhance returns for their customers like public pension funds, mutual fund managers and investment banks. The shareholder model is not valid for other economic sectors like, for instance, manufacturing industries, where investments tend to be made based on the long run profitability. Shareholder model is actually a nineteenth-century vestige (Masaru, Chapter 7), which used to be appropriate when entrepreneurs use to own majority of the shares and were often engaged themselves in the management of their own companies. Corporation laws in most countries, industrialized and non-industrialized nations alike, are still based on the ownership structure of the nineteenth century, despite the fact that ownership structure has radically changed since then, as pointed by Berle and Means (1932). This is "the primitive model of corporation" (Blair, 1995, p. 234) and a kind of Stone Age capitalism for a former Hoechst manager.[8] Most importantly, evidence tends to suggest that the shareholder model affects the US industries competitiveness. Short-term profit views of the 1990s and beyond seems to have weakened American competitive capability on the global market. Porter (1992) thought that the US system first advances the goals of shareholders, interested in near-term increase of their wealth, even at the expense of the long-term performance (Blair, 1995, p. 232).

Charreaux (Chapter 2) shows that "departing from the shareholder's CG model, theories are evolving toward more complex models involving all stakeholders and attributing greater importance to the productive/cognitive aspects of value creation." This evolution, influenced by that of the theories of the firm, leads to considering human capital as being more and more significant since the formation of the competitive advantage seems to be based mostly on skills. This also leads to a better understanding of corporate operations and CG systems evolution and questions dominant SOX paradigm. According to Charreaux, alternative paradigms do exist and are much more promising.

SOX were not promulgated to reinforce management CG obligations. As indicated previously, however, the problem of CG is above all, an issue of corporate democracy, whose responsibility belongs to shareholders and exercised through their elected board of directors. Any legal initiative which would not deal with the board of director's structure and functioning is likely to miss the point in CG reform, the way the SOX sees it.

SOX specific CG orientation

As indicated in this book, CG visions seem to vary with countries and regions. In the majority of countries such visions were structurally borrowed from the American model, where, as we know, the dominant orientation concept is usually related to the maximization of shareholders' wealth. In other environments, on the other hand, the dominant orientation concept has to do with all stakeholders' interest in defense and the achievement of certain collective well-being. As indicated before, efforts of improving CG were, however, mainly initiated from the United States and had thus concerns, particularly the American environment, they naturally have led to rules typically believed to be suitable for the American Environment. SOX vision of CG, for instance, does not necessarily seem to be related to any moral consideration or to any philosophical principle. SOX, like any other American legislation, adapts itself to facts of life and to requirements of the field.[9] Within the American law, for instance, an individual may plead "guilty" for a robbery act, "not because he feels guilty, but only because he might be wishing to put a term at an investigation which may lead to a discovery of more serious crime." Similarly, an innocent individual may also plead guilty for a small crime he would not commit (Délga *et al.*, Chapter 6), only by fears for not being able to prove his innocence and thus risking a higher sentence.[10] American law, to some extent, seems only to be a kind of a quasi procedural recourse to social arbitration, for which good, bad and even ethics are completely a non-existent concept.[11] SOX CG vision seems to stand away from philosophical or moral design, its primary objective resides in reaching a pragmatic result. This kind of governance is not something we can describe as conviction or conscience CG; where one would seek to make good triumph over evil. Social investment would however prove to be useful when corporate image improvement would, for instance, lead to customer satisfaction and loyalty. It is important, however to understand that SOX has never claimed imposing moral principles within organizations' management. SOX objective is forcing corporations, mainly under threat of sanctions and imprisonment, to comply with the rules.

On another level, although, good CG is supposed to be beneficial to all corporations big and small, the American CG system relates only to large corporations. Of course, exorbitant implementation cost, of some SOX provisions, seems without common measurement with the capacity of spending of the majority of small companies throughout the world, and this may invite them to abstain from complying with its provisions. This fact alone militates in favor of easy application standards adoption. In fact, small companies especially those belonging to under developed economies, need more monitoring in order to realize significant CG progress.

Another serious problem may face all those countries willing to adopt CG provisions similar to SOX and integrate them into their own CG reform, especially when they intend to apply them within their existing legal system. Obviously, such initiatives' success will be dependent on their ability to adjust their environment to fit the American environment, with regard to market sophistication and much inefficiency and aberrations, would certainly result from the importation of SOX provisions. Délga *et al.* (Chapter 6), for instance, mention that French law does not recognize the existence of the so-called independent board members, while world rating agencies refer to this category of board members to classify companies ethically. In France independent board member designation has no legal value. Either, the so-called independent board members are like other board members, elected with the same conditions and having the same prerogatives, or they are not. Consequently, in the French law, they cannot represent a special category of board members. Another fundamental legal divergence can also be mentioned in case of corporate asset abuses, existing in most national legal systems, but practically absent in the United States system, it is also the case of CEO dismissal indemnities, illegal in several countries, but legal in the United States.

It is then comprehensive why some would blow the whistle and warn against uniform CG rules throughout the planet, because, according to them, they often contradict national legal systems.

SOX impact on national CG systems

Legislative efforts and academic research to reinforce CG emanated, essentially from Anglo-Saxon environments, especially from the United States. Quite naturally they were oriented to safeguarding the American environment. American legislative initiatives (SOX and New York Stock Exchange (NYSE) requirements) have, however set a pace against which most other legislations have found a proper response for developing their national system. The American CG system has such mechanisms as:

i   efficient markets;
ii   diffuse shareholding;
iii corporate gigantism; etc.

Such conditions cannot be met, however, in environments, other than the United States, as pointed out by Délga *et al.* (Chapter 6), as well as Yoshimori (Chapter 7) and Simon Ho (Chapters 8 and 9). Usually, countries captive of their older history would base their CG reforms on different basis like:

i   family property;
ii   transactions based on the personal relation and word given; and
iii preponderance of an inefficient public sector.

For this reason, the most important agency problem in the United States resides in the relation between the management/board, on the one hand, and external shareholding, on the other. Within such a relationship, management strives toward the maximization of its own utility at the expense of external shareholding. In most others country, like Japan or continental European countries, and where corporate ownership is concentrated in the hands of major banks and other large financial institutions, agency relations are quite different. Agency relations are also different in emerging Asian economies or MENA countries, where ownership is typically concentrated in very few family hands. Family shareholding tries also to maximize its own utility at the expense other stakeholders, through non-declared intermediaries or by even using doubtful means. In such cases major agency problems lie between ownership/board control and minority shareholding. In other environments, such as the Chinese or Commonwealth Independent States, the most important agency problem is a multi-dimensional one. It exists between the State, as majority shareholder, and external minority shareholders. Protection of minority shareholders' rights constitutes one of the economic key considerations in those countries.

From an agency theory point of view, management is a shareholders' agent, whose mandate is the maximization of shareholders' wealth and is only responsible to shareholders. In case of success, like in the case of failure of agent actions on principal are thus clear. Indeed, a new contract, a cost decrease, a profit increase or a value improvement is indisputable proof of good performance and the reverse is true. SOX seems to question the mercenary character of the traditional agency relationship and reintroduced an agency system with several principals, to whom the agent is accountable at the same time.

Although SOX concerns only big American corporations listed in exchanges, gradually, however, it became a source of inspiration of most national initiatives of CG reforms, partly because of its primacy and partly because of the unexpected American official support. American officials are fundamentally convinced that economic development requires a sound CG system, and are prepared to help anybody willing to adopt SOX provisions.[12] They also place all their weight to convince international organizations of the rightness of their vision.[13]

SOX has profound effects on financial accounting and auditing practices, not only in the United States but also elsewhere. It has improved the scope and quality of auditor independence (Public Accounting Oversight Board, PACOB), and has reinforced OECD CG guidelines. While it is doubtful that SOX has eliminated all corporate frauds, more and more companies are, however, pursuing improvements in CG, based on the belief that this is the route to follow, consistent with their own self interest – wealth maximization. On the other hand, although the SOX success in increasing the reliability of financial reporting remains to be proven, there is, however, no doubt that the way boards of directors, corporate managers and external auditor's approach their responsibility has changed drastically and greater efforts are now made ensuring timely and accurate financial information provided to investors. For these reasons the SOX has impacted tremendously all CG reforms across the world.[14]

The next section will emphasize the great diversity of national systems of governance and will reinforce our belief that countries should adopt the corporate model which can best be harmonized with their own socio-economic and political environment.

Characterestics of national CG systems

A common concern with CG quality seems to be shared by most modern world economies and we are witnessing quite a large number of CG legislative reforms, sharing, most of them, with the same source of inspiration, namely the SOX. We have decided to concentrate in this book, on CG reforms, considered to be representative of specific areas or groups of countries, or carrying a particular CG message.

As underlined previously, current interest for CG is a direct consequence of the confidence crisis having recently shacked financial markets. CG has become a major international problem, following first the Asian financial crisis of 1997 and the 2002 black series of corporative scandals, having shacked major Western economies. Very quickly weak CG has proved to be transcending borders and affecting a much larger number of organizations. Actually even if Western economies had constituted corporate frauds major territory, other economies are far from innocent. As a matter of fact, some corporations seem to persist in their wrong behavior, without being worried by the so-called reforms.

CG reforms, initiated everywhere in the world hardly start to give results. Let us recall that what are aimed for here, are CG system improvements and not the state of their perfection. This section summarizes national CG experiments of countries covered by this book, namely the United States, Canada, France, Japan, China, Hong Kong, Turkey, the MENA region, the EU and economies in transition of the former Soviet Bloc, emphasizing their great diversity and the fundamental SOX influence.

CG in the United States is often associated with the recent SOX. While SOX is undoubtedly important, its significance can best be understood in the context of the existing frameworks under corporate and securities law (Nelson, Chapter 4). Indeed, Current legislation in the United States simply adds to the governance measures already in place pursuant to corporate law and securities regulation. This legislation is composed of SOX, but also the NYSE initiatives. Generally speaking, SOX attempts to improve the independence of external auditors and corporate directors so that they are better able – and more likely – to prepare public disclosures in form and substance required by US securities regulations. There are also provisions intended to enhance the care with which corporate officers prepare required public disclosures … . Recent NYSE initiatives, on the other hand, attempt to improve the degree of independence among directors of corporations listed there so that they are better able – and more likely – to meet the performance standards currently applicable to directors under corporate law (i.e. duties of care and loyalty), but the NYSE listing requirements do not change those standards and do not have the force of law.

Canada, geographically located next to the US, but also sensitive to some European influence, faces a constant tension among these competing cultures (Brown, Chapter 5). This is true in every major field, and CG is no exception. While, however, the US has adopted a "rules-based" approach to governance, prescribing standards down to the last small detail and enforcing these through a strong adversarial justice system. Canada has chosen to adopt a principle-based governance framework, where a consensus is reached among diverse players (including regulators, investors, corporations and governments).

In terms of principle area, Canada's corporations show the greatest strengths in the principle areas of leadership and stewardship, and empowerment and accountability. Boards and executives in Canada typically set the corporation's mission, vision and strategic direction together, explicitly codify a code of conduct, and formalize responsibilities and authorities (in terms of reference, job descriptions and delegation of authorities).

Analysis of the French CG system indicates that SOX provisions, introduced by EU directives and especially their application pose serious problems, with regard to CG design itself, at different levels like at the board members independence level, corporate asset abuses, management responsibility, etc. The biggest French fear is to see the French law invaded by SOX concepts, by definition, strange, and are likely to break French law harmony. Most people in France believe that it is possible to collaborate in the development of the international corporate law, without disavowing a legal and cultural, system. Some also regret the confusion introduced by SOX within concepts of ethics, morals and pragmatism.

In Japan, contrary to what occurred in the majority of western countries, where democracy was torn off through a length and tearing process of several centuries of wars, democracy was imposed by the allied forces. But what Japan has set up is not a democracy, neither in spirit nor in reality. It remains, in Japan, an important gap between the law and the reality of its application. Obvious contradiction was kept intact during several decades by the academicians, lawyers, politicians and above all, by the business community. The lack of maturity thus seems to constitute the fundamental reason of CG inefficiency in Japan. The recent reform of the Japanese commercial law which took effect in April 2003 constitutes, certainly, only but one step, toward correction of the situation.

The more striking characteristic of the Japanese CG reform is certainly the discretion given to large companies, in their choice for one or the other, of two types of board structure – the innovating type and the conventional type. The second new aspect is that the first type of structure is literally modeled on the American system. On the other hand, the conventional structure is practically identical to the traditional Japanese model, even if this one contains certain improvements, but whose impact is marginal. The Japanese experiment shows the extent to which it is necessary to allow each country to develop its own CG system, a kind of system which would reflect its own needs and would respect its own culture.

In Hong Kong, enhancing a CG system is a priority, particularly in terms of protecting minority shareholders' interests. The government and all relevant sectors have attached much importance, and dedicated considerable efforts, to reforming legislation, rules and guidelines to keep them up to date. Significant progress has been made toward building a sound and solid CG foundation for Hong Kong, especially, refining of the regulatory framework, improving the internal governance mechanisms, the raising of ethical standards of market participants, securing top management's commitment and cultivating a healthy corporate culture.

In China, even if quite a large number of measures inspired significantly by the SOX provisions, were adopted in order to improve CG, China still shows much delay in the field of CG. In fact, corporate shareholding and CG are new concepts in China (Ho, Chapter 8). The "corporatization" or "privatization" of state-owned enterprises in China has led to new agency problems generating conflicts of interest among different stakeholders of a firm. It seems that the influence of the controlling shareholders and insider control are the key issues of CG in China, but other major problems include ineffective regulatory enforcement, lack of independent board and controls, lack of incentive for executives, low corporate transparency and disclosure quality, shortage of independent and quality auditors and intermediaries, insufficient protection of smaller investors' interests, and low business ethical standards. Generally, while aspiring to more corporative governorship, China tries to preserve its fundamental values and to avoid certain pitfalls observed in other countries, by vigilance and the audacity of which it accustomed us.

Turkey's legal and institutional framework for CG has improved over the past few years, mainly under intense international pressure. In addition, transparency and disclosure standards are comparable to those in other emerging markets and recent legislation can be expected to have further positive effects. In terms of structural reform, the most notable change has taken place in the financial sector reforms and in improved supervision of the banking sector. Recent improvements in Turkish CG standards are still serving as a basis to fill the gap between the law and the desired corporate behavior. This state of affairs is clearly visible in a number of areas where the effectiveness of recent reforms remains highly limited.

There are two obstacles to further improvement in Turkish CG practices. The first is related to the trends in capital flows favoring developed Anglo-Saxon markets and consequential decrease in significance of emerging market companies in strategic portfolio investments. The second obstacle is highly concentrated ownership and low floatation rates, both of which deter investors from entering the Turkish market.

The fate of CG in economies in transition cannot be dissociated from the movement of "Privatization," having affected the former Soviet Union. Such movement has gone through three phases. The first phase or "Mass Privatization" has resulted in the establishment of "modified" stakeholder models dominated by managers, States and banks. The second phase or "Cash Privatization" shifted the corporate decision-making process to the major shareholders who were quick to take under their control all production chains via high-concentrated ownership. The third phase of privatization underscores States' priorities, which range from privatization of the largest strategic companies to nationalization of previously privatized companies. In the view of the Commonwealth of Independent Countries (CIT), because of a lack of capital both internal and external, there is a need of upgrading its CG system to international level, and the State has a major role to play, mainly by improving the regulatory framework to meet companies interests and international capital providers.

The MENA region, as a specific cultural, economic and historical environment today faces many challenges in the field of CG. The implementation of market-based CG is one priority, and strengthening the functions and duties of the boards of directors is yet another. Both objectives require special attention in all MENA countries. On the one hand, family ownership is the dominant form and on the other, major shareholders and related parties have often exercised the greatest resistance to change, in spite of the benefits, which can be brought about by well-functioning markets and improvement of the CG framework, regarding director qualifications and independence; and establishing specialized board committees. The situation is, however, changing and rather rapidly. Results from a 2007 IFC-Hawkamah survey of 11 MENA countries with stock exchanges: Morocco, Tunisia, Egypt, Jordan, Lebanon, West Bank, Bahrain, Kuwait, Oman,

Saudi Arabia and the UAE confirm this wind of change. Minority shareholders seem to be normally protected in most countries in the sample. Boards in most MENA countries are, however, performing poorly. Accounting and auditing are acceptable and so is transparency of ownership and control, although auditing standards are of a poor quality and so, regulatory environments. The overall assessment is mitigated. The top three barriers to CG in MENA countries seem to be: the lack of qualified specialists to help with implementation; the lack of information or know-how and the lower priority given to CG.

The EU CG system is mainly inspired by the US legislation (SOX) which sets the scene for the most important national systems in the world. For this reason, transparency, efficient reporting, shareholders' protection, board efficiency, auditing quality, etc. are all on the menu.

Privileging market primacy orientation, the EU CG system presents the following theoretical foundations: first it is based on a principle-based governance approach, where a consensus is reached among Member States; second the adoption of detailed binding rules is excluded; and third, compliance is based on the "comply or explain" approach originating from England. This approach enables companies to reflect on sector- and enterprise-specific requirements, and for the markets to assess the explanations and justifications provided. Despite the challenged orientation, serious and constant efforts were made by the Commission toward the development of a strong, reliable European model of CG which should essentially be enshrined in European and national legislation. The catch up is impressive, success was the result in most areas and benefits are yet to emerge. The Commission is already exploring channels for simplification. It adopted toward this end, on 10 July 2007, a communication "setting out proposals for possible measures to simplify the EU 'acquis' in the areas of company law, accounting and auditing."[15] Interested parties are invited to comment on the communication and the proposals by mid-October 2007.

National CG systems presented in this book can be put into three categories. First, we have the category of countries having made the choice of adopting their own CG system, because internal pressures of a moral, economic or political flavor. In this class we find the United States, Canada and France. Second, we have the category of countries having made the choice of adopting their own CG system for financial reason. In this class we can count China and Hong Kong. In fact, China like Hong Kong, see in CG, a way of accessing more easily to the international capital market and being a major part in its network. Finally, we have countries having made the choice of adopting their own CG system, because of external pressures, either from the European Community (EC), in the case of Turkey, from international organization, in the case of the MENA countries and CIS, or from the US, in the case of Japan.

The future of national systems of CG

As can be seen in reading this book, national systems of CG are numerous. Different corporate systems coexist all over the world, the American corporate system,[16] for instance, owes obedience to shareholders, and other stakeholders, like workers, have only a small say in the conduct of corporate affairs. It also put the emphasis on conformity to the rules. In most European corporate systems shareholders have less power and bankers along with workers have more say in the conduct of corporate activities.[17] The Japanese corporate system leaves even less room to shareholders in corporate strategic decisions. It seems, however, that there is no ideal system; different countries in different times may need different CG systems. Different corporate systems are also required by changes in boundaries between public and private shareholding, like in China or Russia. The American system is currently, however, setting the tone to any one willing to reform its national system of CG, either directly or through international agencies.

Délga *et al.* (Chapter 7) underline that the internalization of the American system of CG tends to institutionalize uniform CG provisions across the planet. After the first hour of euphoria, people are starting to question the relevance of SOX provisions, especially outside of their home environment. On a predictive level, however, there are various responses to the question of convergence of national systems of governance. Aoki (1995), in view of the effects of globalization, identifies four scenarios:

i   the convergence by reciprocal imitation;
ii   the destabilization of a system due to the integration of elements harmful to coherence and resulting in a protectionist attitude;
iii   the disappearance of dominated systems;
iv   the emergence of a hybrid system with its own institutional architecture, of which the European integration is an incomplete example.

American CG system supporters most often predict a type (iii) scenario; "the arm's length" American system would ultimately prevail due to its greater efficiency while the other theoretical perspectives are far from sharing this conclusion. The regulation theory, for example, claims that the "arm's length" system may dominate, not because of its greater efficiency but rather because of its destabilizing effect provoked by the integration of certain of its elements into other national systems. Most analyses consider the hypothesis of evolution toward a single form – either by progressive convergence or by the disappearance of dominated forms – as hardly plausible, as much due to the cultural and political rigidities as the contingent character of the efficiency of the systems according to the stage of economic development. The complete hybridization hypothesis also seems barely probable. All recent CG system reforms, although influenced to differing degrees, by the American CG system, were all seeking the preservation of their fundamental cultural values. For others the supremacy of the American system, if ever it materializes, will not be because of its greater efficiency, but rather because of the destabilizing effects caused by the integration of some of its elements within the other national systems. Actually, all CG systems present their own advantages and disadvantages, pending on the economic advance of their proper environment.

It would be a big mistake to attempt to impose one country's CG system on countries with different corporate environments. There are the classical difficulties associated with transplants but an imported CG model – involving, as it does, different cultural, political and economic assumptions – has some additional problems. For the first times in the modern economic history, developing economies can make their voice heard. They should try to preserve their own vision of governance.

All nations, regardless of their cultural differences would find it rewarding to seek an optimal CG model, the most suitable for their economic advance and their cultural and political conditions.

Conclusion

Given market globalization and information technology development, it is expected that CG practices will converge more and more. It is necessary, however, to give enough time to such convergence to materialize efficiently. It may be reasonable to say that the CG system of any country has its advantages and limitations and that cross fertilization through comparative studies among countries should be performed to the mutual benefit of all.

Companies in exchanges can, obviously, recourse to either internal and/or external corporate mechanisms, as insured by the board, financial markets, rating agencies, auditing firms, banks and institutional investors, playing a significant role in detecting fraudulent behavior and reducing information asymmetries. Shareholders of non-listed companies can benefit from none of the previous CG external mechanisms and they seem to be neglected by the majority of national systems of CG. This situation is also obvious especially when we consider current efforts of international agencies to improve CG in developing countries. They are advocating dynamic exchanges, diffused shareholdings and so on, whereas often there are no real exchanges and no real shareholders in those environments. In our opinion, addressing the CG issue in developing environments is like addressing the issue of development itself. Rich countries and international organizations have all the reasons to underscore the fundamental role of governance in development, but they should find a way to adapt their requirements to the conditions of developing countries. Due to the complexity of the issue, the road map toward the attainment of such objectives should be worked out with each developing country. Of course, basic CG principles like transparency, corporate democracy, etc., should be respected by all.

Notes

1 It is amazing that until now only the second action of CG has drawn the attention.
2 As was then reported by the financial press, *The Wall Street Journal*, etc.
3 Indeed, analysts have assisted Enron in 69 completed or uncompleted acquisition transactions and the issuing of 138 bonds and were employed to provide investment advice on Enron.

4 Of course several models for approximating market value were suggested: net present value, etc. they all suffer a major weakness the impractical use in real life operations.

5 Over $5 million of profits from these options has been frozen while investigators try to identify who bought them.

6 Max Weber (21 April 1864–14 June 1920).

7 Respondents thought that corporations should sacrifice a part of their earnings for the benefits of employees and the local community, since they also contribute to their fortune.

8 *Business Week*, 11 March 1996, p. 43.

9 The concept, good or evil, is almost strange to SOX.

10 In the United States people would plead not guilty, not because they are really innocent, but because they are convinced that proofs of their culpability are difficult to establish.

11 Délga *et al.* Chapter 6.

12 SOX effect appeared in particular on the level of the supervision of auditing firms, auditors' independence, internal audit, conflicts of interest and management responsibility.

13 Global Corporate Governance Forum meetings of the World Bank (WB), Reports on the Observance of Standards and Codes (ROSC) issued by the International Monetary Fund (IMF) and the WB to gain some insight with regard to CG gains, etc.

14 We should note, however, that the extreme international popularity of the SOX was not really sought, at least not at the beginning.

15 Communication on a simplified business environment for companies in the areas of company law, accounting and auditing of 12 July 2007.

16 The American corporation model is a capital market institution, with its primary duty to its shareholders (Kay, 1993, p. 66).

17 In some European countries union representatives serve as board members.

Bibliography

Abdel-khalik, A. R., Wong, K. A. and Wu, A. (1999) The Information Environment of China's A and B Shares: Can We Make Sense of the Numbers?, *The International Journal of Accounting*, 34: pp. 347–489.

Aboody, D. (1996) Market Valuation of Employee Stock Options, *Journal of Accounting and Economics*, 22: pp. 357–391.

Aboody, D., Barth, M. E. and Kasznik, R. (2004) Firms' Voluntary Recognition of Stock-Based Compensation Expense, *Journal of Accounting Research*, 42, No. 2: pp. 123–150.

Aboul-Atta, N. (2003) Corporate Governance Means of Development: The Egyptian Experience, Center for Private International Enterprises, *Economic Reform Magazine*, Vol. 8.

ACCA (2002) *Responsibility in Business: Attitude to Corporate Governance in China and South East Asia*, Direct, Association of Chartered Certified Accountants, pp. 5–6.

Accounting Principles Board (1970), Statement no. 4: *Basic Concepts and Accounting Principles Underlying Financial Statements of Business Enterprises*, New York, AICPA.

Acemoglu, D., Johnson, S. and Robinson, J. A. (2001) The Colonial Origins of Comparative Development: An Empirical Investigation, *American Economic Review*, 91: pp. 1369–1401.

Acemoglu, D., Johnson, S. and Robinson, J. A. (2002) Reversal of Fortunes: Geography and Institutions in the Making of the Modem World Income Distribution, *Quarterly Journal of Economics*, 117: pp. 1231–1294.

Admati, A. and Pfleiderer, P. (1998) *Forcing Firms to Talk: Financial Disclosure Regulation and Externalities*, Graduate School of Business, Stanford University: Working Paper, No. 67.

Agence des douanes et du revenu du Canada (ADRC) (1996) *Benefits to Employees – Stock Options*, Ottawa.

Aguilera, R. and Jackson, G. (2003) The Cross-National Diversity of Corporate Governance: Dimensions and Determinants, *Academy of Management Review*, 28, No. 3: pp. 447–465.

Aharony, J., Lee, C. W. J. and Wong, T. J. (2000) Financial Packaging of IPO Firms in China, *Journal of Accounting Research*, 38: pp. 103–126.

Ahmed, A., Takeda, C. and Thomas, S. (1999) Bank Loan Loss Provisions: A Maximization of Capital Management, Earnings Management, and Signalling Effects, *Journal of Accounting and Economics*, 28: pp. 1–25.

Aksu, M. and Kosedag, A. (2005) *The Relationship Between Transparency and Disclosure Scores and Firm Performance: Evidence from Istanbul Stock Exchange*, Sabanci University, Working Paper, www.sabanciuniv.edu.

Alchian, A. A. and Demsetz, H. (1972) Production. Information Costs, and Economic Organization, *American Economic Review*, 62, No. 5: pp. 777–795.

Alchian, A. and Woodward, S. (1988) The Firm is Dead, Long Live the Firm, *Journal of Economic Literature*, 26: pp. 65–79.

Alles M., Kogan, A. and Vasarhelyi, M. (2004) *The Law of Unintended Consequences? Assessing the Costs, Benefits and Outcomes of the Sarbanes–Oxley Act*, Vol. 1, 2.

AlYafi, M. (2005) *Corporate Governance Trend*, No. 9, Fall: pp. 64–72.

Amable, B. (2000) Institutional Complementarity and Diversity of Social Systems of Innovation and Production, *Review of International Political Economy*, 7, No. 4: pp. 645–687.

Amable, B. and Petit, P. (1999) *Identifying the Structure of Institutions to Promote Innovation and Growth*. Cepremap, Working Paper, No. 9919.

Amable, B., Barré, R. and Boyer, R. (1997) *Les systèmes d'innovation à l'ère de la globalisation*, Economica.

American Institute of Chartered Accountants (AICPA) (1994) *Improving Business Reporting: A Customer Focus*, Meeting the Information Needs of Investors and Creditors, Comprehensive Report of the Special Committee of Financial Reporting, American Institute of Certified Public Accountants.

Amin, D. I. (1993) Jump Diffusion Option Valuation in Discrete Time, *Journal of Finance*, 48, No. 5: pp. 1833–1863.

Anonymous (2001) Corporate Governance in Hong Kong – the Road to Reform Following the Asian Financial Crisis, *International Financial Law Review*, 35, No. 4: pp. 53–59.

Anonymous (2005) *MENA Ownership Structures.*

Aoki, M. (1980) A Model of the Firm as a Stockholder–Employee Cooperative Game, *American Economic Review*, 70, No. 4: pp. 600–610.

Aoki, M. (1984) *The Cooperative Game Theory of the Firm*, Oxford: Clarendon Press.

Aoki, M. (1988) *Information. Incentive and Bargaining Structure in the Japanese Economy*, Cambridge and New York: Cambridge University Press.

Aoki, M. (1990) Toward an Economic Theory of the Japanese Firm, *Journal of Economic Literature*, 23, No. 1: pp. 1–27.

Aoki, M. (1995) *The Japanese Firm as a System of Attributes: A Survey and Research Agenda.* Revue d'Économie Industrielle No exceptionnel, hors-série, pp. 83–108.

Aoki, M. (2000a) *Information and Governance in the Silicon Valley Model*, Corporate Governance: Theoretical and Empirical Perspectives, Cambridge, MA: MIT Press, pp. 169–195.

Aoki, M. (2000b) *Information, Corporate Governance, and Institutional Diversity: Competitiveness in Japan, the USA, and the Transitional Economies.* Oxford and New York: Oxford University Press.

Aoki, M. (2001) *Toward a Comparative Institutional Analysis*, Cambridge, MA: MIT Press.

Apple Daily (2002) *More Corporate Disclosures, Better Stock Prices*, April 17.

Ararat, M. and Verlag S. (2004) Social Responsibility in a State Dependent System in A. Habisch, J. Jonker, M. Wegner and R. Schmidpeter (eds) *CSR in Europe*, Germany, pp. 247–257.

Ararat, M. and Ugur, M. (2002) Corporate Governance in Turkey: An Overview and Some Policy Recommendations, *Corporate Governance*, 3, No. 1: pp. 58–75.

Archibald, T. (1972) Stock Market Reaction to Depreciation Switch-Back, *The Accounting Review*, 47, No. 1: pp. 22–30.

Audit Committee, Combined Code (2003) *A Report and Proposed Guidance by an FRC-appointed group chaired by Sir Robert Smith.*

Ball, R. (1999) *Challenges Facing Accounting in China*, Keynote Address at the 1999 CAPA Conference, Dailian, China.

Ball, R. and Brown, P. (1968) An Empirical Evaluation of Accounting Income Numbers. *Journal of Accounting Research Autumn*, pp. 159–177.

Ballon, R., Tomita, I. and Usami, H. (1976) *Financial Reporting in Japan.* Working Paper, No. 18.

Banker, R., Chang, H. and Pizzini, M. (2004) The Balanced Scorecard: Judgmental Effects of Performance Measures Linked to Strategy, *The Accounting Review*, 79, No. 1: pp. 1–23.

Banker, R., Poter, G. and Srinivasan, D. (2000) An Empirical Investigation of an Incentive Plan that Includes Non Financial Performance Measures, *The Accounting Review*, 75, No. 1: pp. 65–92.

Bao, B. H. and Chou, L. (1999) The Usefulness of Earning and Book Value in Emerging Markets: Evidence from Listed Companies in the People's Republic of China. *Journal of International Financial Management and Accounting*, 10: pp. 85–104.

Baranger, G. (2004) *Le rapport Spécial du Président du Conseil d'administration sur le Fonctionnement du Conseil et les Procédures de Contrôle Interne.* Bull. Joly sociétés § 27: pp. 169 and up.

Barclay, M. and Holderness, C. G. (1989) Private Benefits from Control of Public Corporations, *Journal of Financial Economics*, 25: pp. 371–395.

Barclay, M. and Holderness, C. G. (1992) Negotiated Block Trades and Corporate Control, *Journal of Finance*, 46: pp. 861–878.

Barro, R. and August, J. (1996) *Determinants of Economic Growth: A Cross-Country Empirical Study*, National Bureau of Economy Research, Working Paper, No. 5698.

Barro, R. J. and McCleary, R. M. (2003) *Religion and Economy Growth*, National Bureau of Economy Research, Working Paper, No. 9682.

Bartov, E., Radhakrishnan, S. and Krinsky, I. (2000) Investor Sophistication and Patterns in Stock Returns After Earnings Announcements, *The Accounting Review*, 75: pp. 43–63.

Beaver, W. (1968) Alternative Accounting Measures as Predictors of Failure, *The Accounting Review*, 43, No. 1: pp. 113–122.

Beaver, W. (2002) Perspective on Recent Capital Market Research, *The Accounting Review*, 77, No. 2: pp. 453–474.

Beaver, W. and Dukes, R. (2002) Inter Period Tax Allocation and Delta Depreciation Methods: Some Empirical Results, *The Accounting Review*, 48: pp. 549–559.

Bebchuk, L. A., and Roe, M. J. (1999) A Theory of Path Dependence in Corporate Ownership and Governance, *Stanford Law Review*, 52, No. 1: pp. 127–170.

Becht, M., Bolton, P. and Roëll, A. (2002) *Corporate Governance and Control*, National Bureau of Economic Research: Working Paper, No. 9371.

Beck, T. and Levine, R. (2002) Industry Growth and Capital Allocation: Does Having a Market- or Bank-Based System Matter?, *Journal of Financial Economics*, 64: pp. 147–180.

Beck, T. and Levine, R. (2004) Stock Markets, Banks, and Economy Growth: Panel Evidence, *Journal of Banking and Finance*, 28, Iss. 3, March: pp. 423–442.

Beck, T., Demirguç-Kunt, A. and Levine, R. (2002*) Law and Finance: When Does Legal Origin Matter?*, National Bureau of Economic Research, Working Paper, No. 9379.

Beck, T., Demirguç-Kunt, A. and Levine, R. (2003a) *Bank Supervision and Corporate Finance*, National Bureau of Economy Research, Working Paper, No. 9620.

Beck, T., Demirguç-Kunt, A. and Levine, R. (2003b) Law, Endowments, and Finance, *Journal of Financial Economics*, 70, No. 2: 454–471.

Beck, T., Demirguç-Kunt, A. and Levine, R. (2001a) *Law, Politics, and Finance*, World Bank – Country Economics Department, Working Paper, No. 2585.

Beck, T., Demirguç-Kunt, A. Levine, R. and Maksimovic, V. (2001b) *Financial Structure and Economic Development: Firm. Industry and Country Evidence* in A. Demirguç-Kunt and R. Levine (eds) Financial Structure and Economic Growth: A Cross-Country Comparison of Banks, Markets and Development, Cambridge, MA: MIT Press.

Beck, T., Levine, R. and Loayza, N. (2000) Finance and the Sources of Growth, *Journal of Financial Economics*, 58, Nos 1–2: pp. 261–300.

Berglöf, E. and von Thadden, L. (1999) *The Changing Corporate Governance Paradigm: Implications for Transition and Developing Countries*, Stockholm Institute of Transition Economics, Working Paper, No. 10.

Berkman, H., Cole, R. and Fu, J. (2002) *From State to State: Improving Corporate Governance When the Government is a Large Block Holder*, University of Auckland and University of New South Wales, Working Paper.

Berkowitz, D., Pistor, K. and Richard, J. F. (1999) *Economic Development, Legality, and the Transplant Effect*, University of Pittsburg, Working Paper.

Berle, A. and Means, C. C. (1932) *The Modern Corporation and Private Property*, New York: Macmillan.

Berlioz, G. and Daigre, J. J. (1996) Le gouvernement d'entreprise: quelles conséquences pour les conseils d'administration des sociétés françaises? *Les Petites Affiches*, 20, No. 140: p. 23.

Bernard, V. L. and Thomas, J. (1989) Post-Earnings Announcement Drift: Delayed Price Response or Risk Premium?, *Journal of Accounting Research* (Supplement) 27: pp. 1–48.

Bernard, V. L. and Thomas, J. (1990) Evidence that Stock Prices Do Not Fully Reflect the Implications of Current Earnings for Future Earnings, *Journal of Accounting and Economics*, 13: pp. 305–340.

Bhagat, S. and Black, B. S. (1998) The Relationship Between Board Composition and Firm Performance in K. Hopt, M. Roe and E. Wymeersch (eds) *Comparative Corporate Governance: The State of the Art and Emerging Research*, Oxford, UK: Clarendon Press and New York: Oxford University Press.

Bhattacharya, S. and Chiesa, G. (1995) Proprietary Information, Financial Intermediation, and Research Incentives, *Journal of Financial Intermediation*, 4: pp. 328–357.

Birdsall, N. and Nellis, J. (2003) Winners and Losers: Assessing the Distributional Impact of Privatization, *World Development*, 31, No. 10: pp. 1617–1633.

Black, B., Kraakman, R. and Tarassova, A. (2000) Russia Privatization and Corporate Governance: What Went Wrong?, *Stanford Law Review*, 52: pp. 1731–1808.

Black, B. S., Hang, H. and Kim, W. (2002) *Does Corporate Governance Matter? Evidence from the Korean Market*, Standard Law School, Korea University and KDI School of Public Policy and Management, Working Paper.

Black, F. and Scholes, M. (1973) The Pricing of Options and Corporate Liabilities. *The Journal of Political Economy*, 81: pp. 637–659.

Blair, M. M. (1995) *Ownership and Control: Rethinking Corporate Governance for the Twenty-First Century*. Washington, DC: Brookings Institution, pp. 262, 273.

Blair, M. M. (1999) *Press Firm Specific Human Capital and Theories of the Firm* in M.

Blair and M. J. Roe (eds) Employees and Corporate Governance, Washington DC: Brookings Institution, pp. 58–90.

Blair, M. M. and Stout, L. (1999) A Team Production Theory of Corporate Law, *Virginia Law Review*, 85, No. 2: pp. 247–328.

Block, S. B. (1999) A Study of Financial Analysts: Practice and Theory. *Financial Analysts Journal*, July/August: pp. 86–95.

Bloom, D., Ratnikov, K. and Osipov, S. (2003) Areshev Coudert: Brothers llp Ownership Changes in Russia: What is it? How to Defend Against it? (Передел собственности «по-российски»: что это такое и как ему противостоять), *Financial Analyst*, No. 3: pp. 98–110.

Bloomfield, R. J. (2002) The Incomplete Revelation Hypothesis and Financial Reporting, *Accounting Horizons*, 16, No. 2: pp. 233–243.

Bodie, Z. R., Kaplan, S. and Merton, R. C. (2003) For the Last Time: Stock Options Are an Expense, *Harvard Business Review*, pp. 63–71.

Bodurtha, J. (2002) *Dilution and Multiple-Issue Tranches Inherent in Employee Stock Option Valuation*, McDonough School of Business, Georgetown University, Working Paper.

Botero, J., Djankov, S., La Porta, R., Lopez-de-Silanes, F. and Shleifer, A. (2003) *The Regulation of Labor*, National Bureau of Economic Research, Working Paper, No. 9756.

Bourdieu, P. (1989) *La noblesse d'État*, Les Éditions de Minuit, 10.

Bourse de Toronto, TSX. (2002) *Revised Requirements: Guidelines and Practice Notes*.

Boyer, R. (2001) The Diversity and Future of Capitalisms: A Regulationist Analysis in G. M. Hodgson, M. Itoh and N. Yokokawa (eds) *Capitalism in Evolution – Global Contentions East and West*, London: Edward Elgar, pp. 100–121.

Boyer, R. (2002) *Variété du capitalisme et théorie de la régulation*, L'année de la régulation, No. 6: pp. 125–194.

Boyer, R. and Saillard, Y. (2002) *Théorie de la régulation: l'état des savoirs*, Paris: La Découverte.

Bradshaw, M. (2004) How Do Analysts Use their Earnings Forecast in Generating Stock Recommendations?, *The Accounting Review*, 79, No. 1: pp. 25–50.

Brokhovich, K. E., Parrino, A. R. and Traparin, T. (1996) Outside Directors and CEO Selection, *Journal of Financial and Quantitative Analysis*, September 31: pp. 337–355.

Bruno, A. (2001) *Adam Smith, vie, œuvre et concepts*, Éditions Ellipse, 84.

Burkart, M., Gromb, D. and Panunzi, F. (1997) Large Shareholders, Monitoring, and the Value of the Firm, *Quarterly Journal of Economics*, 112: pp. 693–728.

Bushman, R. and Smith, A. J. (2001) Financial Accounting Information and Corporate Governance, *Journal of Accounting and Economics*, 32, No. 1–3: pp. 237–333.

Bushman, R. and Smith, A. J. (2003) Transparency, Financial Accounting Information, and Corporate Governance, *Economic Policy Review*, 9, No. 1: 76–90.

Bushman R., Indjejikian, R. and Smith, A. (1996) CEO Compensation, the Role of Individual Performance Evaluation, *Journal of Accounting and Economics*, 21: pp. 161–193.

Bushman, R., Piotroski, J. and Smith, A. (2001) *What Determines Corporate Transparency?*, University of Chicago, Unpublished Paper.

Butterworth, C. and Zartman, W. (2001) *Between the State and Islam*, Cambridge University Press.

Byrne, J. (1996a) How High Can CEO Pay Go?, *Business Week*, April: pp. 100–106.

366 *Bibliography*

Byrne, J. (1996b) The Best and Worst Boards, *Business Week*, November: pp. 82–105.

Cadbury, A. (1992) *Report of the Committee on the Financial Aspects of Corporate Governance*, Gee and Co. Ltd.

CalPERS. (1998) *Corporate Governance Principles and Guidelines*, California Public Employees' Retirement System.

Campos, E. and Hilton, L. (1994) *Information Aggregation and Economic Development: The Case of East Asia*, University of Western Ontario, Papers in Political Economy, Vol. 50, pp. 53.

Canadian Institute of Chartered Accountants (CICA) (2002) Section 3870, *Stock-Based Compensation and Other Stock-Based Payments.*

Carlin, W. and Mayer, C. (2003) Finance. Investment and Growth, *Journal of Financial Economics*, 69, No. 1: pp. 191–226.

Casper, S. (2001) The Legal Framework for Corporate Governance: Contract Law and Company Strategies in Germany and the United States in P. A. Hall and D. Soskice (eds) *Varieties of Capitalism: The Institutional Foundations of Comparative Advantage*, Oxford: Oxford University Press, pp. 387–416.

Castanias, R. P. and Helfat, C. E. (1991) Managerial Resources and Rents, *Journal of Management*, 17, No. 1: pp. 155–171.

Cha, L. (2003) How to Implement the Modern Enterprise System of Listed Companies?, *Caijing Magazine*, No. 76: pp. 46–47.

Chambers, R. (1968) Measures and Values: A Reply to Professor Staubus, *The Accounting Review*, October: pp. 239–247.

Chang, S. J. (2003) Ownership Structure, Expropriation, and Performance of Group Affiliated Companies in Korea, *Academy of Management Journal*, 46, No. 2: pp. 238–253.

Charreaux, G. (1995) Modes de contrôle des dirigeants et performance des firmes, *Revue d'Economie Industrielle*, 1er trimestre: 135–172.

Charreaux, G. (1996) Pour une véritable théorie de la latitude managériale et du gouvernement des entreprises, *Revue Française de Gestion*, November–December: pp. 50–64.

Charreaux, G. (1997) Le Gouvernement des entreprises: Corporate Governance, Théories et Faits, Paris, *Économica*, pp. 421–469.

Charreaux, G. (2000) Nouvelle Économie et Gouvernance, Rapport Moral sur l'Argent dans le Monde 2000, *Association d'Économie Financière*, pp. 315–321.

Charreaux, G. (2002a) Variation sur le Thème à la Recherche de Nouvelles Fondations pour la Finance d'Entreprise, *Finance Contrôle Stratégie*, 5, No. 3: pp. 5–68.

Charreaux, G. (2002b) L'Actionnaire comme Apporteur de Ressources Cognitives, *Revue Française de Gestion*, 28, No. 141: pp. 75–107.

Charreaux, G. (2003) Le point sur les réseaux d'administrateurs et de dirigeants, *Banque and Marchés*, September–October, No. 66: pp. 47–51.

Charreaux, G. and Desbrières, Ph. (1998) Gouvernance des Entreprises: Valeur Partenariale contre Valeur Actionnariale, *Finance Contrôle Stratégie*, 1, No. 2: pp. 57–88.

Chartered Accountants of Canada and Toronto Stock Exchange (TSX) (2001) *Beyond Compliance: Building a Governance Culture (Saucier Report).*

Chartered Institute of England and Wales (1999) *Turnbull Report*, London.

Cheffins, B. R. (2001) Does Law Matter? The Separation of Ownership and Control in the United Kingdom, *Journal of Legal Studies*, 30, No. 2: pp. 459–484.

Chen, C. J. P., Chen, S. and Su, X. (2001) Is Accounting Information Value-relevant in the Emerging Chinese Stock Market?, *Journal of International Accounting, Auditing and Taxation*, 10: pp. 1–22.

Chen, C. J. P., Gul, F. A. and Su, X. (1999) A Comparison of Reported Earnings under Chinese GAAP vs. IAS: Evidence from the Shanghai Stock Exchange, *Accounting Horizon*, 13, No. 2: pp. 91–111.

Chen, D. H., Fan, J. P. H. and Wong, T. J. (2003) *Do Politicians Jeopardize Professionalism? Decentralization and the Structure of Chinese Corporate Boards*, Department of Accounting, Hong Kong University of Science and Technology, Working Paper.

Chen, K. and Yuan, H. (2000) *Earnings Management and Capital Resources Allocation: Evidence from China's Accounting-based Regulation of Rights Issues*, Hong Kong University of Science and Technology and Shanghai University of Finance and Economics, Working Paper.

Chen, K. C. W., Wei, J. K. C. and Chen, Z. H. (2003) *Disclosure, Corporate Governance and the Cost of Equity Capital: Evidence from Asia Emerging Market*, Hong Kong University of Science and Technology, Working Paper.

Chen, X. and Jiang, T. (2000) Diversification of Ownership, Firm Performance and Capital Structure: An Empirical Study (in Chinese), *Economic Research*, No. 8: pp. 28–35.

Chen, X., Lee, C. W. J. and Li, J. (2003) *Chinese Tango: Government Assisted Earnings Management*, Tsinghua University, Working Paper.

Chen, X. Y. and Xu, Y. T. (2001) Ownership Structure, Firm Performance and Protection of Shareholders' Interests (in Chinese), *Economic Research*, No. 11: pp. 3–11.

Chew, D. H. (1997) *Studies in International Corporate Finance and Governance Systems*, New York: Oxford University Press.

Chinese Private Enterprises Research Project (2003) A Report of the Survey on Chinese Private Enterprises, *Caijing Magazine*, February, No. 77–78: pp. 138–160.

Chollet, J. (2001) Revue des modèles d'options et des tests sur les bons, *Fineco*, 11: pp. 97–128.

Chow, C. (2002) *Invest in Corporate Governance: A Perspective from the HK Asset Management Industry*, 2002 Symposium on Corporate Governance and Disclosure: The Impact of Globalization. The School of Accountancy, The Chinese University of Hong Kong.

Claessens, S. and Fan, J. P. H. (2003) Corporate Governance in Asia: A Survey. *International Review of Finance*, 2: pp. 21–48.

Claessens, S. and Laeven, L. (2003) Financial Development, Property Rights, and Growth, *Journal of Finance*, 58, No. 6: pp. 2401–2436.

Claessens, S., Djankov, S. and Nenova, T. (2000) *Corporate Risk Around the World, World Bank*, Working Paper, http://econworldbank.org/docs/l024.pdf.

Claessens, S., Djankov, S., Fan, J. and Lang, L. (2000) The Separation of Ownership and Control in East Asia Corporations, *Journal of Financial Economics*, 58, Iss. 1–2: pp. 81–112.

Coase, R. (1960) The Problems of Social Cost, *Journal of Law and Economics*, 3: pp. 1–44.

Coase, R. (1937) The Nature of the Firm, *Economica*, pp. 386–405.

Coastes, R. (1972) The Predictive Content of Interim Reports: A Time Series Analysis. Empirical Research in Accounting: Selected Studies, *Supplement to Journal of Accounting Research*, pp. 132–144.

Coffee, J. (1999a) Privatization and Corporate Governance: The Lessons from Securities Market Failure. *Journal of Corporate Law*, Fall: pp. 1–39.

Coffee, J. (1999b) The Future as History: The Prospects for Global Convergence in

Corporate Governance and Its Implications. *Northwestern University Law Review*, 93: pp. 641–707.

Coffee, J. (2000) *Convergence and Its Critics: What are the Preconditions to the Separation of Ownership and Control*, Columbia Law School, The Center for Law and Economic Studies, Working Paper, No. 179.

Coffee, J. (2001a) The Rise of Dispersed Ownership: The Roles of Law and the State in the Separation of Ownership and Control, *Yale Law Journal*, 111, No. 1: pp. 1–82.

Coffee, J. (2001b) *Do Norms Matter? A Cross-Country Explanation of the Private Benefits of Control*, Columbia Law School, The Center for Law and Economic Studies, Working Paper, No. 183.

Cohen, E. (2003) *Après Enron, gouvernance et éthique, Le pacte de la transparence*, Paris: Ernst and Young, Editions de La Martinière, p. 110.

Cohen, M. (2002*) Les nouvelles attributions des comités d'entreprise depuis la loi de modernisation sociale*, Droit social No. 3, la loi de modernisation sociale et le droit du travail, numéro spécial: 298 et suivantes.

Coleman J. S. (1990) *Foundations of Social Theory*, Cambridge, MA: Harvard University Press.

Colinet, F. (1994) *Pratique des comptes consolidés*, Dunod des Experts Comptable Collection Fonctions de l'entreprise, 4th edn.

Collins, W., Rozeff, M. and Dhaliwal, D. (1981) The Economic Determinants of the Market Reaction to Proposed Mandatory Accounting Changes in the Oil and Gas Industry, *Journal of Accounting and Economics*, March: pp. 37–71.

Committee on Corporate Governance UK (2002) *The Combined Code Principles of Good Governance and Code of Best Practice*, Derived from the Committee's Final Report and from the Cadbury and Greenbury Reports.

Congress of the United States (2002) *Sarbanes–Oxley Act*, 23 January.

Conrad, A. F. (1976) Corporations in Perspective, *Official Journal of the European Communities*, No. L 26/1.

Core, J. E., Holthausen, R. W. and Larcker, D. F. (1999) Corporate Governance, Chief Executive Officer Compensation, and Firm Performance, *Journal of Financial Economics*, 51: pp. 371–406.

Core, J. E., Wayne, R. G. and Larcker, D. F. (2003) Executive Equity Compensation and Incentives: A Survey, *Economic Policy Review*, 9, No. 1: pp. 27–50.

Coriat, B. and Weinstein, O. (1995) *Les nouvelles théories de l'entreprise*, Le Livre de Poche, Librairie Générale Française.

Cornell, B. and Chapiro, A. (1987) Corporate Stakeholders and Corporate Finance, *Financial Management*, No. 16, Spring: pp. 5–14.

Corporate Governance Workshop (2003) Global Corporate Governance Forum Middle East and North Africa (October).

Cox, J. C. and Ross, S. A. (1976) The Valuation of Options for Alternative Stochastic Processes, *Journal of Financial Economics*, 3: pp. 145–166.

Cox, J. C., Ross, S. A. and Rubinstein, M. (1979) Option Pricing: A Simplified Approach, *Journal of Financial Economics*, 7: pp. 229–263.

CSRC (2000) *Information Disclosure and Corporate Governance in China*, OECD/World Bank Second Asian Corporate Governance Roundtable, Hong Kong.

Cyert, R. M. and March, J. G. (1963) *A Behavioural Theory of the Firm*, Englewood Cliffs, NJ: Prentice-Hall.

Daigre, J.-J. (2004) *Transparence et gouvernement d'entreprise*, Le droit des sociétés.

Dalloz, Coll. Dossiers: 15 et suivantes, 497 et seq.

Dallas, G. (2002) *Evaluating Asian Corporate Governance in an International Context*, 2002 Symposium on Corporate Governance and Disclosure: The Impact of Globalization. The School of Accountancy, The Chinese University of Hong Kong.

Daniels, R. and MacIntosh, J. (1991) *Towards a Distinctive Canadian Corporate Law Regime*, Osgoode Hall Law Journal, 29: pp. 863–933.

Danışmanlık, A. Ş. (2005) *İyi Şirket*, IMKB 50 Endeksi Şirketleri Kurumsal Yönetim Web Analizi, Mimeo.

De Jong, H. W. (1997) The Governance Structure and Performance of Large European Corporations, *Journal of Management and Governance*, 1: pp. 5–27.

de Vries, K. (2002) *Combat contre l'irrationalité des managers*, Paris: Editions d'Organisation.

DeAngelo, L. E. (1988) Managerial Competition. Information Costs, and Corporate Governance: The Use of Accounting Performance Measures in Proxy Contests, *Journal of Accounting and Economics*, 10: pp. 3–36.

Dechow, P., Hutton, A. and Sloan, R. G. (1999) An Empirical Assessment of the Residual Income Valuation Model, *Journal of Accounting and Economics*, 26: pp. 1–34.

Dechow, P., Hutton, A. and Sloan, R. G. (2000) The Relation Between Analysts' Forecasts and Long-Term Earnings Growth and Stock Price Performance Following Equity Offerings, *Contemporary Accounting Research*, 17, No. 1: pp. 1–32.

Demirgüç-Kunt, A. and Maksimovic, V. (1998) Law, Finance, and Firm Growth. *Journal of Finance*, December, 53, No. 6: pp. 2107–2137.

Demirgüç-Kunt, A. and Maksimovic, V. (1999) Institutions, Financial Markets and Debt Maturity, *Journal of Financial Economics*, 54: pp. 295–336.

Demirgüç-Kunt, A. and Maksimovic, V. (2002) Funding Growth in Bank-Based and Market-Based Financial Systems: Evidence from Firm-Level Data, *Journal of Financial Economics*, 65: pp. 337–364.

Dempsey, S., Herbert, J., Hunt III, G. and Schroeder, N. W. (1993) Earnings Management and Corporate Ownership Structure: An Examination of Extraordinary Item Reporting, *Journal of Business Finance and Accounting*, pp. 479–500.

Demsetz, H. (1969) Information and Efficiency: Another Viewpoint, *Journal of Law and Economics*, 12: pp. 1–22.

Demsetz, H. (1991 [1988]) *The Theory of the Firm Revisited* in O. E. Williamson and S. Winter (eds) The Nature of the Firm, New York: Oxford University Press, pp. 159–178, publié initialement in *Journal of Law, Economics and Organization*, 4: 141–163.

Demsetz, H. and Lehn, K. (1985) The Structure and Corporate Ownership: Causes and Consequences, *Journal of Political Economy*, 93: pp. 1155–1177.

Denis, D. K. and McConnell, J. J. (2002) *International Corporate Governance*, Purdue University, Working Paper.

Dey Report (1994) *Where the Directors*, Toronto Stock Exchange (Toronto).

Dezalay, Y. and Garth, B. (2002) *La mondialisation des guerres de palais. La restructuration du pouvoir d'état en Amérique Latine: entre notables du droit et Chicago boys*, Le Seuil, p. 49.

Dhaliwal, D. S., Salamon, G. L. and Smith, E. D. (1982) The Effect of Ownership Versus Management Control On The Choice of Accounting Methods, *Journal of Accounting and Economics*, 4: pp. 41–53.

Dipiazza, S. A. (2002) *How to Gain Public's Confidence Again – A Model for Future Corporate Financial Reporting* (in Chinese) 21st Century Economic Report, China.

Dittmar, A., Mahrt-Smith, J. and Servaes, H. (2003) International Corporate Governance and Corporate Cash Holdings, *Journal of Financial and Quantitative Analysis*, 38, No. 1: pp. 111–123.

Djankov, S. and Murrell, P. (2000): *The Determinants of Enterprise Restructuring in Transition: An Assessment of the Evidence*, Washington, DC: World Bank.

Djankov, S., La Porta, R., Lopez-de-Silanes, F. and Shleifer, A. (2002) The Regulation of Entry, *Quarterly Journal of Economics*, 117, No. 1: pp. 1–37.

Djankov, S., La Porta, R., Lopez-de-Silanes, F. and Shleifer, A. (2003a) *The New Comparative Economics: A First Look*, CEPR Discussion Paper, No. 3882.

Djankov, S., La Porta, R., Lopez-de-Silanes, F. and Shleifer, A. (2003b) Courts Rules, *Quarterly Journal of Economics*, 118, No. 2: pp. 453–462.

Dolgopyatova, T. (2000) Development of Corporate Control Model in Russian Industry, *Economic Journal of Highest School of Economics*, No. 3: pp. 369–384.

Domtar (2002) *Et que disent les chiffres*, Domtar 2002 Annual Report, Montréal.

Dosi, G. (1990) Finance. Innovation and Industrial Change, *Journal of Economic Behavior and Organization*, 13: pp. 299–319.

Dosi, G. (1994) Boundaries of the Firm in G. Hogdson, W. Samuels and M. Tool (eds) *The Elgar Companion to Institutional and Evolutionary Economics*, Vol. 1, Aldershot: Edward Elgar, pp. 229–237.

Dosi, G. and Marengo, L. (2000) On the Tangled Discourse Between Transaction Cost Economics and Competence-Based Views of the Firm: Some Comments in N. Foss and V. Mahnke (eds) *Competence, Governance, and Entrepreneurship*, New York: Oxford University Press, pp. 80–92.

Dupuy, F. (1998) *Le client et le bureaucrate*, Dunod des Experts Comptable Collection Fonctions de l'entreprise, 2nd edn.

Durnev, A. and Kim, E. H. (2002) *To Steal or Not to Steal: Firm Attributes, Legal Environment and Valuation*, University of Michigan Business School, Working Paper.

Dyck, A. and Zingales, L. (2004) Private Benefits of Control: An International Comparison, *Journal of Finance*, 59, No. 2: pp. 537–600.

Dye, R. (1988) Earnings Management in an Overlapping Generation Model, *Journal of Accounting Research*, Autumn: pp. 323–352.

Easterly, W. and Levine, R. (2003) Tropics, Germs, and Crops: How Endowments Influence Economy Development, *Journal of Monetary Economics*, 50, No. 1: pp. 3–39.

Eccher, E. and Healy, M. (2000) *The Role of International Accounting Standards in Transitional Economies: A Study of People's Republic of China*, MIT Sloan School of Management and Harvard Business School, Working Paper.

Eccles, R. G. and Mavrinac, S. C. (1995) Improving the Corporate Disclosure Process. *Sloan Management Review*, Summer: pp. 11–24.

Elam, R. (1975) The Effect of Lease Data on the Predictive Ability of Financial Ratios, *The Accounting Review*, Spring: pp. 25–43.

Elger, E. (1980) Accounting-Based Risk Measurement: A Re-Examination, *The Accounting Review*, Summer: pp. 389–408.

Eliasson, G. (1990) The Firm as a Competent Team, *Journal of Economic Behaviour and Organization*, 13: pp. 275–298.

Elitzur, R. and Yaari, V. (1995) Executive Incentive Compensation and Earnings Manipulation in a Multi-Period Setting, *Journal of Economic Behaviour and Organization*, 26: pp. 201–220.

Ellerman, D. (1999) *Voucher Privatization as the Cold War by Other Means*, Voprosi Economiki, August, No. 8: pp. 212–231.

Ellsworth, R. R. (1985) Capital Markets and Competitive Decline, *Harvard Business Review*, 2, No. 1: pp. 28–42.

Estevez-Abe, M., Iversen, T. and Soskice, D. (2001) *Social Protection and Skill Formation: A Reinterpretation of the Welfare State* in P. A. Hall and D. Soskice (eds) Varieties of Capitalism: The Institutional Foundations of Comparative Advantage, Oxford: Oxford University Press, pp. 145–183.

EU (2007a) *Proportionality Between Ownership and Control in EU Listed Companies*, External Study Commissioned by the European Commission from Shearman & Sterling LLP.

EU (2007b) *Report on High Level of Company Experts on a Modern Regulatory Framework for Company Law in Europe*, Brussels, 4 November.

European Commission (2004) *Progress Report on Turkey's Progress Towards Accession*, SEC, 1201.

European Corporate Governance Network. (1997) *Preliminary Report on the Separation of Ownership and Control: A Survey of Seven European Countries*, Brussels, October.

Fama, E. F. (1970) Efficient Capital Market: A Review of a Theory and Empirical Work, *Journal of Finance*, May: pp. 383–417.

Fama, E. F. (1980) Agency Problems and the Theory of the Firm, *Journal of Political Economy*, 88, No. 2: pp. 288–307.

Fama, E. F. (1991) Efficient Capital Market II, *Journal of Finance*, 46, No. 5: pp. 1575–1617.

Fama, E. F. and French, K. (1992) The Cross-Section of Expected Stock Returns, *Journal of Finance*, 47: pp. 427–465.

Fama, E. F. and Jensen, M. C. (1983a) Separation of Ownership and Control, *Journal of Law and Economics*, No. 16: pp. 301–325.

Fama, E. F. and Jensen, M. C. (1983b) Agency Problems and Residual Claims, *Journal of Law and Economics*, 26: pp. 327–349.

Fan, D., Lau, C. M. and Wu, S. (2000) *Corporate Governance Mechanisms of Chinese Firms: Incentives and Performance*, Proceedings of the Conference on Chinese Management, The Chinese University of Hong Kong and The Hong Kong University of Science and Technology.

Fan, J. P. H. and Wong, T. J. (1999) *Corporate Ownership and the Informativeness of Accounting Earnings*, School of Business and Management, The Hong Kong University of Science and Technology, Working Paper.

Fauver, L., Houston, J. and Naranjo, A. (2003) Capital Market Development. International Integration, Legal Systems, and the Value of Corporate Diversification: A Cross-Country Analysis, *Journal of Financial and Quantitative Analysis*, 38, No. 1: pp. 135–157.

Feltham, G. A. and Ohlson, J. A. (1995) Valuation and Clean Surplus Accounting for Operating and Financial Activities, *Contemporary Accounting Research*, II, Spring: pp. 689–732.

Feltham, G. A. and Ohlson, J. A. (1996) Uncertainty Resolution and the Theory of Depreciation Measurement, *Journal of Accounting Research*, 34: pp. 209–234.

Fikret-Pasa, S., Kabasakal, H. and Bodur, M. (2001) Society, Organizations, and Leadership in Turkey, *Applied Psychology: An International Review*, 50, No. 4: pp. 559–589.

Filatov, A. (2006) *Collective Portrait of Independent Director in Russian Companies*, Independent Directors Association.

Financial Accounting Standards Board (1995) *Statement of Financial Accounting Standards No. 123. Accounting for Stock-Based Compensation*, Stamford, CT.

Finnerty, E. (1976) Insiders and Market Efficiency, *Journal of Finance*, September: pp. 1141–1148.

Finnerty, J. D. (2003) *Valuing Employee Stock Options: A Comparison of Alternative Models*, Financial Executives Research Foundation Inc., Executive Report.

Firth, M., Tam, M. and Tang, M. (1999) The Determinants of Top Management Pay, *OMEGA*, 27, No. 6: pp. 617–635.

Fischer, P. E. and Verrecchia, R. R. (1999) Public Information and Heuristic Trade, *Journal of Accounting and Economics*, 27: pp. 89–124.

Fisher, S. M. (1978) Call Option Pricing When the Exercise Price is Uncertain, and the Valuation of Index Bonds, *Journal of Finance*, XXXIII, No. 1: pp. 169–176.

Foss, K. and Foss, N. J. (2000) The Knowledge-Based Approach and Organizational Economics: How Much Do They Really Differ? And How Does It Matter? in N. Foss and V. Mahnke (eds) *Competence, Governance, and Entrepreneurship*, Oxford: Oxford University Press, pp. 55–79.

Foss, N. J. (1996a) Firms, Incomplete Contracts, and Organizational Learning, *Human Systems Management*, 15, No. 1: pp. 17–26.

Foss, N. J. (1996b) Capabilities and the Theory of the Firm, *Revue d'Economie Industrielle*, No. 77: pp. 7–28.

Foss, N. J. (ed.) (1997) *Resources, Firms and Strategies*, Oxford Management Readers, Oxford: Oxford University Press.

Foss, N. J. and Mahnke, V. (eds) (2000) *Competence, Governance, and Entrepreneurship*, Oxford: Oxford University Press.

Foster, G. (1977a) Quarterly Earnings Data: Time Series Properties and Predictive Ability Results, *The Accounting Review*, January: pp. 1–21.

Foster, G. (1977b) Valuation Parameters of Property-Liability Companies, *Journal of Finance*, June: pp. 823–836.

Foster, G. (1980) Accounting Policy Decisions and Capital Market Research, *Journal of Accounting and Economics*, March: pp. 26–62.

Franks, J., Mayer, C. and Rossi, S. (2003) *The Origination and Evolution of Ownership and Control*, European Corporate Governance Institute, Finance Working Paper, No. 9.

Fransman, M. (1998) Information, Knowledge, Vision and Theories of the Firm in G. Dosi, D. J. Teece and J. Chitry (eds) *Technology, Organization and Competitiveness – Perspectives on Industrial and Corporate Change*, Oxford: Oxford University Press, pp. 147–191.

Frederic, W., James, E. and Keith, D. (1992) The Four Faces of Corporate Citizenships, *Business and Society Review*, Boston: Blackwell, 100, No. 1: pp. 1–99.

Freeman, R. E. (1984) *Strategic Management: A Stakeholder Approach*, Darden Business School Working Paper, No. 101–102.

Friedman, M. (1953) *The Technology of Positive Economics, Essays in Positive Economics*, Chicago, IL: University of Chicago Press.

Fukuyama, F. (1995) *Trust*, New York: Free Press.

Fung, G. F., Han, B. and Sen, B. (2002) An Empirical Study on Ownership Concentration of Chinese Listed Firms (in Chinese), *Economic Research*, No. 8: pp. 12–18.

Galai, D. (1989) A Note on Equilibrium Warranty Pricing Models and Accounting for Executive Stock Options, *Journal of Accounting Research*, 27: pp. 313–315.

Garvey, G. T. and Swan, P. L. (1994) The Economics of Corporate Governance, Beyond the Marshallian Firm, *Journal of Corporate Finance*, 1, No. 2: pp. 139–174.

Gertner, R., Guibbson, R. and Sharfstein, D. (1988) Simultaneous Signalling to the Capital and Product Markets, RAND, *Journal of Economics*, 19: pp. 173–190.

Geske, R. (1979) The Valuation of Compound Options, *Journal of Financial Economics*, 7: pp. 63–81.

Giacalone, R. and Rosenfeld, P. (1991) *Applied Impression Management, How Image-Making Affects Managerial Decision-Making*, Thousand Oaks, CA: Sage Publications Inc.

Gibson, M. S. (2001) *Incorporating Event Risk into Value-at-Risk*, Trading Risk Analysis Section, Division of Research and Statistics, Federal Reserve Board, Working Paper.

Gill, A. (2002) *Corporate Governance in Emerging Markets – Saints and Sinners: Who's Got Religion?*, 2002 Symposium on Corporate Governance and Disclosure: The Impact of Globalization, The School of Accountancy, The Chinese University of Hong Kong.

Glaeser, E. and Shleifer, A. (2002) Legal Origins, *Quarterly Journal of Economics*, 117 No. 4: pp. 1193–1229.

Glaeser, E. and Shleifer, A. (2003) The Rise of the Regulatory State, *Journal of Economic Literature*, 41, No. 2: pp. 401–425.

Goldberg, I. and Watkins, A. (2000) *Enterprise Restructuring*, The World Bank, ECSPF.

Golovin, V. and Taran, A. (2006) *Too Many OTP Acquisitions*, Ukraine: Delo, December.

Gompers, A. P., Ishii, J. L. and Metrick, A. (2001) *Corporate Governance and Equity Prices*, Harvard Business School, Harvard University and University of Pennsylvania, Working Paper.

Gourevitch, P. (2003) The Politics of Corporate Governance Regulation, *Yale Law Journal*, 112, No. 7: pp. 1829–1880.

Gourevitch, P. and Hawes, M. (2002) The Politics of Choice Among National Production Systems, *L'Année de la Régulation*, No. 6: pp. 241–270.

Gourevitch, P. and Shinn, J. (2004) Explaining Corporate Governance: The Role of Politics (forthcoming).

Gray, S. J. (1988) *Towards a Theory of Cultural Influence on the Development of Accounting Systems Internationally*, Abacus, March: pp. 1–15.

Grandori, A. (2001) Neither Hierarchy nor Identity: Knowledge-Governance Mechanisms and the Theory of the Firm, *Journal of Management and Governance*, 5: pp. 381–399.

Grossman, S. and Hart, O. (1986) The Costs and Benefits of Ownership: A Theory of Vertical and Lateral Integration, *Journal of Political Economy*, 94: pp. 691–719.

Gul, F. and Zhao, R. (2001) *Ownership, Board Structures and Firm Performance: Some Evidence from Chinese Listed Companies*, Department of Accountancy, City University of Hong Kong, Working Paper.

Guriev, S., Lazareva, O., Rachinsky, A. and Tsukhlo, S. (2003) *Corporate Governance in Russian Industry*, Moscow: Institute of Economies in Transition.

Guriev, S., Lazareva, O., Rachinsky, A. and Tsukhlo, S. (2004) *Corporate Governance in Russian Industry*, Moscow: Institute of Economies in Transition.

Guyon, Y. (1998), *Corporate Governance*, Paris: Répertoire Dalloz, Sociétés, February.

Guyon, Y. (2000) *Corporate Governance*, Paris: Répertoire Dalloz, Sociétés.

Haidar, J. I. (2006) A *Case for MENA Representation on the IASB*, Middle East, XLIX, No. 34, 21 August: pp. 23–32.

Hall, B. J. and Murphy, K. J. (2000) *Stock Options for Undiversified Executives*, National Bureau of Economic Research, Working Paper, No. 8052.

Hall, P. A. (1999) The Political Economy of Europe in an Era of Interdependence in

H. Kitschelt, P. Lange, G. Marks and J. D. Stephens (eds) *Continuity and Change in Contemporary Capitalism*, Cambridge: Cambridge University Press, pp. 135–163.

Hall, P. A. and Gingerich, D. W. (2001) *Varieties of Capitalism and Institutional Complementarities in the Macroeconomy: An Empirical Analysis*, Harvard University, Department of Government, Working Paper.

Hall, P. A. and Soskice, D. (eds) (2001) *Varieties of Capitalism: The Institutional Foundations of Comparative Advantage*, New York: Oxford University Press.

Hall, P. A. and Soskice, D. (2002) Les variétés du capitalisme, L'année de la Régulation, No. 6: 47–124, traduit de, An Introduction to Varieties of Capitalism in P. A. Hall and D. Soskice (eds) *Varieties of Capitalism: The Institutional Foundations of Comparative Advantage*, New York: Oxford University Press, pp. 1–68.

Hall, S. C. and Stammerjohan, W. W. (1997) Damage Awards and Earnings Management in the Oil Industry, *The Accounting Review*, 72: pp. 47–65.

Hansmann, H. (1996) *The Ownership of Enterprise*, Cambridge, MA: The Belknap Press of Harvard University Press.

Hart, O. and Moore, J. (1990) Property Rights and the Nature of the Firm, *Journal of Political Economy*, 98, No. 6: pp. 1119–1158.

Hashimoto, M. (2002) *Commercial Code Revisions: Promoting the Evolution of Japanese Companies*, NRI Papers, No. 48.

Hausbrich, J. and April, G. (1994) Risk Aversion, Performance Pay, and the Principal-Agent Problem, *Journal of Political Economy*, 102: pp. 258–276.

Haw, I. M., Qi, D. and Wu, W. (1998) *Value-Relevance of Financial Reporting Disclosures in an Emerging Capital Market: The Case of B-Shares and H-Shares in China*, The Chinese University of Hong Kong, Working Paper.

Haw, I. M., Qi, D., Wu, W. and Zhang, W. (1998) *Earning Management of Listed Firms in Response to Securitiy Regulations in China's Emerging Capital Market*, The Chinese University of Hong Kong, Working Paper.

Hawkamah, the Institute for Corporate Governance (2007) *Corporate Governance in the GCC: Country Reports and Comparative Survey: An Investor's Perspective*, www.hawkamah.org/publications/cg_reports/governance_survey/index.html.

Haye, R. (1998) The Impact of Trading Commission Incentives on Analysts' Stock Coverage Decisions and Earnings Forecast, *Journal of Accounting Research*, 36, No. 2: pp. 299–320.

He, J. (1998) An Empirical Study of Corporate Governance of Listed Companies (in Chinese), *Economic Research*, No. 5: pp. 23–30.

He, S. W. and Xu, M. B. (2000) *State-owned Enterprises Reforms and Strategic Re-organizations*, Beijing: China Financial and Economic Publisher.

Healy, M. (1985) The Effect of Bonus Schemes on Accounting Decisions, *Journal of Accounting and Economics*, 7: pp. 85–107.

Healy, M. and Wahlen, J. M. (1999) A Review of the Earnings Management Literature and Its Implications for Standard Setting, *Accounting Horizons*, 13: pp. 365–383.

Henry, M. C. and Springborg, R. (2001) *Globalization and the Politics of Development in the Middle East*, Cambridge: Cambridge University Press.

Hermalin, B. E. and Weisbach, M. S. (2003) Board of Directors as an Endogenously Determined Institution: A Survey of the Economic Literature, *Economic Policy Review*, No. 1: pp. 67–75.

Hess, D. and Luders, E. (2001) *Accounting for Stock-Based Compensation: An Extended Clean Surplus Relation*, ZEW, Manheim, Discussion Paper, No. 01–42.

Hicks, A. and Kenworthy, L. (1998) Cooperation and Political Economic Performance in Affluent Democratic Capitalism, *American Journal of Sociology*, 103, No. 6: pp. 1631–1672.

Hines, D. (1982) The Usefulness of Annual Reports: The Anomaly Between the Efficient Markets Hypothesis and Shareholder's Surveys, *Accounting and Business Research*, Autumn: pp. 296–309.

Hirschman, A. (1972) *Face au déclin des entreprises et des institutions*, Editions Ouvrières.

Hiscox, M. J. and Rickard, S. J. (2002) *Birds of a Different Feather? Varieties of Capitalism, Factor Specificity, and Interindustry Labor Movements*, Harvard University, Working Paper.

HKEJ (2001) China is Drafting Its Rules on Corporate Governance, *Hong Kong Economic Journal*, July: 24.

HKEx (2002) *Proposed Amendments to the Listing Rules Relating to Corporate Governance Issues*, Consultation Paper, January.

Ho, S. S. M. (2000) The Role of Ownership Structure and Disclosure in the Asian Financial Crisis (in Chinese), *Communication in Finance and Accounting*, No. 1: pp. 22–25.

Ho, S. S. M. (2002a) *Corporate Ownership and Governance of Listed Firms in China*, Centre for Accounting Disclosure and Corporate Governance, The Chinese University of Hong Kong.

Ho, S. S. M. (2002b) Business Fat Cats Face Fleecing, *South China Morning Post*, Business 2.

Ho, S. S. M. (2003a) *A Tale of Chinese Private Enterprises. New Finance* (in Chinese), Centre for Accounting Disclosure and Corporate Governance, The Chinese University of Hong Kong.

Ho, S. S. M. (2003b) *Corporate Governance in Hong Kong: Key Problems and Prospects*, Centre for Accounting Disclosure and Corporate Governance, The Chinese University of Hong Kong.

Ho, S. S. M. (2003c) *Corporate Governance in China: Key Problems and Prospects*, Centre for Accounting Disclosure and Corporate Governance, The Chinese University of Hong Kong.

Ho, S. S. M. and Lam, K. (2003) *Directors' Ownership, Board Structures and Executive Compensations*, School of Accountancy, The Chinese University of Hong Kong, Working Paper.

Ho, S. S. M. and Wong, K. S. (2001a) A Study of Corporate Disclosure Practice and Effectiveness in Hong Kong, *Journal of International Financial Management and Accounting*, 12, No. 1: pp. 75–102.

Ho, S. S. M. and Wong, K. S. (2001b) A Study of the Relationship Between Corporate Governance Structures and the Extent of Voluntary Disclosure, *Journal of International Accounting, Auditing and Taxation*, 10: pp. 139–156.

Ho, S. S. M. and Wong, K. S. (2002) *The Perceived Value of Voluntary Disclosure Items and Firms' Disclosure Practice*, School of Accountancy, The Chinese University of Hong Kong, Working Paper.

Ho, S. S. M. and Wong, K. S. (2003) Perceptions of Corporate Reporting and Disclosures, *International Journal of Corporate Governance and Disclosures*, 2: pp. 224–236.

Ho, S. S. M. and Xu Hai Gen (2002) Corporate Governance in China in C. K. Low (ed.) *Corporate Governance: An Asia-Pacific Critique*, Hong Kong: Sweet and Maxwell, pp. 269–302.

Ho, S. S. M., Lam, K. and Heibatollah, S. (2003) The Investment Opportunity Set, Director Ownership, and Corporate Policies: Evidence from an Emerging Market, *Journal of Corporate Finance*, 11: pp. 40–48.

Ho, S. S. M., Lam, K. and Sami, H. (2002) The Investment Opportunity Set, Director Ownership, and Corporate Policies: Evidence from an Emerging Market, *Journal of Corporate Finance*, 10, No. 3: pp. 383–408.

Ho, S. S. M., Scott, R. H. and Wong, K. H. (2003) *Hong Kong Financial Systems*, 2nd edn, Oxford: Oxford University Press.

Hodgson, G. M. (1988) *Economics and Institutions*, Cambridge: Polity Press.

Hodgson, G. M. (1989) Institutional Rigidities and Economy Growth, *Cambridge Journal of Economics*, 13, No. 1: pp. 79–101.

Hodgson, G. M. (1998) Competence and Contract in the Theory of the Firm, *Journal of Economic Behavior and Organization*, 35: pp. 179–201.

Hodgson, G. M. (1993) *Economics and Evolution: Bringing Life Back into Economics*, Cambridge: Polity Press.

Hodgson, G. M. (2001) The Evolution of Capitalism from the Perspective of Institutional and Evolutionary Economics in G. M. Hodgson, M. Itoh and N. Yokokawa (eds) *Capitalism in Evolution – Global Contentions – East and West*, Cheltenham: Edward Elgar, pp. 63–82.

Hofstede, G. H. (1980) *Culture's Consequences: International Differences in Work-Related Values*, Beverly Hills, CA: Sage Publications.

Hofstede, G. H. (1983) The Cultural Relativity of Organizational Practices and Theories, *Journal of International Business Studies*, 14, No. 2: pp. 75–89.

Hofstede, G. H. (1991) *Cultures and Organizations: Software of the Mind: Intercultural Cooperation and Its Importance for Survival*, London: McGraw-Hill.

Holderness, C. G. (2003) A Survey of Blockholders and Corporate Control, *Economic Policy Review*, 9, No. 1, pp. 51–61.

Hollingsworth, J. R. and Boyer, R. (eds) (1997) *Contemporary Capitalism: The Embeddness of Institutions*, Cambridge: Cambridge University Press.

Hong, H., Kaplan, R. and Mandelker, G. (1978) Puling vs Purchase: The Effects of Accounting for Mergers on Stock Prices, *The Accounting Review*, January: pp. 31–47.

Hong Kong Institute of Company Secretaries (1998) *The Limit of Governance*, Company Secretary, January: pp. 15–18.

Hong Kong Society of Accountants (1996) *Hong Kong Accountants*, Special Issue on Corporate Governance, September/October.

Hong Kong Society of Accountants (1997) *Second Report of the Corporate Governance Working Group*, January.

Hosoda, N. (1994) Some Technical Checking Points in Financial Statements Analysis. *Kigno Kaikei*, 46, No. 2: pp. 13–14.

Hu, J. and Goergenm, G. (2001) *Study of Ownership Concentration, Control and Evolution in Chinese IPOs*, University of Manchester Institute of Science and Technology, Working Paper.

Hull, J. C. (1997) *Options Futures and Other Derivatives*, 3rd edn, New York: Prentice Hall, Inc.

Hull, J. C. and White, A. (1987) The Pricing of Options on Assets with Stochastic Volatility, *Journal of Finance*, 4: pp. 281–300.

Hull, J. C. and White, A. (2004) How to Value Employee Stock Options, *Financial Analysts Journal*, January–February: pp. 114–119.

Hunt, H. (1985) Political Determinants of Corporate Inventory Accounting Decisions, *Journal of Accounting Research*, 23: pp. 448–467.

ICAEW (2003) *Combined Code of Corporate Governance*, July.

IFC (2006) *Corporate Governance Practice Survey in Russia*, Report.

IFC-Hawkamah (2007) *Corporate Governance in the GCC: Country Reports and Comparative Survey.*

Ijiri, Y. (1975) *Theory of Accounting Measurement, Study in Accounting Research*, 10. American Accounting Association.

International Institute of Finance (IIF) (2005) *Corporate Governance in Turkey*, 14, No. 4: pp. 325–349.

Iversen, T. and Soskice, D. (2001) An Asset Theory of Social Policy Preferences, *American Political Science Review*, 95, No. 4: pp. 875–893.

Jaffe, J. S. (1974) The Effect of Regulation Changes on Insider Trading, *The Bell Journal of Economics and Management Science*, 5: pp. 93–121.

Jalil, T. J. (2005) *Corporate Governance in Jordan, Recent Development*, Corporate Governance Forum, Rabat, Morocco, 14–15 September.

Jensen, J. and Meckling, W. (1976) Theory of the Firm: Managerial Behaviour, Agency Cost and Ownership Structure, *Journal of Financial Economics*, October: pp. 305–360.

Jensen, M. C. (1998) *Foundations of Organizational Strategy*, Cambridge: Harvard University Press.

Jensen, M. C. (2001) Value Maximization, Stakeholder Theory, and the Corporate Objective Function, *European Financial Management*, 7, No. 3: pp. 297–317.

Jensen, M. C. and Meckling, W. (1992) Specific and General Knowledge, and Organization Structure in L. Werin and H. Wijkander (eds) *Contracts Economics*, Oxford: Basic Blackwell, pp. 251–274.

Jensen, M. C. and Murphy, K. J. (1990) Performance Pay and Top Management Incentive, *Journal of Political Economy*, No. 98: pp. 225–264.

Jensen, M. C. and Ruback, W. (1983) The Market for Corporate Control: The Scientific Evidence, *Journal of Financial Economics*, 3: pp. 305–360.

JICPA (2002) *Oversight and Independence of CPA Auditing in Japan* (available at JICPA site).

JICPA (2003) *Accounting and Disclosure System in Japan* (available at JICPA site).

Johnson, J. L., Daily, C. M. and Ellstrand, A. E. (1996) Board of Directors: A Review and Research Agenda, *Journal of Management*, 22, No. 3: pp. 409–438.

Johnson, S., Boone, P. and Breach, A. (2000a) Corporate Governance in the Asian Financial Crisis, 1997–98, *Journal of Financial Economics*, 58, Iss. 1–2: pp. 141–186.

Johnson, S., La Porta, R., Lopez-de-Silanes, F. and Shleifer, A. (2000b) Tunneling, *American Economic Review Papers and Proceedings*, 90, Iss. 2: pp. 22–27.

Joint Committee on Corporate Governance (JCCG) (2001) *Beyond Compliance: Building a Governance Culture Final Report.*

Jones, J. (1991) Earnings Management During Import Relief Investigations, *Journal of Accounting Research*, 3 No. 2: pp. 193–228.

Kabasakal, H. and Bodur, M. (1998) *Leadership, Values and Institutions: The Case of Turkey*, Bogazici University, Istanbul, Turkey, Research Papers.

Kalotay, K. (2006) *The Role of Foreign Direct Investment in Transition, United Nations Economic Commission for Europe*, Geneva: May.

Kamin, J. Y. and Ronen, J. (1978) The Smoothing of Income Numbers: Some Empirical Evidence on Systematic Differences Among Management-Controlled and Owner-Controlled Firms, *Accounting, Organization, and Society*, 3 No. 2: pp. 141–157.

Kaplan, R. S. and Palepu, K. G. (2003) Expensing Stock Options: A Fair-Value Approach, *Harvard Business Review*, December: pp. 105–107.

Kaplan, R. S. and Roll, R. (1972) Investors' Evaluation of Accounting Information: Some Empirical Evidence, *The Journal of Business*, April: pp. 237–245.

Kaplan, S., Schenkel, A., von Krogh, G. and Weber, C. (2001) *Knowledge-Based Theories of the Firm in Strategic Management: A Review and Extension*, MIT, Working Paper.

Kay, J. (1993) Keeping up with the market, *The Economist*, 11 September, p. 66.

Kenworthy, L. (2002) *Institutional Coherence and Macroeconomic Performance: A Comment*, American Political Science Association Annual Meeting, Boston, August.

Khanna, T. and Palepu, K. (2000) *Emerging Market Business Groups, Foreign Investors, and Corporate Governance*, NBER, Working Paper, No. 69995.

Kim, O. and Suh, Y. (1993) Incentive Efficiency of Compensation Based on Accounting and Market Performance, *Journal of Accounting and Economics*, 16: pp. 25–53.

Kim, W., Lim, Y. and Sung, T. (2004) *What Determines the Ownership Structures of Business Conglomerates, On the Cash Flow Rights of Korea's Chaebol*, ECGI Finance, Working Paper, No. 51/2004.

Klapper, L. and Love, I. (2001) *Corporate Governance: Investor Protection and Performance in Emerging Markets*, World Bank, Working Paper.

Klassen, K. J. and Mawani, A. (2000) The Impact of Financial and Tax Reporting Incentives on Option Grants to Canadian CEOs, *Contemporary Accounting Research*, 17, No. 2: pp. 227–262.

Kogut, B., Walker, G. and Anand, J. (2002) Agency and Institutions: National Divergences in Diversification Behavior, *Organization Science*, 13, No. 2: pp. 162–178.

Kornai, J. (1990) *The Road to a Free Economy: Shifting from a Socialist System, The Example of Hungary*, New York: Norton.

Kornai, J. (2000) *Ten Years After 'The Road to a Free Economy'*, the author's self-evaluation.

Kothari, S. and Sloan, R. (1990) *The Price-Earning Lead-Lag and Earnings Response Coefficients*, University of Rochester, Research Notes.

Krivogorsky, V. (2000) Corporate Ownership and Governance in Russia, *Journal of International Accounting*, pp. 331–353.

La Porta, R., Lopez-de-Silanes, F. and Shleifer, A. (1999a) Corporate Ownership Around the World, *Journal of Finance*, 54, No. 2: pp. 471–517.

La Porta, R., Lopez-de-Silanes, F. and Shleifer, A. (2000c) *Government Ownership of Banks*, National Bureau of Economic Research, Working Paper, No. 7620.

La Porta, R. L., Lopez-de-Silanes, F. and Shleifer, A. (1999c) Corporate Ownership Around the World, *Journal of Finance*, LIV, No. 2: pp. 471–517.

La Porta, R., Lopez-de-Silanes, F., Shleifer, A. and Vishny, R. W. (1997a) *Trust in Large Organizations*, American Economic Review, Papers and Proceedings, pp. 333–338.

La Porta, R., Lopez-de-Silanes, F., Shleifer, A. and Vishny, R. W. (1997b) Legal Determinants of External Finance, *Journal of Finance*, 52, No. 3: pp. 1131–1150.

La Porta, R., Lopez-de-Silanes, F., Shleifer, A. and Vishny, R. W. (1998) Law and Finance, *Journal of Political Economy*, 106, No. 6: pp. 1113–1155.

La Porta, R., Lopez-de-Silanes, F., Shleifer, A. and Vishny, R. W. (1999b) The Quality of Government, *Journal of Law, Economics and Organization*, 15: pp. 222–279.

La Porta, R., Lopez-de-Silanes, F., Shleifer, A. and Vishny, R. W. (2000a) Investor Protection and Corporate Governance, *Journal of Financial Economics*, 58, Nos 1–2: pp. 3–27.

La Porta, R., Lopez-de-Silanes, F., Shleifer, A. and Vishny, R. W. (2000b) Agency Problems and Dividend Policies Around the World, *Journal of Finance*, 55, No. 1: pp. 1–33.

La Porta, R., Lopez-de-Silanes, F., Shleifer, A. and Vishny, R. W. (2002) Investor Protection and Corporate Valuation, *Journal of Finance*, 57, No. 3: pp. 1147–1170.

Lambert, R. (1994) Income Smoothing as Rational Equilibrium Behaviour, *The Accounting Review*, October: pp. 234–248.

Lamoreaux, N. R. and Rosenthal, J. L. (2000) Organizational Choice and Economic Development: A Comparison of France and the United States During the Mid-Nineteenth Century, Working Paper, www.cepr.Org/meets/wkcr/5/575/papers/rosenthal.pdf.

Lang, L. H. P. (2002) A Road to Serfdom in 2002 Symposium on Corporate Governance and Disclosure: The Impact of Globalization, *The School of Accountancy*, The Chinese University of Hong Kong.

Lang, L. H. P. and Young, L. (2001) *Minority Interest, Majority Concern*, Corporate Governance International, 1: pp. 44–49.

Langlois, R. and Foss, N. (1999) *Capabilities and Governance: The Rebirth of Production in the Theory of Economy Organization*, Kyklos, 52: pp. 201–218.

Langlois, R. N. (2001) Knowledge, Consumption, and Endogeneous Growth, *Journal of Evolutionary Economics*, 11, No. 1: pp. 77–93.

Launeadeau Labrecque/Ray and Berndtson (2003) Available at www.rayberndtson.ca/.

Lazonick, W. (2000) *From Innovative Enterprise to National Institutions: A Theoretical Perspective on the Governance of Economic Development*, INSEAD, Working Paper.

Lazonick, W. and O'Sullivan, M. (1998) *Corporate Governance and the Innovative Economy: Policy Implications*, STEP Report ISSN 0804–8185, Oslo.

Lazonick, W., and O'Sullivan M. (2000). *Perspectives on Corporate Governance. Innovation and Economic Performance*, European Institute of Business Administration, INSEAD, Working Paper.

Le Bars, B. (2003) *La rénovation du statut des associations d'actionnaires et d'investisseurs: un épiphénomène révélateur du besoin d'évolution en droit des sociétés*, Rev. Sociétés, 22: pp. 428–442.

Le Nabasque, H. (2003) *Commentaire des principales dispositions de la loi No. 2003–706 du 1er août 2003 sur la sécurité financière intéressant le droit des sociétés*, Bull. Joly, § 185: pp. 859–873.

Leban, R. (2005) *Business Management: Principles and Best Practices*, Paris: Editions d'Organisation.

Lee, K. (1993) Property Rights and the Agency Problem in China's Enterprises Reform, *Cambridge Journal of Economics*, 17: pp. 179–194.

Leftwich, R. (1981) Evidence on the Impact of Mandatory Changes in Accounting Principles on Corporate Loan Agreement, *Journal of Accounting and Economics*, March: pp. 3–36.

Legendre, P. (1974) *L'amour du censeur: Essai sur l'ordre dogmatique*, Le Seuil.

Lev, B. (1992) Information Disclosure Strategy, *California Management Review*, 34, Summer: pp. 9–32.

Levasseur, M. and Quintard, A. (1992) *Finance*, 3rd edn, Paris: Economica, pp. 30–55.

Levine, J. (1997) Financial Development and Economic Growth: Views and Agenda, *Journal of Economic Literature*, 35: pp. 688–726.

Levine, R. (1999) Law, Finance, and Economic Growth, *Journal of Financial Intermediation*, 8: pp. 36–67.

Levine, R. and Zervos, S. (1998) Stock Markets, Banks and Economic Growth, *American Economic Review*, 88: pp. 537–558.

Levitt, A. (1998) *The Numbers Game*, Speech delivered at the NYU Center Law and Business, New York.

Li, J. C. (2000) Incentives Schemes and Corporate Performance (in Chinese), *Accounting Research*, No. 1: pp. 24–30.

Li, T. J. and Hwang, T. H. (2001) *Chinese Corporate Governance: An Empirical Study on the COE/Chairman Duality Issues in 490 Chinese Listed Firms* (in Chinese), Academic Research, No. 2: pp. 31–37.

Li, T. P. (2001) *Major Shareholder Control, Earnings Management and Dropping Performance of Listed Firms*, PhD Thesis, The Shanghai University of Economic and Finance.

Li, W. (2001) *Corporate Governance* (in Chinese), Nankai University Press.

Li, Y. G., Chao, S. P. and Li, W. J. (2001) Studies on Composition of Board of Directors and Firm Performance of Listed Firms (in Chinese), *China Industrial Economics*, No. 5: pp. 48–53.

Licht, A. N. (2001) The Mother of All Path-Dependencies Toward a Cross-Cultural Theory of Corporate Governance Systems, *Delaware Journal of Corporate Law*, 23: pp. 147–205.

Licht, A. N., Goldschmidt, C. and Schwartz, S. H. (2002) *Culture, Law, and Corporate Governance*, Hebrew University of Jerusalem, Department of Psychology, Working Paper.

Lin, C. (2000) *Public Vices in Public Places: Challenges in Corporate Governance Development in China*, OECD/World Bank Second Asian Corporate Governance Roundtable, Hong Kong.

Lin, C. C. (2003) *Determinants and Changes of Ownership Concentration and Its Relationship with Firm Performance* (in Chinese). Proceedings of the Second International Symposium on Empirical Research in Accounting, Chongqing.

Lin, Y., Cai, F. and Li, Z. (1995) The Core of SOE's Reform is Creating a Competitive Environment (in Chinese), *Journal of Reform*, No. 3: pp. 342–355.

Lo, K. J. (2003) Economic Consequences of Regulated Changes in Disclosure: The Case of Executive Compensation, *Journal of Accounting and Economics*, 35, Iss. 3: pp. 205–314.

Loasby, B. J. (2001a) Cognition, Capabilities and Cooperation, *International Journal of Management and Decision Making*, 2, No. 1: pp. 35–48.

Loasby, B. J. (2001b) Organisations as Interpretative Systems, *Revue d'Economie Industrielle*, No. 97: pp. 17–34.

Louis Harris Associates (1996) Opinion poll conducted on 1004 American citizens, February.

Loyd, H. and Rosenfield, P. (1979) Solvency: The Forgotten Half of Financial Reporting, *Journal of Accountancy*, January: pp. 48–54.

Lu, W. B. and Zhu, H. J. (2001) A Study on the Firm Performance Changes and Ownership Structure of IPO Firms (in Chinese), *Financial and Economic Studies*, No. 7: pp. 45–52.

Lundvall, B. A. (1992) *National Systems of Innovation*, London: Pinter.

Lynn, E. T. (2000) *Chief Accountant U.S. Securities and Exchange Commission*, New York: US Securities and Exchange Commission.

Machlup, F. (1967) Theory of the Firm: Marginalist, Behavior, Managerial, *The American Economic Review*, January: pp. 1–33.

McNichols, M. and Wilson, G. P. (1988) Evidence of Earnings Management from Provision for Bad Debts, *Journal of Accounting Research*, 26 (Supplement): pp. 1–31.

MaConnell, J. and Servaes, H. (1990) Additional Evidence on Equity Ownership and Corporate Value, *Journal of Financial Economics*, 27: 234–254.

Mander, J. (2001) *Le code de conduite de l'entreprise, Dans le procès de la mondialisation*, sous la direction de E. Goldsmith and E. J. Mander, Fayard.

Mar, P. and Young, M. N. (2000) *Corporate Governance in Transition Economies: A Case Study of Two Chinese Airlines*, Department of Management, Faculty of Business Administration, Working Paper.

March, J. G. (1991) Exploration and Exploitation in Organizational Learning, *Organization Science*, 2: pp. 71–87.

March, J. G. and Simon, H. A. (1958) *Organizations*, New York: Wiley.

Markham, J. W. (2002) Super-Regulator: A Comparative Analysis of Securities and Derivatives Regulation in the United States, Great Britain and Japan, *Brooklyn Journal of International Law*, 28, No. 2: pp. 319–410.

Masahiko, A. I., Aoki, M. and Kim, H. K. (1995) *Corporate Governance in Transitional Economies: Insider Control and the Role of Banks*, Washington, DC: The World Bank.

Mawani, A. (2003a) Tax Deductibility of Employee Stock Options, *Canadian Tax Journal*, 51, No. 3: pp. 1230–1258.

Mawani, A. (2003b) Cancellation of Executive Stock Options: Tax and Accounting Income Considerations, *Contemporary Accounting Research*, 20, No. 3: pp. 495–517.

Mehran, H. (1995) Executive Compensation Structure, Ownership, and Firm Performance, *Journal of Financial Economics*, 38: 123–138.

Menash, Y., Song, X. and Ho, S. S. M. (2003) Is There a Long-term Payoff to Greater Corporate Disclosure? The USA Experience, *Journal of Accounting and Public Policy*, 22, No. 2: pp. 107–150.

Merton, R. C. (1973) Theory of Rational Option Pricing, *Bell Journal of Economics and Management Science*, 4, pp. 141–183.

Merton, R. C. (1976) Option Pricing When Underlying Stock Returns are Discontinuous, *Journal of Financial Economics*, 3: pp. 125–144.

Milgrom, P. and Roberts, J. (1992) *Economics, Organization and Management*, New York: Prentice-Hall.

Millstein, I. M. and MacAvoy, P. W. (1998) The Active Board of Directors and Performance of the Large Publicly Traded Corporations, *Columbia Law Review*, 98, No. 1283: p. 5.

Ming, P. (2002a) *CEO Kings Daily Pay 0.82 Million* (in Chinese), Hong Kong: Hong Kong Baptist University.

Ming, P. (2002b) *HK Corporate Governance Ranking Just behind Singapore* (in Chinese), Hong Kong: Hong Kong Baptist University, 12 June.

Ministry of Justice (2003) *Japanese Corporate Law: Drastic Changes in 2000–2001 and the Future*, www.moj.go.jp/ENGLISH/CIAB/jc101–1.

Mitarai, F. (2002a) *An Interview: Beikokuno oroka kurikaesuna – CEO tono nareai* (Literally, "Don't Repeat the American Folly – Cozy Relations between the CEO and Outside Directors"), Tokyo: Nikkei Sangyo Shimbun, pp. 10–13.

Mitarai, F. (2002b) *Canon no idenshi soshite waga keieitetsugaku* (Literally, "Canon's Genes and My Management Philosophy"), Tokyo: Hakumon Chuou, pp. 4–14.

Mobius, J. M. (2002) Corporate Governance in Hong Kong in C. K. Low (ed.) *Corporate Governance: An Asia-Pacific Critique*, Hong Kong: Sweet & Maxwell, pp. 269–302.

Mohr, R. (1983) The Segmental Reporting Issue: A Review of the Empirical Research, *Journal of Accounting Literature*, Spring: pp. 39–71.

Molz, R. (1998) Managerial Domination of Boards of Directors and Financial Performance, *Journal of Business Research*, 16: pp. 235–249.

Monks, R. A. and Minow, G. N. (1996) *Watching the Watchers: Corporate Governance for the 21st Century*, Cambridge, MA: Blackwell.

Morck, R., Shleifer, A. and Vishney, R. W. (1988) Management Ownership and Market Valuation: An Empirical Analysis, *Journal of Financial Economics*, 20: pp. 293–315.

Morck, R., Yeung, B. and Yu, W. (2000) The Information Content of Stock Markets: Why Do Emerging Markets Have Synchronous Price Movements?, *Journal of Financial Economics*, 58: pp. 215–260.

Morck, R. A. and Minow, G. N. (2001) *Power and Accountability*, Cambridge, MA: Blackwell.

Morck, R. K. and Stangeland, D. A. (1994) *Corporate Performance and Large Shareholders*, Institute for Financial Research, Faculty of Business, Université de l'Alberta, Working Paper, No. 4:94.

Mori, M. (1994) Risk-oriented Auditing and Networking of Auditing (in Japanese), *Kigyou Kaikei* (Corporate Accounting), 46, No. X: pp. 25–33.

Mowery, D. and Nelson, R. (1999) *The Sources of Industrial Leadership*, Cambridge: Cambridge University Press.

Murphy, K. J. (1998) *Executive Compensation*, Marshall School of Business, University of South California, Working Paper.

Naciri, A. (2000) *Earning Management from Bank Provision for Loan Losses*, UQAM, Working Paper.

Nb, D. (1978) An Information Economics Analysis of Financial Reporting and External Auditing, *The Accounting Review*, October: pp. 910–920.

Nellis, J. (1999) Time to Rethink Privatization in Transition Economies?, *Finance and Development*, June, 36, No. 2, pp. 16–19.

Nelson, R. R. (1993) *National Innovation Systems: A Comparative Analysis*, New York: Oxford University Press.

Nelson, R. R. (1998) An Agenda for Growth Theory: A Different Point of View, *Cambridge Journal of Economics*, 22: pp. 497–520.

Nelson, R. R. (2002) Bringing Institutions into Evolutionary Growth Theory, *Journal of Evolutionary Economics*, 12: pp. 17–28.

Nelson, R. R. and Sampat, B. N. (2001) Making Sense of Institutions as a Factor Shaping Economic Performance, *Journal of Economic Behavior and Organization*, 44, No. 1: pp. 31–54.

Nelson, R. R. and Winter, S. G. (1982) *An Evolutionary Theory of Economic Change*, Cambridge MA: Harvard University Press.

Nelson, R. R. and Winter, S. G. (2002) Evolutionary Theorizing in Economies, *Journal of Economic Perspectives*, 16, No. 2, Spring: 23–46.

Nenova, T. (2003) The Value of Corporate Votes and Control Benefits: A Cross-Country Analysis, *Journal of Financial Economics*, 68, No. 3: pp. 325–351.

Nestor, S. (2003) *International Corporate Governance Convergence*, Washington, Center for International Private Enterprise (CIPE), pp. 45–62.

Nicita, A. and Pagano, U. (2002) *Finance and Technology: A Comparative Institutional Analysis of the Firm*, Universita degli Studi di Siena, No. 361.

Nicoletti, G., Bassanini, A., Ersnt, E., Jean, S., Santiago, P. and Swaim, P. (2001) *Product and Labour Markets Interactions in OECD Countries*, OECD Economics Department, Working Paper, No. 312.

Nicoletti, G., Scarpetta, S. and Boylaud, O. (2000) *Summary Indicators of Product Market Regulation with an Extension to Employment Protection Legislation*, OECD Economics Department, Working Paper, No. (1999)18.

Nihon, K. S. (1993) *To Whom Does the Company Belong?* Tokyo: Asahi Shimbun.

Nihon, K. S. (1999) *To Whom Does the Company Belong?*, 1993 Okuda, Hiroshi. Keieisha yo, kubikiri surunara seppuku seyo, Bungei Shunju, pp. 152–162.

Niskanen, W. (2007) *Enron's Last Victim: American Markets*, New York Times, p. A2.

Noiville, C. (2003) *Du bon gouvernement des risques*, Le droit et la question du risque acceptable, Paris, PUF, coll. Les voies du droit.

North, D. C. (1990) *Institutions, Institutional Change and Economic Performance*, Cambridge, MA: Harvard University Press.

Nrayanan, M. (1985) Managerial Incentives for Short-term Results, *Journal of Finance*, 40 No. 5: pp. 1469–1484.

OECD (1998) *OECD Proceedings on Corporate Governance State-Owned Enterprises and Privatization*, Paris: Organization for Economic Cooperation and Development.

OECD (1999) *OECD Principles of Corporate Governance*, Paris: Organization for Economic Cooperation and Development.

OECD (2004) *Corporate Governance Principles*, Paris.

OECD (2005) The International Experts Meeting on Corporate Governance of Non-listed Companies, Istanbul, Turkey, on 19–20 April.

OECD (2006) *Corporate Governance of Non-Listed Companies in Emerging Markets*, Paris: Organization for Economic Cooperation and Development.

OECD and Hawkamah (2007) *Statement From the Meeting of the Middle East and North Africa Task Force on Corporate Governance of Banks*, The Middle East and North Africa (MENA) Task Force on Corporate Governance of Banks held its first meeting on 19 February 2007.

Ohlson, J. (1995) Earnings, Book Values and Dividends in Security Valuation, *Contemporary Accounting Research*, 11: pp. 661–687.

Oison, M. (1982) *The Rise and Decline of Nations – Economic Growth, Stagflation and Social Rigidities*, New Haven, CT: Yale University Press, trad. française, Grandeur et décadence des nations, Bonnel Editions, 1983.

Okuda, H. (1999) *Keieisha yo, kubikiri surunara seppuku seyo* (Literally, "Managers! If You Axe Your Employees, You Must Do Harakiri!"), Tokyo: Bungei Shunju, pp. 152–162.

Okuda, H. (2002) *Mazu keieishaga rinrikann wo* (Literally, "Ethics of Managers First!"), Tokyo: Nihon Keizai Shimbun.

Olson, M. (1982) *The Rise and Decline of Nations – Economic Growth, Stagflation and Social Rigidities*, New Haven, CT: Yale University Press, trad. française, Grandeur et décadence des nations, Bonnel Editions, 1983.

O'Sullivan, M. (2000) *The Innovative Enterprise and Corporate Governance*, Cambridge Journal of Economics, 24, No. 4: pp. 393–416.

O'Sullivan, M. (2001) *Contests for Corporate Control – Corporate Governance and Economic Performance in the United States and Germany*, Oxford: Oxford University Press.

Pagano, M. and Volpin, P (2001a) *The Political Economy of Corporate Governance.*

384   *Bibliography*

Center for Studies in Economics and Finance, Universita Degli Studi Di Salerno, Working Paper, No. 29.

Pagano, M. and Volpin, P. (2001b) The Political Economy of Finance, *Oxford Review of Economic Policy*, 17, No. 4: pp. 502–519.

Pagano, U. (1993) Property Rights, Asset Specificity, and the Division of Labour Under Alternative Capitalists Relations in G. M. Hodgson (ed.) *The Economics of Intitutions*, Aldershot: Edward Elgar, pp. 440–467.

Pagano, U. A. (2002) *Legal Positions and Institutional Complementarities*, Universita degli Studi di Siena, No. 360.

Pagano, U. and Rossi, M. A. (2002) *Incomplete Contracts. Intellectual Property and Institutional Complementarity*, Universita degli Studi di Siena, No. 355.

Pappe, Y. (2000) *Oligarchs, Economic Review, 1992–2000*, Moscow: Highest School of Economics.

Pappe, Y. and Galukhina, Y. (2006) Russian Corporation: From Oligarch Structures to Participants of World Market, *Neprikosnovenniy Zapas*, Nos 4/5: pp. 16–29.

Pasechnyk, T. (2004a) Ownership Concentration in Ukrainian Industry, *Finance of Ukraine*, No. 3: pp. 128–134.

Pasechnyk, T. (2004b) Equity Capital of Integrated Corporate Groups of Ukraine, *Social-Economic Research Review*, OSEU, Odessa, No. 18: p. 300–305.

Paskhaver, A. and Verhovodova, L. (2006) *Privatization Before and After Orange Revolution*, Warsaw: CASE, Center for Social and Economic Research.

Paskhaver, A., Verhovodova, L., Voronkova, T. and Ageeva, O. (2003) *Problems of Development of Financial Industrial Groups of Ukraine*, Report on order of World Bank, Center for Economic Development, Ukraine.

Patry, M. and Poitevin, M. (1995*) Pourquoi les investisseurs institutionnels ne sont pas des meilleurs actionnaires dans La prise de décision dans les entreprises au Canada?*, Document de recherche d'Industrie Canada, Canada: University of Calgary Press.

PECC (2002) *Guidelines for Good Corporate Governance Practice*, Pacific Economic Cooperation Council.

Pedersen, T. and Thomsen, S. (2003) Ownership Structure and Value of the Largest European Firms: The Importance of Owner Identity, *Journal of Management and Governance*, 7: pp. 27–55.

Penrose, E. (1959) *The Theory of the Growth of the Firm*, Oxford: Oxford University Press.

Perez, R. (2003) *La gouvernance corporative*, La Découverte, collection "Repères": pp. 5, 273.

Perkins, D. (1994) Completing China's Move to Market, *Journal of Economics Perspectives*, 8, No. 2: pp. 23–46.

Perry, S. E. and Thomas, H. W. (1994) Earnings Management Preceding Management Buyout Offers, *Journal of Accounting and Economics*, 18: pp. 157–179.

Peyrefitte, A. (1995*) La société de confiance*, Odile Jacob Éditeur.

Peyrelevade, J. (1999) *Le gouvernement d'entreprise ou les fondements incertains d'un nouveau pouvoir*, Paris: Economica.

Pinçon, M. and Pinçon, M. (2002) Voyage en grande bourgeoisie, *Journal d'enquête*, Paris, PUF, chap. III.

Pistor, K. and Xu, C. (2003a) Incomplete Law, *Journal of International Economic Law*, 23, No. 4: pp. 791–871.

Pistor, K., Keinan, Y., Kleinheisterkamp, J. I. and West, M. D. (2003a) *The Evolution of*

Corporate Law: A Cross-Country Comparison, Columbia Law and Economies, Research Paper, No. 232a.

Pistor, K., Keinan, Y., Kleinheisterkamp, J. I. and West, M. D. (2003b) *Innovation in Corporate Law*, Columbia Law and Economics, Research Paper, No. 321.

Poe, M., Shimizu, K. and Simpson, J. (2002) Revising the Japanese Commercial Code: A Summary and Evaluation of the Reform Effort, *Stanford Journal of East Asian Affairs*, 2: pp. 71–95.

Porter, M. (1990) *The Competitive Advantage of Nations*, New York: Free Press.

Porter, M. (1992) Capital Disadvantages: America's Failing Capital Investment System, *Harvard Business Review*, September–October.

Pound, J. (1993) The Rise of the Political Model of Corporate Governance and Corporate Control, *New York University Law Review*, 68, No. 5: 1003–1023.

Pourciau, S. (1993) Earnings Management and Non Routine Executive Changes, *Journal of Accounting and Economics*, 16: pp. 317–336.

Prahalad, C. K. (1994) Corporate Governance or Corporate Value Added?: Rethinking the Primacy of Shareholder Value, *Journal of Applied Corporate Finance*, 6, No. 4: pp. 40–50.

Previt G., Bricker, R., Robinson, T. and Young, S. (1994) A Content Analysis of Self-Side Financial Analyst Company Report, *Accounting Horizon*, June: pp. 55–70.

Putnam, R. (1993) *Making Democracy Work: Civic Traditions in Modem Italy*, Princeton, NJ: Princeton University Press.

Qi, D., Wu, W. and Zhang, H. (2000) Shareholding Structure and Corporate Performance of Partially Privatized Firms: Evidence from Listed Chinese Companies, *Pacific Basin Finance Journal*, pp. 587–610.

Qian, Y. (1996) Enterprise Reform in China: Agency Problems and Political Control, *Economics of Transition*, 4, No. 2: pp. 427–447.

Qian, Y. (1994) The Reform of Corporate Governance and Financing in China in M. Aoki and Qian, Y. (eds), *Corporate Governance in Transitional Economies: Insider Control and the Role of Banks* (in Chinese), Beijing: China Economic Press.

Radygin, A. (2004) Evolution of Forms of Integration and Management Models: Experience of the Largest Russian Corporations and Groups, *Russian Management Journal*, No. 4, pp. 35–58.

Radygin, A., Entov, R., Abramov, A., Mezheraups, I., Malginov, G.and Sizov, A. (2006) *External-Mechanisms of Corporate Governance: Some of the Practical Problems*, Moscow: Institute of Economies in Transition.

Rajan, R. G. and Zingales, L. (1998a) Power in a Theory of the Firm, *Quarterly Journal of Economics*, 113, No. 2: pp. 387–432.

Rajan, R. G. and Zingales, L. (1998b) Financial Dependence and Growth, *American Economic Review*, 88, No. 3: pp. 559–586.

Rajan, R. G. and Zingales, L. (1998c) Which Capitalism? Lessons from the East Asian Crisis, *Journal of Applied Corporate Finance*, 11: pp. 40–48.

Rajan, R. G. and Zingales, L. (2000) The Governance of the New Enterprise in X. Vives (ed.), *Corporate Governance*, Cambridge: Cambridge University Press, pp. 201–232.

Rajan, R. G. and Zingales, L. (2001) *The Great Reversals: The Politics of Financial Development in the 20th Century*, University of Chicago, Working Paper, No. 8178.

Rajan, R. G. and Zingales, L. (2003) The Great Reversals: The Politics of Financial Development in the 20th Century. *Journal of Financial Economics*, 69, No. 1, July: 5–50.

Rao, S. R. and Lee-Sing, C. R. (1995) *Les structures de régie, la prise de décision et le rendement des entreprises en Amérique du Nord dans La prise de décision dans les entreprises au Canada*, Document de recherche d'Industrie Canada, Canada: University of Calgary Press, pp. 53–121.

Rappaport, A. (1986) *Creating Shareholder Value*, New York: The Free Press.

Roldos, J. E. (2004) *Pension Reform, Investment Restrictions, and Capital Markets*, Washington, DC: IMF, p. 31.

Roe, M. (2000) *Political Foundations for Separation Ownership from Control*, Stanford Law Review.

Roe, M. J. (1990) Political and Legal Restraints on Ownership and Control of Public Companies, *Journal of Financial Economics*, 27: pp. 7–41.

Roe, M. J. (1994) *Strong Managers, Weak Owners: The Political Roots of American Corporate Finance*, Princeton, NJ: Princeton University Press.

Roe, M. J. (1996) Chaos and Evolution in Law and Economics, *Harvard Law Review*, 109, No. 3: pp. 641–668.

Roe, M. J. (1997) The Political Roots of American Corporate Finance, *Journal of Applied Corporate Finance*, 9, No. 4: pp. 8–22.

Roe, M. J. (2000) Political Preconditions to Separating Ownership from Corporate Control, *Stanford Law Review*, 53: pp. 539–605.

Roe, M. J. (2001) Rents and Their Corporate Consequences, *Stanford Law Review*, 53, No. 6: pp. 1463–1494.

Roe, M. J. (2002) *La structure de l'actionnariat: les limites de la théorie juridique. Revue Française de Gestion*, No spécial L'actionnaire adapté et traduit de Corporate Law's Limits, Columbia Law School, Working Paper, No. 186,

Roe, M. J. (2003) *Political Determinants of Corporate Governance – Political Context, Corporate Impact*, Oxford: Oxford University Press.

Roll, R. (1977) A Critique of the Assets Pricing Theory's Test: Part I: On Past and Potential Testability of the Theory, *Journal of Financial Economics*, March: pp. 129–176.

Ross, S. (1979) Disclosure Regulation in Financial Markets, in F. Edwards (ed.) *Issues in Financial Regulation*, New York: McGraw-Hill, pp. 177–202.

Rubinstein, M. (1995) On the Accounting Valuation of Employee Stock Options, *Journal of Derivatives*, Fall: 42–66.

Rutherford, M. (1994) *Institutions in Economics: The Old and the New Institutionalism*, Cambridge: Cambridge University Press.

Sachs, J. D. (2001) *Tropical Underdevelopment*, National Bureau of Economic Research, Working Paper, No. 8119.

Saidi, N. (2004a) *Corporate Governance and Business Ethic in Lebanon*, Launch of RDCL "Code of Business Ethic," Beirut, 28 April.

Saidi, N. (2004b) *Corporate Governance in MENA, Improving Transparency and Disclosure*, The Second Middle East and North Africa Corporate Governance Forum, Beirut, 3–5 June.

Sainsaulieu, R. (1992) *L'entreprise, une affaire de société*, Presses FNSP.

Samuelson, P. and Norhaus, W. (1998) *Microeconomics*, New York: Irwin McGraw-Hill.

SandP and CGFT (2005) *Transparency and Disclosure Survey*, Turkey.

Sarbanes/Oxley (2003) Sarbanes–Oxley Act available at http://fl1.findlaw.com/news.findlaw.com/hdocs/docs/gwbush/sarbanesoxley072302.pdf.

Satskaya, Z. (2006) *Big Talks about Small Business*, Expert Russia, December, No. 12: p. 120.

Schleifer, A. and Vishny, R. H. (1996) Largest Shareholders and Corporate Control, *Journal of Political Economy*, 68: pp. 654–677.

Schleifer, A. and Vishny, R. H. (1997) A Survey of Corporate Governance, *Journal of Finance*, 52, No. 2, June: pp. 737–783.

Schmidt, D. (2004) *Les apports de la loi de sécurité financière au droit des sociétés*, Paris: Bull. Joly sociétés, § 62.

Schrand, C. (2004) Discussion of Firms' Voluntary Recognition of Stock-Based Compensation Expense, *Journal of Accounting Research*, 42, No. 2: pp. 151–158.

Schwartz, S. H. (1999) A Theory of Cultural Values and some Implications for Work. Applied Psychology, *An International Review*, 48, No. 1: pp. 23–49.

Scott, D. (1941) The Basic Accounting Principles, *Accounting Review*, December: p. 341.

Shaker, F. (2004) *Good Governance in Banks and Its Implications for Governance in Private Corporate*, Conference on "Good Governance and Development in Arab Countries", Istanbul, 10–11 February.

Shastitko, A. (2004) *Problems of Corporate Governance and Features of Corporate Control Dissemination in Russia*, Informational-Analytical Review, Moscow, No. 54.

Shleifer, A. and Vishny, R. W. (1989) Management Entrenchment: The Case of Manager-Specific Investments, *Journal of Financial Economics*, 25, No. 2: pp. 123–139.

Shleifer, A. and Vishny, R. W. (1997) A Survey of Corporate Governance, *Journal of Finance*, 52: pp. 737–783.

Shkurupiy, K. (2000) *The Corporate Governance Environment in Ukraine and Its Impact on Corporate Performance and Finance*, OECD, First Meeting of the Eurasian Corporate Governance Roundtable, Kyiv, Ukraine, October.

Simon, H. (1983) *Administration et processus de décisions*, Paris: Economica.

Simon, H. A. (1947) *Administrative Behavior: A Study of Decision-Making Processes in Administrative Organizations*, Chicago: MacMillan.

Sing Tao Daily (2003) *Frauds Commonly Exist in Mainland Enterprises: A Market Lacking Credibility*, 8 January, p. A-18.

Smith, A. (1817) *The Theory of Moral Sentiment*, 31st edn, Boston: Wells and Lilly.

Smith, A. (1776) *Inquiry into the Nature and Causes of the Wealth of Nations*, www.adamsmith.org/smith/won-index.htm.

Sourial, M. S. (2003) *Corporate Governance in the Middle East and North Africa and Future Challenges*, Proceedings of the 10th Symposium on Accounting Disclosure and Transparency, King Saod University, pp. 21–37.

South China Morning Post (1998) *Accountants Want Better Disclosure*, 30 July, Business Section, p. 2.

South China Morning Post (1998) *Newcomers Quick Off Mark with Honourable Mentions, Best Annual Report Awards Special*, Supplement, Business Section: 7, 28 November.

South China Morning Post (2002) *PCCW Directors' Pay Dwarfs Rivals*, 4 January, p. 1.

South China Morning Post (2003) *PCCW Directors' Pay Dwarfs Rivals*, 4 January, p. 1.

S&P (2002) *Transparency and Disclosure Survey*.

S&P (2007) *Expansion of State Companies: Corporate Governance and Economic Efficiency*.

S&P and CGFT (2002) *Transparency and Disclosure Survey*, Turkey study.

S&P and CGFT (2005) *Transparency and Disclosure Survey*, Turkey (forthcoming).

Steinfeld, E. S. (1998) *Forging Reform in China. The Fate of State Owned Industry*, Cambridge: Cambridge University Press.

Steward, J. K. and Walsh, J. P. (1996) The Governance and Control of Voluntary Corporate Spin-Offs, *Strategic Management Journal*, No. 17: pp. 25–39.

Stiglitz, J. E. (1999a) Quis custodiet ipsos custodies?, *Challenge*, November/December, 42, Iss. 6: pp. 26, 42.

Stiglitz, J. E. (1999b), *Whither Reform? – Ten Years of the Transition*, Proceedings of the Annual World Bank Conference on Development Economics, Washington, DC: World Bank, pp. 26–42.

Stiglitz, J. E. (2003) *Quand le Capitalisme Perd la Tête*, Paris: Fayard, p. 416.

Stigler, G. (1964) Public Regulation of the Securities Market, *Journal of Business*, 37: pp. 117–142.

Streeck, W. (1992) *Social Institutions and Economic Performance: Studies on Industrial Relations in Advanced European Capitalist Countries*, London: Sage.

Stromberg, G. (1998) *Témoignage devant le Comité Sénatorial Canadien sur les Banques*, Les Échanges et le Commerce, May 14.

Stulz, R. and Williamson, R. (2003) Culture, Openness, and Finance, *Journal of Financial Economics*, 70, No. 3: 342–356.

Stymiest, B. (2002) *Speech to the 2002 general meeting of the CEO of the Toronto Stock Exchange.*

Su, D. W. (1999) *Leverage Insider Ownership and the Under Pricing of Chinese IPOs*, University of Arkon, Working Paper.

Su, D. W. (2000) *Corporate Finance and State Enterprise Reform in China*, University of Akron, Working Paper.

Sun, Q. and Tong, W. H. S. (2005) China Share Issue Privatization: The Extent of Its Success, *Journal of Financial Economics*, 70: pp. 183–222.

Sun, Q., Tong, J. and Tong, W. H. S. (2002) How Does Government Ownership Affect Firm Performance: Evidence from China's Privatization Experience, *Journal of Business Finance and Accounting*, 29: pp. 1–27.

Sun, Y. Z. and Hwang, J. F. (1999) Ownership Structure and Firm Performance of Listed Firms (in Chinese), *Economic Research*, No. 12: pp. 23–30.

Sunder, S. (1973), Relationship Between Accounting Changes and Stock Prices: Problem of Measurement and Some Empirical Evidence, *Empirical Research in Accounting*, Selected Studies, pp. 1–45.

Sunder, S. (1975) Stock Prices and Risk Related Accounting Changes in Inventory Valuation, *Accounting Review*, April: pp. 305–315.

Sweeney, A. P. (1994) Debt-Covenant Violations and Managers Accounting Responses, *Journal of Accounting and Economics*, 17: pp. 281–309.

Szakmary, A., Ors, E., Kyoung, J. K. and Davidson III, W. N. (2003) The Predictive Power of Implied Volatility: Evidence from 35 Futures Markets, *Journal of Banking and Finance*, 27, Iss. 11: pp. 2151–2175.

Taboglu, E. (2002) Corporate Governance, accessible at www.taboglu-law.com.

Tai, B. Y. K., Au-Yeung, O. K., Kwok, M. C. M. and Lau, L. W. C. (1990) Non-compliance with Disclosure Requirements in Financial Statements: The Case of Hong Kong Companies, *International Journal of Accounting*, 25, No. 2: pp. 99–112.

Tam, O. K. (1994) *The Corporate Governance Structure of Chinese Enterprises* (in Chinese), Beijing: Commercial Press.

Tanor, R. (2000) *Turk Sermaye Piyasasi*, Cilt I, Beta Yayinlari, Istanbul, Vol. I, pp. 18–28.

Tarif, J. (2005) *Corporate Governance in Jordan (Recent Development)*, 14–15 September, Rabat, Morocco.

Teece, D. J., Rumelt, R., Dosi, G. and Winter, S. (1994) Understanding Corporate Coherence, *Journal of Economic Behavior and Organization*, 23: pp. 1–30.

Teubner, G. (2001) Legal Irritants or How Good Faith Ends Up in Divergences Rather Than Unifying Law in P. A. Hall and D. Soskice (eds) *Varieties of Capitalism: The Institutional Foundations of Comparative Advantage*, Oxford: Oxford University Press, pp. 417–441.

The Economist (2001) *Asian Business: In Praise of Rules*, print edition New York, 7 April: pp. 2–18.

The Economist (2007) *Insider trading, Hints, tips and handcuffs*, print edition New York, 8 March: pp. 10–12.

Thomas III, L. G. and Waring, G. (1999) Competing Capitalism: Capital Investment in American, German, and Japanese Firms, *Strategic Management Journal*, 20: pp. 729–748.

Thornton, D. (2002) *Jo the CEO's options*, National Post, 17 July.

Tian, G. L. H. (2001) *State Shareholding and the Value of Chinese Firms*, London Business School, Working Paper.

Toba, S. (1993) *Gajoen Kanko Affair – Its Implications and Remaining Tasks* (in Japanese), Tokyo: Kansayaku, No. 324: pp, 176–189.

Toronto Stock Exchange (2002) *Revised Requirements, Guidelines and Practice Notes, TSX Company Manual, M. Corporate Governance*, 28 November.

Toronto Stock Exchange (TSX) and the Canadian Institute of Chartered Accountants (CICA) (2001) *The Saucier Report.*

Tricker, R. (1995) *Hong Kong, China and Corporate Governance – A Laboratory for the World*, Proceedings of the Seventh Annual Conference of Accounting Academics, Hong Kong Society of Accountants, pp. A41–A53.

Trueman, B. and Titman, S. (1988) An Explanation for Accounting Income Smoothing, *Journal of Accounting Research*, (Supplement): pp. 127–139.

Ugur, M. (1999) *The European Union and Turkey: An Anchor/Credibility Dilemma*, Aldershot: Ashgate Publishers.

Ugur, M. and Ararat, M. (2004) *Macroeconomic Instability and Corporate Governance Quality in Turkey: Scope for Optimism?*, Working Paper, Mimeo.

Vaghefi, R. M., Woods, L. and Da Prile, N. (2001) Creating Sustainable Competitive Advantage: The Toyota Philosophy and Its Effects, online publication of *Financial Times*, 7 October 2001.

Vanberg, V. J. (1994) *Rules and Choice in Economics*, Routledge.

Vatinet, R. (2002) *De la loi sur les nouvelles régulations économiques à la loi de modernisation sociale: une montée en puissance du comité d'entreprise?*, Droit social, No, 3, la loi de modernisation sociale et le droit du travail, numéro spécial: 279 et suivantes.

Verner, N. (2007) Good Buy Weapon, *Ukrainian Business Review "Kontrakty"*, No. 17, April.

Wang, X., Xu, L. and Zhu, T. (2001) *Is Public Listing a Way Out for State-Owned Enterprises? The Case of China*, City University of Hong Kong, The World Bank, Hong Kong University of Science and Technology, Working Paper.

Watts, R. (1977), Corporate Financial Statements, a Product of the Market and Political Process, *Australian Journal of Management*, April: pp. 53–75.

Watts, R. and Zimmerman, J. (1978) Towards a Positive Theory of the Determination of Accounting Standards, *The Accounting Review*, 53: pp. 112–133.

Webb, David (2003) Webb-site.com Launches Project Poll, 23 March, available online at http://webb-site.com, last accessed June.

Wei, K. (2000) Incentives for Senior Executives and Performance of Listed Firms (in Chinese), *Economic Research*, No. 3: pp. 32–49.

Weisbach, M. (1988) Outside Directors and CEO Turnover, *Journal of Financial Economics*, No. 20: pp. 431–460.

Weston, J. F., Siu, J. A. and Johnson, B. A. (2001) *Takeovers – Restructuring, and Corporate Governance*, 3rd edn, Upper Saddle River, NJ: Prentice Hall, p. 187.

Westphal, J. (2002) Independent Directors Reduce Performance of the Board of Directors, *Wall Street Journal*, 27 August.

Wilkins, T. and Zimmerman, I. (1983) The Effect of Leasing and Different Methods of Accounting for Leases on Credit Evaluations, *The Accounting Review*, October: pp. 749–764.

William, S. M. and Tower, G. (1998) *Voluntary Disclosure Practice: An Empirical Investigation of the Impact of Societal Variables*, Proceedings of the Eighth Annual Conference of Accounting Academics, Hong Kong Society of Accountants, pp. 1–16.

Williamson, O. E. (1984) Corporate Governance, *Yale Law Journal*, 93: pp. 1197–1230.

Williamson, O. E. (1985) Employee Ownership and Internal Governance: A Perspective, *Journal of Economic Behavior and Organization*, 6: pp. 243–245.

Winter, S. (1991) On Coase, Competence, and the Corporation in O. E. Williamson and S. Winter (eds) *The Nature of the Firm*, Oxford: Blackwell, pp. 179–195.

Wirtz, P. (2002) *Politique de financement et gouvernement d'entreprise*, Paris: Economica.

Wiwattanakantang, Y. (2001) Controlling Shareholders and Corporate Value: Evidence from Thailand, *Pacific-Basin Finance Journal*, 9: pp. 323–362.

Wong, K. A. and Pu, W. (2002) *Ownership Structure and Corporate Performance: Evidence from the Chinese Stock Market*, National University of Singapore, Working Paper.

World Bank (1999) *Corporate Governance: A Framework for Implementation – Overview*, Washington, DC

World Bank (2002) *Transition – the First Ten Years: Analysis and Lessons for Eastern Europe and the Former Soviet Union*, Washington, DC.

World Bank (2003a) *Report on the Observances of Standards and Codes Morocco, ROSC (2003)*, Washington, DC.

World Bank (2003b) *World Development Indicators (WDI)*, Washington, DC.

World Bank (2004a) *Report on the Observances of Standards and Codes Egypt, ROSC (2004)*, Washington, DC.

World Bank (2004b) *Report on the Observances of Standards and Codes Hashemite Kingdom of Jordan (Jordan) ROSC (2004)*, Washington, DC.

World Bank (2006a) *Report on the Observances of Standards and Codes Tunisia, ROSC (2006)*, Washington, DC.

World Bank (2006b) A Decade of Measuring the Quality of Governance, Governance Matters 2006, *Worldwide Governance Indicators*, Washington, DC.

Wu, S. K. (2002) The U-Shaped Relationship Between Ownership Structure and Firm Performance: An Empirical Study of Listed Firms, 1997–2000 (in Chinese), *China Industrial Economics*, No. 1: pp. 80–87.

Wu, S. and Cui, H. (2002) *Consequence of the Concentrated Ownership Structure in Mainland China: Evidence of Year 2000*, City University of Hong Kong.

Wu, S. K., Bao, K. and Jia, Y. M. (1998) The Separation or Division of Board Chairman and CEO (in Chinese), *Economic Research*, No. 8: pp. 21–28.

Wu, S. K., Lau, C. M. and Fan, D. (2001) An Empirical Study on Non-Executive Directors and Firm Performance (in Chinese), *China Industrial Economics*, No. 9: pp. 69–76.

Wurgler, J. (2000) Financial Markets and the Allocation of Capital, *Journal of Financial Economics*, 58: pp. 187–214.

Wyatt A. (1983) Efficient Capital Market Theory: Its Impact on Accounting, *Journal of Accountancy*, February: pp. 56–65.

Xiao, Z. (1999) Corporate Disclosure Made By Chinese Listed Companies, *The International Journal of Accounting*, 34: pp. 349–373.

Xu, X. N. (1997) Establishing Corporate Governance Mechanism and Capital Market with Legal Persons as Its Main Body (in Chinese), *Journal of Reform*, No. 5: pp. 98–111.

Xu, X. N. and Wang, Y. (1996) *Ownership Structure, Corporate Governance and Firms' Performance: The Case of Chinese Stock Companies*, Amherst College and the World Bank, Working Paper,.

Xu, X. N. and Wang, Y. (1999) Ownership Structure and Corporate Governance in Chinese Stock Companies, *China Economic Review*, 10: pp. 75–98.

Yablonovskaya, T. and Zaderey, N. (2006) *Deal of Small and Medium, Expert Ukraine*, No. 48, December: p. 97.

Yakovlev, A. (2003) Corporate Governance and Restructuring of Companies in Russia: Formal and Informal Interests of Owners, *Economic Journal of the Highest School of Economics*, Moscow, No. 2, pp. 221–230.

Yang, G. (2001) Chinese Enterprises Survey, *Sino-China Management*, No. 6: pp. 18–23.

Yeh, Y. H., Lee, T. S. and Woi, D. (2001) Family Control and Corporate Governance: Evidence from Taiwan, *International Review of Finance*, 2: pp. 21–48.

Yu, T. C. (2001) *Ownership Structure, Governance Efficiency and Firm Performance* (in Chinese), *China Industrial Economics*, No. 5: pp. 54–62.

Yuen, K. L., Wang, K. F. and Liu, M. (2000) *An Empirical Analysis of Stock Option Incentives of Listed Firms and Related Issues* (in Chinese), Collection of Papers on Chinese Capital Markets (co-edited by S. X. Liu and P. Shen), Beijing: Social Science Literature Publisher, pp. 494–507.

Yurtoglu, B. (2000) *Ownership, Control and Performance of Turkish Listed Firms*, Emprica, No. 27: pp. 193–222.

Yurtoglu, B. (2003) Corporate Governance and Implications for Minority Shareholders in Turkey, *Corporate Ownership and Control*, 1, Iss. 1, Fall: pp. 72–86.

Yurtoglu, B. (2004) Corporate Governance and Implications for Minority Shareholders in Turkey, *Corporate Ownership and Control*, 1, Iss. 1, Fall.

Zalewska, A. (2006) *Is Locking Domestic Funds Into the Local Market Beneficial? Evidence from the Polish Pension Reforms*, CMPO, Working Paper, No. 06/153.

Zeira, J. (1999) Informational Overshooting, Booms, and Crashes, *Journal of Monetary Economics*, 43: pp. 237–257.

Zhang, C. (1995a) Insider Control and Chinese Enterprise Reform (in Chinese), Beijing: *Journal of Reform*, No. 3: pp. 12–22.

Zhang, C. (1995b) Reform of SOEs' Corporate Governance: A Financial Perspective (in Chinese), Beijing: *Journal of Reform*, No. 3: 67–78.

Zhang, W. (1993) *Decision Rights, Residual Claim and Performance: A Theory of How the Chinese Economy Works*, Nuffield College, Oxford, Mimeo.

Zhang, W. (1996) Ownership, Governance Structure and Principal-Agent Relationship (in Chinese), *Economic Research Journal*, No. 9: 23–39.

Zhang, W. (1998) *China's SOE Reform: A Corporate Governance Perspective*, Institute of Business Research, Peking University, Working Paper.

Zhang, W. (1999) *Property Right, Corporate Governance and Performance: An Evaluation on China's SOE* (in Chinese), Shanghai: Shanghai Fareast Publishing House.

Zhu, W. Z. and Zhang, F. (2001) An Analysis of Business Performance Changes Before and After IPO (in Chinese), *Economic Research*, No. 11: pp. 45–52.

Zimmerman, J. (1980) Positive Research in Accounting, N. Nair and T. Williams (eds) *Perspective on Research*, Madison, WI, Graduate School of Business, University of Wisconsin, pp. 107–128.

Zingales, L. (1998) *Corporate Governance* in P. Newman (ed.) *The New Palgrave Dictionary of Economics and the Law*, London, Stockton Press.

Zingales, L. (2000) In Search of New Foundations, *Journal of Finance*, 55, No. 4: pp. 1623–1653.

Zhukov, A. (2006) *Corporate Governance – Harmonization of Russian and European Standards*, Conference Report, London, p. 7.

Index

LaVergne, TN USA
02 April 2010
178054LV00001B/35/P